MISSION TO OSLO

DANCING WITH THE QUEEN, DEALMAKING WITH THE RUSSIANS, SHAPING HISTORY

TOM LOFTUS

FORMER AMBASSADOR TO NORWAY

LITTLE CREEK PRESS

MINERAL POINT, WISCONSIN

Little Creek Press
5341 Sunny Ridge Road
Mineral Point, WI 53565

ORDERING INFORMATION
Quantity sales. Special discounts are available on quantity purchases by corporations, associations, and others. For details, contact info@littlecreekpress.com

Orders by US trade bookstores and wholesalers.
Please contact Little Creek Press or Ingram for details.

Printed in the United States of America

Cataloging-in-Publication Data
Names: Tom Loftus, author
Title: Mission to Oslo: Dancing with the Queen,
Dealmaking with the Russians, Shaping History
Description: Mineral Point, WI Little Creek Press, 2024
Identifiers: LCCN: 2024912202 | ISBN: 978-1-955656-78-8
Classification: POLITICAL SCIENCE / International Relations / Diplomacy
BIOGRAPHY AND AUTOBIOGRAPHY / Memoirs
HISTORY / Europe / Nordic Countries

Book design by Little Creek Press

On the cover: The author dancing with HM Queen Sonja in the ballroom of the Waldorf Astoria, New York City, on the State Visit of Their Majesties, October 1995. Photo credit: Anita and Steve Shevett, courtesy American Scandinavian Foundation.

This memoir is a truthful recollection of actual events in the author's life.

To Norwegian immigrants
and their descendants.

PRAISE FOR *MISSION TO OSLO*

66 Tom Loftus pulls back the curtain and shows us the realities involved in the operation of an ambassador's life. From the logistics of Winter Olympics last-minute accommodations to the decisions of who sits where at a formal dinner to negotiating the perilous details of NATO policy, this is a fluid, literate, and revealing account."
—George Hesselberg, journalist and writer on Norway

66 Protocol in diplomacy, what it is and how it is observed, is brought to life because Tom is a gifted storyteller."
—Fred DuVal, former deputy chief of protocol, U.S. State Department

66 Both the content and your writing style, terse and humorous, are entertaining and kept me reading along at a good pace."
—Katharine Lyall, former president of the University of Wisconsin System

66 This is an extraordinary effort by you; the events and the details you recount during your tenure in Oslo are astonishing! This would be a tour de force for that alone."
—Ambassador Larry Taylor, former ambassador to Estonia

The memoir reflects the ambassador's close relationship to his ancestral homeland in his travels throughout Norway and in his ndship and interaction with leading Norwegian politicians. The oir is told in a chronological diary form and each listed topic is d with knowledge and engagement, and throughout displays nse of humor Loftus has. The memoir is an excellent read."
S. Lovoll, Ph.D., professor emeritus of history St. Olaf College, field, Minnesota, and the University of Oslo

“Wow, Tom! This is incredible! When I got to your manuscript, I couldn't put it down. You clearly were at the core of critical events and I felt privileged to get the personal perspective you provided. This should be required reading for those who want to go into diplomacy and public service.”

—Dennis Dresang, professor emeritus of public affairs and political science at the University of Wisconsin

“I first knew Ambassador Tom Loftus as a master state legislator who got things done and charmed both sides in the process. His new book, *Mission to Oslo: Dancing With the Queen, Dealmaking With the Russians, Shaping History,* is a lively accounting of what the word 'diplomat' actually means. Yes, it's dinner with Yasser Arafat and tea with Nelson Mandela, but it's also sweating the small stuff, like working on your Norwegian accent and waking up worrying you'd just killed a famous dinner guest who's allergic to shellfish. Mostly, it means doing the gritty work of furthering shared interests that make the world safer, like crafting an agreement between the U.S., Norway, and Russia to reduce the possibility of a nuclear waste disaster in the Arctic. This witty and insightful memoir is a master class in how to forge true alliances.”

—Dave Iverson, journalist, filmmaker and author of *Winter Stars: An Elderly Mother, An Aging Son and Life's Final Journey*

“Tom describes the backstory of what happened in the U.S. Embassy in Oslo when the International Campaign to Ban Landmines and I were jointly awarded the Nobel Peace Prize in 1997. President Clinton, who would not sign the land mine treaty, was well served by Tom's diplomatic skills in soothing feathers, honoring Americans, and being a great host on a great day.”

—Jody Williams, 1997 Nobel Peace Prize Laureate

“Wow! So many great stories and so many interesting and famous people. You have a gift for writing in a way that pulls people in and makes them feel a connection to you.”

—Ambassador Daniel Speckhard, former ambassador to Belarus and Greece and deputy assistant secretary general at NATO

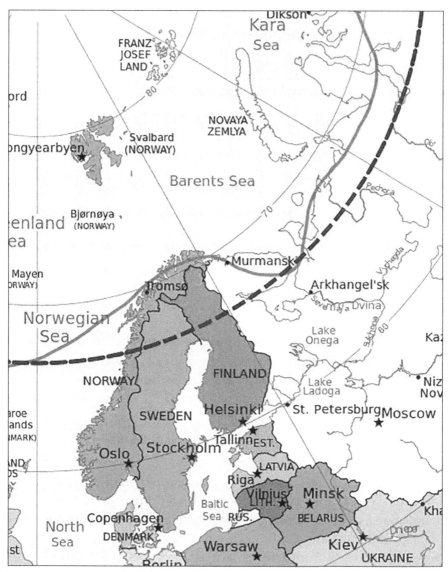

Norway above the Arctic Circle. Credit: Map Norway

Credit: Nations Online Project

FOREWORD
A PROMISE OF PEACE

The four years from 1993 through 1997, my time as ambassador to Norway and the first four years of the Clinton presidency, were the most optimistic and opportune time of the 20th century for Europe and the United States.

In this memoir, you will witness events and meet the people whom history tapped on the shoulder to take on the task of securing peace among nations. A peace that promised to be more than just the absence of war.

President Bill Clinton was 47 and Vice President Al Gore was 45; they had arrived when their time had come. (I was 48.)

The Europe that had been divided into east and west at the end of World War II, with borders and ideology frozen ever since in a Cold War, ended suddenly in 1989. Germany was now reunited. The countries of West Germany and East Germany were gone. West and East Berlin were no longer—it was now just Berlin.

The Soviet Union was no more. It was very shaky, but Russia was a democracy led by Boris Yeltsin. He had just survived a coup attempt. Poland, Hungary, and the Czech Republic were now independent of Soviet Communist rule and were seeking to secure that new status by joining NATO and the European Union—and quickly, for fear the ghosts of Germany and Russia past would come back to life and threaten them again. The three Baltic countries of Estonia,

Latvia, and Lithuania were freed, having suffered fifty years of harsh occupation, first by Nazi Germany and then the Soviet Union. They wanted desperately to prevent a recurrence of what history had taught them: Russia would come again.

Cartographers were much in demand.

Norway, the only member of NATO bordering the Soviet Union, now had in Russia a new friendly neighbor wanting to establish trade and needing help dismantling nuclear weapons and securing their radioactive waste. The Soviet ICBMs (intercontinental ballistic missiles) and nuclear submarine fleet were there, just across the Arctic border near the city of Murmansk. The nuclear bombs on missiles and in submarines meant to destroy the United States had been taken off target. So had our land-based and submarine-launched missiles that were meant to destroy the Soviet Union.

In South Africa, Nelson Mandela was out of jail after 27 years and had negotiated the end of white apartheid government with President F.W. de Klerk, and a free election for a new South Africa was scheduled. Mandela and de Klerk were awarded the Nobel Peace Prize in Oslo in 1993. Mandela became the first president of the new South Africa in June 1994.

In October 1993, there was the Handshake on the White House Lawn. It marked the signing by the prime minister of Israel, the foreign minister of Israel, and the chairman of the Palestine Liberation Organization of the Oslo Accords—a roadmap for peace in the Middle East. The secret negotiations were initiated and facilitated by Norwegian diplomats. These three were awarded the Nobel Peace Prize in Oslo in 1994.

The not-so-distant thunder at this post-Cold War picnic was a bloody ethnic conflict in the Balkans. Some bad actors let off leash by the breakup of Yugoslavia had gained control of Serbia and were bent on creating "Greater Serbia" via the mass murder of Bosnian Muslims.

Dear reader, you will meet the three leaders the world was counting on to bring peace to the Mideast.

Fasten your seatbelt for a ride on an icy road with First Lady Hillary Clinton to the Winter Olympics in Lillehammer.

Be with me in the White House for the return of the young Norwegian prince FDR helped with his homework during World War II who is now The King of Norway.

Walk the path with one of the Norwegian saboteurs who blew up the heavy-water plant in Nazi-occupied Telemark, ending Hitler's quest for the atomic bomb.

Join me at a private suite in Oslo's Grand Hotel for tea with Nelson Mandela, and have dinner with a movie star who won an Oscar for best actor.

Meet Gro Harlem Brundtland, the prime minister of Norway, the most influential woman political leader of the 1990s. A force to be reckoned with.

And lastly, get out your recipe box and a wine glass. The menus of diplomatic dinners are in store, along with wine pairings. All at Villa Otium, the American Ambassador's Residence that sits on its own city block.

Enjoy.

PREFACE

How did it come to pass that I decided to write a memoir thirty years after the time I served as the United States ambassador to Norway from 1993 through 1997?

The inspiration came when I opened the ten boxes of personal papers that had been shipped home with me. The Wisconsin Historical Society wanted the papers, and they needed them organized according to their instructions, which included a list of documents the society did not want.

Opening them for the first time, I discovered my assistant in Oslo, Sue Meyer, who had also been my assistant during my time as Speaker of the Wisconsin Assembly from 1983-1991, had included my daily schedule for each of the 1,460 days I was posted in Oslo. They were organized in folders by the month.

The schedules were hour-by-hour and included such details as every lunch and dinner I hosted, the guests, the menu, and the seating chart. Every trip I took by car, plane, or train was there—the time I arrived and the time I departed. The same was true for important guests like former President Jimmy Carter, who came three times, First Lady Hillary Clinton, who came to represent the United States at the 1994 Lillehammer Winter Olympics, and Nelson Mandela, with whom I had tea. Also included was the appointment hour for the fitting for a morning coat to wear to present my credential to The King. Included was the cost of the rental.

One of the many notable visitors to Oslo was John Kenneth Galbraith, Harvard professor and President Kennedy's ambassador to India. He was a houseguest, and we became fast friends and had long talks. He brought, as a gift, his memoir of his time in India. He had gone through the whole book and underlined for me the parts I should take as lessons. He was foremost a teacher.

Galbraith thought his memoir would be a collection of letters from India sent to JFK assembled in chronological order. It didn't make sense to proceed when the dreams of the Kennedy presidency were ended with the assassination.

"But I thought it would be most instructive of all to tell in a day-to-day fashion just what an ambassador does..."

I followed that advice, and my schedules and the diary I kept, along with notes of meetings and events, made this memoir easy to do—a pleasure to write.

PART ONE
SETTING THE STAGE

CHAPTER 1
BECOMING AMBASSADOR

FIRST, THE OVAL OFFICE

In February of 1993, I was in the Oval Office with President Bill Clinton. It was a bright winter day less than a month after his inauguration. It was just the two of us, and we were still amazed that after meeting each other in 1987 and going through several campaigns that led up to the 1992 victory, here we were standing in this room. We said to each other pretty much in unison, "Can you believe it?" He gave me a tour of the office. "Here is where Nixon's secret tape recorder was. Here is the medicine cabinet where I keep my asthma medicine. And the desk is the 'Resolute Desk,' a gift to President Hayes in 1880 from Queen Victoria."

I asked to be appointed ambassador to Norway. I did not offer a choice. He had been briefed and knew the question was coming. And, like seasoned politicians everywhere—and we were that—you never say "no," and you try to imply "yes." He said, "You'd be good at that."

Some weeks later when there was no communication, and after two senators and several people from the campaign inquired, finally Clinton said, "Where's Loftus?" My file was found on the "no" stack. A friend, a staff person who had been with Clinton in the governor's office in Little Rock, found it and knowing Clinton's wretched handwriting recognized right away what had happened—he had written on my file, "Not a bad idea." The staff person who recovered it from the desk after our meeting had read it to say, "No, a bad idea." My nomination was sent on to the State Department to start the process that would lead to Senate confirmation seven months later.

THE NOMINATION

When President Clinton OK'd my nomination,[1] the vetting began. A stack of papers to fill out on tax history, investments, Army records, proof of my college degrees by producing the actual graduation certificates, a set of fingerprints ($5—the police chief in my hometown of Sun Prairie, Wisconsin, did it himself), marriage license, and my medical history, plus I needed an extensive physical with numerous tests.

Next, an FBI agent showed up at my office holding my college transcripts, asked me each place I had lived since age 18, said I should in short order provide a list of every trip I had taken outside the country with the exact dates since age 18. And, were there any he would be interested in? I said the first time I went to a foreign country I walked. It was over the bridge to Juarez, Mexico. I was a military policeman at Fort Bliss in El Paso, and off duty we spent our free time in Juarez.

By this time—1993—I was what is called "widely traveled." After getting my first passport, I had pledged to myself to use it. Of interest to the FBI were several trips. One was a trip to Communist China in 1983. I was the majority leader of the Wisconsin Assembly then, and this was a trade mission with Republican Gov. Lee Sherman Dreyfus. Another was a trip to Honduras and Nicaragua in 1984, just at the start of the Contra/Sandinista Civil War. It was a fact-finding trip I led with the former governor of Wisconsin and ambassador to Mexico, Patrick J. Lucey. I'd been to East Berlin twice, in 1985 and again in 1989. I happened to be in West Berlin when the wall opened, and I walked across the border. Also, Peru, Columbia, Bolivia, Ecuador, Taiwan (twice), Japan, Thailand, South Korea, Israel, Norway, and many times to Germany.

The next day a former colleague from the state Assembly called and said the FBI had called him and asked if I drank a lot. I said, "Thank God he did not ask about you!" After this vetting and obtaining the highest level of secret clearance, I was assigned a space in a State Department program for ambassadors-to-be. This came with special permission to begin Norwegian language classes with a tutor in Madison rather than attending the language school in Washington.

My tutor was LuAnn Sorenson, who was a graduate student in the Scandinavian Department at UW-Madison. She was young but wise enough to focus on my accent. At age 48, I was not going to become fluent or even pretty good, but to be able to do my best with the accent would, it turned out, be a key to my being welcomed home, so to speak.

Ambassador school was four weeks on and off. Spouses were included, and we spent the time at a hotel in D.C. School contained very practical information on duties and responsibilities. It was going to be just like being the Assembly Speaker: responsible for everything. There was a lot about the budget for entertaining. Expenses not directly related to the mission I would pay for personally. More on this later, but I would eventually learn that if we labeled something "wine" no questions were asked. There was an option to take out an $18,000 advance on salary to be paid back through lower paychecks over a year, and I signed up.

I did have briefings on the economy and politics of Norway, visited the CIA, was briefed on their rather extensive operations involving Norway, and received a briefing from the Pentagon on the pre-positioned equipment in bunkers hollowed into the mountains at a series of airports throughout Norway for supplying F-16s when the Soviets invaded. What turned out to be the issue that would consume most of my energy and the work of the embassy started at this point with the Navy's briefing on U.S. and Soviet nuclear submarine activity in the Arctic.

The State Department's attitude was that if we had gotten far enough in our lives that a president would nominate us, we would instinctively know what to do—no training or briefing would substitute. The purpose of school was really to get to know my future colleagues in Europe and be introduced to the State Department structure. I would be in the European section.

And it was during this time that I made a personal decision that from then on, I would eat the European way, holding the fork in my left hand and the knife in my right. This small gesture paid big dividends in increasing my comfort level with Norwegians and other diplomats in Oslo.

SENATE CONFIRMATION

When ambassador school ended, my nomination was to be sent to the Senate in time to make the deadline for the last floor period before a recess. One problem: It was the day of the deadline, and the papers had to be signed by the president—except he was on the golf course in Martha's Vineyard.

The answer: Tee up Bruce Lindsey. Bruce was there at the course. He had been Clinton's chief of staff in the Arkansas governor's office, then campaign director, and now was assistant to the president. My friend and longtime political mover and shaker Madison attorney, Brady Williamson, called Bruce, and Bruce commandeered a golf cart. He crossed one fairway after another shouting "Fore!," found the president, and got the signature.[2]

The hearing before the Senate Foreign Relations Committee was uneventful. There was a Democratic majority in the Senate and Democratic president, and the four of us up for the hearing that day were well known. I was introduced to the committee by Wisconsin Sen. Herb Kohl, an old friend, whom I had supported in his campaign in 1988. I was then Assembly Speaker and chair of the Dukakis for President campaign in Wisconsin.

Then, nothing. I, Alan Blinken nominated for Belgium, Swanee Hunt for Austria, and Dan Spiegel for the U.S. mission in Geneva, had a "hold" placed on us by a senator who, as was allowed under Senate custom, did not disclose his name. This prevented our nominations from coming up for a vote on the floor.[3] What the hell? The four of us got on the phone and called every senator we knew to find out who this senator was and get this hold off. Each day we had a conference call reporting our discussions and planning the next move. Historically nominees were supposed to be silent and await their fate. In politics, fate is fought for.

I'd never ever heard of the senator who placed the hold. Mitch McConnell, a freshman Republican from Kentucky, wanted two staff people in the State Department who had been with the Clinton campaign fired. And the four of us were being held hostage until that happened.

Sen. George Mitchell of Maine was the Senate majority leader, and we all knew him. He had come to Wisconsin in November 1988 after the election to ask my help in persuading Herb Kohl to vote for him for majority leader. George Mitchell was and is a wonderful human being. He fought for us. He threatened to bring our nomination to the floor and ask for a vote for cloture. He called me and said, "Tom, you were the Speaker. It is hard for you to understand the little authority I have here." A deal was finally struck with the State Department inspector general. The two employees were not going to be fired. However, they found other employment.

PRESIDENT'S LETTER OF INSTRUCTION

A detailed memo prepared for me containing practical information was my guidebook. It included a four-page "letter of instruction" from the president.

> As my representative, you along with the Secretary of State, share with me my constitutional responsibility for the conduct of relations with ...The postwar era is drawing to a close... our nation faces a historic opportunity to help shape a freer, more secure and more prosperous world in which our ideals and way of life can truly flourish. As President, I intend to advance these objectives... and I look to you, as my personal representative in Norway, as my partner in this task.

The letter was very clear on another subject:

> (A)s Commander in Chief, I retain authority over United States Armed Forces. I charge you to exercise full responsibility for the direction, coordination, supervision, and safety, including security from terrorism, of all Department of Defense personnel on official duty in Norway.... (T)he security of your Mission is your direct, personal responsibility. I expect you to report with directness and candor. I am sure you will represent the United States with imagination, energy and skill. You have my full personal confidence and best wishes.

The other 40 pages covered ethics, gifts, my salary, travel outside Norway, the budget for official Residence expenses, including the staff of three maids, a chef, two laundresses, a gardener, and a driver,

Edmund Steiro, who would be my constant companion for four years, and a car: a 1988 Cadillac Brougham "...it is lightly armored and equipped with a variety of security enhancements."

About this car. It was so heavy that one winter day after I first arrived, when leaving the Israeli ambassador's residence high up on Holmenkollen, the internationally known ski-jumping venue, Edmund couldn't stop it. We slid down the icy road, schussing past the ski jump, pulling the emergency brake to slide the back end at the curves, and the defroster on full blast could only clear a small patch in the thick, bulletproof windshield. We asked for a new car and soon a black Chevrolet Impala with a V8 and no armor arrived. Cloth seats.

The State Department said the Cadillac could not be sold or junked for security reasons. A brilliant idea! How about giving it to His Majesty, The King? State said, "We like the way you are thinking over there." Next time we saw the Caddy it was on TV arriving at the Palace carrying the president of Finland on a state visit.

My base salary was $115,700. Added to this was a "post differential" of 35 percent, the max under the formula used by State as Oslo was ranked the most expensive city in the world to live in. I was reimbursed for costs incurred in operating the Residence in excess of a required "contribution" of 5 percent, deducted from my salary. I was able to save some money, make the maximum IRA contribution, and buy savings bonds for my two sons, Alec and Karl.

Most important was "the ambassador's personal secretary." I could hire exactly one person: a personal secretary. It was discouraged, but that person could be hired outside the career service. I was delighted when Sue Meyer, who had been my assistant for 12 years in the Legislature, the treasurer of my campaign for governor, part of our family, and knew the players in the White House, agreed to join us.

Since all the staff needed for hosting meetings, events, lunches, and dinners were in place, it meant the budget for representational costs such as dinners, receptions, wine—anything for the purpose of representing America—was plenty, as long as we did not host events in restaurants or hire halls.

The ambassador's duties, responsibilities, and rights, when in the host country, are spelled out quite clearly in a remarkable economy of words by the Vienna Convention on Diplomatic Relations: "(T)he person of (an Ambassador) shall be inviolable. He shall not be liable to any form of arrest or detention. The Receiving State shall treat him with due respect and shall take all appropriate steps to prevent any attack on his person, freedom or dignity."

As are the rights and obligations of the host country: "The sending State must make certain that the agreement of the receiving State has been given for the person it proposes to send as head of mission...the receiving State is not obligated to give reasons to the sending State for a refusal of agreement." It is also where you find it is the right of the host country to kick out any member of the staff they see fit with no explanation required. Relates mostly to spies.

The most important part of the Vienna Convention is this guarantee: "(T)he official correspondence of the mission shall be inviolate," and the "diplomatic bag shall not be opened or detained.

SECRETARY OF STATE: DO WHAT NEEDS TO BE DONE

I also received a letter from Secretary of State Warren Christopher before departing for my post:

> *November 4, 1993*
>
> *The Honorable Thomas A. Loftus*
> *Sir:*
> *The President, by and with the advice and consent of the Senate, has appointed you Ambassador Extraordinary and Plenipotentiary of the United States of America to Norway, and the commission evidencing your appointment to this office is enclosed.*

It went on to say that upon arrival I was to meet with the foreign minister and make arrangements for the presentation of my letter of credentials to the head of state, His Majesty King Harald.

And any mother would have in her heart the hopes of the last sentence:

> *Entire confidence is entertained that during your incumbency the cordial relations existing between the two governments will be even further strengthened.*
>
> *Sincerely yours,*
> *Warren Christopher*

Plenipotentiary means that one has the power to act on behalf of the government, including the president. But more importantly, the title plenipotentiary, in practice, meant I had the power of independent action. No waiting for instructions. Do what the situation calls for.

IT'S OFFICIAL!

On November 10, 1993, I was sworn in as the ambassador to the Kingdom of Norway by Federal Judge Barbara Crabb in the Wisconsin State Capitol building. "The crowd which surrounded the rotunda, and spilled over into the upper galleries, heard a gracious Loftus acknowledge friends and family in his acceptance of the post," according to the *Sun Prairie Star*.[4]

The Grieg Men's Choir sang the Norwegian and American national anthems. The choir was founded by Norwegian immigrants in Madison in 1925 to preserve the heritage of Norwegian music and culture.

Former governor and ambassador to Mexico, Patrick Lucey, my mentor in politics, was there to introduce me. I ended my remarks by saying, "(T)o all you friends and relatives. We go with all of you in our hearts. The Norwegians have a lovely phrase used when meeting a friend again after a special occasion like this. It is 'takk for sist,' meaning thanks for the last time we were together. My wife Barbara and I will be greeting you with that salutation when we return and see you all again." Judge Crabb said it was one of her best days as a judge. It was a treat to be the first to address me as "His Excellency, the ambassador to Norway." A reporter asked if I saw a person stepping forward to fill my role as inspirational leader of the Democratic Party. When you lose an election like I did for governor in 1990, you lose an election. When you lose and the president makes you an ambassador you are looked back on as an inspirational leader, apparently.

There was a photo on the front page of *The Milwaukee Sentinel* the next morning of son Karl, age 6, who was chewing bubble gum, blowing a huge bubble during my speech.

FAMILY IS PART OF THE PACKAGE

At the ambassador-to-be sessions in Washington, D.C., there was a discussion on the role of the spouse. Best we could tell, it was to be like Ginger Rogers—do everything Fred Astaire did but backwards and in high heels, with no pay.

The discussion was cut short and went from abstract to knowing nods when a veteran member of the State Department, who had been an ambassador in several countries, said, "It is the same as the role of the first lady in the White House, and the ambassador's Residence is America's White House in a foreign country."

We then went on to a session on the Art in the Embassies program. Each new ambassador is to assemble a collection of art for his or her residence. Whatever you want, preferably from your home state, that you can borrow for a few years from artists, museums, friends or from your own collection. Art in the Embassies will pick it up, pack it, insure it, ship it, and arrange for its installation. The reverse when you leave your post. These changing displays of American art would be written about, featured in the media and seen by generations of Norwegian guests.

My wife, Barbara, set about this very pleasant task. Shortly after we arrived in Oslo, the art came and was installed. There is great art everywhere. There are few places with great walls to hang it. And the Residence in Oslo had great walls. Eventually Barbara produced a photo booklet of the art with a blurb on the artists that acknowledged each lender. This was presented to guests and became part of the Art in the Embassies archives.

Barbara was comfortable being a public person, forged by being the Wisconsin Assembly Speaker's wife and traveling the state in my campaign for governor in 1990. She was good at public speaking, and she was well traveled. This included going off to the French Alps in her early 20s to work for a family running their household, but really to have a place to live and time off to ski. Her skiing proficiency would prove a boon.

Son Alec was 12 years old when we left for Norway. He was adventuresome, gregarious, and, like his mother, an avid skier.

Karl was 7. He was Tom Sawyer. His life of playing in the backyards and nearby woods, with his two cousins, Mike and Mark Wolfgram, who lived one house away, was a boy's dream life.

My father and mother had bought a cottage on Lake Delton near Wisconsin Dells in 1956, when I was 11, and it was only 45 minutes from our house. This place, used by the whole extended family, was where Alec and Karl had a kid's paradise on summer weekends. This is where Karl became hooked on fishing.

The boys would miss their grandparents and doting aunts, my sisters Shirley Wolfgram and Jerry Wagner, who lived only a few blocks away. Jerry took loving care of the boys while we campaigned. Their other aunt, my sister Wendy Loftus, was waiting for them in

Norway.

Wendy was my younger sister, and she had traveled to Norway after college to find her roots and learn Norwegian. She found a husband, Jens Stub. Their boy, Christoffer, was Karl's age. Wendy had a master's degree in social work from the UW and was now running a neighborhood center for the elderly in Oslo.

Wendy, you will learn, liked to tap dance. She had a routine. It turned out the best place to tap was on the tiled kitchen floor of the Residence.

PREPPING FOR DIPLOMACY: MY BACKGROUND

My time as Assembly Speaker, the longest-serving Democratic Speaker in Wisconsin history, made me a good fit for being an ambassador. I was accustomed to and comfortable with being in charge. And I had learned to embrace ambiguity.

My time in the Army and my college years at UW-Madison in the late 1960s were, as I look back, also important experiences.

But first, why did I want to serve as ambassador to Norway and only Norway? My roots are there; it's my ancestral home.

The Loftuses come to America

Norway was the country from which my grandfather, Edward Lofthus, came to America in 1885. He was just a little boy. There was his father Ole and mother Margit, and his brothers and sisters: Albert, Signe, Knut, Alice, Ole, Sara, and Amanda. The family came from Telemark—the drinking, dancing, fiddle-playing, not-that-far-removed-from-paganism inland county. They came from a farm with a house that had a loft. Thus, the name Lofthus[5] changed to Loftus in America. They ended up in Brooklyn, Wisconsin, a small farming town near Stoughton just southeast of Madison, and settled there with several other Norwegian immigrant families. Some Danes too.

Just a few years later, my grandmother, also a little girl, and her family immigrated and ended up in Brooklyn. Her name was Heletie Birkeland. They were from Åna-Sira on the southwestern coast of Norway, a tiny fishing town in a cozy fjord near Stavanger. This was the Bible Belt of Norway. Only in America would my grandfather and grandmother have ever met.

Telemark is breathtakingly beautiful—mountains, woods, and green valleys with sheep grazing on the hillsides. There are wooden stave churches—"stave kirke"—from medieval times. There are Lutheran churches to be sure, but the old ways still play out like a shivaree at a wedding. Green hay is draped over the fences to dry. The farmhouses have intricate paintings of winding roses—"rosemåling"—decorating the insides that were painted by traveling artists. Åna-Sira is similarly beautiful with its wooden fishing boats and birch forests, thus my grandmother's name Birkeland. But they all left for America. Only Ireland was poorer than Norway at this time. And, you can't eat beauty.

For a short history of the relationship between Norway and America, see Appendix A.

Before college and career, the military

I was drafted within weeks of flunking out of college in the spring of 1965, and in December was sent off for eight weeks of basic training at Fort Leonard Wood in Missouri. The start of a two-year obligation. After being issued a duffle bag full of clothes, a buzz haircut, and shots for jungle diseases, we were assigned to large tents placed on wood platforms with a pot-bellied coal stove for heat. There were not enough of the WWI-era wooden barracks to house the wave after wave of arriving draftees.

There was an IQ test of sorts which had pretty easy questions, and I was plucked out of my group because of my test score to go to a leadership training course of ten days. We would be the leaders in the barracks to roust out the others in the morning and line them up for breakfast. "Take all you want. Eat all you take." Same for all the other lineups, from marches to mail call.

Three weeks into basic, I was deathly ill with pneumonia and pleurisy. After my one month stay in the wooden barrack designated a hospital, my group had already left for the final training before Vietnam. I waited with another guy, feeding and banking the coal furnaces of the barracks for the next scheduled basic training class.

After those eight weeks, leaving with some notoriety after setting a record for number of days on kitchen police (KP) due to my unappreciated smart remarks to the drill sergeants, I was off to Fort Bliss in El Paso to train as a forward observer for artillery, a short lifespan job in Vietnam. Well into this training, with the Army needing military policemen (MP), my class was assembled in the parking lot outside our artillery company HQ, and the five tallest, which included me, were sent off for MP training. I learned how to spit-shine my boots, direct traffic, shoot a .45 (received a marksman medal), fold the flag, and write up an accident report for court. This was taught brilliantly by a retired high school English teacher to a group of us where many had not graduated high school and only I and Don Russell, the "Wolfman," from Evansville, Indiana, had ever been to any college. Weeks of this training delayed me again and by the time the wheel of fate came to me, I did not have enough time left in service to spend the requisite year in Vietnam.

Fort Bliss was a big base with heavy car traffic, so it was like being a cop in a city, except most everyone was a teenager or in their early 20s. For some reason, there were only a few ambulances, and we ended up taking kids to the hospital who had tried very inefficient ways of harming themselves to get a discharge—drinking brass polish or jumping off the second floor. We started with two men in a squad, eight-hour shifts, and soon, it was twelve-hour shifts and one man in a squad. Fellow MPs left for Vietnam and the ones coming back, a lot of dog handlers, were only with us to muster out and didn't pull duty. They were still on edge—"spooked" was their description.

Soldiers were paid in cash and because of this we stood guard at the pay stations on payday. To free up this day for duty, MPs were paid the day before. On that day, with our cash in hand, groups of buddies walked across the bridge over the Rio Grande to Juarez for tequila, street food, and, among other things, bullfights. I saw a picador killed, the charging blood-streaked black bull hitting him full in the back. Two bucks to get in. The matador was Raul Contreras, nicknamed "Finito." I kept the poster.

The stockade, full up with returned AWOLs (absent without leave), was understaffed and there had been a riot—more of a protest—and I was sent there for a stint overseeing five guys in a separate cell area who were suicide risks. We ate at our own table in the mess hall, and I counted the forks and spoons before and after the meal. No knives. My main tool to keep this gentle group happy was listening to their stories and handing out filter cigarettes, something denied to those in the stockade because of the riot.

Having enough of this, I volunteered for what was thought to be the only job worse than the stockade, and it was to be sent out to the MP outpost in the desert of New Mexico, McGregor Range, a one-million-acre missile training range of tumbleweeds, sunken launch silos, snakes, and coyotes.

The desert was heaven. We had no officer in charge, only a three-stripe sergeant who gave us a clip of five rounds for our pistols before each shift and made sure we signed for each bullet going out and coming in. "Don't shoot unless shot at, preferably hit, and don't chase speeders as you will likely kill yourself." There was a swimming pool and movie theater. German NATO troops came for training on Hawk anti-aircraft missiles, as did the Japanese Home Guard. The former drank beer and marched around at midnight singing. The Japanese once launched a Hawk uprange, the wrong way, and it came screaming back over the base compound. They claimed it was an accident.

Sitting on a small hill a few miles downrange was a large telescope once on a Navy ship and we used it to explore the moon on clear nights. The horse track, Ruidoso Downs, was a cheap day trip. White Sands Missile Range was not far away and one night my fellow MP "Z" from South Philly and I drove our squad miles past our patrol border to the site of the first atomic bomb test and sat on the rock designating the spot. There was a bar between the range and El Paso on highway 54, where we spent our off time when not making trips to Juarez. Two days before Christmas 1967, I was discharged and hit Route 66 in my red Mustang (V8 three speed on the floor) and never looked back.

UW-Madison prepared me to be ambassador

Some courses and professors at UW-Madison were very important to me in finding my way in the world of diplomacy. These were the years 1968-1972.

Professor Leon Epstein, who became my mentor and champion at the UW, taught British politics and the political party systems in Western democracies. From this, I gained a basic knowledge of the parliamentary system and how parliaments, through political parties, worked in practice.

There was a required course in international law for political science majors that was taken in the law school with law school students. It focused on disputes between countries and treaties. We read case studies.

I needed five credits one semester to fill out my schedule, and a five-credit course in the political history of Africa was handy.

It focused on colonialism of the European powers and current liberation movements. One can learn a lot about France, Britain, Germany, Belgium, Portugal, Italy, and Spain by looking behind the gloss that was passed off as the history of their colonialism that was taught in America up until the late '60s.

I forget the title of another worthwhile class, but call it a class in political thinkers where we read their original works: Rousseau, Burke, Locke, Machiavelli, Marx and Engels, and the political writings of Martin Luther. The latter was of great help to understand Norwegian history and Lutheran as the state religion of Norway. And to appreciate the continuing testy relationship between Norway and the papacy, which was on full display when Pope John Paul visited Norway in 1989. (28,000 Catholics in the whole country.)[6]

Luther's basic political idea is the relationship of the church to the state. He states that the secular kingdom has no authority in matters pertaining to the spiritual kingdom. And vice versa. This builds on the words of Jesus in Matthew, "Render therefore unto Caesar the things which are Caesar's; and unto God the things that are God's." This "two kingdoms" idea roiled the Vatican as the Church thought it should wear both crowns.

There was no test in this course. The professor said reading Marx was punishment enough.

PERHAPS IT WAS PROPHETIC...

Perhaps it was prophetic. During a debate in my race for Wisconsin governor in October 1990, a reporter on the panel of questioners asked me, "If elected, would you pledge now to serve out the four-year term?" I said yes, unless I was appointed ambassador to Norway. This wasn't rehearsed. It just came out of my mouth. Three years later to the month it happened. How?

In 1988, I was the chair of the Dukakis for President campaign in the Wisconsin primary and general elections. We became great friends. He lost to George H.W. Bush. Dukakis won Wisconsin and 17 other states. The electoral vote math was such that this eighteen-state base for a Democrat suggested that in 1992 the right Democrat could win the presidency.

My candidate was Bill Clinton. He was by now a political partner and a friend. He had supported my bid for governor. And he was making a name for himself by promoting a more centrist Democratic

Party in speeches around the country. Very eloquent speeches.

The bump in Clinton's road to the White House was his clunker of a speech at the 1988 Democratic Convention in Atlanta, where Dukakis was nominated.

I had been part of a vocal group of insiders in the Dukakis campaign urging that Clinton be chosen to give the speech nominating Dukakis. He got the second speech—the policy speech: Praise Dukakis, then applause, list every piece of legislation supported by Democrats that would lead to the American utopia. Then applause. A nod to notable former and current Democratic politicians, their families, and the names of their pets. Then more applause. I went backstage just before Clinton was to go out to give this speech to wish him luck. I specifically did not say "break a leg."

Back in my seat in the Wisconsin delegation section—I was chair of the delegation for Dukakis—Clinton went on so long he was booed. The immediate conclusion among the media cognoscenti covering the convention was that this meant Clinton's political future was behind him. What to do?

Hillary Clinton and the Arkansas delegation were seated one level of rows behind our delegation. I asked my aide Stephanie to clamber best she could through the crowd, find Hillary and tell her it was a good speech. Stephanie said, "But it wasn't." I said, "OK, then tell Hillary that I liked it." As in, "Tom really liked Bill's speech."

I had arranged for Clinton to meet the Wisconsin press at our convention hotel early the next morning. My thought of course had been that the press, still awestruck at the brilliant speech, could be the first to report a political star was born. That didn't happen, but he came and made the best of it, and the press stories were kind, as they still had the first shot at him.

The booing made him a celebrity of sorts, which led to an invitation to appear on *The Tonight Show Starring Johnny Carson*, where his self-deprecating, aw-shucks, perfectly timed one-liners had Johnny cracking up; then Clinton played the saxophone, a jazzy version of "Summertime." He got a standing ovation from the band and whoops from the audience. Johnny Carson gave him 12 minutes and 18 seconds of time before a national audience. When you look at it now, you know why he became president. He went from he "coulda been a contender," to a contender for future president.[7]

Before he announced his run for president in October of 1991,

Clinton suggested it would help if I came to Little Rock and told my fellow Speaker in the Legislature there that Clinton's campaign pledge to stay the full four-year term, if he was re-elected governor of Arkansas in 1990, could be finessed.

I was not in office now but still the titular head of the Democratic Party in Wisconsin and a valuable fellow—my campaign apparatus, list of funders, volunteers, and voter ID files were there for Clinton. I could tell the Speaker: Just say all the work had been done, the promises kept, the budget passed, and the governor should run for president. The pledge didn't matter now. America needed him more than Arkansas.

Shortly after I landed in Little Rock, I was at lunch with Bill and Hillary at the governor's residence. A detail of convicts in prison togs were tending the lawn. Sweet tea was served. Then to meet Bruce Lindsey and Betsy Wright in the governor's office. They were the keepers of the Rolodex for the race for president. Two special people.

It was on that visit that I realized that maybe it was possible I would end up in Norway. We had a take-in lunch in the Speaker's office. There was a painting on the wall of a cockfighting arena. The scene: Only one rooster was in the pit. A poster on the wall in the background said "Vote."

Clinton devoured a triple-decker chicken salad sandwich on white bread, talking all the while. I thought: This guy can be elected. Clinton asked me to organize and chair the 1992 Clinton for President campaign in the Wisconsin primary. Mostly volunteers and mostly made up on the fly. Someone called me from Eau Claire and wanted to volunteer. I said, "You are now the campaign director for northern Wisconsin."

Schedules? Typical was the day I was introducing him at a rally at the airport in La Crosse, and he had yet to board the plane to get there from Cincinnati. All this was colorfully detailed later in a series of newspaper articles in the *Wisconsin State Journal,* the morning daily in Madison. I had taken a chance on Clinton winning and agreed the *Journal's* reporters could be on the inside of the campaign and follow me wherever, but only if the stories ran after the primary election was over. (Clinton loved this newspaper series.)

The last campaign appearance he made in the primary was in Milwaukee at the technical college. We were in the underground parking garage waiting for the cars—Bill had on the leather Harley

Davidson jacket he had been presented (Harleys are made in Milwaukee)—and I said, "If you become president, I'm joining you." I did not phrase this in the form of a question.

The Wisconsin win was crucial. Had we lost Wisconsin, and we almost did, it would have been another story. Clinton also won in New York that day, and the two victories ended the hopes of Gov. Jerry Brown of California, the last candidate in the race who could deny Clinton the nomination. The margin of the Clinton win in Wisconsin was 37 percent to 35 percent.[8]

In the general election, I was put on the national campaign committee. No responsibility, just go to meetings and sit there with the potted plants and be a recognizable name in Democratic politics. Perfect.

CHAPTER 2
PEOPLE, PLACES AND CUSTOMS

VILLA OTIUM, MY DIPLOMATIC HOME IN OSLO

"We have acquired the finest place in Christiana (now called Oslo) at a very reasonable figure...it will give us added prestige in Norway. The press, which has given prominent space to the purchase, speaks of it as a special courtesy towards Norway, stressing the view that it is evidence of the importance the United States attaches to this mission and of its sincere desire to cultivate and preserve the friendly relations subsisting between the two countries."[9]

The year was 1923. The cost of the ambassador's Residence, Villa Otium, was $125,000 and included 3.5 acres of parkland and gardens, the Otium. There was a view of the Oslo Fjord to the south and Frogner Park was adjacent to the north. The library would be the ambassador's office. There was a separate large garage with a second-floor apartment suitable for offices.

The first American ambassador to the new country of Norway, Herbert H.D. Pierce, set up shop in 1906 in two furnished rooms at the Victoria Hotel. This was not unusual, as the U.S State Department did not own one property in Europe. The homes of the ambassadors and the space to entertain were such an embarrassment that in 1910 business leaders and civic groups formed the American Embassy

Association to lobby Congress to buy buildings "over which the Stars and Stripes can float as American soil..."

Villa Otium was built in 1908 for Hans Andreas Nikolai Olsen, who had been in charge of the Russian operations of the Nobel family oil company, one of the largest in the world. He married a niece of Alfred Nobel. He was named the Norwegian consul general in St. Petersburg when Norway became independent. When he retired, he wanted a grand home in Oslo meant for comfortable living and social events. After a design competition, Henrick Bull, a notable Norwegian architect of the time, was chosen. The design was in the popular Art Nouveau style.

Ambassador Laurits Swenson, who served from 1911 to 1913, had searched for several years, settled on Villa Otium as the best option, and lobbied the State Department for the purchase. "It featured two halls and two salons, reception room and sitting room, dining room, library, office, fifteen bedrooms, three bathrooms, servant's quarters, a modern kitchen and a pantry, laundry and storage space."

Think of the American ambassador's Residence like the White House in both function and as a symbol of America.

The Residence, from bottom to top

The basement was as large as the footprint of the house, plus there was a workspace for the gardener under the terrace. There she had her tools and fertilizer and such. There was a bank of florescent lights over a wooden worktable to start plants from seeds and force bulbs. The garden had 100 rose bushes in her care.

Two furnaces—behemoths—one had been converted from coal. No air conditioning as there was no need. A hulking mangle dominated the washing room, where two veteran matrons came as needed, three times a week sometimes, to wash and iron the tablecloths and napkins. Another room was just to hang them to dry.

A sauna was almost hidden, as it was the bombproof room that Ambassador Harriman was to go to if the Germans invaded Oslo. The steel door, closed when the sauna was on, did not invite relaxation—what if it got stuck?!

The wine cellar was in the basement but had to be accessed from outside the house down a set of steps where a thick oak door with a padlock had to be opened with a key that was forever being misplaced. Perhaps it could hold 500 bottles, but only the racks next to the door were used, as I had to buy the wine and then be reimbursed when it was consumed. My practice was just-in-time inventory, and my assistant Sue would bill the embassy for reimbursement so quickly after an event that I had no out-of-pocket cost.

The entrance was a room with two long racks for hanging coats, several umbrella stands, a full-length mirror, and the leather-bound guest book on a standing desk. In winter, women guests would bring their shoes in bags and leave their wet boots under the racks. Full-length mink coats were common and practical for protection from the weather and slush on the streets while shopping and waiting for the bus or trolley. The cost was not great and likely the lovely coats had once been their grandmothers'.

Most guests arrived by taxi because of the strict drunk-driving law. When invited to the American ambassador's home for dinner where there would be champagne and wine, perhaps cognac, and talking with the smart set, why sit there with a glass of mineral water? Take a taxi.

There was one guard in a small side room to look after us and monitor the cameras placed around the property. For as long as anyone could remember, the guards had been retired Oslo policemen. Willy had been there the longest, through five ambassadors. Always good for a story and to chat up guests as they waited. As a boy during the German occupation, he had been a runner of coded messages for the Resistance.

Guests came into the first room and were greeted by myself and Barbara, and then the person or persons being hosted next in line, usually American or Norwegian officials and notables. May-Britt Ivarson, the protocol doyenne, would often hover behind me to introduce the guests and say something about them I could use in my welcoming toast—some familiarity that would make their night special. Or mention when we had met before, a prompt for me to say "takk for sist"—thank you for the last time we were together.

There was a large fireplace that provided ambiance, heat, and risk. Often it wouldn't draw because of the heavy moist air in the winter, and the house would fill with smoke causing an opening of windows to the cold. Several times I came down the spiral stairs from the family quarters to be greeted by a pigeon standing inside the fireplace. Fell down the chimney. The lesser-known Santa Claus breed of pigeon.

The first salon was meant for gathering while standing and

chatting with others, a glass in hand. When the signal for dinner was given, there was a casual promenade through the sitting room over the Persian carpet following the path worn down to the threads from high heels, past the Steinway that had hosted many a virtuoso, the lid a pattern of round stains from cocktail glasses, and into the dining room aglow with candles refracting light off the silver and glassware—and then the anticipation of finding your place card and meeting the others at your table. How exciting. The house, the piano, the guard, the maids, the chef, where the name cards are placed, all needed for successful diplomacy. As essential as a canvas is to the artist.

The family suite of rooms on the second floor included a master bedroom, a dressing room with two walls of closets, a master bathroom bigger than a New York City apartment, a sitting room with a television, two other bedrooms, and another bathroom. There was a tiny kitchen; it must have been a maid's resting room or for storage originally, as there was only a two-burner hot plate, a sink and an ancient refrigerator that belonged in a museum. But this is where the boys had their cereal in the morning before school, or if they got up in time to avoid the usual mad dash the two blocks to catch their city bus, I would make French eggs—butter on both sides of white bread, cut out the center, put in a frying pan, crack an egg in the opening, fry, flip, and fry again. Top with Karo syrup. Croque enfants.

At the other end of the hall from the family rooms was a spectacular guest bedroom, with its own big bathroom, and a balcony overlooking the gardens. This balcony had an ingenious fire escape. It appeared to be a pipe to the ground, like an eave spout, but opened up to a ladder when a latch was released. I demonstrated this to each guest. Jimmy Carter, trained as an engineer, took particular interest in the mechanism. Fire was always on my mind as we always had candles lit for events, and, of course, there were fireplace embers. Often, I would get up in the middle of the night and check, finding that a candle somewhere had been missed and was still flickering.

The marble terrace overlooking the garden, two-thirds the length of the house, was the scene of many a reception and could accommodate enough tables for a lunch for 30. The garden was a large open yard of great use for events like the Fourth of July celebration where several hundred invited guests had room to mingle with ease.

When you looked back at the house from the garden, you would notice a granite relief with two putti, sometimes confused with cherubs, holding rose stems, with a vase of roses between them. The rose in Norway is symbolic and plentiful because the climate is one of the rose-friendliest in the world. Hence, rosemåling, the art of the Norwegian people.

THE U.S. EMBASSY: WHAT IT IS AND HOW IT WORKS

My day in my office at the U.S. Embassy in Oslo always started the same. Sue Meyer, my assistant, would have waiting on my desk three stacks of cables: a pile from other Nordic[10] embassies, which I read religiously, and other European embassies; a stack from State and other government agencies, with wide circulations from which I would pick and choose based on subject; and a third, a short stack that I had to read and sign with my name and date. These were sometimes marked "Secret: Ambassador's Eyes Only," with a warning of limited circulation. The other ambassadors, who had received that same cable that morning, were listed. If there were cables from elsewhere in the world where Oslo had been added to the circulation, there was a reason for it, and I read those.

Mixed in among the three stacks were cables from Moscow. It was essential to our embassy that I read the ones from Moscow as more and more of our embassy's focus was on everything dealing with the Norwegian-Russian border. After the stacks were disposed of, and only then, would Sue hand me the *International Herald Tribune*.

The U.S. Embassy staff

The staff of the embassy when I arrived numbered 135—roughly 40 percent American in diplomatic positions and 60 percent Norwegian as support staff. The diplomatic staffing of the embassy reflected a focus driven by the fact that Norway is the only NATO member with a border with Russia. Norway is the size and shape of California. There is a geographically spread-out string of airfields and mountain bunkers stuffed with materiel waiting for the F-16s and land forces to arrive quickly if Norway is threatened. There is also a diplomatic touchiness related to the operational presence in the Norwegian Sea of U.S. Navy nuclear powered submarines. The military attaché at the embassy was a submariner.

Every Tuesday morning at 10:00, the Country Team met in the

conference room off the ambassador's office. I was at the head of the table. My assistant Sue Meyer was behind me taking notes. To my right was the deputy chief of mission (DCM), Bill McCahill. Next to him were Rob Weisberg, administration; the head of our combined Political and Economic Section, Harold "Hal" Meinheit; and Consular Eli "Nick" Lauderdale. At the other end from me was the defense and naval attaché, U.S. Navy Captain Richard "Dick" Vidosic; Office of Defense Cooperation Air Force Colonel Daniel "Dan" Penny; then the head of the U.S. Information Service, the press person Michael Scanlon (a Mainer); and Foreign Commercial Service officer Scott Bozek. And to my left was the CIA station chief. All talented, dedicated, experienced, and with a sense of humor. It is how they got these very special postings.

There was a report from each person on the week past and a brief on the week ahead. If there was a visitor of note coming the arrangements were discussed. Sometimes there was such a visitor every day. Also, almost every day came a directive from State, or any agency of the U.S. government or other embassies for démarches, meaning we were to deliver a message or ascertain a position on an issue from the Norwegian government. I would always deal with the prime minister, the foreign minister, and the defense minister. Then there was triage and a message returned if necessary.

These were quite informal meetings with quips rewarded. (You can tell Russian spies as they have the best gold teeth.) We were all friends and all in this together. Much of my schedule was decided at the Country Team meetings by the need for my presence to meet a visitor, host a dinner or lunch, be at an event, or travel. There was a lot of travel.

The deputy chief of mission is the No. 2 diplomat in the embassy. He or she is the chief adviser to the ambassador and the chief of staff. When there is no ambassador, the DCM becomes the chargé d'affaires. The chargé has the same diplomatic privileges and immunity as an ambassador.

I was delivered to the trusted and veteran hands of DCM Bill McCahill when I arrived in Oslo on November 13, 1993. Bill had a perfect educational background for diplomacy: a BA degree in religion. He had been the executive assistant to Secretary of State Alexander Haig and George Shultz and executive assistant to NATO General Secretary Lord Carrington.

For any ambassador to be successful, he or she has to let the DCM run the place. Bill did it with aplomb and humor.

Bill had the smile, the calmness, and knew what he wanted next in his career. He had a Ph.D. in South Asian Studies from Harvard and spoke Chinese. DCM in China was the goal. It was good for me to know this from the get-go.

The defense attaché is responsible for military-to-military relations. He or she reports to the ambassador. The office is part of the Defense Intelligence Agency (DIA) in the Department of Defense. The attaché's responsibility is to gather information related to military matters that will inform policymakers. The DIA synthesis of this intelligence often ends up as a part of the president's daily briefings. The defense attaché in Norway was almost always a submariner, as was our experienced attaché, Navy Captain Dick Vidosic. The activities of nuclear submarines, ours and the Russians, were the soup du jour of this office.

The intelligence officer was Commander Al Nadolski. Young, brilliant, an Annapolis grad—not a submariner. I came to rely on him as my special diplomat. The Cold War was no more. Overnight the policy changed from the Soviet Union as the enemy to finding constructive ways to engage the new Russia through their Northern Fleet.[11] The two policy goals were to make the Partnership for Peace work and help the Russian Navy secure its nuclear materiel. For two navies at odds for 50 years, it was a shocking change of mission and culture. Our job in Oslo was, in partnership with Norway, to help find the calmer waters the end of the Cold War promised. Al was good at this new maneuvering.

The U.S. Embassy building

The embassy building in Oslo sits on Henrik Ibsen's street on the same sloping hill as the Palace, which is just a short walk away through the Royal Park.[12] From my large corner office on the top floor, I could see the flag that when raised indicated His Majesty King Harald was in residency. The Norwegian Foreign Ministry is nearby at Victoria Terrasse, an architectural landmark built in 1890. It was the HQ of the Gestapo during the occupation.

The architect of the embassy was Eero Saarinen, a Finnish-American famous for the Gateway Arch and Dulles Airport. He was born in the Grand Duchy of Finland, Russian Empire, in 1910. He became an American citizen in 1940.

This embassy was perhaps the most striking example of architecture meant to symbolize "This is America" during the Cold War with the Soviet Union. Most important was the library with a separate entrance, which took up the ground floor. Free and open, books not censored, no overtly ideological tracts, a place to study. Dozens of Norwegians in the government, Parliament, and Foreign Service told me of their time as students studying and doing research in this library.

The building was a parallelogram.[13] No square corners. Even the elevators were cockeyed. My office was all windows on the two sides facing the street and was shaped like a large wedge of cheese. Very expensive cheese. I could see the blue trams going downtown and back and hear their bell signaling the stop just outside the embassy's front door. The center of the building was a hollow triangle with an atrium up to the top-floor ceiling with a gong hanging from a chain dangling over a koi pond. Great sport was to bang this gong to produce an echo.

It was a working office building that had an underground garage with a motor pool where oil could be changed and cars repaired, and that ensured that my Chevy was always in our control. There was a full kitchen with an in-house cook and a dining hall for the staff and to use for entertaining. There was a post office for APO mail, and a small Post Exchange store.

There was a special room for the Marines to store and clear their weapons at the end of a shift, making sure there was not a bullet in the breach by shooting into a barrel of sand. Amazing how far the sound travels when a gunshot goes off inside a barrel. They still used the Colt 45 I carried in the Army—a brute of a pistol very dangerous to the person carrying it.

The consular section, where passports and visas were handled, was on the street level with its own entrance. There was a real estate section to manage the buildings we owned—the embassy, the ambassador's Residence, the deputy chief of mission's residence, three large villas—and the many apartments we leased. "In constant need of repair" was their motto.[14] This was compounded by the Norwegian system where the lessee is responsible for upkeep.

The Department of Commerce had an office in the embassy to help American business.

A general responsibility that did not have a separate office was the duty to see to it that Americans, including those in jail, had their interests protected within the laws of Norway and international law.

FOOD, DRINK, AND DIPLOMATIC DINNERS

(T)o share food with friends or strangers is a great equalizer. Around the table, social ranks fade. Rivals and opponents share the intimacy of the table, sometimes merging into friendly guests.
— *"The Art of the Chicken," Jacques Pepin,* Harvest, 2002

The food

Julia Child said she only really mastered the cooking of fresh ocean fish during her time in Oslo, from 1959-1962, when her husband Paul was a cultural attaché at the embassy during his last two years before he retired from the State Department.[15]

Fresh fish dominated the menu at the Residence: grouper, halibut, and Arctic char. The preparation was simple and sauces were kept to a minimum. If there was a salad, it would be peppery arugula with just a misting of vinaigrette. For informal occasions, there could be mussels mariniere. Dust off your copy of *Mastering the Art of French Cooking,* and you will find the recipe.

Mussels, called blue shells for their color, were gathered a few times by Edmund and me, taking the boat just far enough out in the Oslo Fjord to the nearest small rock island then sticking a push broom down in the water and pulling up dozens of mussels that would latch on to the bristles.

Duck breast was another staple. Surprisingly tasty because of the fat content and could be seared and served pink in the middle. A chef's friend.

A real treat was reindeer. A filet tasting of nuzzled moss and lichen. No other way to describe as that is their diet. It could be cut with a fork. Also served rare. Reindeer is a very small creature and does not have the taste of venison. It is wild but herded by the Sami in northern Norway.

The signature dessert was cloudberries with cream. Cloudberry bushes were wild and grew in the mountains. They are white with tiny seeds like a raspberry and picked only by trolls. (OK, made that up, the troll part).

But the daily food of Norway was still quite familiar to me, except for one staple: shrimp. I'd eaten shrimp in the U.S., but Norway's fresh shrimp was a different experience altogether. Barbara and I went the first time to Norway in 1977 to visit my sister, Wendy, and be tourists. We had first spent some time in London and then caught the overnight ferry from Newcastle to Bergen. It was the day Elvis died. At the dock, my sister, Wendy, was waiting for us, and we walked a few steps to a fishing boat selling steamed shrimp caught that morning. So sweet it demanded the meat in the tail be sucked out. A noon lunch was often a bowl of fresh shrimp set in the middle of the table to share, and you peeled it and placed it on one slice of white bread with a dollop of mayonnaise and a lemon wedge.

Norwegian sandwiches are open face. A slice of bread with butter and Jarlsberg cheese is lunch for the worker in the factory, on the farm, or in the office.

Lefse, a Norwegian flatbread made with potatoes, flour, butter, and milk that we ate slathered in more butter and sprinkled with sugar in church basement dinners, was still around, but now as a hot-dog wrap sold at 7-Eleven.

Lutefisk, the dried cod cured in lye that Norwegian immigrants brought with them and had shipped over, was also common at Christmastime in both America and Norway. In my church, Bristol Lutheran, the communal Lutefisk dinner was in the church basement. Lutefisk is reconstituted in salty water and has a fishy aroma. This olfactory assault would seep up from the church basement to the parishioners above and could linger until Palm Sunday. The word "gelatinous" is a synonym. There is a law in Wisconsin prohibiting lutefisk from being named a hazardous material. (Not making this up.)

The cod drying in the winds off the ocean in north Norway hanging from racks that look like tents is not for lutefisk. This is for shipment to Catholic countries like Portugal and Brazil for making bacalao, the common dish for meatless Fridays. 'Twas a pope that spawned the Norwegian dried cod industry and saved the world from lutefisk.

A pastry known to all was a roll with a yellow pudding in the center called a sunshine roll, and kids walking to school would get one on the way. Caraway was in everything including breads, cheese, and aquavit. An often-used spice and a treat for me was cardamom, especially in the wheat rolls Wendy would bake. It was also in the title of the children's book *Folk og røvere i Kardemomme by (When the*

Robbers Came to Cardamom Town), which was our textbook for learning to read and speak Norwegian. A lot of wisdom in that book, and it added greatly to my understanding of Norwegians.

At a mountain hotel on your ski vacation or summer sojourn, you would find on the breakfast table: two baskets of eggs (one hard- and one soft-boiled), dark bread, Wasa (a crispbread), Jarlsberg cheese, gjetost or brunost (a soft sweet cow's or goat's milk cheese that looks like a block of peanut butter), caraway cheese, lingonberry jam, pickled herring, pickled beets, a waffle with sections the shape of hearts, butter and more butter, paper thin slices of ham (much like parma), prunes, cucumber slices in a vinegar and sugar solution, gravlax with a sweet dill mustard sauce nearby, orange juice, and weak coffee with real cream and sugar cubes nearby. A coffee cake or two.

At Christmas time, there was the julebord. This was not for family, but rather the office party. I usually attended 10 of them—each branch of the military expected me as did the Norwegian American societies—and hosted two or three. On the table would be aquavit, some alcoholic punch, juleøl—a dark but sweet beer brewed for the holidays—ribbe (roasted pork belly), pinnekjøtt (salted lamb ribs), boiled potatoes, pickled sour red cabbage slaw, and much of the list from the breakfast bord (table). Desserts that could be easily handled like cookies but usually not traditional Christmas desserts.

All this was eaten and drunk standing up. There would be toasts and songs as the aquavit settled in.

The drink

The host will typically begin by rising to give a brief welcome to the table "Velkommen til bords" speech to the guests. The host or hostess lifts the glass, makes eye contact with each of the guests around the table and says "Skål."[16]

There is more, much more. For me as host of the dinner, the brief welcome meant I would say something personal and complimentary about the guest of honor. If we had met before that would be mentioned. All this was vetted by May-Britt Ivarson, the embassy's protocol doyenne, so there were no faux pas. For example, an imbroglio of the first order: What if I referred to his wife when she was his samboer, "the one who lives together"? A legally recognized union. What do you think that conversation would be like when they got home? My goal was to make people feel at ease and get a smile, perhaps a polite laugh, and be self-deprecating, as that and the wine would address the Janteloven— the need to not appear to be better than others.

At each table, there would also be a round of looking at eyes and during the meal a lifting of a glass could also allow a glance and a mutual sip between individuals. No clinking of glasses. Too intimate. "Please, we're Lutheran here."

Now for me this seemingly off-the-cuff patter of understated flattery was second nature. But pity the guest of honor as he or she would have to give a "takk for maten" speech (thank you for the food). This would dampen the appetite of many a guest of honor thinking ahead of the remarks, in English, in front of the American ambassador and the gathered guests, many of whom would be well known and likely friends. Yet, all did very well, including the Americans.

The wine was always from California and to this day an oaky Chardonnay will give me a woozy sensation like being around a cigar. After dinner, there was cognac, always Larsen. It was from France, but the company was founded by Jens Reidar Larsen, a Norwegian, who was on his way to immigrate to America but never did as the ship stopped in Bordeaux where he found a wife and in 1926 founded Larsen Cognac. I always brought a bottle or two at Christmas to the police station where those responsible for my safety were headquartered.

The quite smooth Norwegian brewed beer is called pils (pilsner) and Rignes was my favorite as it was available at Ullsvik's grocery on East Washington Avenue in Madison when I was growing up. A six-pack of Rignes was a staple when my parents would have a get-together around Christmas. However, the real Norwegian gift to beer was lettøl, a great-tasting reduced-alcohol beer. Because of the severe penalties for drunken driving, a history of prohibition and Lutheran damnation of drunkenness, and the fact that alcohol is taxed based on its alcohol content, lettøl was born and offered everywhere, including diplomatic dinners.

Oh, and home brew. Brewing beer in rural areas to evade the taxman is still a sport, enjoyed since the time of Danish rule. If a guest brought a jug of home brew as a gift, I knew I had been granted entrance into some clandestine lodge. Sharing a glass of this yeasty mead was like the secret handshake.

Norwegian aquavit usually only made an appearance on the Christmas julebord. It's typically offered ice cold as a snort, in a fancy shot glass. The rest of the year it is kept in the freezer. And, it had to be Linie. This means "line," and the line was the equator, and genuine Aquavit has to travel twice across in a cask. The roll of the ship sloshes the spirit in the cask, and along with the changing weather gives it the special taste. Discovered 200 years ago when some of this cargo didn't get unloaded in Japan and returned to Norway, where the only sensible thing to do was to drink it.

DRESSING THE PART

A 40-long suit off the rack with a 34 waist fit me like I might have been the model. I came to Norway with a good wardrobe for the climate—similar to Wisconsin but cooler in the summer. A below-the-knee length cashmere overcoat I had bought at KaDeWe in Berlin in 1985 and a trench coat were always in style and provided warmth plus rain and wind protection.

All was well haberdashery-wise in Norway. I could continue to order shirts and ties from the mail order company Lands' End through APO. But then came the invasion of the double-breasted suit. Suddenly I needed new suits. Not to worry.

Most embassies including Oslo's had an arrangement where a fellow from one of the Savile Row tailors in London would stop in every two months with a book of swatches. At the first visit, your measurements were taken and placed on file. Choose a material and style and the suit would come quite quickly through the mail. Very reasonable as there were no taxes or duties. All this tucked into the treaty that proscribed a host country from imposing their taxes on diplomatic missions. So double-breasted it was. A bespoke suit is heaven.

As Speaker, a candidate for governor, and ambassador, I was photographed all the time. The march through three decades of photos of me in suits is archival. What I didn't have was the closet of clothes and shoes Norwegians have for boating, skiing, hiking in mountains, walking about the city in winter in continual mist, and hunting birds and deer. The Norwegian wool sweater covered a lot of these needs. I did have a Harris Tweed but alas, from the days when I was a slimmer 39 long.

There was a Helly Hansen shop by City Hall for the rain gear, hiking and skiing pants, and jackets. Coats were picked up on travels—a green hunting coat with shotgun stock padding on the right shoulder when Alec and I went to Copenhagen so he could go to Tivoli and the Ripley's Believe It or Not Museum. Somewhere along the way, I acquired a loden wool cape-type coat.

Shoes were an issue as in the winter it was either wet or the sidewalks were covered in dangerous ice. This was solved by ordering two pairs of Rockport waterproof walking shoes—one for rain and one with grips on the soles like crampons for ice. I would very often walk to the embassy and Edmund Steiro would bring dress shoes in the Chevy.

Oh, and neck scarves. I never could get the hang of the European style of looping a wool scarf, so my hanging scarf was very American and another unintended trademark.

THE NORWEGIAN PRESS

"I had nothing but the most pleasant and cooperative relations with the many newspaper editors and reporters I came to know…many of them had lived in the United States…It was my observation from experience that the journalists of Norway were governed by a sense of social responsibility. They did not wish to make trouble out of slips, and valued as much as I did the clear understanding between our two countries. If I, on my part, had the slightest misgiving about the propriety of any statement, they were too glad to protect me."[17]

This was the experience of Ambassador Florence Jaffray Harriman in 1940, and it was mine as well.

As ambassador, it was my job to be available to the press. Reporters and editors who wrote about foreign affairs were invited to appropriate receptions, dinners, and lunches.

Many a good story could be gotten while holding a glass of California wine and chatting with guests at the United States ambassador's Residence.

Michael Scanlon was the embassy press attaché. He made sure that when a reporter called there was an answer ASAP. Mike had a background as a newspaperman in Maine. "Just the facts please." He liked to call himself a "Mainer."

Per Egil Hegge was *Aftenposten's* legendary journalist and raconteur. Upon meeting him for the first time he appointed himself my "explainer of things." We became fast friends. *Aftenposten* is the afternoon paper in Oslo and, like *The New York Times*, is the paper of record. It is read throughout the country.

The journalist spent his whole career at *Aftenposten*, starting as the newspaper's correspondent in London and then Moscow, until he was kicked out for reporting on Aleksandr Solzhenitsyn. His reporting included quite a scoop: Solzhenitsyn dictated his acceptance statement for the Nobel Prize for Literature to Per Egil despite the fact that Solzhenitsyn usually avoided foreigners.

Per Egil then went on to head *Aftenposten's* Washington, D.C., bureau. A much friendlier beat.

He was back in Oslo when I became ambassador and had free rein at the paper; he was purportedly the culture editor. Per and his wife were quite a pair and the two of them at a reception were easily spotted and soon surrounded by those who knew he would be telling a delicious story about a politician or other violator of the rules of Janteloven—thinking oneself is better than others.

Per Egil loved Washington, D.C., and understood Americans. An invitation to his home was a ticket to a salon. The assemblage would enjoy the wit, the wine, and his noted cooking. One half-expected to catch a glimpse of Gertrude Stein and Alice B. Toklas in the garden.

I would say something like, "What do you think of the rumored next prime minister?" And I would get the history of the person, his or her family, the talk about town, and what it might mean for the United States. Minor peccadilloes were not off limits. An ambassador does well by keeping in mind that reporters are people too. Per Egil was an exemplar of the profession.[18]

THE NORWEGIAN LANGUAGE

There was no written Norwegian language until the 1860s. Danish was the official written language and was used by government, business, and the Lutheran Church.

Ivar Aasen, a self-taught philologist, decided he would travel the country, listen to the spoken word used in the rural areas, and meld this into a new written Norwegian national language. This was called Landsmål—"the language of the country"—and was eventually named Nynorsk—"the New Norwegian language." This was not popular in the cities and an alternative, a mixture of Danish and Norwegian, was developed, which became known as Bokmål—"book language."

What to teach? There were two official languages. Students had a choice and almost all chose to be taught in Bokmål. And this is the language most used in newspapers and books and what is taught to foreigners. My Norwegian language tutoring was in Bokmål.

Norwegian literature brought the new language to the world's attention. The poet Bjørnstjerne Bjørnson won the Nobel Prize for literature in 1903 and Norwegian author Sigrid Undset won the literature prize in 1928 for the beloved stories of the medieval heroine Kristin Lavransdatter.[19]

Henrik Ibsen brought Norwegian plays to every stage on the globe with *A Doll's House* in 1879 and *Hedda Gabler* in 1890. Edvard Grieg's *Peer Gynt Suites*, which he wrote for the Ibsen play *Peer Gynt*, became a symphony standard and in turn publicized the play.

The exploits and the bestselling books that followed by the polar explorers Fridtjof Nansen in the 1890s and Roald Amundsen in the first two decades of the 20th century were in great demand by publishers and were translated into dozens of languages. Translators who could bring the nuanced Norwegian to life in another language became much in demand. All helped to spawn the robust Norwegian publishing enterprises that thrive today.

PART TWO
DIARIES OF THE AMBASSADOR

The diary entries from my tenure as ambassador, which I have relied on extensively in this memoir, were created like this: A tentative schedule would be created, and my personal assistant, Sue, would pencil this in my date book. After the event actually happened, she would put it in ink; I would often add my handwritten notes one or two days after the event; if the embassy produced a cable on the event or there were news articles, I would add from them. Lunches, dinners, etc., were noted and the person for whom the event was held identified. The guest list and often the menu were filed separately. Except for chapters on dealing with nuclear waste and the push to enlarge NATO, my time in Norway is relayed in chronological order in this memoir.

CHAPTER 3
EARLY DAYS: NOVEMBER AND DECEMBER 1993

ARRIVING IN OSLO

We arrived in Oslo November 13, 1993 at 7 a.m. on Delta, first class from JFK, and were met by Deputy Chief of Mission Bill McCahill and his teenage son. And we met Edmund Steiro, my driver (who would be my driver and confidant for four years). A black Cadillac (lightly armored) took us to the Residence, and there were "wows" all around. Alec explored and claimed a large bedroom on the third floor as his.

PRESENTING CREDENTIALS TO THE KING

On November 18, the day I was to present my credentials to His Majesty King Harald V, a small announcement from the Palace noted it was on his schedule. One sentence in the newspapers stated that at 11 a.m. I would be received.

Measurements had been taken and morning dress had been rented, and I was handed a sheet of paper on conventions of conduct. "The King will offer his hand first." All arranged by May-Britt, the ineffable protocol director. Morning dress is a daytime tuxedo. Think of the groom figure atop a wedding cake. A black coat with tails, vest, gray perfectly creased pants, regular tie, and black dress shoes. Important for me on this day were my cap-toe Florsheim shoes that I had shined and buffed to a sheen using the horsehair brush I still had from my days as a military policeman.

The car from the Palace arrived according to schedule at 10:30 a.m. and the chamberlain rang the doorbell at 10:31. At 10:55, I was in the anteroom outside HM's reception room.

The Palace is not a grand affair. Do not think of Buckingham or some other stone edifice in the English countryside. It was built in 1845 for Carl Johan, king of Sweden and Norway during their union, as he would need a place to stay should he visit. It became the residence of the new Norwegian monarch after independence from Sweden in 1905.[20]

HM King Harald was standing when the large wooden door was opened and his real, genuine "glad to meet you" smile lit up the room. Six feet tall and you could see the fitness from years of sailing. I was taken aback. There stood a man who looked like my mother's father, my grandfather Viggo Neilsen who had immigrated from Denmark with his brother Axel to Wisconsin in 1902.

HM was quick and easy with a laugh and had dimples worn to creases from smiling. We chatted a long time about the things of the day and the new president, Bill Clinton. What was he like? We would see each other often, he said as we parted.

Back to the Residence and champagne toasts all around with the embassy staff. May-Britt was relieved I had caused no international incident she knew of yet. I stayed in morning dress for a long while. We had it for 24 hours.

MEETING THE PRIME MINISTER

Gro Harlem Brundtland (GHB) was in her third year of her third term as prime minister (PM) when I arrived in Norway and met her in November 1993. She had been prime minister for eight months in 1981 when she was 42 years old—Norway's first female prime minister. Brundtland was PM again from 1986 to 1989, and after a Conservative Party-led coalition fell apart after one year, Labour was again in power in 1990. The Labour Party was now the dominant party in Norwegian politics and Gro Harlem Brundtland was by far the dominant figure in the Labour Party.

I had followed Norwegian politics and had been to Norway several times prior to becoming ambassador, but my knowledge of GHB came from my time in the Wisconsin Legislature in the decade of the '80s when I was Assembly Speaker and several landmark pieces of environmental protection legislation were passed. Important in this environmental decade and the generation in the trenches fighting for change was knowledge of the "Brundtland Report." Not that we knew the details, but that we knew *of* it.

In 1987, the report *Our Common Future* was published by the World Commission on Environment and Development. Prime Minister Brundtland was the chair—thus it became known in the press as the Brundtland Report. The powerful political idea that the environment and development could co-exist became known as "sustainable development," and this, as a political philosophy and a manifesto of the Labour Party, was what one needed to grasp to understand Gro Harlem Brundtland.

I knew enough to talk in our first meeting on November 19, 1993, about my background in the environmental battles. And, a seasoned politician knows after years of campaigning, speeches, and debates that there is that "thing" that can define one politician to another: I was at the first Earth Day, and the founder of Earth Day, Wisconsin Sen. Gaylord Nelson, was a friend and mentor. Say no more. "How refreshing to talk to an American ambassador about the environment," was her comment that has stuck with me.

The prime minister's office is a spartan affair in a functional building with furniture easily recognizable to an American as Scandinavian. Like all meetings to come, a bottle of sparkling water, always the Norwegian brand Farris, was on the table and coffee offered. I had practiced saying "kaffe med fløte." Coffee with cream.

When she smiled, the mood in the room brightened. I was a change. President Clinton was a change. The Cold War was over. Norway's border with the Soviet Union in the Arctic and the NATO alliance no longer had to suck up all the oxygen in a room in meetings between the U.S. and Norway.

An introductory meeting is not where policy is discussed. The goal of both parties is to form a professional friendship. That is what an ambassador should strive for. There were two others in the meeting: Morten Wetland, a political adviser, and Jonas Gahr Støre, the liaison to the Cabinet. They were smiling.

Morten's title was state secretary, and this meant he was a political appointee and important in Labour Party hierarchy. It was obvious the trust Gro had in him by the way she said his name—like it was all capital letters—when she needed a word or a policy reminder.

Jonas was director general of the prime minister's office, somewhat similar to a U.S. president's chief of staff. I would come to know Jonas in time, but Morten and I became fast friends on that day. If I had to guess why looking back, it likely was when I talked about my first real job in politics. It was as a speechwriter. Morten was the speechwriter—in Norwegian, English, and German. It is a cabal of souls who try to explain the president or prime minister in words they can own. The speechwriter is "in the room" and hears it all and goes forth to make persuasive prose out of babble.

THANKSGIVING DINNER WITH YASSER ARAFAT

Yasser Arafat was coming to Oslo on November 25, 1993, at the invitation of the Norwegian government to be feted and treated like a head-of-state-to-be. This was all-important, as it was necessary at every opportunity to reinforce the Oslo Peace Accords through promoting Arafat, Peres, and Rabin since this peace was a work in progress that relied not on words on paper but on faith in three people and symbols.

The Oslo Accords were a road map for peace and further reconciliation between Israel and the Palestine Liberation Organization (PLO) secretly negotiated in 1993 by a team of Norwegian and Palestinian academics under the auspices of the Norwegian Foreign Ministry. The accords were signed by President Clinton, Israeli Prime Minister Yitzhak Rabin, and PLO Chairman Yasser Arafat in a ceremony on the White House Lawn on September 13, 1993.[21]

The essential breakthrough was that Israel and the PLO would recognize each other as the negotiating partners, meaning that the PLO recognized the state of Israel as legitimate and Israel recognized the PLO as representing the Palestinian people. The Norwegian officials involved were Deputy Foreign Minister Jan Egeland, Terje Rød-Larsen, and Mona Juul.

For me as the U.S. ambassador, the important thing to note is that

I was now free to meet and conduct relations with PLO Chairman Yasser Arafat as a representative of the president of the United States. I—as the living symbol of the U.S.—was to be at the dinner in the receiving line next to PM Brundtland as Arafat arrived.

There was some cable chatter from State as to how I was to address Arafat—all ignored, as his title was chairman. No need to catch me mouthing some accolade that would come back to hit us in the face. My driver Edmund came up with the good idea that we could put American flags on the front fenders of the Chevy. We never did that except for very important events, like visits of heads of government.

We got to Akershus fortress in plenty of time for the dinner, and we were at the arched stone entrance built for horse and carriage—but the Chevy with the flags was too wide to go through. Edmund had to get out and take off the flags. By this time, with other ambassadors in their cars waiting behind us, it was too late to put them back on. Such is life, said Edmund.

There were a dozen press and TV cameras crowded around as Arafat came in and took my outstretched hand. "It is a pleasure to meet you Mr. Chairman," I said. He did not let go of my hand; our handshake and wide smiles were frozen until every TV camera and news photographer left the scene. Not your traditional Thanksgiving.

TEA WITH NELSON MANDELA

I was in my office. It was noon on December 10, 1993. I was waiting to go to the large ornate room that is the whole ground floor of Oslo City Hall for the Nobel Peace Prize ceremony at 1 p.m.[22]

My secretary came in and said, "Nelson Mandela is on the phone and would like to talk to you."

Mandela, then the president of the political party the African National Congress, or ANC, was to receive the Peace Prize, which was to be shared with South Africa's President Frederik Willem de Klerk for their efforts to end apartheid. I did not doubt it was Nelson Mandela. My thought was, "OK, now what has happened that I haven't been told about?"

He said, "Thank you, Mr. Ambassador, for taking my call," and asked if I could meet him in his suite in the Grand Hotel 30 minutes after the ceremony as there was an important issue to discuss.

I was there early. He greeted me, and I was in his thrall. I felt in the presence of goodness. He offered me tea and poured our two cups.

He took milk. I took milk.

He had notes. I had not a clue.

He explained that there was a critical issue in the negotiations to be decided in the next two days at the round of discussions of the General Agreements on Tariffs and Trade, GATT, now going on in South Africa.[23] If the U.S. position to put a tariff on textiles prevailed, it would mean the loss of several hundred thousand jobs in the South African factories making clothes for export.

I asked if I could please use the phone. There is a secret number to call a special White House operator, and I called it and said I needed Mickey Kantor right away. Mickey was the U.S. trade representative who was handling the GATT talks. I knew Mickey from the Clinton campaign as we were both in it from the start. In 10 minutes, Mickey was found.

"Mickey, I am here in Oslo with Nelson Mandela in his suite in the Grand Hotel. He has just been awarded the Nobel Peace Prize and he is asking if we can change our position on textiles for South Africa in GATT, and I told him we probably would do that. Here, I will put him on the phone."

Back with me on the phone, Mickey said, "Well what can I do, I said yes, but we have to talk again tomorrow."

The next day, I was back at Mandela's suite with Mickey on the phone telling me, "OK, tell Mr. Mandela it is a deal but no mention to the press or anyone else."[24]

In April, there would be the first free election in South Africa and Nelson Mandela would surely be elected president. How was he to build a new South Africa if at the start the U.S. killed a major sector of the economy?

After this news, Mr. Mandela was relaxed; I was relieved, and we talked up a storm. It was so meaningful at this incredible moment that I could tell him that in the Wisconsin Legislature we had fought for the divestment of stocks in the state's pension fund of U.S. companies doing business in South Africa.[25] Mr. Mandela said when in prison he was aware that American state legislatures had been involved in the divestment movement, and it had been important. Then we took photos.

Back in my office I wrote a note to President Clinton: "Don't fire Mickey," went on to describe what had happened, and ended by saying, "Nelson Mandela owes you one."

FROM PARTY TIME TO MIDEAST CRISIS

It was the night of the chief of station's holiday julebord given for leaders of the Norwegian Intelligence Service.[26] The relationship between this agency and the embassy is most important. Its responsibilities are both civilian and foreign and it is under the Ministry of Defense. Norway is one of the few countries in the world where the intelligence agencies have a special relationship with the United States. My relationship with Defense Minister Jørgen Kosmo had to be one of complete trust. We had to be friends. But it very quickly became "Jørgen and Tom."

There was another reason I was looking forward to this party. Just before I arrived the Norwegian press had reported that several agents of the Norwegian intelligence had actually been paid by the U.S. and without forewarning this had been abruptly stopped as a post-Cold War money-saving move. There were also press stories on the financing of what was commonly known as the spy ship *Marjata*. This embarrassment had to be acknowledged.

Intelligence agencies have the best food and on the long candlelit table was every Norwegian delicacy, from the time of the Viking mead hall to the holiday spread at the posh Theater Cafe. The wine was not plonk, shall we say. Eating and drinking for my country.

But then a call from the deputy chief of mission, Bill McCahill. We were to leave immediately and go to the foreign minister's home with a message from U.S. Secretary of State Warren Christopher. Johan Jørgen Holst, Norway's foreign minister, should call Yasser Arafat that night as something had "gone completely to hell." The call was in reference to the follow-on negotiations to finalize the language of the Oslo Peace Accords.

We were already halfway up Holmenkollen, the mountain rising above Oslo, near the ski jump. The roads were the usual two ruts of ice worn into crusted snow. A dark night. Not a twinkle. My driver, Edmund, had never been to this address before, and we got lost.

We were greeted by Holst, his wife Marianne Heiberg, and their young son Edvard, still up and demanding attention in the midst of the excitement. Holst studied at Columbia, had a Ph.D. in history from Oslo University, and was acknowledged to be a brilliant scholar and statesman. He had been the defense minister before Jørgen Kosmo. Holst was recovering from a medical episode and had not been out of the hospital long. He was pale and sat the whole time in his armchair. But his eyes were bright, and he was relishing the prospect of another serious talk with Yasser Arafat.

The next day DCM Bill McCahill told me Holst had stayed up all night talking to Arafat, and we had a readout of the call for a cable to send back to Washington.

CHAPTER 4
FAREWELL TO PEACEMAKER JOHAN JØRGEN HOLST

NORWAY'S PEACEMAKING FOREIGN MINISTER IS DEAD

"The President was saddened to learn yesterday of the death of Norwegian Foreign Minister Johan Jurgen Holst...[he will be remembered] for his leading role in the Israeli-PLO negotiations that led to the breakthrough in the Middle East peace process last September. The President was proud to have the opportunity to honor Minister Holst at the White House signing ceremony on September 13."[27]

DIGNITARIES RSVP FOR HOLST FUNERAL

A cable: Secretary of State Warren Christopher will attend Holst's funeral on January 22. We also learn Peres and Arafat will attend.

THE FUNERAL

The Holst funeral was held at the Oslo Dome Church. My heart was pounding. My ears were hearing something for the first time. Tears broke. The sound of the orchestra and singers rose to the top of the dome and filled it and then it crashed down on us. Again and again. Every vestibule, communion cup, the baptism font, and crack inside the 400-year-old walls of the church filled with the sound, and there was nowhere for it to go. Trumpeting angels had surely lifted Holst at this moment.

The program listed the music as *Mikis Theodorakis/Pablo Neruda: Los Libertadores fra Canto General*. Neruda's poem is about the struggle for justice on earth, not about angels and the promise of heaven. Every other item—the psalms, the prayers, the eulogies—were printed in Norwegian on the left side of the program and English on the right. Not this. It was Spanish on the left and Norwegian on the right.

During the funeral, Warren Christopher gripped his hands together tightly trying to hold on but then lost his compass of North Dakota stoicism. He had been born there in 1925. One parent had Norwegian roots. Their Lutheran church was of the austere branch. We had first met in Little Rock after Bill Clinton's election when he was heading the transition, and I told him I was going to ask for the Norway job. We talked in the car after the funeral about the criticism he was getting for not being good with the press—not chatty, no good quotes. Loquacious and North Dakota are close only in the dictionary. We concluded it was not what he said today, it was that he was here in Oslo at this funeral that mattered to the peace process, to the people of Norway, and to the Holst family. Being there is the job of diplomats.

I had met Shimon Peres in Israel in 1988 during a trade mission trip with Wisconsin Gov. Tommy Thompson. Peres was the minister of foreign affairs then and spent a great deal of time talking with Tommy and me in his office.[28]

Holst's successor was to be Bjørn Tore Godal, the minister of trade and shipping. He had yet to be officially sworn in to his new post. Godal was important and talented and had been groomed by the Labour Party, but he had not been involved in the peace process.

Arafat told the press only "small differences" remained. Peres predicted a breakthrough when they would meet the following week in Davos. No agreement was reached in Davos.

CHAPTER 5
HILLARY COMES TO
THE OLYMPICS

JANUARY 27, 1994: "URGENT"

To: Will Itoh, Executive Director, National Security Council
From: William C. McCahill, Jr., Deputy Chief of Mission

Dear Will,

Many thanks for coming back to us so quickly last night. Tom called Gro with the news, and she was absolutely ecstatic. When I followed up with Morten Wetland this morning, he said the PM's main interest was that Mrs. Clinton enjoy her stay in Norway, that she does things that she herself really found interesting, and she not feel burdened by protocol or other events she would rather avoid. So we have a deep well of Norwegian good will and enthusiasm to make this visit work really well...There will be many logistics problems to resolve.

That was an understatement. First Lady Hillary Clinton and daughter Chelsea would have a trailing entourage of staff, press, and security and the opening ceremony was in two weeks. And, we had to find a hotel as there was not a room left in Lillehammer at this late date. And the drive. Uff da.

In summer, the scenery on the 2 1/2-hour drive north to Lillehammer from Oslo is a feast for the eyes. A Monet of fields of hay that slope gently down to the shore of Lake Mjøsa, where the sky is reflected. Dotting the green fields are the 19th-century white-painted manor houses of the landowners and the small wooden cottages of the tenant farmers, "bønder."[29] That is in the summer. In the winter, the roads are usually so icy that tires embedded with steel studs are the norm. If cold could be scenery, this is what it would look like.[30]

Each country sends a representative to the Olympics, often the head of state. That the new first lady of the United States would represent America was a good-news headline. A real compliment to Norway. A winter thunderbolt thrown from Valhalla with a note tied to it stating that the Olympics would be a success. (But no mention of a hotel.)

First Lady Hillary Clinton was almost like the president himself coming because she was a force in the White House and could influence decisions. She could make decisions. Others could now imagine a word with her at a reception, perhaps: "Madame first lady, my prime minister very much would appreciate one of the early calls the president makes with world leaders." It is passed on and briefings would be written. This less-than-official but more-than-not-official chat is what is called a meeting on the "margins" of another meeting. Many times, I was instructed to pull someone aside during the milling-around, drinking-an-aperitif prelude to a dinner or event and inform so-and-so about such-and-such and report the answer. So-and-so would have been briefed by his people that the question was coming. Very important these side meetings for greasing the wheels of diplomacy. Marco Polo probably had side meetings.

For Gro Harlem Brundtland, this was the opportunity to establish a friendship. A personal relationship with a soul in kind. No sitting American president had ever visited Norway, but this was close. The first item put on the agenda was a breakfast between the two of them.

AN ENTOURAGE OF STARS

The White House Office of the Secretary: "President Clinton today announced the delegation to the 1994 Winter Olympic Games in Lillehammer, Norway."

In addition to the first lady and myself there was Florence Griffith Joyner, known as Flo Jo, a superstar of track and former Olympic medalist—someone who would be recognized by other athletes as a peer and example of what they hoped to become. Also, Tom McMillen, former member of the House, college basketball all-American, and member of the 1972 U.S. Olympic team.[31]

And, wow, Dawn Steel, the former head of Columbia Studios. The first woman to head a major movie studio and known for bringing America such iconic films as *Flashdance* and *Top Gun* when she was head of production at Paramount. Now an independent producer, her film *Cool Runnings*, a comedy about a Jamaican bobsled team making it to the Olympics, was a smash hit in theaters right now.

On the list with a name straight out of Mark Twain, perhaps Dickens, was Irby Clifford Simpkins Jr., the publisher of the *Nashville Banner* newspaper who would become part of Olympic Lore—at least my lore.

THANKS BE TO ODIN, GOD OF HOTEL RESERVATIONS

There was a hotel. Thank you, Odin.[32] The embassy staff had organized a team, called every hotel within a few miles of Lillehammer and were tipped off that the Hotel Nevra was empty. How could that be? The ownership control of the hotel was in some sort of legal limbo in Sweden.

The hotel was Norway in a nutshell. A høyfjellshotell (high mountain hotel). A traditional but relatively new mountain resort hotel with its own small ski hill. Rooms had rosemåling. And it was set off—eight miles up into the mountains so security was good. The Norway pines with branches weighted with snow that seemed to signal "Welcome Hillary" added to the decor. You would send a postcard from this hotel.

A call to the lawyers. A deal was made. The next day the embassy team had electricians and our own security people at the hotel upgrading the telephones and casing the place for the best rooms for H and C.[33]

THE DEVIL IN THE DETAILS

Trying to firm up the schedule. The rule in politics, diplomacy or travel of the first lady is that one gets a schedule and follows it. Details are the mother's milk of success.

From: Ambassador Loftus
To: Lawrence Payne, White House Advance

This needs to be corrected asap before any schedule is released publicly. The names of The King and Queen are spelled wrong. They are Harald and Sonja.

To: Lawrence Payne, White House Advance
From: DCM McCahill

The Ambassador will present Hillary with a Norwegian sweater for use at Olympic events...The King, Queen and PM will all be wearing LOOC (Lillehammer Olympic Organizing Committee) sweaters with matching anorak jacket and pants...we will get Hillary and the Ambassador official USOC (United States Olympic Committee) coats and boots...check and double check the size so we know the coats and boots will fit...Hillary in the men's locker room after the hockey game on the 10th, I don't think so!...FYI the ambassador's son Alec will attend the game—he is 12 1/2 and presumably knows something about hockey...the speed skating venue and the hockey venue are spelled wrong...and where is Chelsea throughout this schedule? She is not mentioned...

My last note was on the motorcade from the airport to Lillehammer: "No flashing red lights, no sirens, no motorcycles, and no speeding."

A CALM BOBSLED TEAM

The schedule is set, and the White House advance team has done a great job. The first lady was to be an emissary in a foreign country, a rare event in American history.

Every hour of every day to the minute is accounted for and the staff persons responsible for the site advance and the press advance are listed. The plane's manifest has Hillary and Chelsea, now and for the duration listed as HRC and CVC, the members of the official delegation, and, can I ever thank you enough Odin, two old friends and Clinton campaign colleagues: Melanne Verveer,[34] now HRC's chief of staff, and Fred DuVal,[35] a friend since the 1976 Morris "Mo" Udall for president campaign. Fred was now the deputy chief of protocol for the State Department. They were battle-tested and calm. Fred had a smile that could disarm a polar bear. We would be a three-person bobsled team of laid-backness.

The embassy had its own manifest of embassy and WH staff with telephone numbers, pager numbers, fax numbers—each car or van had a number. It was four pages long. Telenor, Norway's mobile phone vendor for our cell phones, was on call 24 hours.

PROTECTING THE FIRST LADY

The first time I met Hillary at an airport, it was early in Bill Clinton's primary campaign, when she came to Madison to speak to students at the UW Law School at the invitation of Donna Shalala, then UW-Madison's chancellor. She arrived in a small prop plane and was driven the short distance to campus in my father's Oldsmobile.

The first lady's arrival at the airport outside Oslo was quite different. There was a receiving line and a bouquet of flowers presented by Kjeld Vibe, the always-cordial and smiling Norwegian ambassador to the United States. Your favorite uncle.

It was 9:45 p.m. by the time we started on our way to Lillehammer in a motorcade. First in line was the Norwegian police escort, setting a pace well below the speed limit. Next were Hillary, Chelsea, myself, Barbara, and the delegation in a large van, then the Secret Service van, and at the end was Edmund driving my black Impala with Sue and Alec in the car. Then the incident.

A service vehicle from Telenor tried to pass Edmund. At first Edmund blocked the way, expecting the driver would note the diplomatic plates with the number indicating this was an American Embassy vehicle. He decided this was too much a risk for Sue and Alec and backed off.

When the truck passed, the Secret Service van's back door and side windows opened and suddenly five stubby automatic rifles were pointed at the driver, and the truck forced to the ditch. "Å, Herregud!" the driver must have said many times ("Oh, my God!").

We were not aware of this in our van, where we were chatting away in high spirits about the adventure to come. We arrived at the Hotel Nevra at midnight.

STARS ARE STAR-STRUCK

February 12, 1994, a very busy day. Cold but sunshine all the brighter reflected off the snow—the perfect snow for the Olympics. At breakfast with the prime minister, a friendship was made that would be true and important for Norway. Morten and I agreed it was a great start to the relationship with the Clinton administration. Little did we two know then how important this Gro and Hillary friendship would turn out to be.

Then, off to greet the gathered American athletes in the Olympic Village disco. More than 100 decked out in red, white, and blue with dazzling smiles so happy after their hard work to know the games would soon begin. The first lady of the United States was there to cheer them, and such a revered athlete as Flo Jo was in the official delegation. Hillary then had a private audience with Their Majesties The King and Queen. This is when the invitation to visit the White House was delivered on behalf of the president. In an aside before this meeting, I said to Hillary that Queen Sonja was not one to be hanging on the arm of The King. She had studied fashion design, and you could tell it. Her degree was in French, English, and art. And she had let it be known her expectation was half the Palace staff were to be women.

This all before 1:30 in the afternoon. At 3:20, we are in the VIP tent to don Olympic jackets, say goodbye to warmth and take our place for the opening ceremony in the American section of the metal bleachers at the bottom of the downhill ski run. The sun sets now, and it is darkness.

There is a 1,000-year history of the Norwegian people and pageantry is part of the poetry of the generations. You can hear it sung in the national anthem, which is a poem written in 1859 by Bjørnstjerne Bjørnson, the Walt Whitman of Norway.

Yes, we love this country
as it rises forth,
rugged, weathered, over the water,
with the thousands of homes,
love, love it and think
of our father and mother
and the saga-night that lays
dreams upon our earth.

The brightly lit ski run on the mountainside shone like a full moon. The announcers were Liv Ullmann,[36] the goddess of Scandinavian film (*Scenes From a Marriage*) and Thor Heyerdahl, the adventurer and author of *Kon Tiki* and *Aku Aku*. It was an honor to be in their presence.

Suddenly, there appeared, a few at first, then wave after wave of figures outlined against the night skiing down the hill. When they came closer, you could see they were wearing traditional costumes[37] and telemarking back and forth in graceful turns. Soon you could hear them. They were playing Hardanger fiddles, and there in the middle were a bride and groom and a pastor acting out a wedding. In unison, the assembled thousands took the ice-cold air into their lungs and roared approval.

Then, there was a twinkle of light at the top of the slope, and soon it grew brighter and closer and there was the skier with the Olympic Torch. He handed it to the 21-year-old Crown Prince Haakon Magnus, who sprinted up the steps of a tower of Greek columns and lit the flame. The games had begun.

At 9:30, our happy delegation made it to dinner and sat near the fire. There were awestruck exclamations retelling the beauty and marveling at the organization of the event. None had been to Norway before, and now, they thought they had found that mythical place in the snowy mountains that was called Shangri-La. Stars themselves, they were starstruck.

OOPS, WRONG KING

At 10:45 a.m., we are back in our row of seats at the base of the downhill. It's sunny and cold. We are hoping American Tommy Moe will win a medal, perhaps gold, in the downhill. There is a steady stream of others in this VIP section coming by to introduce themselves to Hillary, and Flo Jo gets her share as well. Albert, the prince of Monaco, sidles in to shake hands with Hillary. He is a longtime Olympian and would compete in the bobsled for Monaco later in the games. I confess that after he left the subject of our conversation turned to his mother Grace Kelly and her movies.[38]

We took turns in the VIP tent where it was warm. Princess Anne, the daughter of Queen Elizabeth and who was the leader of the British contingent, was there on my turn, and we had a chat. "Cold, isn't it?" She had on a scarf and was gripping with both hands a cup of hot tea.

Tommy Moe wins the gold. The Norwegians take some pride too as Moe is a common Norwegian name, and it was assumed his grandparents had immigrated.

A very audible whisper made the rounds throughout the sections:

"There is the king." Before I knew it, *Nashville Banner* publisher Mr. Irby Clifford Simpkins Jr. bolted from his seat and went up to the man and said: "King, it is an honor for me to be here, and I congratulate you and your country on the marvelous hosting of these games." The man said: "Thank you, but I am the king of Spain."

At 7:45 p.m., we are seated at the USA vs. France hockey game. Hillary is in the team parents' section. Pat Richter, the UW athletic director, and his wife are there. Their son Barry is on the team. Alec sits next to Chelsea. I find out I am assigned the seat next to George Steinbrenner, the owner of the Yankees. We prattle on through the game. As most in Wisconsin my age can, I rattle off the names and positions of the 1957 Milwaukee Braves team that went to the World Series and beat the Yankees 4-3. That was an icebreaker. The hockey game ended in a 4-4 tie.

A FALL, BUT LATER THE GOLD

Perhaps Dan Jansen was destined to be an Olympic speed skater, as he was born in West Allis, Wisconsin, the home of the only speed-skating practice facility in the United States.

We were to meet Jansen—just Hillary, me, and Barbara in a private room—immediately after the 500-meter event. Jansen held the world record and was the favorite to win the gold. We had to get into the room before the event and watch on the closed-circuit TV. He was leading the race and then fell. A dreaded outcome as the press had repeated over and over that in the 1988 Olympics, he had fallen in both the 500- and 1,000-meter, where he was leading at record-breaking speed.

He came in the room still in his racing suit, and we were consoling and Hillary was saying how proud she was to be with him. I said all of Wisconsin was still in his corner. His wife and baby were there with him, and he started to apologize. "No need, no need," we blurted out. Photos were taken. Four days later, Dan Jansen won the gold in the 1,000-meter.

At 3:30 pm February 14, Hillary does one last interview with CBS News, and then we depart for the airport. Hugs all around and everyone is beaming. Wheels up at 5:00 p.m. I am very happy for the embassy staff as hosting the first lady in the middle of an Olympics was no small task. For two years, the embassy's Country Team had been planning for the event. Deputy Chief of Mission Bill McCahill headed this effort and handled it with aplomb. It had been only 10 days before the February 12 opening ceremonies and just a week after the secretary of state had left Oslo following Holst's funeral that we had learned the first lady would lead the official delegation. In Bill's report to Washington when the Olympics were over, he detailed not only the U.S. Embassy's efforts, but a description of how "little Norway" pulled off what was already being called the best Winter Olympics ever. A big part: "True sportsmanship and friendliness on the part of the happy and well-informed Norwegian fans as the home team garnered medal after medal," not to mention sunshine for all 16 days. Oh, and the Army was mobilized.

I copied Ambassador Walter Mondale in Tokyo. Good for him to know the folks in the old country did well.

CHAPTER 6
DAY TO DAY IN THE AMBASSADOR'S LIFE

VISIT FROM A UW ALUM

Tor Reiten pays a visit to introduce himself. A UW alumnus '68. Was on the track team—now a heart doctor. After undergraduate studies at Madison, he was going to go to medical school in Germany, but the mayor of Madison, Henry Reynolds, a cousin of his mother, persuaded him to go to med school back in Madison. Still has his runner's physique. A smile you would want for your doctor to have. I happily agree to visit him in Lårdal, where he lives and practices medicine.

AS COLD WAR SUBSIDES, BRITISH SCHOOL CLOSES

The British school where Alec goes is closing and there's a parents meeting April 6. It's another sign of the end of the Cold War. Students at the British and German schools and the U.S. Department of Defense school, which is also closing, will join the international school and double the enrollment. The U.S. Embassy is negotiating with the Pentagon to donate all the assets of their school.

THE MULTI-LINGUAL DUTCH AMBASSADOR

Dinner hosted April 7 for Barbara and me by the Dutch Ambassador. He had been the DCM in the Dutch Embassy in D.C. and knows America quite well. His post before Norway was Cuba. Great stories about Castro. The Dutch ambassador's residence is close by, one of the classic villas surrounding Frogner Park: white stucco, dark-tiled roof, several pot chimneys. Some schnapps and cigars after dinner—a deadly combination. The ambassador is tall with a gray mustache and speaks seven languages: Dutch, French, Spanish, German, Italian, Russian, and Norwegian. We agree to play tennis soon at the clay courts in Frogner just across the street.

QUAFFING FOR MY COUNTRY

I host a California wine-tasting reception the evening of April 18, 1994. California vintners are making a first-ever attempt for market share. Because alcohol in Norway is taxed on the alcohol content, California wines are competitive with European wines on price. There is a ban on advertisement of alcohol, and it is only available in a state-run liquor store, the Vinmonopolet (the wine monopoly). To get a good shelf position and to prompt people to ask for a specific wine, as one cannot take the bottle from the shelf, it must be asked for and the person at the counter fetches it from the stock room, so the strategy is to get your wine reviewed in the weekly column of the wine critic for the largest daily paper, *Aftenposten*. All of this folderol is a hangover from prohibition laws and Lutheran tsk-tsk.

The wine critic is present. He suffers not from lack of invitations by ambassadors. There are several restaurateurs. They can bypass the Vinmonopolet and buy direct. Quaffing for my country.

MANDATORY SCHOOL SUBJECT: SKIING

Tour elementary and high schools April 19 with Education Minister Gudmund Hernes, who earned a Ph.D. in sociology from Johns Hopkins University and is one of the bright, young new thinkers of the Labour Party. Sociology is a Norwegian forte. The discipline has some roots in the Lutheran pastors who traveled about to congregations and kept written records of the living conditions of the people. These chronicles are still studied. It was quickly Gudmund and Tom.

Gudmund is very tweed jacket, with a trademark goatee leisurely on its way to the color gray. Erudite. He introduces me to two sayings he is very fond of repeating. He tells Norwegian students: "If you want to improve education in Norway then leave," meaning go away to study or travel or do something, and then come back. The other: "When you meet an American you risk making a friend for life."

Kindergarten, "barnehage," starts with 4-year-olds and it can be held partly outdoors even in winter. (There was such a "barnepark" just across the street from our house, and we could hear children playing). At age 7, school starts and goes until age 19. The last year of high school is akin to the first year of college. English is taught from the first day as the "second first language." Texts and classroom teaching are often in English. Sports are in clubs not connected to the school. And cross-country skiing is the main sport. "Norwegians are born with skis on their feet." (Karl at age 8 had to go away for a week to "learn to ski camp." It was mandatory.)

RICHARD NIXON'S DEATH REVERBERATES

Richard Nixon dies. Sue to double check on when flags at half-mast. Make sure guards at our Residence notified!

CONDOLENCES, THEN THE OPERA

I was first to sign the embassy's condolence book for President Nixon.

We attend Norwegian Opera's performance of *Barber of Seville* in Norwegian. It will not replace Italian, but it works very well with such talented performers. We understand not much but know when to laugh and clap in unison as the audience gives the clue. A Campari and soda at intermission. Goes well with opera.

THE CULTURAL EVENT OF THE YEAR

April 30 was the opening of Somrene i Normandie (Summers in Normandy) at Blaafarveværket (Blue Color Works).

It promised to be the cultural event of 1994 Hosted by the French Embassy and the French Ministry of Culture, it was the opening of an exhibition of impressionist paintings by French and Norwegian artists who spent summers at Normandy. They were there for the light. Familiar names such as Monet, who grew up in Le Havre; Corot; Guillemet; and famous Norwegian artists Thaulow, Peterssen, and Skredsvig.

HM Queen Sonja would open the event. There were to be 400 invited guests. It was a must that the corps diplomatique be well represented, especially the American ambassador, as my absence might be construed by some as an affront to the French. Quite ticklish are French-American relations.

Blaafarveværket was the site of the cobalt mines and processing works producing blue pigment for glass and porcelain industries worldwide. In the 1800s, it was the largest company in Norway with 2,000 employees. Norwegian-Americans will know the cobalt color from the Bing and Grøndahl Christmas-themed porcelain plates that were collected and proudly displayed each holiday season.

I knew well the Romantics, the 19th-century landscape artists, as they had pride of place in Oslo's National Museum, but I did not know the Norwegian impressionists, with the exception of Christian Skredsvig because he was from Vinje in Telemark where the Lofthus farm was. His painting *The Poet Vinje's Home* is on every postcard sold in the town.

The Queen was resplendent in layered shades of white and tones of black. A narrow-brimmed hat with a cream band was on for her arrival, which was photographed to the nth and would be featured in the papers.

She gave her remarks to open the exhibit in French. Expected, yet valiant and much appreciated by the French ambassador and his wife. I was silently cheering her on as it was clear that many of the expat French community in Oslo were present as well as a former French minister of culture and just perhaps some were judging how well she spoke the language rather than what she said. It was a sunny day. The light was just right for the event of the day.

The most familiar Romantic-era painting to Norwegian-Americans would be *Bridal Procession on the Hardangerfjord* by Adolph Tidemand and Hans Gude. We had a copy of this painting in our house when I was growing up. Noted for paintings of scenes of breathtaking beauty of the mountain waterfalls and fjords, the Romantics introduced the beauty of Norway to the rest of Europe, bringing to the country other painters and many tourists seeking the harmony of nature.

CHAPTER 7
AMBASSADORS MEET IN BRUSSELS

The meeting of all European ambassadors—the chiefs of mission—held from April 13-15, 1994, came at a critical time. The once Soviet Union, now the Russian Federation, was still becoming whatever it was going to be; the war in the Balkans was in a stage of slaughter; the expansion of NATO and the EU were open questions. Would there be a new, integrated Europe—or what, exactly?

The schedule was packed. All the presentations were to be by our fellow ambassadors.

It was the first time most of us would meet one another in our role of ambassador. Assistant Secretary of State for European and Canadian Affairs Steve Oxman had called the meeting.

The meeting was held in Truman Hall, the residence of the ambassador to the North Atlantic Treaty Organization that is named in honor of President Harry S. Truman, one of NATO's founders. The owner of the country estate sold it to the U.S. at a bargain because "your country saved mine in WWII."

OLD HANDS REPORT

The old hands would talk the first night, April 13, and the rest of us would give reports on our countries at dinner the second night. From my notes:

Steve Oxman: "The fall of Communism not the end of history. Could just be the beginning of an instant replay. Partnership for Peace has prevented a re-division of Europe."

Richard Holbrooke, Germany, the view from Bonn: "The German consensus: They cannot be the eastern border of Europe. Will focus on expanding EU to Poland and Hungary."[39]

Pamela Harriman, France: "The last time Averell (Harriman) and I met with Tito he said this would happen when he left (meaning the breakup of Yugoslavia). This humbled those unaccustomed to being humble. France would be a leader in EU expansion."[40]

Tom Pickering, the Russian Federation: "Assumption versus reality. Economy not fatally sick. A misdeveloped economy. Seventy-five years of chronic error. Now a convertible currency, money economy. Elections count. Not voting no longer seen as a protest. Election in '96. Yeltsin wants to preside over transition to successor. Near abroad—Russians must be treated decently by the very people they oppressed. Not easy. Ukraine potential civil war."[41]

Nicholas Rey, Poland: "PfP (Partnership for Peace): Their military can be a Lego that could fit into NATO. Market reform and democracy go hand-in-hand. There is 'reform fatigue.' Pocketbook issues drive elections. Solidarity and Walesa now a nonplayer. Need to focus on political parties, not personalities. Past Communists now for reform. They want to be 'inside Europe.'"[42]

Stuart Eizenstat, U.S. ambassador to the European Union: "EU not a nation state. Don't hold it to that standard. But it is a democracy-builder among nation states. The common currency is coming. EU cannot lead on major foreign policy issues, even in their own backyard. EU more pessimistic about Russia than U.S. A fear of Ukraine."

JFK'S SISTER—AND MEMORIES OF JFK

In the meeting room there was an open chair next to Jean Kennedy Smith, President Kennedy's sister whom Clinton had appointed ambassador to Ireland. I quickly took this place as this was an opportunity to tell her about my being a fellow in the early 1990s at the Institute of Politics, the school at Harvard devoted to JFK and public service, established in 1966 as a living memorial to the president.[43]

Our conversation at the Brussels' meeting quickly went to the 1960 Democratic primary in Wisconsin when JFK won over Hubert Humphrey, called at the time "Wisconsin's third senator." This win would propel him to the nomination. Also legendary, because Democratic Party Chairman Patrick Lucey broke with precedent and endorsed JFK in the primary. He became and remained a Kennedy family confidant his whole life. [44]

Jean told me she campaigned in Wisconsin in that April primary campaign. Teddy went down the ski jump on the west side of Madison. I told her Lucey was governor when I was elected the first time in 1976 and "he has been coaching me on what to do ever since." (Lucey was appointed ambassador to Mexico in 1977.)

We sat together much of the time. We took a chatty walk during one of the breaks: "So Ireland is the second time you have lived in an ambassador's residence."... "My father and I the only father-daughter ambassador combination."[45]

As we walked, I told Jean the cheesehead story. At the 1988 Democratic Nominating Convention in Atlanta, I was in our delegation's hotel strategy room—the bar--and was informed that John F. Kennedy, Jr., was looking for the head of the Dukakis delegation from Wisconsin. Me. Two in our delegation had fashioned hats of cardboard like wedges of yellow cheddar cheese. Their photos were in all the papers. When I introduced JFK Jr. to them, he asked if they would give him one of the hats for a story he was writing. The response: "No way!" Cheeseheads were born.

What we both knew, and did not need to be said, was that Jean and her siblings had regularly visited their sister Rosemary, who had been a resident at St. Coletta School for Exceptional Children in Jefferson, Wisconsin, since 1949. (Rosemary died in 2005.)

Jean told me about the embassy and Ireland and her goals and prospects of peace in Northern Ireland. "Clinton is the hope. It is good he is young."

And I told her: "Loftus can be an Irish name. And I am often accused of being Irish. Vikings, you know." (Lofthus in Norway. Lofthouse in Ireland.)

A bit of conversation about the criticism of her on the Gerry Adams incident.[46]

And, I had one great story to tell of JFK and my father. It was like a miracle I could tell this to JFK's sister.

I had called my sister Jerry, the family archivist, to have her read from the May 13, 1962, *Milwaukee Journal* to check my memory.

At a fundraiser for JFK in Milwaukee, my father Adolph and Lew Brooks, partners in the farm machinery business, were there at the behest of Pat Lucey, still the Democratic Party chair.

As cocktail hour was ending just prior to the dinner, "after sipping a single daiquiri, Mr. Kennedy started toward the door but got into a discussion with Adolph Loftus, a Sun Prairie farm machinery salesman who told him: 'You've got to do something for the farmer.'

'What do you have in mind?' the president asked.

'If you get the farmer $4 a hundred for milk, that'd be fine.'

'Everybody has different ideas on the farm problem,' Mr. Kennedy said."

Both Lew and Adolph loved to tell the story, punctuating it by noting that at $100 per person for the event, Pat Lucey still had a cash bar.

I GIVE MY REPORT—AND JEAN'S

By dinner time the last night, we all knew each other quite well, as that was one goal of the gathering, and we had the current thinking from the American perspective about NATO and EU expansion.

Most important to me, and of lasting importance, were to be the reports from each ambassador about the view of things from their country. We sat around a horseshoe-shaped table in the ornate dining room and all of us who did not present in the earlier sessions gave our short presentations.

Bob Hunter, U.S. ambassador to NATO gave this message: "EU only a fledgling capacity for security actions. France accepts U.S. leadership. PfP announced by president signals U.S. is going to lead. Enlargement yes. Need for militaries to de-communize. We have one Greece and one Turkey and that is enough for any alliance. Russia welcomed to PfP and could have a special relationship to NATO. We have a tremendous stake in seeing PfP work. NATO expansion will go 100 percent with EU expansion."

I had notes on Norway for when my turn would come. I quoted Norwegian Prime Minister Gro Brundtland from her January 10, 1994, statement at the meeting of NATO Heads of State and Government in Brussels. "We are embarking on an evolutionary process toward a future expansion of NATO ... The U.S. Partnership for Peace proposal provides a brilliant answer. ... PfP membership could function as preparation for NATO membership." I know her well enough to know that use of the word "brilliant" is not a casual remark. Labour Government's EU application is also "a desire to cooperate fully in its foreign and security policy cooperation." Just across Norwegian border with Russia "there are 100 nuclear submarines and 60 obsolete ones...and practically no storage or handling for warheads or fuel."

I add that the immediate problem is Russian policy, on hold for the moment, of dumping in the Barents Sea the low-level radioactive liquid that is used to cool sub reactors. I am making it my priority to focus the U.S. Embassy, especially our Navy team, on helping and leading the effort to get a deal on no dumping of the sub reactor coolant. We will have extensive reporting on the EU accession negotiations. Come visit us! (They did.)

Jean Kennedy Smith sat next to me and just before it was my turn she said: "Please give my report. I am not going to talk. You know it all by now anyway." Jean didn't ask me to talk for her because she was bashful. Everything she said or didn't say would be in the minutes and cables. For example, did she say or was she silent as to whether she would continue to break the rules by again traveling to Northern Ireland despite the strenuous objections of the U.S. Embassy in the UK, or continue to meet with Gerry Adams, the head of the IRA's political wing, even though State Department policy forbade it, considering Adams a terrorist mouthpiece?[47]

And I gave her report after giving mine. There was a roomful of raised eyebrows. I haven't the faintest memory of what I said and took no notes. Not one person said a thing to me about this, then or later. (Forgive me, Ireland.)

CHAPTER 8
GRO GOES TO THE WHITE HOUSE

AN HONORARY DEGREE FROM UW-MADISON

In December 1990, I was in Oslo on a personal trip. This was shortly after losing the election for Wisconsin governor in November (I came in second). I carried with me a letter from UW Chancellor Donna Shalala to deliver to Gro Harlem Brundtland offering her an honorary degree.

I met with Ambassador Loret Miller Ruppe, a fellow Wisconsinite, and she graciously arranged the delivery of the letter and invited me to join her at the Nobel Peace Prize Ceremony on December 10, 1990 in Oslo City Hall.[48]

The recipient, for his role in ending the Cold War and the fall of the Berlin Wall, was Mikhail Gorbachev, president of the Soviet Union. He didn't show up. The situation in Moscow was so fluid that a coup was feared. Perhaps when he was out of the country, he would be prevented from returning. His acceptance speech, which credited the new way of thinking, "perestroika," for the breakthroughs, was read by the deputy foreign minister.[49]

Fast forward to my letter of April 1994:

April 20, 1994
Donna Shalala, Secretary
U.S. Department of Health and Human Services

Dear Donna,

In December of 1990, you were kind enough to ask me to deliver a letter to Prime Minister Gro Harlem Brundtland offering her an honorary degree at the University of Wisconsin. Well, she has accepted.

On May 17, Syttende Mai, Norwegian national day, she will be with President Clinton at the White House...

The rest of the schedule was: May 18, meet with members of Congress, including the Speaker, and a speech at the European Institute. May 19, Chicago for a speech at the Chicago World Affairs Council and meet the governor. On the 20th, Madison for a reception and then on the 21st she would give the commencement speech for the College of Letters and Science and receive her honorary degree.

I had been working on the trip and lobbying for the May 17 date.

SINCE PREZ CAN'T COME TO PM, PM WILL GO TO PREZ

The U.S. Embassy was primed for this trip to the White House because we had recently prepared for a visit from the U.S. president to Norway.

Late in 1993, when it was set that there would be a Clinton/Yeltsin summit in Moscow January 15, 1994, there was a commitment that the president would stop in Oslo on the way back to D.C. All the background memos were written, and preparations made. It was to be the first visit by a sitting U.S. president to Norway. I mentioned that often. Presidents like this type of first. The visit didn't happen. Oslo was canceled for a meeting in Geneva with Syrian President Hafez al-Assad regarding Mideast peace.

When the president thought he was coming to Oslo, he asked about Professor Johannes Andenaes, a Norwegian legal scholar whose writing Clinton had admired when a law student at Yale. We found Professor Andenaes and the book with the article the president specifically mentioned.

Professor Andenaes wrote a very thoughtful inscription and had been on the visit schedule to present the book to the president. A logical pivot now was that Prime Minister Gro Harlem Brundtland would hand this book to the president in the White House meeting.

SHIPS OF STATE WILL PASS IN THE NIGHT

On April 20, 1994, the same day I wrote Donna Shalala telling her Gro had accepted the honorary degree from UW, and she would be in the White House on May 17, I wrote Jimmy Carter a letter expressing regret I would not be in Oslo to meet him when he and Rosalynn visited May 17.

Carter was coming to Oslo to present the Norwegian people a special award from the Carter-Menil Human Rights Foundation for the Oslo Accords. It would be a 10-foot-high monumental sculpture titled *Marriage* by the late American artist Tony Smith.

In recognition of the work of those individuals involved in the Oslo Accords, there would also be a $100,000 donation to the Institute for Applied Science, FAFO, a Labour Party-oriented think tank.

IRISH GET ST. PAT'S DAY, NORWEGIANS GET SYTTENDE MAI

The White House did very much want Gro to be welcomed. Of course, Norway was itself admired, and the first lady had been a guest at the Olympics. But Gro was one of very few female heads of government and was herself admired as a global environmental leader. But I was lobbying for a specific date—one that also fit into the visit to Madison. With the trip cancellation as a chit and the unwitting help of the prime minister of Ireland, I was able to get Gro into the White House on May 17.

On St. Patrick's Day, March 17, the Irish prime minister was in the White House and feted in a ballyhoo of epic proportions. And that is no blarney. Clinton and Sen. Kennedy invited and entertained every Irish pol there. A red carpet embedded with four leaf clovers was rolled out down Pennsylvania Avenue from the White House to the Congress. (OK, I made that up.)

My case, irrefutable logic to a politician, was if the Irish PM gets in on St. Pat's Day, then the Norwegian PM gets in on Syttende Mai.

WHALING CAN'T BE IGNORED

The preparation machinery of briefing memos, letters, and phone calls was fired up and the script written. Since most of the players in this dress rehearsal stage were friends, and there were no big issues between the two countries, it was a pleasant task.

I wrote Gro's advisor Morten Wetland a briefing letter, the type a fellow speech writer would need. I diplomatically did not mention whaling in the letter, but assured Morten in a call that this was a subject Clinton would have to bring up in our White House meeting.

In 1993, Norway had returned to commercial whaling, breaking the moratorium of the International Whaling Commission. The killing would be limited to minke whale and occur only in waters between Iceland and Norway. Norway claimed this small whale was not endangered and could be "sustainably harvested."

Norway was getting a lot of bad press for its move worldwide and especially in the U.S., but was on solid ground, so to speak, with public opinion at home. There was a T-shirt worn around Oslo that had printed on it: "If we had dolphins we would kill them too."

For a short history of Norwegian whaling, see Appendix B.

MAY 17, SYTTENDE MAI, FINDS GRO IN WHITE HOUSE

The short trip to the White House from National Airport was typical.

There was the Washington, D.C., afternoon melody of the sirens of black cars speeding through red lights. Impressive to the visiting autocrat of a minor country, but a bit embarrassing to Gro. There were quite a few anti-whaling protesters holding uncomplimentary placards standing along the iron fence on Pennsylvania Avenue outside the White House.

It was a cloudy day, but the Oval Office with its blues and yellows had an inviting warmth about it. The low coffee table had a couch on either side and a chair at each end.

President Clinton, his allergies evident as it was prime pollen time, sat in the chair opposite Gro. Her adviser Morten Wetland and I were on one couch and Vice President Al Gore and Norwegian Ambassador Kjeld Vibe on the other. A serving set of White House china with cups, a creamer, and small bowl with sugar cubes for coffee was very welcoming. The cups and saucers were white with a gold rim and imprinted with the seal of the president.

We did not know Al Gore would be joining the meeting. He was a fan of Gro's and it was probably expected he would be there to say something about whaling. He had the morning paper, which had a front-page piece on the PM's visit and the whaling issue on his lap, but under his briefing book. We got the message.

The president was delightful in giving a recap of his wonderful visit to Norway when he was a college student. He said some nice things about me. The VP repeated the U.S. position on observing the whaling moratorium, and then he stated the Norwegian position, so it was understood that he had put some work into knowing what it was and why it was. Gro was consistent with her previous explanation that the science allowed sustainable whaling and Norway was in accord with international law. With that over, we went on to other topics.

Gro can be official, and she can be charmingly candid. This was a charmingly candid day.

The other topic she was going to talk about, she announced, was her recent conversation with the pope. I am sure Morten was saying to himself, "What?" There was no doubt Clinton and Gore wanted very much to listen. Not many of these conversations came their way.

In summary, the conversation was about HIV/AIDS in Africa, and the helpless position women were in with the Catholic Church edict on condoms, forbidden because they were birth control. This was a human tragedy unfolding and the pope should use his power to do something about it. It was a public health issue. His answer was not helpful, she said.

She relayed this conversation, so Clinton and Gore would know it had happened. And that she spoke to the pope as a doctor[50] who happened to be the PM of a country that gives a lot of money to alleviate suffering around the world.[51]

It was a very cheery meeting. Three politicians in their prime. At the end, Gro presented the book from Professor Andenaes. Clinton went on about this a bit. It was a good gift. Now Hillary had a Norwegian sweater from the Olympics, and Bill had a law book from a revered Norwegian legal scholar. Perfect.

VP Gore joined in the press conference customary after such visits. The questions about possible sanctions on Norway were deftly sidestepped. The president was asked if he was going to visit Norway. "I hope I'll be able to go back. I went when I was a young man. I loved it. I'd love to go back someday. One of the best trips I ever made in my life."

PM: NORWAY SHOULD BE IN THE EU

The PM's May 18 speech to the European Institute focused on why Norway sought to join the European Union. In short, for a seat at the table. To be in the room when economic and security decisions are made. She expressed support for expanding the EU to the east if Norway were to become a member, something the EU had wanted to hear. Most importantly for this audience, she articulated her view of the EU:

> I see the Union as Europe's modern contribution to the civilization of inter-state relations...with new principles of shared sovereignty and solidarity.
>
> The EU has become the key institution in shaping Europe's future. This is recognized by Russia and is a major reason underlying the Norwegian government's decision to apply for membership." The point being, membership would help foster cooperation with Russia as Norway would become an EU country bordering Russia.
>
> That border, about 192 kilometers long, is the only border between a NATO country and Russia. The northwestern part of Russia is an important gateway to Western Europe. Russia's principal ports of Murmansk and Arkhangelsk are here...Our ambition is to restore normality and trade ..."

She added to this message that the joint U.S., Norway, and Russia naval exercise—Pomor—that had happened just one month prior, was an example of the way forward with Russia in military cooperation.

Dick Norland, the head of the Norwegian desk at the State Department, was at the speech. An experienced hand who knew news when he heard it, Dick sent me a note not on the speech, but on Gro's answer to a question asked by a Norwegian reporter: Would she "throw in the towel" if the referendum vote failed? "No, the Government will not resign over this issue," she replied.[52]

GRO AND TOM MEET HOUSE SPEAKER FOLEY

Tom Foley, the Speaker of the House, was from the state of Washington and represented the area that included Spokane. He was Irish on both sides and not the first House Speaker with this pedigree. The late Tip O'Neill, may the wind still be at his back, seemed even in heaven to have a guiding hand on the gavel.

On May 18, it was a reunion for Foley and me of our pairing at a catastrophe of a political event. At the October 1988 debate in Los Angeles between Massachusetts Gov. Mike Dukakis and Vice President George H.W. Bush, the Dukakis campaign had us in the "spin room" as a twosome to answer questions from the press after the debate. We were ready. A quiver full of quotes pretty much all saying Dukakis won.

Except debate moderator Bernard Shaw of CNN asked what became known as "the question." "Governor, if Kitty Dukakis were raped and murdered, would you favor an irrevocable death penalty for the killer?" Dukakis went into a discourse on his longstanding opposition to the death penalty. Someone nearby said, "Get the hook. He's done."

Gov. Dukakis was a great friend. Thank goodness, as I had spun one spin too many to a *New York Times* reporter. I said "lost" in some context I thought immune. Quoted in the front-page story. I was the chair of the Dukakis campaign in Wisconsin, and he won the state by a healthy margin. It set the stage for Bill Clinton.

Gro was a welcome guest in Speaker Foley's office. Every Speaker's day is clogged with meetings on minutiae. The prime minister of Norway stops in, and it is like a letter from home. He wanted to listen to her on any topic, talk about the weather, but don't leave soon. Stay a while. Have some coffee. Let's take some pictures. Over 400,000 Norwegian-Americans ended up in Washington. Gro wanted to know about the chances for Hillary's health insurance in the Congress. She smiled a lot.

The Irish really do make good pols.

GRO AND TOM VISIT CHICAGO'S "LITTLE NORWAY"

We were picked up at Chicago's O'Hare airport on May 20 by Illinois state troopers and driven into the city to start our visit. The officer driving us observed the speed limit, stopped at red lights and employed no sirens or flashing lights. He addressed Gro as "ma'am" and me as "sir." Destination number one: "Little Norway."

The immigration of 800,000 Norwegians to America over the course of 100 years was called a "rural-to-rural" movement. They came from rural areas in Norway and settled in rural areas in America. Yet by 1930, Chicago's "Little Norway" tallied 56,000 and was the third-largest Norwegian population in the world after Oslo and Bergen. It was concentrated around Humboldt Park and Logan Square. The Norwegian language newspaper *Skandinaven* had a larger circulation than any paper in Norway. And this enclave of immigrants to America might be a candidate for the most studied, recorded and dissected of any.[53]

We were to visit the Norwegian-American Hospital. Historically a must-stop for prime ministers and members of the monarchy visiting America. The hospital was established by the Norwegian community to serve Norwegian immigrants. It was quite noteworthy as the hospital of the first graduate of Chicago's Women's Hospital Medical College in 1889, Dr. Helga Ruud. She came to Chicago to become a doctor, as women were not allowed to study medicine in Norway. Dr. Ruud was called in the press "one of the City's most distinguished petticoat surgeons." She was a lifelong friend and disciple of Jane Addams of Hull House. Dr. Ruud was at the hospital until 1945, a 50-year tenure.

In 1994, a lot of Lutheran church steeples were to be seen peeking above the modest houses on the streets of Humboldt Park. There seemed to be one on every block, but precious few Norwegians. They had melted away into other more upscale neighborhoods and the suburbs. The statue of Leif Erikson was still in the park.

The hospital continued to serve well each wave of those moving in before they moved out of Humboldt Park. There were now many Puerto Ricans.[54]

Gro switched from PM to medical doctor and was very interested in the hospital, how it worked, what the health care focused on and did people have health insurance. Hillary Clinton's efforts to design a new health insurance scheme in the United States was of much interest to her and would come up at each appropriate opportunity during the trip.

The visit was appreciated by the staff of the hospital.

UW-MADISON GIVES GRO HONORARY DEGREE

Early on the morning of May 20, the PM and I flew to Madison from Chicago in plenty of time for a luncheon hosted by the UW Scandinavian Studies Department held on the 19th floor of Van Hise Hall.

The view is of the beautiful campus spread along the shore of Lake Mendota. There were the sailboats of the student sailing club and seemingly on cue the rowing team glided past in a practice match.

Picnic Point juts out into the lake and there hidden in the canopy of mature oaks spread out over 83 acres is Eagle Heights, a cosmopolitan neighborhood of 1,050 apartments for graduate students with families. They are from all over the U.S. and dozens of foreign countries.

The view from the top floor of the tallest building on campus was nice, but the prime minister of Norway was the focus of the room packed with students studying Norwegian language and literature and their faculty. Professor Harald Naess, who guided the Scandinavian Studies Department for 32 years from 1959 until his retirement in 1991, was our host. (His son Petter is the director of the embassy library in Oslo.)[55]

The happy chatter in Norwegian of this kindred crowd was like a family reunion with Gro asking as many students as she could their story and how it was they were studying Norwegian.

At 2 p.m. we moved to the reception at the Alumni Lounge, also hosted by the Scandinavian Studies Department. This was a big affair. There were invitations to make sure people with special connections to Norway would be there, but it was also open to the public. People just had to register to get a head count.

The Norwegian ambassador to the United States, Kjeld Vibe, had now joined us. I gave some opening remarks and then Ambassador Vibe introduced the PM. And here is what she said that was featured in a local newspaper. "Coming to America, I feel like coming to my second nation, after my own."[56]

There was no receiving line. Just a crush of well-wishers wanting to meet the Norwegian prime minister and get a chance to tell of their family connection with Norway. Their grandparents came from the tiny town of Balestrand on the Sognefjord, or Telemark, or Osterøy island near Bergen. Or they studied in Norway. Or their son or daughter had been an exchange student.

Fascinating for Gro was when I introduced her to Dr. Rolf Quisling. Sverre, Abe, Gunnar, and Rolf Quisling founded the Quisling Clinic in 1933.[57] The Quislings were the most prominent Norwegian-American family in Madison. They were respected doctors. A comparison with the Mayo brothers and the Mayo Clinic would be fair. First Gro asked about the relationship to Vidkun Quisling, the Norwegian traitor who ran the occupation government for Nazi Germany. Yes, a slight connection if you go back far enough on the family tree. Then Gro the medical doctor took over and asked questions about health insurance in America, and Dr. Quisling asked questions in return about the practice of medicine in Norway.

At 5 p.m., UW Chancellor David Ward introduced PM Brundtland at the Honorary Degree Ceremony at the Field House (basketball arena) and said the degree was earned by those "who live extraordinary lives." Almost all honorary degree recipients had been UW alumni so it was a special recognition.[58] She was escorted to the stage by Professor Harald Naess. The graduation cowl was placed on her shoulders. She joined the other degree recipients on this commencement weekend: 3,230 bachelor's degrees and 1,620 Ph.D., master's and professional degrees awarded.

Dinner was hosted by Chancellor Ward and his wife Judith. Dear friends. David was born in Manchester, England, studied at the University of Leeds, and came to UW-Madison on a Fulbright Travel award. He stayed, earned a Ph.D. in geography and joined the faculty. David was liked and proved to have a knack for running things. He kept calm and carried on. He knew full well the wisdom of the adage that academic politics are so hard fought because the stakes are so low.

UW Chancellor Donna Shalala made him the provost, and when she left the Board of Regents had no hesitation in choosing him as chancellor. A change from the flamboyant Shalala. She fit the time then, and David fit the times now.

I first met Judith Ward when she was on the staff of the Legislative Fiscal Bureau. She, along with her colleagues, provided the analyses that were the highway maps of how to get from the introduction of a state budget through passage. They made me look brilliant—at times a low bar, as all I did was read the memos.

The chancellor's house, built in 1911, was a gift to the UW in 1924. Never look a gift house in the mouth; this would be the exception. A welcoming red brick classic on the outside. The inside was a patchwork of temporary fixes to the wiring, plumbing, and kitchen. There were bats in the attic. Somehow it was made to work for dinners and other events. An army of students were employed to serve, weaving between tables as close as those in a railroad dining car. What did Gro ask? If she could see the living quarters. The Norwegian prime minister does not have an official house. Gro lives in a modest house on the west side of Oslo. David stayed calm. Judith gave her a tour of the bedrooms and quaint bathrooms. Of particular interest was Judith's room of her own. An inviting garret on the top floor with a writing desk, personal books, and an exercise machine. This tour, a first for the Wards, but a great story.

GRO DELIVERS UW COMMENCEMENT SPEECH

Chancellor David Ward kindly informed me in a letter several weeks before the UW visit that I was to kindly inform the PM she would have 20 minutes for her commencement speech to the graduate students—Ph.D., master's, and professional.

A time limit is a gift to the speech writer and the speech giver. Morten Wetland, the PM's top aide and speechwriter, knew the points Gro wanted to make, and I had sent him a list of things about Wisconsin and the UW he could pick and choose from for the warm-up.

(Also noted was that UW alumnus former Secretary of State Lawrence Eagleburger was to be the commencement speaker for the undergraduates.)[59]

Gro's speech was well crafted and a rare feat, as it was able to be read as well as spoken. It connected the PM to America, Norway to America, Wisconsin to Norway, the UW to Norway, and brought President Clinton in for best actor in a supporting role.

Excerpts:

> (T)he Lillehammer Olympics were probably the biggest thrill in the world of sports since the Badgers won the Rose Bowl on January First.

> I once had the privilege to attend an American university myself and to experience commencement as you are doing. The University was Harvard...I am told that Harvard ranks about equal to Wisconsin...The year was 1965 and I received my master's degree in public health.

President Clinton naturally appointed a son of Wisconsin and a grandson of Norway as his ambassador to my country. He is here with us today, and you know him well, Ambassador Tom Loftus.

Almost every family in Norway has ties with the USA. They are the fibers in the fabric which has been woven by people and time between your country and mine.

These bonds, our alliance in war and peace, our commitment to freedom, democracy and social justice and our shared values are among the reasons why I was so pleased to celebrate our national day—the 17th of May—in Washington as the guest of the president of the United States.

And the takeaways:

(T)he 'Scandinavian model' has attracted a great deal of interest because it combines three elements: the improvement and expansion of social, health and educational services; maximum participation in the work force, especially for women; and, through active state intervention, sustained full employment. These elements have been realized within the framework of an open economy and international cooperation.

The word 'public' has no negative connotation in Scandinavia. A strong public sector is viewed as the most reassuring of tools. Market forces are good at allocating resources effectively, but they cannot build community purpose or instill social responsibility, or assert the larger vision only people can have of a just and equitable society.

My appeal to you today is to become involved in public life. You should serve your country and your community and maintain a social conscience so that you do not become indifferent to the plight of your fellow citizens.

CHAPTER 9
FLIGHT TO A VOLCANO

I was in the jump seat behind the co-pilot in the Norwegian Air Force C-130 Hercules, and there on the far horizon was a white speck on the ocean. In the clearest air on the planet, you see a white as white as angel wings. As we neared, it revealed itself as a snow-covered mountain rising up like meringue on the island of Jan Mayen. This was the volcano.

When we touched down on the gravel landing strip after the 500-mile flight from Bodø we were closer to Greenland than Norway. Beerenberg is the name of the volcano, the northernmost active volcano on earth, the most recent eruption being in 1985.

Jan Mayen is part of Norway. This is why a group of ambassadors from Oslo were flown here on one of the eight flights a year that resupply the weather reporting station's small contingent of meteorologists, technicians, and one nurse.

From the 1600s on, written accounts of visitors to Jan Mayen were by Dutch explorers and about whaling. Jan Mayen was the name of a Dutch whaling ship captain. The commercial and scientific interest in the unexplored Arctic by Europe's empires in the quest for whales, furs, coal, and the dream of a Northeast passage came to the fore in the International Polar Year of 1882-83, when there was an Austro-Hungarian North Pole Expedition that made extensive maps of Jan Mayen and established an outpost of the empire.

In WWI, Jan Mayen had some military value as a weather-reporting location during the war. Thus, in the tidying up after the First World War, the victors through the League of Nations gave control of Jan Mayen to Norway. In 1921, Norway opened the weather station.[60]

By this time in my tenure in Norway, I too had joined those with a fascination with the Arctic. When you breathe in Arctic air for the first time and see for the first time the curve of the earth over the horizon, you understand more of Fridtjof Nansen and Robert Peary and why they just had to reach the North Pole.

When we boarded the plane for the return, we were given a small volcanic rock with Jan Mayen lettered on it in white paint. A cherished item for me.

CHAPTER 10
PM: WOMEN'S RIGHTS
ARE HUMAN RIGHTS

Near the end of 1994, it was already apparent that this year was to be a turning point in Norwegian history and for Prime Minister Gro Harlem Brundtland.

The Oslo Peace Accords, a framework seeking to end the Palestinian-Israeli conflict, had brought Norway worldwide acclaim. PM Brundtland had emerged as an international leader, the looked-to woman head of government. Margaret Thatcher and "Thatcherism" were gone. What Gro did and said now counted and was a responsibility and opportunity. The opportunity was not wasted.

On September 5, 1994, in Cairo, Egypt, Gro gave the keynote address to the United Nations International Conference on Population and Development.[61]

> We now possess a rich library of analysis of the relationship between populations and growth and poverty...we know the policies that don't work...We are not here to repeat them... When we adopt a plan of action, we sign a promise to make men and women equal before the law and to promote women's needs more actively than men's until equality is reached.... Women will not become more empowered

merely because we want them to be...with 95 percent of the population increase taking place in developing countries the communities that bear the burden of rising numbers are those least equipped to do so...(the action plan) must promise access to education and basic reproductive health services, including family planning as a universal human right...Sometimes religion is a major obstacle but morality becomes hypocrisy if it means accepting mothers suffering or dying in connection with unwanted pregnancies and illegal abortions...

Gro Brundtland threatened the whole male order of things, and the reference to religion caused heartburn in Rome, but it was the phrase "a universal human right" that resonated. And she knew it.[62]

The Universal Declaration of Human Rights had been adopted by the UN in 1948, declaring the rights and freedoms of all human beings. It led to the development of human rights law. It is found in many treaties and some constitutions. There are precedents that bind. If you want something to eventually become a human right, use the language Gro used. And use it when and where it counts.

CHAPTER 11
HOLLYWOOD COMES TO OSLO

I had just left lunch on November 28, 1994, and was standing in front of the Theater Cafe. A taxi pulled up and out stepped Cliff Robertson. Dashing in a trench coat.

He was Mr. Hollywood, a list of iconic films to his credit. Awarded the Oscar for best actor for the movie *Charley*. And famous for being President Kennedy's personal choice to play him in the movie *PT 109*.

It had been some time, but we recognized each other immediately. A friendship can be cemented in one eventful day. In 1976 on the day of the Wisconsin presidential primary, which was down to a contest between Morris Udall and Jimmy Carter, I got a call from the Milwaukee campaign office of Udall's campaign that they were sending Cliff Robertson to me. They had nothing for him to do in Milwaukee. I was one of the congressional district chairs and located in our Madison office. Robertson had been campaigning for Mo Udall across the country.

The problem was that papers and TV stations didn't report campaign events on Election Day. So, I quickly got the theater faculty at the UW to round up students in the acting classes. Cliff would put on a seminar of sorts. This acting class was the event and the excuse to get him live on the noon and nightly TV news. When they interviewed him, he would mention he was in town for the Udall campaign.

I had driven in the out entrance of the parking lot of the building where we met the students. There was a gate. So I had to back out. I opened the door of my AMC Hornet to look behind, and my glasses fell off and were smashed by the tires. The rest of the day's schedule with Cliff I had to wear my prescription sunglasses. (Shouldn't he be the one in the shades?)

That night, still in sunglasses, I was on TV celebrating the victory of Udall and holding up the sunrise edition of *The Milwaukee Sentinel* with the headline "Udall wins Wisconsin." Alas, when the paper ballots finally were reported from the farm counties the next morning, it ended up that Carter had won in a squeaker.

Cliff was in Oslo in 1994 to film *Sunset Boys* with Robert Mitchum and an international all-star cast. The production had already received tons of press, as it was to be one of the biggest-budget Norwegian films ever and was to be directed by Leidulv Risan, a well-known director, screenwriter and professor at the Norwegian film school.

Also noted was that Cliff was the narrator in the soon-to-be-released documentary on Sonja Henie, Norway's most celebrated Olympic champion and international film star. *Sonja Henie: Queen of the Ice* would be shown on national TV in America. Of interest in Norway was that the documentary would include some rare footage of a young Princess Märtha.

Cliff was a gift from heaven for JoDell Shields, the embassy's cultural director. Here was Hollywood in Oslo, and she had him at no cost to her limited budget, as we would have a reception in the Residence charged to my wine cellar. Cliff said, "Whatever you want and where and when you want me to be." The invite went out to Oslo's theater and film actors, producers, and directors, and the newspaper film critics. My fellow ambassadors called and asked to be invited. My Dutch colleague had a daughter in L.A. trying to break into the movies.

It was a blast. The most interesting night. Everyone was on stage so to speak and Cliff was most gracious in wanting to know about the Norwegian theater and film scene.

That night he took Barbara and me to dinner at Le Canard. I had seen almost all his films, including two recent films he had produced and wanted to know more about: *The Great Northfield Minnesota Raid* and *J.W. Koop*. "Tom," he said, "you are a true friend. No one saw those films." He told the story about being in New York filming *Barefoot in the Park* with Jane Fonda and getting a call from the White House asking if he could come down to meet with the president. "That is when he told me I was to play him in *PT 109.*"

Barbara noted how lucky we were that I did not win the governor's race in Wisconsin. "We got a better house. Are making terrific friends. And movie stars take us to dinner."[63]

CHAPTER 12
NORWAY VOTES NO
—AGAIN—ON EU

On December 1, 1994, PM Gro Brundtland greeted me with a strong handshake and a wry smile saying, "What a strange country we have."

This was a reference to the "no" vote on the recent referendum to join the European Union. The vote margin was almost the same as in 1972, and the map of the country showing where the people voted "no" and the places where they voted "yes" was also the same.[64]

I was meeting the PM to deliver a letter from President Clinton on an upcoming matter. We chatted about the politics of the vote, and I recalled to her our trip to Washington and her speech there listing the reasons her government had to seek EU membership. She explained, in so many words, why a "no" vote could just come down to sovereignty.

Norway was a new country—it was only 79 years since the break with Sweden, not even a generation since the end of German occupation, and there was now security with NATO and the Americans. There was another big reason. On the day of the vote, I had noted in my diary that there was no pocketbook reason for Norwegians to vote "yes." The *International Herald Tribune* had just published a country data report on growth, inflation, unemployment, and interest rates. Norway was in good economic shape. It had double the growth rate of any other country in Western Europe.

My driver, Edmund, summed it up: If Norway joined the EU, Germans would come and pick all the cloudberries, EU rules would prohibit steak tartare with a raw egg, and the Spanish would get all the fish.

German Chancellor Helmut Kohl had done everything he could to woo Norway, the last country that could contribute financially to the costs of the EU and would be a partner with Germany. Fishing rights, protection of agriculture, oil would be Norway's alone—whatever it was, Kohl gave Norway a good deal.

The United States had no position on joining, nor should we have, but expansion of the EU was supported and it would be a real plus if such a strong democracy as Norway had a seat at the table.

Our erudite ambassador to the EU, Stuart Eizenstat, who got his start as President Carter's domestic policy adviser, had written an aspirational column in the *International Herald Tribune* about the possibility of a United States of Europe. Sort of a U.S. position. I invited Stu to visit a few weeks before the vote, and we would set up a day for him. And after the meetings, he should spend a few days to travel and see the fjords and mountains, talk to a shop clerk or fisherman, eat a heart-shaped waffle with butter and jam. Get outside Oslo.

Professor Odd Lovoll from St. Olaf College, the historian of Norwegian immigration, was in town and explained to Stu over coffee that this vote would again fall along the old divisions of urban versus rural. The "no" vote in a nutshell: This was something "Oslo wanted." Lunch was with a cadre from the foreign ministry, prominent businesspeople, and academics—the "yes" vote crowd.

Then coffee and sweets in my office with Marit Arnstad, a new young member of Parliament and a "no" vote. Stu said, "You're young, educated, and well-traveled, why are you voting no?" She said, "Because I am young, educated, and well-traveled." I left Stu with the phrase my relatives in Stavanger would use even when they took a trip to Denmark. "We are going down to Europe." Norway is in Europe, but is it part of it?

CHAPTER 13
JANUARY 1995

A VISIT FROM HENRY KISSINGER

Son Alec was on a ski trip with school and son Karl had mono. A dinner for us hosted by the Egyptian ambassador was on the schedule. I was speaking at the opening of the U.S. pavilion at the travel show, and HM Sonja would be stopping by. And Henry Kissinger was on his way to Oslo.

The schedule for Kissinger's visit—January 12-14, 1995—was set from the U.S. Embassy's end. A separate set of events was organized by the Norwegian Foreign Ministry.

The former secretary of state was also the head of Kissinger and Associates, a consulting firm with a who's who of international clients needing access to government leaders at the highest level around the world. These two roles were melded into his schedule.

A near-eruption by Kissinger

I hosted a breakfast at the Residence on January 12, Mr. Kissinger's first morning and, as requested, invited those who were considered to be the captains of industry.

The guests: Ragnar Halvorsen, chairman of DYNO; Finn Hvistendahl, chairman of Den Norske Bank; Gerhard Heiberg of

Norscan Consultants (and chairman of the Lillehammer Olympics); Erik Tønseth, CEO of Kvaerner; and Karl Otto Gilje, CEO of ESSO Norway. All of them had been guests before and had hosted me at one time or another.

Barbara was seated directly across from Mr. Kissinger, and in his follow-up thank you note he mentioned how charming she was.

A traditional American breakfast was served and Mr. Kissinger had three helpings of the fried potatoes. I mentioned this to the chef, Anne-Lise.

Next on the agenda was a visit to the U.S. Embassy, as Kissinger had agreed to speak to the American staff. The small conference room was crowded and many were standing. Several of the senior staff had started their careers when Kissinger was with Nixon. "NATO should quickly take in Poland because history shows that if Poland is left alone both Russia and Germany will try to assert its hegemony. The eastern border with Europe should not end at Germany. NATO should step in to stop Russia's historical predilections," Kissinger opined.

On the Balkan war, Kissinger rolled out a historical argument that there was no real basis for Bosnia as an independent nation and there was no Bosnian language. There was time for one question and I called on Rob Weisberg, the embassy's head of administration. "On Bosnia, why then did you so vigorously support the Republic of Vietnam? ... There never was a historical basis for a separate South Vietnam nor a South Vietnamese language." Shall we say it was spoken in a forceful accusatory tone.[65] Kissinger almost erupted, and spent the rest of the time stating he had always been for peace, etc., etc.

Rob's wife Nergish, also on our staff, came up to me after the meeting and said, "Mr. Ambassador, you had to call on him? When I saw there were only five minutes left, I thought maybe just this once maybe my husband would keep a lid on. But no, no, he couldn't resist going after him."[66]

I said, "Nergish, I am sure I saw Rob's hand go up, but there was glare from the windows and perhaps I was mistaken."

Kissinger makes his case for expanding NATO

Foreign Minister Godal hosted a private lunch at the government guest house in Parkveien. I was very pleased to see Arne Olav

Brundtland there as he was a great fan of Kissinger's writings.

I had asked the former secretary of state to please repeat the view on NATO expansion that he expressed at the staff meeting. I couldn't say it the way he did to the Norwegians, but he could, and I thought it conveyed several of Clinton's thoughts quite well. Key people who would form Norway's stance on NATO enlargement were in that room.

Kissinger repeated his view on NATO expansion and added, "If we worry about upsetting Russia now when they are weak, what will happen when it is strong? Get the Baltics and others in the EU. But get Poland, Czech, Hungary, Slovakia in NATO. ... Forget about Ukraine and Belarus as independent countries."

In response to a question on Russia, the former secretary said: "Perhaps a Pinochet-type government will emerge, authoritarian but fostering market reforms."

At 3 p.m., in the Nobel Institute, Kissinger gave the Kissinger lecture in memory of Johan Jørgen Holst: "Europe's New Historic Challenges and the Prospects for Trans-Atlantic Cooperation." He was treated to a 20-minute primer on Norwegian foreign policy by PM Brundtland as his introduction.

After the speech, I bid farewell to Kissinger and thanked him for the embassy visit and the words on NATO. I noted I had five straight days of travel coming up and needed to prepare, be briefed and have a weekend with Barbara and the boys.

100TH ANNIVERSARY OF THE SONS OF NORWAY

I knew a thing or two about the Sons of Norway, as there were three lodges in Dane County alone—Madison, Stoughton, and Mount Horeb—the latter two in my legislative district.

The organization started in Minnesota as a society to help Norwegian immigrants get medical care during the deep depression of the 1890s. Each family chipped in some money that was pooled to pay the doctor. The group grew quickly and soon there were lodges in Minnesota, Wisconsin, Iowa, Washington, Illinois, the Dakotas, and Canada. In 1981, the Norway lodge was founded.

A mutual insurance company, a charitable foundation, *Viking Magazine*, and a headquarters building in Minneapolis were added over the years. The Sons is the largest Norwegian organization outside Norway. Keeping ties to Norway alive is important to their purpose. It was quite an honor to be invited to speak to their lodge in Oslo on January 16, 1995, the occasion of their 100th anniversary.[67]

AN EIGHT-GUN SALUTE FROM DEFENSE MINISTER KOSMO

Jørgen Kosmo, Norway's defense minister, invited me to visit his hometown of Horten on January 17, 1995, where he had started his political career with the Labour Party. We were to tour Karljohansvern, the nearby historic naval base that was once the headquarters of the Navy.

The 90-minute drive south along the Oslo Fjord took us right to the point where the fjord opens into the Skagerrak, the narrows where the Baltic and the North seas meet. It was easy to see why the Navy was here, as it was the best place on the fjord to defend Oslo and inland Norway from attack.

When my driver Edmund swung the Chevy through the gate, there was Kosmo smiling that devilish smile, a row of cannons behind him, and in quick order I was given an eight-gun salute and piped aboard the Coast Guard cutter at the dock. (I was thinking: Why eight guns?)[68]

The delicious lunch with the officers was lively. Someone always has a relative in America, so there is that story. "Where did my grandparents come from?" And, "What is Clinton like?"

After the war, the main naval base was moved to Bergen, a more strategic place on the Atlantic, to fulfill the NATO mission and in recognition that the Soviet Northern Fleet on the border with Norway was now a threat. "And that is where our oil is," Kosmo helpfully added.[69] Karljohansvern was now mostly a site where the history of the Norwegian Navy is honored with museums and tours.

Jørgen and I settled in with our coffee, and he told me his story. A construction worker, he rose through the ranks of the building workers trade union, became mayor of Horten, and since 1985 had been a member of Parliament. He particularly liked the image of him portrayed in the photo that was all over the Norwegian papers showing up at the NATO summit in 1994 wearing a light beige summer suit, while all the other defense ministers were dressed in dark suits. He told the press, "It was hot that day."

So here we were, a couple of pols from small towns who made it big. Someone has to be the defense minister. Someone has to be the ambassador. "It might as well be us," we concluded.

A ROCKET LAUNCH THAT COULD HAVE STARTED WWIII

I spent January 18-20, 1995, at the Andøya Rocket Range,[70] located on an island 500 miles above the Arctic Circle, to witness the launch of an American research rocket that when it happened, Boris Yeltsin claimed was a nuclear attack! It wasn't me, Boris.[71]

The launch was to be of the powerful Black Brant XII, which would peak at 1,400 kilometers high over the Norwegian island of Svalbard. The purpose was a research project by Cornell University to gather daytime data on the northern lights. They had obtained the rocket under a NASA program.

The launch was scheduled for early morning January 19, but weather conditions that day and the next stopped the countdown, and I returned to Oslo as I had several events scheduled with the departing Russian ambassador the following week.

On January 25, the weather cleared and at 7:24 a.m. the launch went off. Within seconds the Russian early warning radar system near Murmansk tagged it as a possible nuclear missile attack by the United States. The speed and suspicious trajectory of this rocket would not have been seen before by Russian radar. It had been the first-ever launch of a Black Brant from Andøya.

A mid-level automated alert was triggered, and the first steps for the Russian response began. The rocket stayed on its course, with the last stage dropping into the sea 320 kilometers northeast of Svalbard. It did not enter Russian air space. The alert was over before the Russian general in charge that day could get from his nearby office to the command-and-control center.

Word of this alert reached the Russian news service Interfax. It was first reported a rocket had been shot down. This was quickly corrected, but the next day President Boris Yeltsin was quoted as saying he had been given the "black box," the instrument with the keys to launch a nuclear counterattack.

At this time, the Russian economy and government were in shambles, and there were domestic political reasons for the mercurial president to appear strong and in charge.

Within two days the incident was being treated by the world press as a bit of a farce and an example of Russian incompetence. And Yeltsin's black box claim was questioned. It was not a joke, and we are all lucky. A lot could have gone wrong.

A new look at the event suggests not all was so straightforward on January 25, 1995.

The Black Brant is a four-stage rocket. At stage three, the rocket would mimic the look of a Trident missile launched from a U.S. nuclear submarine.

Had this particular Black Brant rocket—shipped in parts, assembled on site, and lying in a warehouse for several weeks—gone off course, there was no capability to destroy it in flight by those who had launched it at Andøya. This fail-safe was not available.

A routine notice on December 21, 1994, to embassies in Oslo from the Norwegian foreign ministry stated there would be "an international scientific rocket campaign" taking place from the Andøya Rocket Range in the time period January 15 to February 10, 1995. The basic information was meant to alert sea-going traffic as to where each of the stages of the rocket was likely to fall into the ocean. No note of the rocket's trajectory or height at apogee was given.

Russian officers in charge that day state that notice of the launch did not reach the right people in the Russian military. Even if it had, the possibility that it would have triggered the Russian early warning system would not have been apparent.

Why worry about one rocket? In a surprise attack, a Trident missile would first launch and set off a high-altitude nuclear explosion to blind Russian radar so the follow-on launch of intercontinental ballistic missiles from the U.S. directed at Russia's missile silos would not be detected in time.

The time from detection of an incoming missile to the decision by authorities to launch a counterattack would have been just a few minutes if Russian missiles were actually to be launched, in order for them to get a safe distance out of a launch silo. Luckily, the Black Brant remained on course and did not enter Russian air space, and the Russian early warning system and those in control of it that day acted appropriately. Had the missile been perceived as a threatening Trident, the outcome could have been disastrous.

On January 26, the day after the incident, I was with the Russian ambassador for his farewell reception. Neither of us mentioned the rocket, Yeltsin, or the black box. Nostrovia![72]

CHAPTER 14
FEBRUARY 1995

75TH ANNIVERSARY OF THE NORWAY AMERICA ASSOCIATION

The 75th anniversary of the Norway America Association on February 1 is a gala event—almost all the 100 invited guests for the honoring reception attend and crowd into the Residence. I am the host along with Canadian Ambassador Robert Pedersen, Education Minister Gudmund Hernes, and Kjeld Vibe, Norwegian ambassador to the U.S.

The lively multitude is a who's who of Norwegians passionate about education as the tie that binds. Their purpose is to encourage and fund Norwegians to study in U.S. and Canadian colleges and universities.[73]

We are very honored that Claus Helberg is with us—he is one of the heroes of Telemark, the group of Resistance fighters who in WWII sabotaged the hydroelectric plant producing heavy water, a necessary ingredient needed by Germany to develop an atomic bomb.

The wine cellar took a heavy hit.

SNORKELS AND GROUNDHOGS

Each Groundhog Day in Norway is a blessing, as nothing happens. My hometown of Sun Prairie, Wisconsin, has long claimed to be the groundhog capital of the world. On the morning of February 2, just before sunrise, a small crowd rousted out by the Chamber of Commerce would gather in the parking lot of Sun Prairie's American Legion building. The groundhog was produced and would see his shadow—or not. Usually, the mayor divined the answer, and local TV—this was carried live—would breathlessly announce whether there would be six more weeks of winter or an early spring.

My last year in office in the Wisconsin Assembly, 1990, the volunteer fire department had a eureka! moment and said, "Hey, this is a good opportunity to demonstrate our new snorkel truck. We'll put the groundhog and Loftus on the snorkel platform and raise them high above the crowd."[74] So there I was swaying in the breeze above the trees, the snorkel fully extended, with the rodent. His name was Jimmy, and I said to him, "Shadow or not I am going with the crowd pleaser." From on high, I announced to great cheering that there would be an early spring.

This is how you become an ambassador.

LUNCH WITH THE NEXT PM?

There are rumors that Gro is going to step down as prime minister and there is no better way to innocently chat about this than to invite to lunch the presumed PM in waiting, Thorbjørn Jagland, the leader of the Labour Party.

Jagland is a sincere person and at ease when there are just the two of us, even when talking English. There have been critiques of his English in the press. (Everyone can speak English better than I can speak Norwegian, but I try and this helps me.) Just saying "takk for sist" brings a smile. A smile is a diplomat's best friend.

Jagland is a member of the Parliament's Foreign Affairs Committee and well versed in U.S. policies under Clinton. He has met many of his counterparts in the U.S. Congress and the Democratic Party.

I ask: "If Gro steps down are you the next PM?" Jagland says, "You can ask such a question because you are an American and have had no diplomatic training." He's smiling, laughs, and is blushing! He gives the party line answer that he expects Gro to be a candidate again in the fall of 1997.

Every time I see him after this, he smiles with a knowing look and has to hold back a chuckle when I say "takk for sist."

TO THE TOP OF THE WORLD

It is the 75th anniversary of the Spitsbergen Treaty on February 9, 1995. Norway's sovereignty over Svalbard is spelled out by the Spitsbergen Treaty of 1920, one of the treaties following the Treaty of Versailles in 1919 that continued the sorting out of things by the victors in World War I. Svalbard is the archipelago, Spitsbergen the main island, and Longyearbyen the capital city.

Svalbard means "icy coast." And it was a sheer cliff of glacial ice that I first saw out the plane window when I flew from Tromsø to Svalbard's capital city of Longyearbyen. Think of the White Cliffs of Dover as ice. This, my first visit, was to pay respects to the sysselmann, the governor who is appointed by the government in Oslo acting on behalf of The King.[75]

On my schedule was also a visit to Barentsburg, the nearby Russian coal-mining settlement. A call on the director and a tour had been arranged. Longyearbyen is a modern Norwegian town with all the amenities, including regularly scheduled air service and a new university center. Snowmobiles are the main form of transportation, and brightly painted houses perch on stilts driven into the permafrost. Longyearbyen is named after John Munro Longyear, a Boston businessman who was visiting Spitsbergen on a cruise with his family in 1901. He noted the mineral potential, bought land, and started a coal company two years later.

Ann-Kristin Olsen is the sysselmann, the first female to hold this post. She had also been the first female police chief in Norway. A lawyer. We were born within three weeks of each other in 1945. We had a long talk over coffee and sweets. "Tourism and research are the future." She had put quite a dent in my ignorance about Svalbard by the time she sent me off armed with a map of historic sites. I went straight away to Ny-Ålesund to see the dirigible mooring tower, which had been my goal from the minute I knew the trip was planned.

The race to the North Pole made Spitsbergen famous. It was here in Ny-Ålesund that the dirigible named Norge, the airship of Norwegian explorer Roald Amundsen, started the flight that carried him and his crew to the North Pole on May 12, 1926, the first "verified" to reach the North Pole.[76]

My next stop was the Svalbard Museum to buy a book on Svalbard's history and a map, a very good reproduction of a Dutch map from the

17th century. There were good exhibitions with concise narratives of the culture and history. Since Barentsburg was my next destination, I took special note: "The community has a characteristic Russian feel, with a set system of blocks of flats and streets. ...The entrance to the mine, the storage area for the coal, and the shipping quay lie in the centre of the town. Barentsburg has a heliport, sports and culture building, a cowshed, hothouse, research station, museum, souvenir shop, medical center, and nursery school. Archaeologists, meteorologists, geophysicists, and glaciologists work at the research station during the summer season. Barentsburg has a Russian consulate."[77]

Potemkin got there ahead of me. The buildings were there but not the people. It was just I, a fellow from the maintenance crew with a ring of keys who unlocked a few buildings, and the world's northernmost statue of Valdimir Lenin.

I was witnessing the human toll of the economic collapse that followed the end of the Soviet Union: There was no need for the coal. There was no money for the salaries. There were no teachers or children to teach. This outpost, where the pay was very good to compensate for the hardships, was emptying out.

Upon my return to Oslo, I sent a thank you letter to Sysselmann Olsen, recalling her hospitality and expressing my gratitude for her counsel, and copied the foreign minister.

THEIR MAJESTIES ROYALLY ENTERTAIN THE AMBASSADORS

His Majesty is the head of state, and the Palace has its own diplomatic duties and agenda. It is to The King that an ambassador presents his or her credentials, rather than to the head of government.

Each year, Their Majesties host a dinner at the Palace for the Diplomatic Corps. It is a special and looked-forward-to event. In February 1995, it was at the Palace in a large hall lit by glittering chandeliers. The lights and Their Majesties' smiles brought a gaiety that erased from one's mind that this was in the darkness of February.

Those ambassadors from countries with a monarchy had a little extra regalia. My Danish colleague even sported a sword. One tuxedoed wag did mention that only the ambassador from the former colonial ruler seemed to need a weapon.

The invitation, menu, and musical interlude program was in French for the occasion. The food Norwegian. The menu was assorted caviar, poached salmon, reindeer filet, a cheese plate, and a cream cake. The wine courses were French, American, Italian, and German. The music selections by the string ensemble showed the same variety. "If I Fell" by Lennon and McCartney and a selection from *The King and I* by Richard Rogers among the tunes. I was at the head table, four places away from His Majesty. This was according to my seniority in the corps diplomatique.

THE LITHUANIAN EMBASSY OPENS

The Lithuanian Embassy opened on February 13, 1995. Ambassador Kornelija Jurgaitienė was my colleague from the newly independent country of Lithuania. She was Lithuania's first ambassador.

Lithuania had seen more than 50 years of Soviet and Russian military occupation. Although my memory of her story is vivid, I asked Kornelija to tell it in her words for these memoirs.

> *Dear Tom,*
>
> *You are right, my Ph.D. focused on American female writers of the South: Carson McCullers, Flannery O'Connor, Eudora Welty. The paradox was that I went into American literature to be as far away from the Soviet society as I could. Nevertheless, as the only competent commission on this subject was in Moscow, I had to write my paper in Russian. I had to have my dissertation blessed first, and only then I got a rare opportunity to make use of the IREX student exchange programme.[78] Thanks to it, I spent some time at Columbia, then Duke universities (the staff there was memorable: When I explained that I wanted to go deeper into the theory of literature as all I was fed in the USSR was social realism, they laughed and said: 'Girl, you are in a wrong place. We are all Marxists here.') I ended up at the University of Southern Mississippi in Hattiesburg—mainly to feel the flavor of the literature of the South. Lithuania declared independence from the Soviet Union at 10:44 p.m. on March 11, 1990. I worked in the Presidium of the Lithuanian Academy of Sciences at that time, in the international relations department. Then I got involved with a group of scientists around the Baltic Sea interested in the political, ecological, and economic transition in the Baltic States.*

We were arranging seminars and producing publications.

In 1993-94, I was chosen as a NATO research fellow in the individual project 'Modern National Identity and the Challenge of Europeanization: The Case of the Baltic States.' I moved to a position in the government and later was invited to be a national programs coordinator at the United Nations Development Program (UNDP), Lithuanian Division, freshly opened in our country. When one of my colleagues from our international team of Baltic scholars became the very first minister of foreign affairs (Mr. Povilas Gylys), he invited me to join as they were still lacking diplomats. Good knowledge of English was a great asset. I was asked to choose from several embassies and picked Norway, where I had once studied for half a year, had close contacts with the Academy of Sciences and Letters, was a little bit familiar with ways of life (that's what I naively thought at that time) and could manage some Norwegian. So this is my way to Norway, from starting the first-ever Lithuanian Embassy in that friendly ally of ours, up to becoming the first-ever female doyenne for corps diplomatique in Oslo in 2000. By the end of that year, I was invited back home by a new minister to become his adviser and the head of Cabinet.

I am still with the foreign ministry and currently the ambassador-at-large covering Baltic regional organizations and the Arctic Council. By the way, I was posted to our embassy in D.C. in 2004-2007 (actually, during this time I was invited and delivered a presentation at the University of Wisconsin-Eau Claire).

Sincerely, Kornelija
April 2022

P.S. Despite the fact that Lithuania had already announced its independence on March 11, 1990, the Soviets were preparing a bloody attack on the Lithuanian government and people in order to negate our Declaration of Independence. On January 13, 1991, Soviet tanks moved out of their barracks in Vilnius to launch an attack on our independence, and in response hundreds of Lithuanians headed to the Lithuanian Parliament and TV tower

*in Vilnius, where they would make a stand against Soviet troops
with their bare hands. More than a dozen died, and hundreds were
wounded. It was only after the lost coup in Moscow in August
1991 that Moscow would recognize the independence of the Baltic
nations. January 13 is now Freedom Defenders Day in Lithuania.*[79]

A VISIT TO THE SAMI PARLIAMENT IN KARASJOK

The year to come is not the sister of the year that passed.—Sami proverb

Karasjok is 500 miles north of the Arctic Circle, near North Cape,
the northernmost point on the European continent. Sami are the
indigenous people of far northern Norway, Finland, and Russia—
called Laplanders in the U.S.

They have lived with and off the great reindeer herds, first hunting
them and now herding them. Moving each season with the reindeer
to the next grazing pastures on their commonly owned land.

Still visible on the mountain plateaus from a thousand years ago is
the hunting method—two low stone fences wide at the opening then
narrowed like a funnel to a cliff where the reindeer would be chased
to plunge to their death. The images of the prehistoric rock carvings
of reindeer hunting were used at the '94 Olympic as emblems.

Now the herding is helped by snowmobiles and helicopters. The
delicate meat is a favorite among the fine diners in Oslo. The soft fur
of the brown-grey hides average about three feet by four feet, goes
with any decor; the hides are thrown over the backs of sofas in stylish
homes the world over.

The Sami had become only recently freed from the government
policy of "Norwegianization," where their culture, language, beliefs,
and even identity were unlearned through boarding schools and
the evangelistic fervor of the Lutheran Church—all in the name of
assimilation.

I knew two things about the Sami before coming to Norway. In
the late 1970s, the protests and civil disobedience by the Sami in
response to a plan for a hydroelectric dam near Alta that would
have flooded a Sami village and disrupted reindeer migration were
widely reported in the American press. In 1981, the Sami and their
allies in environmental groups staged a sit-in, blocking construction
machines at the dam site. There were thousands of protesters, some

chained to the equipment, and in Oslo a determined group of Sami went on a hunger strike in front of Parliament. Several hundred police, quartered in a cruise ship near Alta, removed the protesters from the dam site. In Oslo, the hunger strikers were dragged away. For the first time since WWII, Norwegians were arrested and charged with rioting. Several protest leaders were convicted and sent to jail.

The Labour prime minister, Odvar Nordli, promised a review of the Parliament's decision to stop the unrest, but the dam plans, although altered for the better, went on and construction was finally completed in 1987. But the activism and organization went on as well, and Norwegianization was finally put to rest. In 1988, the Norwegian Constitution was amended to enshrine Sami rights: "It is the responsibility of the Norwegian state to ensure favorable conditions to enable the Sami people to maintain and develop its language, culture and social structures." And the new Sami Parliament was officially opened in 1989 by King Olav.

So here we were, on February 21, 1995, Prime Minister Brundtland and me, at the annual opening of the Sami Parliament. But I was not with the PM. On this day, I was the American ambassador to a people with their own Parliament and sovereignty. A beacon to indigenous peoples worldwide.

The first president of this newest Parliament in the world was Ole Henrik Magga, a politician, and a linguist of the Sami language with a Ph.D. His moral authority radiated; it was almost visible. And he looked like Robert Redford.[80]

The proceedings were in Sami. It is a lilting language, especially when compared to Norwegian. I did not tune in on the headphones to the translation offered in Norwegian. My interest, fascination really, was to observe—to note the rituals and symbols. Would there be any traditions of the British Parliament? What about the Sami anthem, which had sections that were pretty harsh on the Norwegians? The Sami flag was prominent. The Norwegian flag was not.

During this parliamentary session the sun shone brightly. The four months of darkness had only been breached in late January. It was a good sign.

Ole Henrik Magga became a regular and quite anticipated guest at U.S. Embassy events, always careful to wear the brilliantly colored gákti, the traditional clothing worn by the Sami.

Oh, and the other thing. I had seen the Sami film *The Pathfinder*, which had been nominated for an Academy Award in 1990. Check it out.

On October 7, 1997, His Majesty King Harald opened the third Sami Parliament and apologized to the Sami people for the repression they suffered under Norwegianization.[81]

CHAPTER 15
MARCH 1995

IN THE PICTURE FOR GUATEMALAN PEACE NEGOTIATIONS

The March 9 reception for the president of Guatemala, Ramiro de León Carpio, hosted by Foreign Minister Bjørn Tore Godal, marked the start of the negotiations Norway was hosting to bring an end to the Guatemalan Civil War.

Ramiro de León Carpio had initiated the peace talks between the government and rebels of the Guatemalan Revolutionary National Unity. The piece of the United Nations-brokered deal Norway had was to find a process the two sides could agree to for disarming.

I was there along with my colleagues from Mexico and Spain, as we were to be the "friends of the peace process." Over the next several months, we would be summoned for a dinner or lunch or signing of a document to stand behind the negotiators for the two sides and be in the photo. This signaled that our respective governments recognized that progress was being made.

It is an important role for an ambassador to be in the picture. I hadn't a clue what was in these documents. That wasn't my job. I had no need to know. The political officers in the U.S. Embassy put in cables basically what Jan Egeland, the Spanish-speaking, very talented Norwegian go-between, reported to us on progress. This was very sensitive, as any leaks suggesting one side was agreeing to something the other side proposed could cause a setback, a hardening of positions.

The basic Norwegian strategy was to bring the representatives of the two sides to Oslo and put them up in the four-star Holmenkollen Park Hotel, on top of the hill way above Oslo, which was somewhat isolated—good food, great wine. The implication was make a deal or you can kiss this Shangri-La goodbye.

Fortunately, there was a Guatemalan in Oslo who had married a Norwegian, and he was tapped to be Guatemala's ambassador to Norway. Young, charming, and reserved. OK with both sides. We became quite close, as it was his job to get close to the Americans. He was invited to any lunch, dinner, or reception at the Residence that would get him connections that could help him play the hand he had been dealt.

SHIPBOARD ENTERTAINING

March 16, 1995, was like the baseball game where every player was used and every person from the manager to the bat boy had an important role to play.

The *USS Deyo* was still in the Oslo harbor on port call and I sent an SOS to Commanding Officer Commander Jeffrey Maydosz. I needed to host a lunch and it would be impossible to do it at the Residence. Could we do this on board? Yes!

In the evening, there was a reception for the American Field Service.[82] The invitation list was five single-spaced pages of names. The setup would take all day and everyone in the embassy and Residence was at work.

Commander Maydosz said, "At your service and it can be on my nickel." The lunch was an opportunity to gather an eclectic group the embassy needed to thank: Vice Admiral Leonhard Revang, the Norwegian Navy chief of Defense Headquarters staff; State Secretary Sigve Brekke of the Defense Ministry, a young man being groomed for a bright future, who also had a say in defense procurement; Ingelin Killengreen, the Oslo chief of police—the first woman to hold this post, and the person responsible for my safety most of the time; Per Hansen, the port director; and for all of us it was a great honor that Gunnar Sønsteby, a WWII Resistance hero, had accepted this invitation. Helping me host was our Colonel Ruth Phillips, the Army attaché in the embassy—one of the few women to hold such a post in an embassy.

The guests at the reception were AFS students who had been in the United States, those who were going, American students in Norway and their host families, a sports announcer, a jazz pianist, a violinist, the head of the Oslo Police's white-collar crimes unit, a half-dozen journalists, someone representing every industry from shipping to oil, many academics, editors of the three newspapers and staff, and many of the spouses from the embassy, who helped host.

Presidents have lauded AFS, especially John F. Kennedy, who in his short presidency met with the AFS three times, addressing the students at the White House directly about their role in creating a more peaceful world. His talk to them in July 1963 on the south lawn of the White house is inspiring. It is a call to service. He asks who is here from Canada and South America? Asia? Africa? Europe? What about Scandinavia in Europe? Each group of students gives a tremendous roar. A very loud and enthusiastic roar was from the students from Scandinavia.

In my remarks I quoted the speech JFK gave to the crowd of 16-, 17- and 18-year-olds. In 1963, JFK said to them:

> ...when you go home you will not be a friend of the United States but rather a friend of peace, a friend of all people; that you will stand in your community, in your state, and in your country for those principles which motivate us all around the globe, a chance for everyone, a fair chance for everyone and also for a world in which we have some hope for peace. If we are able to do that, this will be the most remarkable generation in the history of the world...
>
> I know what it was like in 1963 when I was 18, and this is a speech that has to be listened to and to hear the roar of a new generation so full of hope.[83]

I delivered the lines with all the vigor I could muster, but left out JFK's last sentence:

"Some day you will come back to the United States, when I am old and gray..."

The sadness endures.

HOSTING DINNER FOR STATE TRADE OFFICES IN EUROPE

The number of U.S. states with trade offices in Europe was expanding quite a bit. Wisconsin has had a trade office in Germany since the late 1970s. I was a champion of this and as Speaker of the Wisconsin Assembly made sure this office had support in the state budget.

The association of these trade offices was meeting in Oslo, and I was keen to show them that the embassy and the ambassador were here to help them be successful. The best way to do this was host a dinner and invite the Norwegian businesses and individuals they should get to know—a Rolodex of contacts they could call upon. These offices promoted their home state businesses in Europe and worked to bring European businesses to their state. A lot of cachet to have these business introductions hosted by the ambassador.

Twelve states were represented by their trade office directors— Iowa, Florida, Illinois, Indiana, Kentucky, Maryland, Michigan, Missouri, New York, Oklahoma, Texas, and Wisconsin, which was represented by Joan Treadaway.

There were 17 Norwegian businesses represented, including the Norwegian-American Chamber of Commerce, which represented Norwegian businesses with operations in the United States.

This list was arrived at by our commercial attaché, Scott Bozek, in consultation with the trade directors. Some had targeted businesses and some had sectors. Scott informed us at the embassy's Country Team meeting briefing on this event that it was "all hands-on deck." So we had 12 from the embassy staff—those dealing with commerce, the defense attaché's officers who were heavily involved in the sale of American weapons systems, and a few others, including Berit Sjølund, the chief of Delta Airlines in Norway and president of the American Chamber of Commerce in Norway, which represented U.S. companies doing business in Norway. Berit was always helpful to us, and we helped her promote the Delta nonstop flight from Oslo to Newark, a flight we desperately wanted to succeed for selfish reasons, among others.

Each table had a trade office director and a host from the embassy staff. At my table, there were Scott and the trade directors of Iowa, Illinois and Wisconsin, along with Eyolf Haug, president of the Norwegian-American Chamber of Commerce, and Berit Sjølund.

Barbara Rendalen, an American living in Oslo we called on often for entertainment, played the Steinway after dinner.

EN ROUTE TO D.C., A STOP IN BRUSSELS

On April 5, 1995, I was to join up with Prime Minister Brundtland in Washington, D.C., for a meeting with Vice President Al Gore. The next day she would give the keynote address at a major conference to mark the 25th anniversary of Earth Day.

The philosophy of the Country Team was I had the luggage, the tailored suits, and the big salary so why not send me out early and add a few stops along the way. So, I stopped in Brussels for two days of meetings.

Day 1 took place at U.S. NATO headquarters with a packed schedule of briefings arranged by Bob Hunter, the U.S. ambassador to NATO. A lunch in my honor included the Norwegian ambassador to NATO, Leif Mevik, and Clyde Kull, Estonia's ambassador to Belgium and their representative at NATO HQ, whom Bob seated next to me.

Ambassador Kull was 36 years old, a graduate of the Moscow State Institute of International Relations and was in the first group of diplomats recruited for the new Ministry of Foreign Affairs after Estonia regained independence in 1990.[84] He asked me about Norway's position on the Baltics joining NATO. I said every signal from the current government indicated support. Sounds like a statement right out of Diplomacy 101: "How to give a fuzzy answer," but accurate and he said helpful.

The menu included Le Saumon Roti Sans Peau aux Jeunes Poireaux a la Hollandaise (AKA Norwegian Salmon).

My second full day, at the U.S. Mission to the European Union, was hosted by our gifted ambassador to the EU, Stuart Eizenstat. I told Stu that although Norway voted "no" on EU membership in the November 1994 referendum, there was no truth to the rumor that his visit to Oslo shortly before the vote tipped the scales to the "no" side. Won a bet with myself—I got him to laugh.

My report to Stu: In addition to the continuing melancholy of the "yes"-side voters, there was emerging a none-too-kind assessment of the status of Norwegian foreign policy four months after the "no" vote.

Nils Morten Udgaard, the respected foreign policy writer for *Aftenposten*, offered his analysis in a column headlined: "A Politically

Castrated State in Europe."

> Four months after the EU-No, Norway has experienced the steepest fall in its foreign policy influence ever in peace time. Norway exists as a politically castrated state in Europe. The EU vote has made the U.S. more important for us. But at the same time, the Norwegian involvement in all the problems of the world is leading to a foreign policy with unclear contours. The real priorities are becoming difficult to see.

> Bjørn Tore Godal is the only minister of foreign affairs who has been in the position for 14 months without visiting the U.S. He knows Yasser Arafat better than the leaders of the U.S.[85]

PARIS, AMBASSADOR PAMELA HARRIMAN, AND THE "RICH COUNTRIES CLUB"

Why oh why am I in Paris? Paris is the HQ of the Organization for Economic Co-operation and Development (OECD). Not in the EU, Norway now by necessity needed to increase its presence in Europe where it had a seat at the table. I now needed to know about the organization.

David Aaron, the U.S. ambassador to the OECD, had prepared a two-day tutorial for me on the workings of the organization, including a lunch with his colleague the Norwegian ambassador. (There was a separate lunch with the Norwegian ambassador to France.)

In 1947, the predecessor organization to the OECD was founded by 20 countries to administer U.S. Marshall Plan funds for the rebuilding of Western Europe after WWII. Norway was one of the founding states. Fostering democracy, free market economic growth, and keeping down Communist influence in countries outside the Soviet Bloc were the focus.

By 1995, the shorthand for the organization had become the "Rich Countries Club." The countries in the OECD now were democracies of varying degrees with developed economies. After the revolutions of 1989, the focus had turned quickly to development aid for the newly independent countries of Eastern Europe, specifically Hungary, Poland, Czech Republic, and Slovakia.

Norway was already an important player in the OECD and Labour

Government Finance Minister Sigbjørn Johnsen was playing a personal role in increasing Norway's influence.

Minister Johnsen and I had become Sigbjørn and Tom after our first lunch, when he delighted in telling me of his hobby of studying the U.S. Civil War, including visiting battlefields. He knew well of Colonel Hans Christian Heg, born in Norway, who led the Fifteenth Wisconsin, the "Norwegian regiment," and was killed at the battle of Chickamauga. So when I noticed a just-published book on the First Minnesota Volunteers, a celebrated Scandinavian regiment, I called the author, Richard Moe, and he graciously sent an inscribed copy that I presented to Sigbjørn.[86]

I arrived in Paris by train from Brussels and went first to the American ambassador's residence where I would be staying. Ambassador Pamela Harriman greeted me, and we sat down to chat over a cup of coffee. I was on the couch under the Renoir. I think. I couldn't just stare at it. Anyway, one of the greats.

We had first met in 1990 when I was running for governor. And we met at the NATO ambassador meeting in the spring 1994 where she was our witness to the history of Europe. That night Dustin Hoffman and Lauren Bacall were coming to a reception, and regretfully, I told Pamela I had a schedule conflict and must attend another event. She knew that, as in politics and diplomacy, success comes when you follow the script.

The next day Pamela was hosting a garden party in the late afternoon. The guests were fashionable and perfectly coiffed women and men in clothes à la mode worn nonchalantly.

Yet all eyes were on Pamela. She was wearing the glamour of her well-known life. She introduced me as her friend the ambassadeur Américain en Norvège. All ambassadors introduce their colleagues as friends, but these were welcome words, as guests asked me how I knew Pamela, rather than mention in a world-weary sort of way that they would probably never get to Norway.

CHAPTER 16
APRIL 1995

25TH ANNIVERSARY OF EARTH DAY WITH GRO, GAYLORD, AND GORE IN D.C.

Vice President Al Gore, Prime Minister Gro Harlem Brundtland, and the founder of Earth Day, former United States Sen. Gaylord Nelson of Wisconsin, would be the speakers at the April 5 conference marking the 25th anniversary of Earth Day in Washington, D.C.

I was not a speaker, but as is often the case, I was writing in my mind the speech I would give. Perhaps a cake recipe capturing the 20th century. The ingredients would be shovels-full of blood-soaked wars; add nightmares of nuclear annihilation; mix in the assassinations of JFK, RFK, and Martin Luther King Jr.; finally, leaven with progress on civil rights, equality for women, and the big new idea that humans owed the planet respect, as captured by two words: Earth Day. It could save the cake.

On the first Earth Day in 1970, I was there on University Avenue in Madison, closed to traffic for the event, as a few thousand students and people of every age and walk of life joined 20 million others across the country. The model was the teach-in, influential gatherings of students and faculty boycotting classes to speak the truth about the Vietnam War.

Gaylord told Gro that his grandfather Christian Nilsson was born in Norway in 1845. She displayed all the pride a Norwegian is allowed in learning that the father of Earth Day was of Norwegian descent.

Gaylord was a very respected, folksy senator who had been in WWII (used as an example of "the greatest generation") and came from the tiny town of Clear Lake, Wisconsin. Former governor of Wisconsin, he was a dear friend, mentor, and political partner. He would rather get a laugh and tell the Earth Day story—the moral reasons for our duty to the environment—than just tell the Earth Day story.[87] One opening line when he was to speak was, "Of all my introductions, that was the most recent."

The first time I met Prime Minister Brundtland in October 1993, we talked about Earth Day. Gro and Vice President Gore had now assumed the mantle of environmental leadership.

Gro and I had a packed two-day schedule meeting with Gaylord and meeting with VP Gore, and a dinner the first night hosted by the Norwegian ambassador to the United States Kjeld Vibe.

The meeting with Sen. Richard Lugar, chairman of the Senate Foreign Relations Committee, was a priority for an update on the Cooperative Threat Reduction Program, legislation he sponsored with Sen. Sam Nunn enacted in 1991 to provide funding and technical help to Russia, Ukraine, Belarus, and Kazakhstan for the deactivation of nuclear warheads.[88]

I had met Sen. Lugar several times, including sitting next to him at a small dinner at the Norwegian ambassador's residence in Washington on an earlier occasion. A most gentle person. With a full head of silver hair, he looked like a senator. A former mayor of Indianapolis, Indiana. The Nobel Peace Prize in the future for him and Sam Nunn?

Gro sketched out Norway's many initiatives in the Murmansk area to assist the Russians with the safe disposal and transport of nuclear weapons materiel. I gave a briefing on disposal programs for radioactive waste from decommissioned Soviet submarines, a task not covered in Nunn-Lugar. And I mentioned the upcoming trip of Sen. Nunn to Oslo on July 4. A three-day program of meetings and travel were planned.[89]

Gaylord, VP Gore, and Gro gave good, impassioned speeches. But the words were not the message. It was that Earth Day was here to stay and it had already influenced another generation.

CELEBRATING MY 50TH, POLAR BEARS AND ALL

The Queen sent me flowers. My sister Wendy gave me a traditional Telemark man's knife embellished with silver on the handle and sheath with my initials engraved and the date. My fun-loving cousins flew over from Stavanger and brought their party clothes and singing voices.[90]

At my birthday party on April 24, 1995, Barbara sang and played the piano. The cousins were a champagne-glass-raising, swaying chorus of harmony. Wendy tap-danced in the kitchen. Trolls gamboled in the countryside. The cognac cupboard was cleaned out. Not even the start of it.

The Royal Norwegian Air Force Arctic rescue team invited Barbara and me to ride along in the helicopter on their spring flight from Tromsø to Spitsbergen, a 300-mile flight. We would stop halfway at Bear Island on April 24th and the crew at the weather station would throw a party and bake a cake.

The 50th birthday in Norway is a big deal. In the old days, if you made it until 50 it was a long life. Born, baptized, confirmed, married, had children—all milestones—but reaching 50, that was your day, spent with your friends celebrating your life. Birthdays after that, ho hum.

The instructions for the flight to Spitsbergen: "Anti-exposure suits are required to be worn over your clothes for the flight...the crew normally wears long johns under their suits... the suits are very hot in buildings, and the crew is known to have lunch in their long johns... there will be dinner at a 'top-notch, white-tablecloth Arctic dining establishment' in Longyearbyen. ...Pack accordingly. It will be very cold."

We flew to Tromsø and were met by the aircraft commander, a dashing lieutenant, and three other young, handsome, grinning crew members. The hulking *Sea King* amphibious helicopter painted bright orange was waiting. This workhorse American-made helicopter designed originally for hunting Soviet subs could be made watertight and land in the ocean. Or on snow, ice, or tundra.

Into our togs, a brief briefing, and we were off due north up the coast, skimming a snow-covered mountaintop, then looking straight down into a fjord of topaz-blue water. My eyes told my stomach we were on a roller coaster. Then soon out over the Barents Sea on our way to the famous Bear Island, Bjørnøya.

By the third week in April, the midnight sun has arrived at Bear Island. The sun sits high in a bright blue sky, I wrote in my journal. On April 24, 1926, Amundsen would have been preparing for his attempt to reach the North Pole in the dirigible *Norge*. He reached it on May 12. We were flying low to the ocean just at the height of a dirigible and witnessing the horizon as Amundsen did.

The coal mines and being a strategic site for weather forecasting brought the island importance in WWI, such that the Spitsbergen Treaty gave Norway sovereignty over the Svalbard Archipelago, including Bear Island.[91]

After some banking of the helicopter "for better views" to the right and then to the left with the door open and Barbara hanging out as far as her safety harness would allow "for photos," we landed near the weather station building, the rotors fluffing the snow up into a white cloud of confetti that then came down over us like we were in a ticker-tape parade in New York. What an entrance.

The cheering team greeted us with shouts of welcome. OK, we were bringing the mail and booze. Not everyone was in the greeting party. The guy 50 yards away with the high-powered rifle on polar bear watch held his attention to the near horizon.[92]

Magne Gundersen, the station chief, welcomed us inside to a waiting table set with a steaming pot of coffee and homemade cinnamon buns. Never have welcomers been so welcoming. We got settled and out of our exposure suits and into our jeans and Norwegian sweaters and were given snowmobile suits, helmets, and sun goggles.

Off on snowmobiles to see a polar bear cave dug in the snow that the mother had recently left. Barbara, whose middle name should be adventurous, climbed down into the chamber. The guy with the rifle was really nervous at this point.

Back to the station and out of those clothes and given towels. "Mr. Ambassador, Madame Ambassador, you are about to join an exclusive club. The Bear Island Polar Bear Club." There was a log shed with a sauna so hot the heat turned to steam when it found its way outside through the cracks in the chinking. A stop there first. Like a last cigarette before the firing squad. Then down to the shore edge where a 10-foot square of open water had been chopped clear of the ice. An aluminum extension ladder stuck out. The rules: Your head had to go under at least once and you had to swim five strokes. This was about all your body could take.

Everyone went in except the guy with the rifle. So cold it burned. The lost tenth circle of hell. Climbing up the frozen metal rungs of the ladder on feet devoid of feeling and racing over the snow to the sauna. Inside it was slippery, as there was now a half-inch of frost on my feet.

At the birthday dinner, certificates were given out first with a toast in Norwegian—tough to follow—but I think it meant we were now something like blood brothers and one adventuresome blood sister. Rare-cooked reindeer filets and Napa red wine and then a cake only describable as butter, sugar, and cream held together with the minimum of flour and on top the number 50 outlined in cherries. I gave a toast—here is to The King, here is to the president and here is to the Royal Norwegian Air Force Arctic rescue crew, and, from your fellow club member, here is to the clan at Bear Island. Skål.

On April 25, we flew on to Longyearbyen and stayed overnight at the Polar Hotel. The next day I went over to inform the sysselmann, Svalbard's governor, that I was there and how I got there. I was not on the manifest of any commercial flight. Barbara went off on a snowmobile trek with the crew and a guy with a gun. Just one month before, in March, two Norwegian girls, college students, were out on a hike and were attacked by a young polar bear. One girl was killed. Neither had a gun.

Polar bears are protected, and the rifle or shotgun is to be used to scare them off, with killing the last resort. A pump shotgun with a stainless-steel barrel and mechanism, one that can hold seven slugs, is recommended. If you have fired off four rounds and a bear is still coming, you will need the other three.

Dinner at the white-napkin restaurant, just a safe, short walk from the hotel, was a seven-course Arctic tasting menu with wine. The chef introduced each course and tasted the wine along with us. Quite a happy fellow by course number five. And inexpensive. Well within the crew's per-diem and the extra stash they had for entertaining Barbara and me. The feast was a fourth of the cost at a swanky joint in Oslo. Why? Taxes were set low by the Spitsbergen Treaty and the Norwegian government waives some taxes and subsidizes business so they will locate in Svalbard.

We took the earliest commercial flights back to Oslo on April 27th in order to arrive late morning. That night, I was to host at the Residence the largest and most important event for the California wine industry ever held in Norway.

AMBASSADOR, ENVOY, PLENIPOTENTIARY, WINE PURVEYOR

The spit buckets were out. Hundreds of wine glasses were placed on tables around the rooms—the furniture had been taken out. The California wineries had delivered their cases of bottles. Sales representatives stood by their wares, corkscrews at the ready.

No more nice little wine tastings—we were going for the throat, so to speak. California wine could compete on price with European wines but there was no advertising allowed of wines in Norway and there were gatekeepers: the buyers at the government-run liquor monopoly Vinmonopolet and the testy tasters who wrote reviews of wine each week in the papers.

So, we invited the people whose job it was to select wines to buy: sommeliers and chefs from a few dozen of the best watering holes and restaurants; and the buyers for the three airlines, government guest house, Royal Palace, hotels, and airport vendors. And then a list of those who had some influence on policy in this area: the Fruit and Vegetable Association, Food Control Authority, Ministry of Agriculture, Cooperatives and Wholesale Association, Ministry of Foreign Affairs, every wine and food writer, Explorer's Club, and Wine Club of Oslo.

And the Vinmonopolet buyers—this group alone bought a million bottles of wine a year, and were quite susceptible to buying the wine the writers featured. We wanted their taste buds unedited.

There were 60 sippers and spitters attending, and they all left happy and singing "California, Here I Come."

A NEW RUSSIAN AMBASSADOR WITH BROKEN BUGS

The new Russian ambassador, Juri Fokine, started in the Russian Foreign Ministry in 1961 when he was 25 years old. His first assignment was at the Soviet Mission at the United Nations in New York. He quickly rose to positions in the Foreign Minister's office, and prior to coming to Oslo, he had been the director of one of the two European departments. A senior diplomat.

I greeted him at the door of the Residence. A great smile and a natural informality—the word nonchalant could be used.

He was making his rounds of courtesy calls as a new ambassador must. We had met at his welcoming reception, but this was a chance to get to know each other. We talked a long time over coffee.

Juri said Norway was a priority for the new Russian Federation for the obvious reasons of a shared border, a friendly history, and the not-so-obvious reason that Norway was a friend inside NATO. A good way to put it, I said.

I told him of my priority of working to get an agreement to end the dumping of low-level-liquid nuclear waste in the Barents Sea by being a partner with Norway in the task. And I told him of my activities in Murmansk. "Interesting," was his comment when I said the Environmental Protection Agency was the lead on this in Washington. Not State or the Navy.

We really hit it off and decided we would have lunch once a month just the two of us and alternate between my digs and his. On the way out I said, "I suppose you have this place bugged?" He said, "Yes, but they don't work." Touché, but really an insider comment, noting that after the fall of the Soviet Union nothing much was working.

CHAPTER 17
MAY 1995

A SPY PLANE FOR THE BODØ MUSEUM AND
THE U-2 INCIDENT 35 YEARS LATER

In January 1994, I had been visited by the mayor of Bodø. He asked if I could procure a U-2 spy plane for the town's museum—if possible, just like the one Gary Powers flew when he was shot down over the Soviet Union in 1960 on his way to the secret airfield in Bodø. Air Force Colonel Posner, the embassy's liaison with the Norwegian Air Force, indicated this should be possible with the ambassador's help. (What? Who do I have to call to get this done?)

I managed to get a decommissioned plane like Powers' from the Air Force for the museum simply by asking.

Now, on May 1, 1995, it was the 35th anniversary of the Powers' incident. The sensational news of the 1960 U-2 downing, and the parading before television cameras of captured pilot Gary Powers was all about the U.S. and the Soviet Union. President Dwight D. Eisenhower eventually issued a mea culpa. Little was reported on the shockwave this produced in Norwegian politics or at the U.S. Embassy in Oslo because little was available in English.

The United States and the Cold War in the High North by Norwegian historian Rolf Tamnes tells the Norwegian story in detail.[93] A secret agreement between the CIA and the Norwegian government allowed the flights, but Norwegian airports "were not to be used in connection with overflights of Soviet territory." The CIA representative in Oslo was Louis C. Beck. He informed Norwegian intelligence only that there would be a flight on May 1, 1960. There had not been overflights before, so there was no reason to believe this would be different.

The Norwegians were stunned to see Khrushchev on TV claiming that the U-2 shot down had been heading to Bodø. "Beck disappeared, and the U.S. Embassy knew nothing."[94] Khrushchev said Norway could be "subject to retaliatory strikes." The Soviet defense minister said: "Think about it. We can hit these air bases so there is nothing left of them."

The United States ambassador, Frances Willis, the first-ever female career Foreign Service officer to serve as an ambassador, said she had not been informed and wrote in a cable that "the involvement of Bodø and Norway came as a shock." The Norwegian government investigated and concluded they had not been informed of this flight.

On May 13, 1960, Norwegian Foreign Minister Halvard Lange handed to Ambassador Willis a pro memoria (a formal note of events) that "permission for the U-2 to land in Bodø had not been sought in advance, and such permission would in any event have been in conflict with the conditions attached to the use of airports for reconnaissance missions.[95]

The U.S. response delivered by Willis on May 18 acknowledged the Norwegian version of events as being correct, adding that in the future the United States would abide by Norwegian restrictions. Moscow came to accept the Norwegian explanation and Eisenhower stopped the U-2 flights.

EXPLODING A SOVIET BUILDING IN LATVIA

It was usually a two-hour drive from Riga, Latvia, to Skrunda. On May 4, I was in the car with America's ambassador, Ints Siliņš. Ahead was the car with the prime minister.

It was a narrow, two-lane road of crumbling blacktop; there were rows of tall trees on either side, each with a stork's nest of woven sticks on the very top. Hundreds of black and white storks circled above us. It was a sunny day, and the shadows from the trees made the road a picket fence of light and dark. A speeding caravan we were. The security in the lead car would force oncoming cars off the road. There were no shoulders.

It was the fifth anniversary of Latvia declaring its freedom, and we were to witness the blowing up of a Soviet radar station, a 14-story building. It was a new facility that was to have been part of their anti-ballistic-missile early-warning system.

The Clinton administration was paying—a piece of a several-million-dollar deal with the Russians to get their military out of Latvia faster. The last Soviet troops had left Latvia less than a year before.

We gathered. A white Chevrolet pick-up pulled up and an American in a hardhat and clad in khaki stepped out and explained that we were about to see an implosion. The charges were set such that the building would collapse inward and fall down where it stood.

And it did. A pile of Cold War rubble and a cloud of white dust. The lone cloud in the blue sky. After the echo of the explosions had gone, storks could be heard screeching.

With Ambassador Siliņš, a career Foreign Service officer,[96] the new American presence in Latvia was in safe hands. He was born in Latvia in 1942 during the German occupation. In 1944, his mother took him and fled the Soviet occupation, and they ended up at an American displaced persons camp in Germany. His father stayed, expecting the Allies would liberate Latvia. The Red Army captured him. He was sent to a concentration camp in Siberia, where he died.[97]

From 1922 until 1940, Latvia was an independent country with an American ambassador. In WWII, Latvia suffered murderous occupations by the Soviets, then Nazi Germany, and then again the Soviet Union.

The U.S. terminated its diplomatic mission in Latvia in September 1940. The end of the Cold War and the restoration of Latvian independence saw a restoration of diplomatic relations and the return of an ambassador.

CELEBRATING THE 50TH ANNIVERSARY OF THE END OF NAZI OCCUPATION

It was a celebration of the 50th anniversary of the end of the occupation, that day in May 1945 when the German general in charge of 350,000 troops simply surrendered to one person, a member of the Norwegian Resistance. The iconic photo of this shows a young man alone standing tall, a Sten gun slung over his shoulder, and the general saluting him.

Was the 50-year anniversary also to be a day of reckoning with the past? Some marking of a reconciliation with those who were with Vidkun Quisling, who nominally headed the Norwegian government under the Nazis, and the other collaborators? Would it address the continuing stigma attached to children of the Norwegian women who had slept with the enemy?

And, what about the Germany of now? The German ambassador was to participate, and the German anthem played. There was vocal resistance to this from veterans of the military and the Norwegian Resistance. The German ambassador was one of the regulars at our doubles tennis match on Saturday mornings. After a game in late April, he said to me, "Tom, I will not be going to the 50th." He wanted me to have this confidence as his friend before it was announced. It was a tough call, certainly reached after much angst in Bonn and was likely a decision taken by Chancellor Helmut Kohl himself.

In the American Embassy, we were not sure what to make of our role or how to report.

Our conclusion was that I was to go where invited and listen. No statement or activities that might intrude.

There were to be Liberation Day ceremonies throughout Norway on May 7. I was invited to Narvik. The battles for Narvik in April 1940 identified a main reason why control of Norway was essential: The port in a deep fjord could host a German battleship, and the railhead for shipping iron ore from Sweden, which supplied the German war machine, was in Narvik. Sweden allowed this transshipment, part of many deals to preserve a compromised neutrality.

For Norwegians, the first battle of Narvik was a victory in which Norwegian, French, British, and Polish troops took the city back from the Germans. They had to withdraw a short time later when the forces were more needed elsewhere in Europe. (America was not in the war at this time.)

His Majesty, the PM, and Defense Minister Kosmo would be at Narvik. The first thing upon seeing me, with a twinkle in both eyes bathed in smoke from his signature hand-rolled cigarette, Minister of Defense Kosmo said, "We will buy the AMRAAM missiles. Don't tell Hughes, they might raise the price." (Advanced Medium-Range Air-to-Air Missile fired from an F-16. Only available from the American defense contractor Hughes since 1991, the Norwegian purchase was one of the first. AMRAAM became the standard for NATO.) He laughed but was serious. The deal was the French would withdraw their bid later in the month before the announcement.

Time in the VIP waiting area with HM was not to be wasted, and I told him The King of Spain story from the Olympics. The royal laugh was such it may have been heard in Madrid.

The day and the dinner for 500 in Narvik were both joyous and somber. The occupation and war had scarred the nation.

On the flight back to Oslo I thought of the speech The King would give the next day, the most important perhaps he would ever give. And, as one who has written and given speeches for decades, I thought of the speechwriter. The words had to be a speech to the nation, of the moment, to be listened to nationwide on radio and television, but also written for the historical record. The speech would be a draft of points that hung together for content and allow The King to easily tailor to his own thoughts, his own history. He was there. All 50 years.

This is the speech that His Majesty The King gave on May 8, 1995, for the 50th anniversary of liberation:

> President of the Storting, Prime Minister, guests from many countries, veterans, officers and soldiers, Norwegian women and men,
>
> Today we celebrate the memory of the greatest day modern Norway has ever known: May 8, 1945. On that day, Norway became free again and peace returned to Europe, after almost six years of war with unfathomable suffering and destruction.
>
> Fifty years ago today, the nightmare ended. Nothing compares with the joy that filled us then. It still resounds in the hearts of all who experienced the day, here in a Norway with flag and song and rejoicing—and among all of us who had longed to return home for five long years and knew on this day that it would not be long until the dream became reality.
>
> In our case, it happened on June 7 when my dear grandfather King Haakon came home to the country he loved. 'Where the home is, there is also the fatherland,' said Christian Michelsen when he welcomed him in 1905. This was how our family felt, this was how the country felt:

We had gotten our homeland back. Everything Norwegians had fought for, longed for, asked for in unease and anxiety, had suddenly become ours again, like an unbelievable gift.

The last great fear we had was also let go: that the over 350,000 soldiers that Hitler had in Norway would continue the war here, after the rest of Europe had found peace. That uncomfortable thought had given Norwegians many sleepless nights. Instead, we experienced a peaceful spring with a dreamlike intoxication of joy. We also woke to a new workday when Norway would rebuild after the war's great destruction, not least in Northern Norway, and all capacity was put into building efforts, with results we can be proud of.

Now, as then, we have every reason to remember what the war cost us in victims and suffering. On the home front, in dangerous missions, people assembled in opposition and grew into a network that was crucial for an orderly transition when freedom came. Women and men contributed equally hard. Norwegians outside of the country, in all branches of defense, fought bravely on the Allied side. The war sailors' contribution cannot be valued highly enough. Many Norwegians suffered in prisons and concentration camps. The will to resist was found in all parts of the country, under hardship and loss.

Their contribution fills us with pride and gratitude. But we must also in gratitude acknowledge that many other people carried much larger burdens than we did. They fought an indomitable fight against the Nazi tyranny—with millions of victims—and also led us to victory and freedom. We owe them eternal gratitude. I thank especially all the nations that are represented here today.

The war was an expensive lesson for us. At that time, we promised each other that never again would anyone find us unprepared to stand up to attack and use of power. We sought security in cooperation with the countries that stood by us. The goal was: no more war! Today we can look back on 50 years of peace in our country and in most of

Europe. But the world is uncertain, and the promise we made must always be renewed and followed through in action.

The war left deep wounds in Norway as well. Many lost their loved ones. Children experienced cruelties that they can never forget. People who made a great war effort didn't get the support they had reason to expect, and even after 50 years, not all wounds are healed. We all have a responsibility to do our part so that the wounds are now healed.

This also applies to countrymen who were on the wrong side. We who lived through the war would not be honest if we agreed with the old saying that to understand everything is to forgive everything. What was wrong doesn't become right just because we understand the reasons and circumstances. But one thing is actions and guilt which must be atoned for—another thing is people who have suffered for what they once did. A conciliatory hand will always be stretched out. It is both a Christian and humane duty. Reconciliation will overcome irreconcilability and hate.

In the time after the war, it was the path to reconciliation the Western world followed—for the first time after a great war. France and Germany, two archenemies through the centuries, became partners in peaceful cooperation. Great Britain, the United States, and other Western countries were founders and participants of democracy building in Europe, which has been crucial for the longest peaceful period in European history.

That was what they fought for, the many who kept our honor shining during the war—a peace that has a place for freedom and humanity. It is therefore a great pleasure to see so many veterans assembled here today—and know that so many are gathered and following us over the whole country. On their behalf, I thank the Government, National Committee, and all the others who made sure this marking of the peace anniversary received celebration and dignity.

But we owe the greatest gratitude to those who gave their lives during Norway's fight for freedom. Akershus Fortress is our national memorial for them. They live yet in our hearts. With their loss of life, they showed what the fight cost. Their sacrifice is the hidden foundation of the free and peaceful Norway that we inherited, and which is our job to continue.

Nordahl Grieg, himself one of our fallen, wrote about them:

We are so few in this country,
every fallen is brother and friend.
We have the dead with us
the day we come again.

Yes, the dead are with us, also on this day of joy. They gave everything so that the joy should be ours. So, we will also share it with them, in reassurance that their sacrifice was not in vain, in gratitude for the model they gave us, and in commitment to the promise that is written in the national anthem:

At the call we too will aid her
Armed to guard her peace.[98]

"AN INVASION OF NICENESS" FROM MADISON

Oslo Mayor Ann-Marit Sæbønes[99] and I had been preparing for the Sister City visit of the people from Madison, Wisconsin, by having several lunches together. "Get ready for an invasion of niceness," was my advice.

The Sister City programs were started by President Eisenhower. In 1962, then Madison Mayor Henry Reynolds initiated a sister city relationship with Oslo.[100] The visitors to Oslo by the Madison group, often led by the mayor, brought back tales of good times with wonderful host families.

The Madison delegates spread good cheer and were welcome guests. The first time I walked into the bar at the Bristol Hotel it came up in the conversation that I was from Madison, and the bartender asked, "How is the gin martini guy doing?" He was referring to Byron Ostby, the longtime beloved honorary consul of Norway in Madison.

Madison was still a city with a large population of those whose parents and grandparents had immigrated from Norway. The UW had many Norwegian alumni and was one of only three universities where the Norwegian language was taught and the literature studied.

One Madison mayor was born in Norway, several were of Norwegian descent, and Mayor Albert Schmedeman had been President Woodrow Wilson's ambassador to Norway from 1913 to 1921.

Mayor Paul Soglin, who had been elected mayor three times in three decades, serving a total of 20 years, perhaps had the best Norway connection—members of his family fled the Nazis and found refuge in Norway before making their way to America. When opportune, he would claim Norwegian ancestry.

Ann-Marit would hold a reception for the Madison group and their host families on the 16th, and I would host this same group at the Residence on the 19th. This was no small cast of characters—75 Norwegians attending from the host families and 60 in the Madison delegation, including Byron Ostby who along with his wife, Helen, helped both Ann-Marit and then Barbara and me with the hosting. A good time was had by all, friends were made and "On Wisconsin" was sung. People from Madison were quite proud to have Oslo as a sister city.

CELEBRATING SYTTENDE MAI

Syttende Mai, May 17, is like the Fourth of July: Independence Day and a national holiday.[101] The embassy was closed and Barbara could finally have the day to herself, as May had been nonstop events; my driver Edmund could be with his kids.

The day is marked in Oslo by a children's parade up the hill to the Palace where Their Majesties and their children, Crown Prince Haakon and Princess Märtha Louise, stand on the balcony waving and smiling until the last child toddles past.

The children, led by their teachers, hold small Norwegian flags in one hand and to a rope with the other—like a ski-hill tow rope to help keep them in line and not wander off. They are dressed in their kid-size national costumes, likely the same bunads handed down from parents and grandparents. No dignitaries in the parade. No jets screaming overhead. This is about the children and the country.

The red, white, and blue sea of fluttering flags. The sunny day. The King on the balcony waving and smiling. These children will remember this day for the rest of their lives.

I walked down to the Palace to be there at 9 a.m. to sign the royal Palace registrar, giving me plenty of time before the start of the parade at 10 a.m. to get in my assigned seat in the inconspicuous bleachers reserved for diplomats.

Sue walked Alec and Karl down to the government guest house behind the Palace and met me after the parade at 12:45 so Alec, Karl, and I could be right on time for the 1 p.m. start of Foreign Minister Godal's Syttende Mai reception for the children of diplomats.

A VISIT TO ÅLESUND, THE TOWN THE KAISER BUILT

The Foreign Ministry sponsored trips for the diplomatic corps to visit places in Norway that would further their understanding of the country. Jan Mayen was one of those trips. Another was two days in historic Ålesund with its nouveau architecture.

The wooden buildings that were Ålesund burned in a horrendous fire on January 23, 1904. The fire was news throughout Europe—10,000 were left without shelter.

Kaiser Wilhelm II, the German emperor and king of Prussia, often spent weeks in summer in Ålesund. The imperial yacht, the *Hohenzollern II*, was a common sight in the harbor. The kaiser sent ships with supplies to build temporary shelters, and soon after produced a plan and the money to rebuild the city in the Jugendstil (Art Nouveau), the architectural style of the day. Teams of architects and builders from Germany and Norway rebuilt the downtown, incorporating the best features of Jugendstil buildings from throughout Europe. Ålesund is a "magical town," says the tourism bureau, and they are right. To walk through the town is to be inspired. Go there.[102]

Day One started at a fish farm, where we gingerly walked out on the wooden plank paths above the huge nets in the fjord teeming with tens of thousands of salmon. The feeding of pellets of meal was constant, shot out from a device resembling a rotating machine gun atop a post.

Then a factory where the most famous Norwegian sweaters were made. A room of automated looms fed with dyed wool from content Norwegian sheep. (My cousins in Flekkefjord would uff da at this, as these sweaters should be hand knit by grandmothers.)

Dinner was hosted by the vice mayor, the charming Mr. Kjell

Skorgevik. He was promoting tourism, and this area had a lot to offer. He was so right. Barbara and I were so surprised at the unique history and beauty of this area inside a country full of uniqueness and beauty.

The next day we embarked on the fjord tour boat to visit Sykkylven and the Ekornes furniture factory, the makers of the ubiquitous stressless chair. We had one in Wisconsin. Why a furniture factory here? The supply of oak and the supply of hides not marked by barbed wire, which is not used in Norway, and the fjord location with easy access to markets by ship.[103]

And perhaps most amazing was the frozen pizza factory of the Stabburet company. It was one continuous belt of machines—the dough is fed in, the sauce spread, the cheese showered on, the diced red peppers sprinkled; the product is frozen and wrapped, stacked in boxes picked up by forklifts to be loaded on refrigerated shipping containers. The operator of the forklift the only human in the process. (Cable to Charlie Chaplin: "Post-*Modern Times* found in Norway.")

That night Foreign Minister Godal hosted the dinner. This is a very efficient way for the foreign minister to visit with each ambassador, who in turn can mention a policy they would like to talk to him about when back in Oslo. Perhaps an opportunity to take him aside for a moment to mention something that best only he hears. Not something to be said in a meeting with notetakers.

And, the Lord Chamberlain and Head of the Royal Household, Sivert Farstad, and his wife were on the trip. The informal and social nature of being on a trip together, away from Oslo, fostered a relationship with the Palace that the ambassadors and the Lord Chamberlain could put to good use when needed.

The diplomacy genius of this particular trip with spouses is that several ambassadors simply did not have the money to travel. Estonia, Hungary, Bulgaria, Poland, and Slovakia were in reality new countries. The Soviet masters were gone and so was the funding. The new ambassadors were engineers, academics, writers, and others who were recruited because there was no taint from the secret police. Once an enemy of the people, they were now tasked to build a new society on a budget. Funding of a trip like this by the Norwegians helped them with their mission.

LAYING A WREATH ON MEMORIAL DAY

From my diary: Memorial Day. The embassy is closed. In the morning, I walk through Frogner Park to Vestre Gravlund—the West Side Cemetery—to be there by 8:30 at the section where the graves of the war dead of many nations are located. There is a plaque indicating the American part and a few rows of white crosses each marking a grave. At 8:45, a band from a Norwegian veteran's group plays. There is an American flag. I lay a wreath and give a short speech in commemoration of those Americans buried here. It is sunny but cold, and I can see my breath.

CHAPTER 18
JUNE 1995

A VISIT FROM AMERICAN ARTIST ROSS BLECKNER

2 p.m. June 10: Attend opening at the Astrup Fearnley Museum of Modern Art of the exhibit of the American artist Ross Bleckner.

4 p.m.: Attend reception for Ross Bleckner hosted by JoDell Shields, embassy cultural attaché.

Note from my diary: Mr. Bleckner has gained fame for his talent and paintings related to AIDS. Astrup Fearnley as a venue is a sign that one has arrived in modern art. JoDell's apartment loved by artists and actors, etc., comfy chic and overlooks the Palace park. Charged to my wine cellar.

THE PRODIGAL GRANDSON RETURNS—
AND HE IS UNITED STATES AMBASSADOR!

The small city of Flekkefjord on the southwest coast from where my grandmother's family emigrated in 1905 invited me to a "Lofthus" day on June 25 held in my honor.

Mayor Egil Normann Eek and the town council hosted a reception at the town hall. My cousins Ranveig Åsebø and her husband Egil were there, as was my sister Wendy's husband Jens Stub, who happened to be a consultant to the town manager that month.

Per Birkeland was the Conservative Party councilman and we

decided we certainly were relatives. Birkeland was my grandmother's maiden name.

The newspaper took photos. Then there was a boat tour of the harbor, full of the old-style wooden fishing boats with a working sail and a small diesel engine. A stop at the local salmon fish farm. Then lunch at the restaurant Skipperhuset—The Sea Captain's House.

Quite interesting was a visit to the Aarenes Laerfabrikk tannery where the special soft and supple leather used for Coach handbags was prepared.

A guided walking tour of the town through the streets of charming houses painted white and set off by rose bushes in bloom in the yards was next. One neighborhood called Hollenderbyen (town of the Dutch) dates from the 18th century when Flekkefjord was a booming port, shipping out oak and pine from the surrounding forests—the oak to build dikes and the pine for houses in Amsterdam.

Then dinner with a group of quite-pleased-to-be-here smiling citizens at the harbor-side Maritim Hotel. The mayor drove me to the airport at Stavanger, and I was back in Oslo by 10 p.m.

DONNA SHALALA AND GRO BRUNDTLAND GET ACQUAINTED

The packed four-day schedule, June 24-27, for the visit of U.S. Health and Human Services Secretary Donna Shalala was for the purpose of forging a personal relationship with Prime Minister Gro Harlem Brundtland and getting to know the players in the government dealing with the World Health Organization. The State Department handles foreign relations, but HHS has carved out for itself one international role and that is that the secretary of HHS represents the U.S. at WHO.[104]

Gro Brundtland and Donna Shalala were two of the most influential women in the world.

Shalala had been one of the very first Peace Corps volunteers in 1964 (Iran). She had been president of Hunter College in New York, and then chosen chancellor of the University of Wisconsin at Madison. She was the first woman to head the UW, which at the time had 42,000 students, 17,000 employees, and a billion-dollar budget. HHS had 125,000 employees and a budget of $539 billion.

I was the Speaker of the Wisconsin Assembly when Donna arrived in 1988. Her energy and charisma charmed the Legislature, faculty, students, and alumni, and, after she fired the football coach and hired a winner, she delighted the fans. We became good friends and fellow Clinton supporters. After she left UW, she was chair of the Children's Defense Fund, working closely with Hillary Clinton. Donna was one of President Clinton's first Cabinet appointments.

PM Brundtland's advisor Morten Wetland and I had a couple of lunches at the Theater Cafe and a drink or two after work at Brasserie Costa to prepare for the Shalala visit. Gro was the host and I needed to know what she wanted out of the visit. I had the scoop on Donna's ideas from David Hohman, head of HHS International Affairs, who advanced her trip.

Saturday

2 p.m.: An exclusive interview at the ambassador's Residence with *Aftenposten's* most influential reporter and columnist, Per Egil Hegge.

4 p.m.: Doubles tennis at Bygdø Tennis club. Donna and myself vs. Dr. Eric Solberg, director Ullevål Hospital and Per Granlund, club instructor. (We lose.)

When we return from tennis, son Alec is shooting baskets in the driveway and Donna challenges him to a game. Fair enough; they are the same height. (Alec wins.)

7:30 p.m.: Dinner hosted by Ambassador and Barbara Loftus in honor of Secretary Shalala. Minister of Health Dr. Werner Christie and Minister of Education Gudmund Hernes attend. Guests are health policy leaders. Dr. Jo Ivey Boufford, Donna's policy adviser, also attends.

Secretary Shalala overnight at Residence.

Sunday

9 a.m.: Doubles tennis at Bygdø Tennis Club. Donna and I versus Navy Commander Al Nadolski and Al's mother, who is visiting from the U.S. (We lose.)

12:30 p.m.: Fornebu Airport. Ambassador and Secretary Shalala meet Gudmund Hernes for two-hour airplane tour of Norway in eight-seat Piper Navajo Chieftain.

5 p.m.: Reception at ambassador's Residence for Donna—guests include UW alumni and university leaders. (Donna delights in telling the group assembled on this sunny afternoon on the terrace that

Gro is a UW alumna—honorary degree—and so is Barbara—degree in history.)

7:30 p.m.: University of Oslo Summer School opening ceremony at the University Aula. Secretary Shalala delivers 15-minute speech.

9 p.m.: Ambassador, Barbara, Donna, David Hohman, and Dr. Boufford dinner on Aker Brygge boardwalk, fjord-side restaurant SS Louise. (Sunshine, wine, reindeer filets, mussels, ice cream.)

Secretary Shalala overnight at Residence.

Monday

(I remind Donna that Gro is a medical doctor and practiced in the area of public health before her career in politics. And it was Donna's invite that led to Gro traveling to Madison to receive her honorary degree.)

9 a.m.: Ambassador and Secretary Shalala meet with Prime Minister Gro Harlem Brundtland in her office. Morten is in the meeting.

10:30 a.m.: Ambassador and Donna visit battered women's safe-house with Health Minister Christie. (Location not to be on schedule!)

1 p.m.: Frambu Clinic specializing in disabled children's medical care. Lunch followed by tour with Minister Christie. Press availability.

7 p.m.: Dinner hosted by PM for Secretary Shalala on sailboat *Johanne Marie*, expected duration three hours in Oslo harbor area. No open water.

Note to ambassador: "Attire: 'elegantly casual,' i.e., no jeans or shorts, comfortable clothes suitable for an old sailboat. Tie not required." (Gro and Donna chat the whole time. Morten and I sit in the back of the boat tie-less trying our best to be "elegantly casual.")

Secretary overnight at Residence.

Tuesday

9 a.m.: Ambassador and Donna tour Radium Hospital with Secretary Christie. The hospital is part of Oslo University. It is one of the largest medical research institutions in Europe, a renowned cancer treatment and research hospital. The cancer drug trials are respected worldwide.

Noon: Fornebu Airport: Secretary Shalala and Dr. Boufford depart Oslo for Stockholm. Ambassador returns to embassy.

CHAPTER 19
CELEBRATING THE FOURTH OF JULY

The only thing atypical about the embassy's Fourth of July celebration in 1995 was that it happened on July Fourth.

Norwegians take several weeks of summer vacation between June 15 and August 15. This includes the PM and the members of the Cabinet. We would consult the PM's office and arrive at a date sometime in the last two weeks of June that she could commit to attend. Luckily this year the Fourth worked.

My day started at 8:30 in the morning at Frogner Park with a speech at the statue of Abraham Lincoln. This bust in a quiet corner of the park was a gift to Norway from the state of North Dakota on July 4, 1914, to commemorate the centennial of Norwegian independence. The governor of North Dakota was there that day in 1914. Among his delegation was Smith Stimmel, who had been one of Lincoln's bodyguards. A poem by the state's poet laureate was read.

During the Nazi Germany occupation of Norway, this statue became a place where on July Fourth, Norwegians would gather and stand in silent protest. For some reason this particular protest was ignored by the authorities.

After my Lincoln speech, I went to the Palace to sign the royal register in honor of The Queen's birthday. She was born on July Fourth in 1937.

The Independence Day reception at the Residence started at 11:30 a.m. Not a cloud in the sky and the sunshine made the lawn a glorious riot of colors: red, white, and blue tents with the hot dogs, the sodas, and the wine. Women were in white summer dresses with a dash of red.

Five hundred and ninety-eight people signed the guest book.

The Marine honor guard started things off marching from the back of the lawn in their dress blues with white hats and gloves and wide smiles. Two had carbines at the shoulder and two held flags forward from the waist.

I gave a speech in Norwegian. Trond, the tutor, and I had been crafting and practicing this talk for weeks, eliminating the words I was having trouble with and getting my diction right. He stood in the back and I could see him mouthing the words as I spoke.

Barbara, who could actually speak Norwegian, introduced me. My sister Wendy prayed.

After the speech 598 people came up to me and said, "I didn't know you were fluent in Norwegian." This flattery was given in pure gratitude that I had made the effort. Only after I talked did the PM make her entrance. It was planned that way.

CHAPTER 20
SEPTEMBER 1995

LUNCHING WITH CONGRESSMAN CHARLIE WILSON

From my diary, September 4, 1995: Delightful lunch with Congressman Charlie Wilson from Texas at Blom Restaurant— long history as a hangout of artists. (This was long before Wilson became a household name as the titular character in *Charlie Wilson's War*.)

The dining room was once the building's courtyard and by now is covered by a glass dome. Wilson, a Democrat, had represented Austin in the House since '73. Resembles Johnny Cash, right down to the black cowboy boots. He has two tumblers of Johnny Walker scotch. Glances at some food. Presents me with a pair of gold cufflinks with the House Seal on them. We talk about David Obey, our mutual friend and his longtime colleague on the Appropriations Committee. Bemoan the nasty turn of events of the '94 GOP takeover of the House, which ended David's chairmanship of the committee. Charlie must be trusted because he has a seat on the House Defense Appropriations Subcommittee. They have the secret pot of money that isn't tracked to help in foreign operations. We swap stories about serving in a state legislature. He was six years in the Texas House and six in the state Senate. We had fought for the same liberal issues— the Equal Rights Amendment and raising the minimum wage. He buys lunch.[105]

REVISITING THE 1979 AFGHANISTAN INVASION WITH ANATOLY DOBRYNIN AND STANSFIELD TURNER

On September 21, 1995, I hosted a private lunch for Ambassador Anatoly Dobrynin and Admiral Stansfield Turner. Vodka was served. Russian vodka.

Dobrynin had been the Soviet Union's ambassador to the United States from 1962 to 1986, from JFK through Ronald Reagan. Stansfield Turner was the head of the CIA for Jimmy Carter.

It was a sunny day in Oslo, and the three of us chatted like old friends, as we had come to know each other over three days at a closed-door conference from September 18-20 hosted by the Nobel Prize Institute recounting the Russian invasion of Afghanistan in 1979.[106] That conference can best be described as, "What didn't we know, and when didn't we know it?"

All of the actors making decisions at that time were at the conference, including the head of the KGB and the head of the White House National Security Council. It was to be a record of the oral history of those in the Soviet Union involved in the fateful decision to invade Afghanistan and those in the Carter administration who decided how to respond.

It was the end of détente, the thaw in the Cold War that began in 1969 as the new policy of President Nixon that had produced the SALT I treaty reducing nuclear weapons. It was the reset after the 1962 Cuban Missile Crisis. The direct telephone link between Washington and Moscow— "the red telephone"—was installed at this time so the leaders of the two world powers could talk and hopefully defuse a crisis that might escalate into war.

That phone must have been off the hook in December 1979 because it became clear from the conference that neither side knew what the other was doing or thinking despite being sure they did.

The Soviets thought the U.S. would know that the invasion of Afghanistan was directed at keeping a Muslim country on their southern border from falling apart, caused partly by the inept and corrupt government they had been propping up and a puppet president who might best be described as a Marxist of the kleptocracy school.

The Carter White House thought this was part of a grand plan to expand the Soviet Empire. They were creating an "Arc of Crisis."

There was even a lecture to the Russians by the head of the National Security Council on Lenin's ideology. The word "bourgeois" was used in a sentence.

The Soviets thought this had nothing to do with détente. They did not want to invade, fearing a repeat of the disaster of their sending tanks into Prague or the American quagmire in Vietnam. Dobrynin at the conference: "We are not here to repeat dogmas of the Cold War...I am trying to tell you how we really thought. There was no discussion in the Kremlin of any Grand Design. There was no discussion in the press—well, the press did not matter—nor in the Politburo, or the Foreign Ministry. I spoke privately with (Leonid) Brezhnev at the time and there was never a single word about it... In one of the meetings Brezhnev even asked me, "Anatoly, where is the 'Arc of Crisis'?"

Well, things fall apart. There was a Western embargo and sanctions on the Soviet Union and President Carter pulled the United States out of the Moscow summer Olympics. The war lasted nine years, over a million civilians were killed and millions more fled as refugees to Pakistan and Iran. The CIA started a not-so-covert action to harass the Soviets—this was Charlie Wilson's war. The fighters against the Soviets became radicalized and when President Mikhail Gorbachev ordered the Soviet 40th Army to return home, what was left in Afghanistan was a mess that turned eventually into the Taliban and al-Qaida.

Dessert that day in 1995 at the Residence was vanilla ice cream over cloudberries. Plus a tad of port.

Dobrynin told stories until three in the afternoon. He had been in Washington 24 years and served under six leaders of the Soviet Union and through six American presidents and seven secretaries of state.

I had recently read his just-published memoirs and asked him to recount the story in the book of his secret meetings with Bobby Kennedy during the Cuban Missile Crisis in 1962, the first year of his ambassadorship in Washington. He brought messages directly from Khrushchev to Bobby and Bobby brought them to his brother—a messaging setup that was critical in arriving at the final deal.[107]

Dobrynin asked Stansfield Turner how he became the CIA director. He said: "I sat next to Jimmy Carter in classes at the Naval Academy."

A fine day in Oslo.

WITH COD ON HIS SIDE IN ICELAND

My trip to Iceland September 26-28 was to get an update on the future of Keflavik, the U.S. Air Base that played an important part in NATO's defense of Norway. I would also meet the Speaker of the Parliament and visit Thingvellir, the historic site of the world's first Parliament in the year 930.

Ambassador Parker Borg met me at the Reykjavik airport. He was in my Senate confirmation hearing group. He was from Minnesota. Parker was a Norwegian-American story. His grandfather Karl immigrated from Sarpsborg, Norway, in 1901 at the age of 19. There were nine children. Karl was the third son. There were cousins in Minnesota, so he went there.

Parker came to the foreign service from the Peace Corps. He was part of the first group to go overseas, and the first former Peace Corps volunteer to become an ambassador. His distinguished career with the Department of State included two tours in Vietnam, ambassador to Mali and a series of tough assignments in counter-terrorism and counter-narcotics.

Parker had the distinguishing honor of being nominated for ambassador to Burma (Myanmar) by President George H.W. Bush in 1991. It didn't happen. There was opposition to sending an ambassador to Burma by Democrats in the Senate because of the military dictatorship, its human rights record, and the house arrest of Aung San Suu Kyi. (She was awarded the Nobel Peace Prize in 1991.)

The Bush administration believed it was best to have a U.S. ambassador in the American Embassy in Burma to bear witness and engage the regime. Parker was eloquent in pressing this policy.

When the Democrats won in 1992, the new Clinton administration chose to send Parker to Iceland, an important U.S. post, because of its strategic North Atlantic location and the presence of a large U.S. air base.

I got off the plane, and we drove less than a mile to the adjacent naval air station, Keflavik, to meet with U.S. Navy Rear Admiral Stanley W. Bryant, the commander of the Iceland Defense Forces. This is the name of the NATO unit dedicated to the defense of Iceland, and Keflavik is the base for air patrols for anti-submarine warfare in the North Atlantic.

There have been as many as 2,000 NATO personnel at the base, mostly Americans. Iceland has a robust Coast Guard but never had an armed force. Its defense is the responsibility of U.S. National Guard units.

The admiral explained that there was mounting pressure to reduce or close the base because of the end of the Cold War. Parker was to sort out the future relationships between the Icelandic government and the U.S. military presence.

The evening was not scheduled, so it was red wine complementing a baked cod dinner with dill sauce and a long conversation with Parker and his wife Anna at the ambassador's residence, which is half of the small building housing the embassy. It is "koselig"—a Norwegian word to describe comfy—and impressive only in its modesty. On the white plaster walls hung several framed watercolors of Minnesota landscapes painted by Parker's father.

Anna was also a Foreign Service officer but required in this situation to be on unpaid leave. In State Department speak they are a "tandem couple."

To start the next day, September 27, we pay a courtesy call on Ambassador Helgi Ágústsson, the permanent secretary of the Icelandic Ministry of Foreign Affairs. Next, a short distance away (everything is a short distance), we meet with the Norwegian Ambassador Nils Dietz, a veteran of thirty-five years in the Norwegian Foreign Service.

A lot of talk about the fishing dispute between Norway and Iceland—called the Cod War in the Loophole. The loophole is a triangle-shaped patch of ocean in the Barents Sea that is just outside the 200-mile economic zones of Norway, Svalbard, and Russia. Draw a line at the outer reaches of each country's zone and what is not touched is the loophole. Icelandic trawlers were now fishing here and Norway was much agitated, arguing these waters were not in the Icelandic zone. Iceland's retort was, I paraphrase, "We can fish here. Nothing you can do about it." Seems each country strongly believed the other in the wrong.

At 11, we meet with Ólafur G. Einarsson, the Speaker of the Icelandic Parliament. The Parliament is called the Althing (means assembly) and is the oldest Parliament in the world, dating from 930. Speaker

Einarsson's powers and duties as Speaker were the same as mine as Speaker of the Wisconsin Assembly. He runs the place. It was a thrill to be with the Speaker, to share stories and our common experiences. We stood together on the Speaker's rostrum. Then he stepped down and took a photo of me.

The building is constructed of Icelandic stone and dates from 1880. The 63 members from five political parties sit close together at three banks of desks arranged in a horseshoe.

The small room has an aura of restraint. Sort of a "we've been around for a thousand years, so don't get too excited" feeling. The light-green walls framed by white borders bear no paintings or ornamentation. An Icelandic flag hangs from a flagpole behind the Speaker's rostrum, and there is a large floral arrangement in the middle of the room. That is it.

In the afternoon, we are off to visit Thingvellir, the site historians have marked as the exact place where the first Parliament met. Parker is driving the embassy's white Chevy Suburban and has a route mapped out to show me the countryside.

Thingvellir is a test for the eyes and the brain to absorb, as you are not looking at scenery but experiencing a place like the Temple Mount. The first sighting is from the cliff on one edge of a vast green valley below with a river the color of cold blue running through. This is the "Assembly Plains."

The striking rock formations are even more dramatic when you learn this is the place where the North American continental plate and the European plate push together and form a sharp ridge.

There is a circle of rocks, the Ting, where the tribal chiefs met to set the laws. This day there were fast-moving clouds that let flashes of sunlight hit the valley as they passed. (Was it like this that first day, the blinking lights some Morse code message from Thor?)

We started back and the car stopped. Now what? We had run out of gas. The first car coming by stopped, the friendly fellow had a can of gas that was cheerfully offered, and we made it home.

Parker and Anna hosted dinner that night at their residence with the chairman of the North Atlantic Salmon Fund, Orri Vigfússon, his wife, and the secretary general of the Ministry of Fisheries, Arni Kolbeinsson, and his wife. I learned that Iceland would not be joining the European Union under any scenario, as part of the deal would be to allow British and Spanish fishing boats access to the fisheries. The fisheries secretary said on this issue he had "cod on his side."

The next morning early, after checking the gas tank, headlights, and turn signals, Parker drove me to the airport.

CHAPTER 21
OCTOBER 1995

ANNIVERSARY OF GERMAN UNITY

It was relaxing for Germany's ambassador to be hosting at his embassy a party in celebration of a good-news event. And it was very important the American ambassador always attend. The new National Day of Germany was October 3, marking the anniversary of German unity in 1990, the result of what was called the Two Plus Four Treaty. In this treaty, East and West Germany agreed on unification and the United States, the UK, France, and the Soviet Union—the four powers that had occupied Germany since WWII—renounced their rights of occupation. An important part of this treaty was that unified Germany had to agree to the existing border with Poland.[108] A lot of sausage, dark bread, hearty beer, and schnapps ladened the tables and there were toasts aplenty.

A NEW CLASS OF THE NORWEGIAN FOREIGN MINISTRY

Each year the embassy would host the incoming class of the Norwegian Foreign Ministry, the "aspirants." This would take place in the embassy cafeteria. This informal setting and a tour of the library, the visa operation, and other areas took away the mystery of the building, which is so imposing from the outside. Each of the embassy sections outlined what they did, answered questions, and handed out business cards with telephone numbers. I would give a welcome and then answer questions on any subject. When meeting these people later in their careers, they would always mention that this event, especially their freedom to ask questions of the American ambassador, had been important to them.

THE KING AND QUEEN VISIT THE U.S.

The plan

The dates for the first-ever visit to the United States by Their Majesties King Harald and Queen Sonja were set for mid-October. Many times as crown prince and princess, they had traveled to America on behalf of Norway, including when the princess opened a traveling Norwegian art exhibit at the University of Wisconsin.[109] I was there but did not meet her.

This would be the most important event of their new tenure and mine. Luck was at work.

The trip would start in New York with a dinner at the Waldorf Astoria with guests galore and a dance band, all organized by the Palace and the Norwegian Friends Association. There would be two weeks of travel and then the State Dinner in the White House with President Clinton the last day.

Perfect. The American Friends of Norway could tend to events in New York, and at the later stops in Minneapolis and San Francisco, there were Norwegian consulates and the Lutheran Seamen's churches to handle events and details. There would also be a stop in Iowa at Vesterheim, the National Norwegian Museum and cultural center in Decorah. I would leave HM after the visit to St. Olaf College in Minnesota and go to D.C. to work on the schedule there, which included a trip by helicopter to the Naval Base at Norfolk. Barbara would meet me for the State Dinner. She had much hosting to do in Oslo as there were important events going on, and the boys had school.

The State Dinner was the idea of great minds working together in self-interest. It would be a dinner in the private quarters with only Their Majesties, the president and Hillary, VP Al Gore and his wife Tipper, the secretary of state, Barbara and me, Norwegian Ambassador Kjeld Vibe and his wife Beate, and Foreign Minister Bjørn Tore Godal and his wife Gro Balas.

This saved the White House from the all-hands-on-deck chore of developing an invitation list that for every person invited would hatch a dozen ingrates. Parsing the list of donors, celebrities, and campaign bigwigs to be invited was avoided. And venerable senators would be saved from another night in the too-tight tuxedo.

It meant Clinton could be himself and tell stories. And it would allow a telling in private by His Majesty of his time living in the White House with FDR as a boy during World War II (See Appendix A). Like Churchill, HM and his mother, Crown Princess Märtha, and his two sisters were an important part of the history of the White House during WWII. I was specifically told Clinton was relishing the thought of this dinner—a hint I should clue in HM.

First stop: Dancing with The Queen in New York

The ballroom at the Waldorf was packed October 11 with tables glittering in china and crystal and very happy people. They were beaming, almost glowing, all decked out in glad rags appropriate for meeting royalty. Men had dark suits. Women had options and had a fashion show going on.

I was to propose a toast welcoming Their Majesties to America on behalf of the president and first lady. HM would then offer a toast to the president, thanking him and the American people for the invitation to visit.

At the end of the dinner, I was to lead Her Majesty to the dance floor and start the dancing. It was a waltz kind of tune. Innocent enough. HM was light as a feather following my lead. No natural, I had to concentrate on my feet. She led me by her following. A real talent.

The waltz did not end, as the band moved without pause to a fox trot in rock boogie tempo. HM held tightly to my hand. We weren't leaving the dance floor. "Oh my," I thought. With her smile that lit up the room and infectious energy, she made me look like a dancer.

To Washington, D.C.

I arrived in D.C. from New York early on the 12th to be there to meet Their Majesties when they arrived later in the morning at Washington National Airport. I hooked up with Fred DuVal, State Department deputy chief of protocol, who had been with the first lady at the Olympics, to meet the flight.

When The King and Queen and their party were settled in to the Willard Hotel, I dashed to the Capitol to meet Congressman Martin Sabo (Minnesota) and Sen. Kent Conrad (North Dakota) to be seated in time at the lunch for His Majesty given by the Norwegian Caucus. Marty is an old friend. He reeled off a few practiced one-liners and The King chuckled throughout the lunch. After lunch, Marty and Kent gave a tour of the Capitol, and in Statuary Hall stopped at the statues representing their states: Minnesota (Henry Mower Rice, the first senator) and North Dakota ("Honest John Burke," an early governor).

In the evening, The King and Queen hosted a dinner at the Norwegian ambassador's residence. Black tie. A small but lively crowd.

Lunch on an assault ship

The October 13 trip in a Navy helicopter from the Pentagon grounds to Norfolk, Virginia, went without a hitch, and the subsequent helicoptering to a small amphibious assault ship, *USS Saipan*, for a lunch for His Majesty hosted by the captain occurred over calm seas. The pre-lunch briefing on the Atlantic fleet in relation to Norway was extensive and no sensitive information was held back. HM was very knowledgeable about all of it, asked good questions, and gave spot-on commentary.

The lunch was in the hanger below the flight deck and there were about one hundred officers and enlisted men. We all stood and the captain gave a welcome, quickly said something to the effect of "Let's eat," and sat down before HM. Briefly, HM and I were the only two still standing. It was America. We sat down.

The Kennedy Center

On October 14, we enjoyed a concert at the Kennedy Center by the Norwegian Chamber Orchestra and a reception hosted by Their Majesties.

Arlington Cemetery and more

In the morning of October 16, I accompanied Their Majesties to Arlington National Cemetery where The King laid a wreath at the Tomb of the Unknown Soldier. In the afternoon, I had a busy schedule of meetings at the State Department, Department of Defense, and the White House.

In the evening at the National Museum of Women in the Arts, The Queen opened an exhibit: "At Century's End: Norwegian Artists and the Figurative Tradition 1880/1990."

Free for dinner and met up with a group including the Norwegian Artist Ida Lorentzen, who had a piece in the show—a friend from Oslo, frequent dinner guest, and The Queen's portraitist.

A gala in Minnesota

My mother Margaret and father Adolph received an invite for dinner in Minneapolis October 18 for Their Majesties hosted by Ambassador Sidney Rand, President Carter's ambassador to Norway and former president of St. Olaf College. Sidney, a Lutheran minister, and his wife Lois are chairs of the Royal Visit Midwest Committee.

A huge gala at the Radisson Plaza. Black tie. My dear friends Roger Moe, the state Senate Majority Leader, and Harry "Tex" Sieben, the former Speaker, are there glad-handing and making everyone feel welcome. Roger asks my mother if there is anything he can do for her. "A brandy old fashioned would be nice," she says.

Gov. Arne Carlson is there to give the welcoming speech. He reminds me that he had made me an honorary Minnesotan and that is why I am at the head table. (That was not true but I thanked him for that courtesy, especially coming from a governor who is Swedish-American.) Music by Cliff Brunzell and the Golden Strings.

The St. Olaf choir wowed in Northfield, Minnesota, and the retelling of the immigrant story of the Lutheran colleges' start in the U.S. and what fine academic institutions they are now was heartfelt.

To Iowa by hook or crook

The trip to Iowa October 19 was a problem. The Minnesota National Guard would not give permission to transport His Majesty over the state line in one of their helicopters. How hard could this be? The governor, the head of the National Guard, the Speaker of the House—a general in the Guard—and the majority leader in the Senate were all friends and political partners. But no budging for us notables. There were federal rules about foreign heads of state. A plane was arranged by the ever-helpful Kjell Bergh, the Volvo dealer and a friend of HM.

Chatting with His Majesty

His Majesty and I spent hours together in VIP rooms waiting for events to start. (Her Majesty had a separate schedule of appearances.) His sense of humor and exquisite American English were delightful. HM looked so serious when in Norway speaking in Norwegian, mostly at official events. He had to. I told campaign stories about Clinton and briefed HM about how we would be relaxed at the dinner.

Finally, I told him the story:

> *Your majesty, we both have Danish grandfathers who married English women named Maud. My grandfather Viggo Neilsen and his brother Axel came to America from Odense in Denmark with their parents to Wisconsin, where they settled on a farm near Madison. Viggo married Dorthea Thompson. They had two children—Mildred, the older and Margaret, my mother. Dorthea died of the Spanish flu in 1917. My mother was 15 months old. Axel had been drafted into the Army and like many other draftees, before he left for France, he married his sweetheart, Maude Electra Parch. She was from those who had come from England and moved on to the Midwest. Axel was at the battles of Meuse-Argonne and Belleau Wood. He made it back. It was decided Mildred would live with her father Viggo, and Axel and Maude would raise Margaret. They farmed nearby. Axel and Maude never had children of their own, and I was their grandson in every way. That is the story.*

It is a good story, he said, and thanked me very much for sharing it.

A State Dinner and a smoke

The limousine with Their Majesties should arrive 15 minutes ahead of the time on the schedule for October 30.[110] There was new security at the White House, with sniffing dogs and looking under the car with a mirror.

Hillary, with help from Fred DuVal and Melanne Verveer, were keen in their attention to every detail and thoughtfulness, sincerely wishing this would reflect the hosting of the first lady at the Olympics.

I had my own task. His Majesty would enjoy a cigarette at some point in the no-smoking White House. I had seen Clinton many times with a cigar. So, the plot was he would invite The King out on the Truman balcony—not part of the White House, I argued with some historic license. Then HM could have a smoke and Clinton could have a puff or two of a lit cigar. It had to be lit.

The limo arrived early that October 30. No dogs. No mirrors. No Clintons on the steps to greet. They rushed out, and it added to the relaxed nature we were striving for—and the president lit up hearing the stories how President Roosevelt had helped him with his homework, and how he had sailed on the Potomac with him in the yacht—and not really remembering there were braces on FDR's legs.

The King said the most vivid memory he had of FDR was at the inauguration in 1945 when he stood behind the president. All three of us children were there, he added. The president noted that was the inaugural at the White House. I slipped into the conversation that Her Majesty was born on the Fourth of July. (My grandfather and his family left from Norway going to America on July 4, 1885.) And the president lit up the cigar on the balcony and HM enjoyed a smoke.

It was a great State Dinner. The menu included: soup made of baked wild wheat with beans and mustard seed pudding accompanied by Saintsbury Chardonnay 1991, as appetizers.

The main course was nut-breaded lamb chops with fried garlic and squash risotto plus salad with red pepper dressing and Parmesan crisps, accompanied by Solitude Pinot Noir 1992.

And for dessert, a basket of pears with raspberry and chocolate sauce and acorn cakes accompanied by Jordan "I" 1989.[111]

CHAPTER 22
NOVEMBER 1995

YITZHAK RABIN IS ASSASSINATED

From my diary November 4, 1995: Prime Minister Yitzhak Rabin is assassinated in Tel Aviv at the end of a rally in support of the Oslo Accords. The assassin is a 25-year-old right-wing law student. He is quoted as saying the agreement's plan to give back territory on the West Bank would "deny Jews their biblical heritage." On November 6, we all watch the funeral on TV in the embassy. The president and first lady are there, as well as Presidents H.W. Bush and Jimmy Carter and Secretary of State Warren Christopher. I see my friend and former colleague in the Wisconsin Legislature, Sen. Russ Feingold, in the official delegation. President Clinton ended his remarks by saying, in Hebrew, "Shalom Haver" (Goodbye, friend).

Watching TV on this day, I remembered well sitting in the audience in the great room in Oslo City Hall on December 10, 1994, when Rabin gave his Nobel Peace Prize lecture. He spoke of his life as a soldier who at age 72 now saw a chance for peace.

MARINES TO THE RESCUE AS BARBARA'S DRESS CATCHES FIRE AT THE BALL

There are days when it is just thrilling and humbling to be an American ambassador. The annual Marine Birthday Ball is one of them. The ball is held around the world in November wherever Marines are stationed. It was the 220th anniversary of the founding of the Marines in November 1995.

For the Marine security guards in over 180 U.S. embassies, it is very special because there are so few of them, and they are all enlisted men. On their own. No officer there to give orders. These Marines are under the supervision of the senior diplomatic officer at an embassy. That was me, and I was mindful of this. That is how they looked at me, and it was important I act accordingly.

The ball was held November 4 in Gamle Logen, the venerable concert hall in Oslo. Usually, people are described as venerable, but I felt this place was a citizen of Oslo. Built in 1836 as the Masonic Lodge and now owned by the city. The main hall where we were was opened in 1844 with a performance by the world-famous Norwegian violinist Ole Bull. It was Edvard Grieg's concert hall.

The Marines cut striking figures in their dress blues. Their girlfriends are in floor-length gowns. Male guests are in tuxedos. Barbara has a gown made especially for this event.

There is a traditional schedule to be followed. Cocktails at 6 p.m. At 7 p.m. a cake-cutting ceremony. With solemnity, I am presented a special sword to cut the first piece, which is then handed to Barbara.

I give my remarks and then a Marine officer visiting just for the occasion reads a message from the commandant. Then the reading of the historic Marine Corps birthday proclamation.[112]

At 8 p.m. is dinner and at 9:30 the band is cued and the dancing begins. A Marine leads Barbara to the floor, and the evening starts in earnest. The hall is glittering, with chandeliers and candles on the tables.

The photographer is kept busy as each Marine and guest want their photo taken plus a photo with me and Barbara. Unfortunately, Barbara is a little too close to a candle during one pose and the back edge of the cowl draped over her shoulders starts on fire.

Not to worry. Marines to the rescue. It is extinguished with aplomb and there is just the trace of a singe. Added to the history of Marine balls.

PENGUINS WON'T FLY

For a year, I have been sent on one démarche after another to inform Norwegians we would like them to sell their Penguin anti-ship missiles to Turkey. This missile, launched from a ship, goes up, then down to hit another ship. The démarches are due to pressure put on the U.S. by Turkey and the Sikorsky helicopter company to lobby the Norwegians. For example, a Norwegian ship in a fjord could launch the missile and hit an enemy ship in the next fjord over. The Norwegians have said "no" every time, citing the irrefutable assumption that if Turkey, a member of NATO, had these missiles, it would likely use them to sink Greek ships sheltering behind one of the small islands that pepper the eastern Mediterranean Sea between the two countries. "Greece is also a member of NATO," is usually mentioned to me in a by-the-way fashion. Finally, I sent a cable saying time to give up.

From my diary November 24, 1995: Quotes from my cable not surprisingly shared with the lobbyist for Sikorsky. (The Penguin also can be helicopter-launched). They are pushing the Norwegian ambassador in Ankara to intervene. The Pentagon had been expecting a yes from the Norwegians and were pushing some lame argument that this sale would be part of "reassuring" Turkey after they made some minor improvements in their terrible record on human rights.[113]

CHAPTER 23
DECEMBER 1995

A SPY CAN STAY OUT OF THE COLD

From my diary December 1, 1995: Told COS (CIA chief of mission) he was not to go nor were any of his people to go to Svalbard for NASA event on their new facility. Even though there was an open invite for embassy staff. Explained I had instructions that said no spies. After Yeltsin dragged out the black box when the rocket was launched from Andøya, they are suspicious of NASA. And Svalbard a special place. I am not the ambassador to Svalbard. No sense to risk screwing this up for NASA.

AT THE FINNISH EMBASSY

Finland's Independence Day is December 6. It celebrates Finland's declaration of independence from the Russian Empire when the Bolsheviks took power in late 1917.

Finland's ambassador to Norway, Jorma Inki, looked a bit like Humphrey Bogart, including the side-of-the-mouth smile. His customary greeting to me was a quite graphic three-word phrase as to what American policy should be toward the Russians. "You can cook a Russian in butter, but he will still be a Russian," was another of his favorites. 1989 might have been the end of the Soviet Union, but Jorma said they are the "same Russians as before."

Jorma wanted me to know that in Finland, 1989 was the 50th anniversary of the Winter War of 1939 when the Finns held the Russian invasion force at bay, fighting them to a bloody, grim ending that saved independence but on terms dictated by Moscow.

There was a knowing laugh when I told Jorma the history of the Finnish immigrant population in Wisconsin and my less-than-successful firsthand experience with their voting habits.[114]

On the Clinton policy in Finland, I relied on Derek Shearer, the U.S. ambassador in Finland. He *was* the policy. A perfect pick for this country with his background in Russian studies and journalism. Derek was a classmate of Bill's at Yale. Derek's brother-in-law was Strobe Talbott, the deputy secretary of state. Derek's cables, patiently written to inform the ignorant rest of us about Finland, were a must-read.[115] I had to cross-country ski a lot for social occasions but Derek had to take nude saunas. What an American!

The other person who informed me on Finland was Arne Olav Brundtland, who specialized in the Nordic Baltic area at NUPI, the Norwegian Institute of International Affairs, where he was a scholar.

My education on things Finnish by Arne Olav was in snippets of conversation at official dinners. Arne Olav was the spouse of the prime minister and often seated next to me. A delightful dinner companion. Delicious were his critiques of the current Labour government headed by his wife. Arne Olav was a member of the Conservative Party.

BOB DYLAN AN ARCHANGEL IN THE TRONDHEIM CATHEDRAL?

Go where you are invited. Good advice for ambassadors and most others. When the bishop invited me to Trondheim a few weeks before Christmas to experience its cathedral, I accepted by return letter. Nidaros Cathedral was the mythical, mystical place where modern Norwegian history could be said to have begun.[116]

The cathedral is on the site of the grave of King Olav, who reigned from around 1015 to 1028, and unified Norway under one king and Christianity. He died in the battle of Stiklestad near Trondheim. Olav was designated a saint by the pope in 1164. After Martin Luther and the Protestant Reformation swept through Norway, the cathedral was expropriated by the newly established Lutheran State Church of Norway in 1537. Olav had staying power, as he remains to this day the patron saint of Norway.

The cathedral was still in gala form as it had just recently, on June 23, 1991, been the place of the consecration of HM King Harald and HM Queen Sonja.

There was another reason I was keen to visit the cathedral in December 1995. The poet A.O. Vinje, who I was claiming might be a shirttail relation, had written a book that had been translated into English called *Travel Memories From Norway 1860.*[117] It chronicled his walk over several weeks from Telemark to Trondheim to witness the coronation of the Swedish king's rule over Norway. There is a lot of Mark Twain in Vinje, including wit well wielded. His description of the people he met along the way, the cathedral, and the swells at the coronation had been stuck in my head. Pithy and ribald, and no romanticizing offered of the ignorant poor of the countryside. "Freedom suffices little in poverty."[118] When Vinje arrived, the cathedral was a wreck.

> Every stone is cracked...on the statue of St. Peter, the nose is gone. Judas has lost his pouch. Luke, an eye and an arm, Matthew is headless. Referring to the cost of building the cathedral special care is taken to offend religiosity and the priests ... who siphoned off their share of the loot of the Viking plunderers, who knew perfectly well how to serve God and themselves at the same time.

On the coronation of the most recent Swede to rule Norway:

> It was much ado and holiness...a red carpet in the street... young beautiful women, looking like flowers in long braids...at ten o'clock the royal procession...the Heralds went in front, dressed like fairytales...The King and Queen in ermine...in the circle around the altar, fifty priests in their chemises...to be standing like I did on the organ over the entrance door taking in the splendor listening to the cascading choir...the saluting from the cannons from the ships in the harbor when it was over...the dancing afterward I would have invited old Odin and the Valhalla bunch...I would walk all this way to Trondheim again, if I got to see such a display again.

On my visit, after a delicious lunch with wine, the bishop delivered me to a young cleric for a learned tour of the cathedral.

The church can seat 1,900 people. The row of statues on the west front was rebuilt by an army of sculptors between 1905 and 1983. Peter has his nose and Matthew his head. At the very top of the north tower, the winged archangel Michael is depicted fighting evil in the form of a dragon. According to the sculptor, the archangel's face is modeled on Bob Dylan's.

Then he walked me through the nave and left me at the altar to go by myself up to the crypt. I walked up in the near dark on the stone steps worn to shininess. There were small rooms with tiny windows. Each had a candle lit that day by someone. My claustrophobia and vertigo would not allow the final staircase; I did not see the crypt—or Bob Dylan.

CHAPTER 24
DEALING WITH SOVIET NUCLEAR WEAPONS AND WASTE

MURMANSK, RUSSIA, WHERE THE EXISTENTIAL THREAT TO AMERICA FOUND A HOME

They shall beat their swords into ploughshares... (Isaiah 2:3-4)

It's hard to beat swords into ploughshares when the swords are nuclear weapons.

The warm current of the Gulf Stream flows northeast through the Atlantic Ocean from Florida, and when it rounds the top of Scotland, it comes down to bathe the whole coast of Norway, making it ice-free in the winter from Oslo to the Arctic. Far above the Arctic Circle, it says hello to Murmansk, Russia, before taking a U-turn back to the Atlantic. This is why Murmansk is Russia's only ice-free port on the Atlantic.

This is where the nuclear submarines loaded with missiles targeted to annihilate America have to be. But they don't lurk there. They hide undetectable under the polar ice cap, or they roam the north Atlantic waiting for the order to surface and launch doomsday. They are shadowed by their American counterparts with the same mission. Or they shadow them. It is cat and mouse, with both sides thinking they are the cat. Titanium tubes hold sailors with no function other than to lay waste to the world above them when told to do so. The expectation is that they will never be told to do so because this mutually assured destruction would be madness.[119-120]

PREPPING FOR MURMANSK

Meet Bob Dyer

The preparations for my first Murmansk trip started with the many visits to Oslo by Bob Dyer, an oceanographer with the U.S. Environmental Protection Agency's Office of Radiation Programs.[121]

Bob was the expert on ocean disposal of radioactive wastes. No desk-sitter or theoretician. In 1972 at age 32, he was the one in a deep submersible who found and photographed at a depth of 7,000 feet in the Pacific Ocean a cache of radioactive waste drums dumped 20 years earlier.

Horn-rimmed glasses, wavy hair as long as he could get away with, and a conspiratorial smile. The first time we met he pulled out a photo of his red Corvette parked on the street in D.C., positioned so the White House was the backdrop.

He had the strategy and in me found someone on the chessboard who could actually move the pieces. We met for the first time in 1994.

An illuminating report on Russian fleet radioactivity

The end of the Cold War and the collapse of the Soviet Union freed from secrecy a trove of documents. Taking quick advantage of this was the Norwegian environmental group Bellona, led by the assertive Frederic Hauge. Think of him as a Woodward-and-Bernstein-type investigative reporter uncovering hidden information one layer at a time.

Bellona published their findings: "The Russian Northern Fleet: Sources of Radioactive Contamination." This detailed 168-page report maps the radioactive trail from the dawn of the age of nuclear submarines to the dumping of their reactors in the Arctic Ocean when the lifespan of the vessel was over. It offered an illuminating summary of the history of the Northern Fleet from inception in 1899 through the wars and then the nuclear age, plus the status of the fleet right up to 1995.[122] The report is a Rosetta Stone of the Cold War.

The report also chronicles the sudden deterioration of living conditions in Murmansk due to the collapse of the Soviet Union and how this devastated the submarine crews, with their salaries now almost worthless and attention to duty lax and morale low, which in turn increased the risk of nuclear accidents, especially the most common accident of fires onboard the submarines.[123]

The ennui affecting the population of Murmansk as a whole is in itself a risk: Who cares about this radioactive stuff when there is no heat and only pickled beets to eat?

Bellona had published first and braced for the consequences later. The first reaction was that one of the writers of the report, Alexsandr Nikitin, was arrested by the NSB (successor to the KGB) and accused of espionage and high treason. Nikitin was a full captain in the Northern Fleet who retired in 1992 and went to work for Bellona in Murmansk in 1994. He had worked at the Department of Nuclear Safety in the Ministry of Defense in Moscow.

Two other Russians on the advisory panel, a retired rear admiral of the Northern Fleet and a nuclear chemist who had worked on nuclear accident cleanup, were under surveillance.

I was using this report, which we had been given in advance of the publication, as the background material for my upcoming trip to Murmansk.

Oh, and my dear friend Norwegian Defense Minister Kosmo was none too happy with me when I started to invite Bellona's Frederic Hauge to receptions at the Residence, including one where Kosmo was present and the two had a tete-a-tete of the robust variety. Hauge raised a lot of questions on Norwegian inaction regarding the handling of radioactive wastes by the Soviets.[124]

FIRST VISIT TO MURMANSK

An American ambassador must receive permission from the U.S. State Department to leave the country he or she is accredited to, and this goes for vacation as well as an official event, such as Nordic ambassadors meeting in Stockholm.

If the ambassador is to go to another country to conduct business related to the country they are in, they must receive the permission of that country's ambassador. So for me to go to Murmansk on August 15, 1995, I needed the OK from the U.S. ambassador in Moscow, Tom Pickering.

By this time, Tom and I had met several times, and I considered him my mentor. His cables were the ones I relied on as my guide on all things Russian.[125] Tom was a career ambassador. This rank is a special appointment by the president, confirmed by the Senate, for career members of the Senior Foreign Service in recognition of distinguished service. This small cadre of diplomats get the tough jobs one after another.

Tom was enthusiastic about my trip and briefed me for an hour. We talked about Foreign Minister Kozyrev, who represented Murmansk in the Duma. I said I was trying my best to get Kozyrev credit for good things that happened, whether he knew about them or not.

Tom knew that from Murmansk I was going straight to St. Petersburg to meet Barbara for a vacation with two other ambassador couples. The first night the U.S. consul was hosting a dinner for us. So happens, said Tom, the consul in St. Petersburg is persona non grata in Murmansk. Seems he told the truth about the local regime there a few too many times. I was to brief the consul on my trip. There would also be the usual post-trip cable from embassy Oslo, sent out by Hal Meinheit, our senior political officer, who would be with me in Murmansk.

I told Tom we had asked if the commander of the Northern Fleet would see me but so far there had been no response. We had characterized this as a courtesy call. I was not there to do business with the Russian Navy, nor could I. The official host of my trip was the CEO of the Murmansk Shipping Company, Vyacheslav Ruksha. I would be his guest and stay overnight on one of the company's nuclear-powered ice-breakers.

I explained to Tom that the stage had been set for my trip when I hosted Mr. Ruksha in the Residence in Oslo when he and several others from the shipping company were in Oslo as guests of the Norwegian Foreign Ministry.

The Murmansk trip was set for August 15 and with approvals and details in hand I met with Russian Ambassador Fokine two weeks prior to brief him. We usually met for lunch with no staff, but this time Hal Meinheit was with me as he would be on the trip and responsible for reporting on the Murmansk meetings. It was important that the Russian Embassy in Oslo be knowledgeable about the trip in order to send a cable to their consul in Murmansk and the Foreign Ministry in Moscow. We wanted no surprises and to make sure Fokine was seen as in the loop.

Hal Meinheit and I left Oslo at 9:45 a.m. for Tromsø to board the flight on the newly inaugurated air connection to Murmansk.

This first-ever air route was on a Norwegian carrier and heavily subsidized by Norway as one more effort to establish a new post-Cold War relationship with that part of Russia on their border.

We arrived at 3:30 p.m. At customs, we presented our diplomatic passports and changed dollars into rubles. Our $100 bills were put through a scanner to see if they were counterfeit. An anxious moment.

The Murmansk Shipping Company car with my name on a sign in Russian in the window met us as we exited the airport. The driver spoke a bit of English and had been instructed to give us a tour of the town.

The first surprise were the pastel-painted buildings in the city center. Like South Beach Florida on the Arctic Ocean. The Lenin statue in the square has him standing high on a plinth and clad in a weather-appropriate long overcoat.

The population of Murmansk, once almost 450,000, has seen more than 100,000 leave since the economy collapsed with the end of the Soviet Union in 1989.

Outside of town on a promontory stands the 116-foot-tall statue of a soldier in a winter greatcoat with a submachine gun slung over his shoulder. He looks west toward the Valley of Glory where the German forces trying to take Murmansk in 1941 were turned back. A fateful decision by Hitler caused this debacle.[126] The statue was dedicated in 1974 on the 30th anniversary of the defeat of the Germans. An unknown soldier is laid to rest here.

It was not clear whether the next stop, a cemetery, was on the official schedule, as it was a bit out of the way. It was where those in the British and U.S merchant marine in WWII are buried and those lost at sea commemorated. These are the seamen of the ships that were sunk by German submarine torpedoes in the Allied convoys to Murmansk loaded with everything from tanks to airplanes to field rations to resupply the Red Army fighting the Germans on the Eastern front. This was commonly called the British cemetery, but there are a number of American graves; Hal and I went into this part and stood silent for a moment. It was overcast with some light rain.

Then the infamous. We drove to the far end of the Atomflot harbor, the home port of the nuclear icebreaker fleet just a few miles from

Murmansk city, to look at the decommissioned cargo ship *Lepse*. It was tied to the dock. A bright yellow sign warning of radioactive material dangled from one of the ropes. "...the holds of the *Lepse* are filled with casks and caissons holding 639 spent nuclear fuel assemblies—equaling hundreds of tons of radioactive materials—a significant portion of which have been damaged, including assemblies that were damaged during offloading from the nuclear icebreaker *Lenin*."[127]

Nearby is one of the liquid-waste storage buildings, where we are dropped off and greeted by the supervisor. We don white coats of light cotton, and a device to measure radiation that looks like a meat thermometer is clipped to the pocket. There is an interpreter. The supervisor explains the process of unloading the liquid waste from the icebreakers and transporting it to the cask. The building is constructed of cement and the casks are cement lined with stainless steel. There are some gauges sticking out the tops. It looks like the room in a brewery where draft beer waits in tanks.

The discussion and my questions are limited to the process for the commercial icebreakers. It would not be diplomatic and the supervisor would have been uncomfortable, and the interpreter too, if I were to ask anything about the Northern Fleet's submarines and their procedures. I knew from the Bellona Report that liquid waste from submarines was also processed at Atomflot.

At the Shipping Company headquarters, I am reunited with Vyacheslav Ruksha. It was like we were separated at birth. A big smile and two minutes of handshake. The same ensemble from our times meeting in Oslo. A black leather jacket. A white shirt and red tie. A taut collar.

We sit down opposite each other with the interpreter. I tell him all about our day and my impressions of Murmansk. We have tea and cakes.

My rule, gained from much experience in dealing with interpreters, is to say what you mean in plain English.[128] "There can be a deal made to help with the costs of safely storing liquid waste."

A handshake. Then smiling like the cat who just ate the canary Vyacheslav said: "You will have dinner tonight on the *Arktika* as the honored guest of the captain."

Dominating the harbor is the nuclear icebreaker *Arktika*, which will also be my hotel for the night. Imposing at 480 feet long, high as a four-story building and appearing all the more masterful as the superstructure is painted red.[129]

Dinner with the captain and a few officers focused on the ship. I paraphrase: Since things have gone to hell there is little of the once-good business of escorting through the ice ships that brought timber and minerals for export up the rivers. We do nothing important now. Breaking through the ice to take rich people to the North Pole for $25,000 each so they can say they were there is not a real job. There were once 180 crew on this ship. No more.

On the wall of the officers' dining room is a framed photograph of a sheikh from the Middle East kneeling on the ice facing Mecca with the *Arktika* in the background. North Pole and the date are written on the photo.

After dinner the captain offers another vodka and a cigarette. He is about 60 with cropped grey hair and has a red hammer and sickle tattooed on the web of skin between his thumb and index finger. After I informed him that I had toured the liquid-waste building he said, deadpan, perfect timing: "You will never need another battery for your watch."

I am presented with a gift at the end of the meal: a bottle of vodka that had been to the North Pole.

FOREIGN MINISTER ANDREI KOZYREV

When Boris Yeltsin took over control of what was left of the Soviet Union from Mikhail Gorbachev and became the first head of the new Russian Federation in 1991, he passed over the old guard of the Foreign Ministry and plucked out the most pro-Western officer he could find for his foreign minister.

This was Andrei Kozyrev, a proponent of democracy and the idea that a new Russia, unlike the Soviet Union, did not need as part of its national narrative the United States as the eternal enemy.[130]

Prior to my first trip to Murmansk, I read enough to grasp why Kozyrev had wanted to be in the Duma. He was the foreign minister but totally dependent on Yeltsin fending off his critics. A seat in the Duma would offer some more protection and give him a domestic pulpit to voice his views.

But why choose to run in the Murmansk constituency? Conventional wisdom—at least mine—had it that this area's voters were basically military personnel of the Northern Fleet and townspeople who were seeing their lives upended by the cuts in military spending promoted by the Yeltsin-Kozyrev policies. Kozyrev put it this way: "Like the baby boomers in the United States, my generation in Russia felt as if it had lived permanently on the brink of annihilation."

Murmansk would be America's target No. 1 as this was where the Soviet ICBMs were, as well as the nuclear missile-carrying submarines. Kozyrev campaigned on the pledge to get Murmansk out from under this threat and bring normalcy to the lives of ordinary people. He could point to success here, as after the signing of the START II treaty in 1993 the ICBMs of each side were taken "off target," meaning Murmansk was no longer Armageddon's flash point.[131]

In one of the best campaign speeches I have read, Kozyrev said this to 1,000 assembled officers of the Northern Fleet:

> Officers, I know that some call me a pro-Western politician...I am pro-Western because I am pro-Russian... what unites countries of the West are democracy and a market economy which supports a high standard of living for their people. I want Russia to continue with its radical reforms on the path to democracy and a market economy... and in this sense I am pro-Western... Officers, your opposite number is the naval base in San Diego, California. Those of you who have been there have noticed the striking difference in the standard of living between San Diego and the naval base here in Murmansk. You are their equal in skill. ...We take pride in that...I dream of a day when we could also take pride in comparing the living conditions of your families and theirs. That is what being pro-American means to me.[132] Kozyrev got 70 percent of the vote.

REACHING AGREEMENT ON NUCLEAR WASTE

The Murmansk Initiative Conference was scheduled for December 13 and 14, 1995, in Oslo. The goal of the initiative, signed by the U.S., Norway, and the Russian Federation was to fund an expansion of the low-level liquid nuclear waste storage facility in Murmansk— the facility I had toured in August—so Russia could sign on to the London Convention, an international agreement prohibiting the ocean dumping of radioactive waste.[133]

The funding was key, as Russia couldn't come up with any cash. Bob Dyer, the scientist and deal-maker for the EPA[134] on this project, had been camped out in my office for three days searching the EPA budget for potential sources of money for the U.S. share and refining the proposed construction design.

The day before the conference at three in the afternoon we met with State Secretary Siri Bjerke, the deputy foreign minister, who was handling the negotiations and the money for the Norwegian side. The Norwegians had been working closely with EPA on this for months. The final joint proposal was discussed and agreed upon.

At five p.m., perilously close to the start of the pre-conference reception, Bob and I met with my by-now-old pal Vyacheslav Ruksha, head of Atomflot, the parent company of the nuclear icebreaker fleet. Atomflot was the owner and custodian of the storage facility that handled liquid nuclear waste from both the icebreakers and the nuclear submarines of the Northern Fleet. The proposal was discussed and agreed upon in time for a glass of wine.

On Wednesday morning December 13, 1995, Russian Ambassador Juri Fokine, Siri Bjerke, and I officially opened the conference.

During the day, the negotiators for the scientific and construction protocols hashed out a plan all three countries could sign.

Juri, Siri, and I reappeared at the dinner for the delegation at the fabled downtown restaurant Dartagnan, stopping first at the entrance to read the prominently posted Michelin Guide review, and then we smiled a lot and toasted with champagne all and sundry. "Congratulations," "Pozdravlyayu," "Gratulerer."

Siri picked up the check. (The auditor at the Foreign Ministry, I am sure, understood when this whopper of a bill showed up on her expense account.)

In Bob Dyer's report he said, "While it is a civilian plant, its military use, including playing an important role in storing the waste generated during the dismantling of decommissioned nuclear submarines, makes this project of special interest for the Norwegian and U.S. partners and for future co-operative projects with the Russian Federation."

The agreement was signed December 14, 1995, at 2:30 p.m. in a ceremony at the Foreign Ministry.

RECEPTION FOR THE GOVERNOR OF MURMANSK OBLAST

Russian Ambassador Juri Fokine's March 13, 1996, reception for Yevgeny Komarov, governor of the Murmansk Oblast—an oblast is similar to an American state—was very well-attended by Norwegian officials of all stripes—Foreign Ministry, Defense Ministry, trade and culture. Juri made a point of introducing me and gushing about the friendly relations of America, Russia, and Norway.

Komarov was the first governor of this region in the new Russia. He had been appointed by Boris Yeltsin in 1991 and was up for election in a few months. During the Soviet Union's existence, the highest authority was the local Communist Party chief. So it was quite a change that oblast governors were now to be elected locally and hold significant executive authority.

The success of the Yeltsin experiment in democracy depended a lot on this federalism producing economic results. Ditching the Communist Party chief and having an election was not the test. Komarov, along with Foreign Minister Kozyrev, who represented Murmansk in the Duma, needed outside help if they were to be successful in bringing back jobs. We—the U.S. and Norway—were doing our best to assist in the economic development of Murmansk through trade and financial assistance to secure nuclear waste and weapons. Norway was even buying fish from this region—fresh, frozen, and pickled.

I wished him well and told of my good experiences on my trip to Murmansk. The Russian Embassy had a photographer on hand and the two of us smiled for the camera. Who knows how that photo ended up being used.

NATO, RUSSIAN GENERALS, AND NUKES IN THE ARCTIC

Bob Dyer and I flew to Kirkenes on the morning of June 24, 1996, for a NATO workshop on "Recycling, Remediation, and Restoration Strategies for Contaminated Civilian and Military Sites in the Arctic Far North."

Although under NATO auspices, this three-day meeting was organized by the Norwegians and the only contaminated sites were in Russia, it was a breakthrough given the Russian participation. Deputy Foreign Minister Siri Bjerke and I spoke at the opening session along with the general who was the head of the Directorate for Ecology and Special Means of Protection, Ministry of Defense, Russian Federation.

Bob talked on the third day on "molten metals technology and quantum catalytic extraction processing"—helpfully summarized by Bob as "nuclear waste processing and recycling—how to do it."

He was joined on his session by two Russian generals talking on the disposition of nuclear waste resulting from the decommissioning of nuclear submarines and two other Russian experts from Moscow: civilians who addressed processing of low-level liquid radioactive waste generated by the nuclear-powered icebreakers.

My old friend, the head of the Murmansk Shipping Company, the icebreaker fleet, Vyacheslav Ruksha, outlined "alternative waste transport plans in Murmansk." Since I was scheduled to be in Estonia and visit the abandoned Soviet nuclear submarine base in Paldiski, the session by a scientist from Finland on "Experiences at Paldiski" was most informative. The Soviets left like thieves in the night, leaving the nuclear hazard for others to clean up.

There were 33 speakers sharing experiences, meeting each other and making friends at lunches and dinners. Especially the dinners. The pre-dinner wimpy aperitif was replaced by cocktails, as how else could Russian vodka be served? I helpfully explained to the Russians this was what Americans called "happy hour." They adopted this phrase and repeated it several times with big smiles. (President Clinton: Please note another breakthrough in U.S.-Russian understanding.)

A DASH TO THE RUSSIAN BORDER WHERE GOD STOOD GUARD

Bob and I took advantage of a break in the NATO conference on June 25 to make a run for the border. The Russian border, one hour's drive to the east.

At the border, the road turns north and there at the end of the road on the shore of the Arctic Ocean is the King Oscar II Chapel. This small stone Lutheran church built in 1869 is exactly 1,600 feet from Russia.

The landscape, on the drive east from Kirkenes on a narrow blacktop road, is the Arctic tundra—patches of grasses and scrub trees, some hearty blue and white wildflowers. The road went up, then down to hug the rolling terrain, and then unexpectedly, the road plunged down several hundred feet, and we were in a green valley.

We descended into a heavenly place of trees and a farm with a red barn; the family was in the field cutting hay. The tractor, a familiar cream-and-red Ford, pulled a side mower, the cutters scissoring back and forth, moved by the tractor's power take-off unit. There was hay that had been cut earlier hanging on a line like a clothesline to dry before storage in the haymow of the barn. From there it would be fed right to the cows or perhaps be part of the brew to make silage.

I asked myself: Even with a short growing season does 24 hours of sun produce one crop of hay? Two? Why not bale the hay with a baler? It was like being home in my heart for me. There is a photo of me sitting on the seat of that model Ford tractor on our Wisconsin farm where we lived when I was born.

The Russian border was not what I expected. It was a 20-foot-high fence of wire mesh, maybe it was 30 feet. There were guard posts perched on high wooden structures like the fire towers in a national forest in the U.S. They were frequent and the silhouettes of the guards with their Kalashnikovs could be seen. We didn't wave or stop and continued on slowly north toward the sea.

After the Soviets had pushed the Germans out of northern Norway during World War II, they went back across their border, built the fence, and here we were fifty years later. The fence is meant to keep people out, as on the other side are Russian military bases with battalions of tanks, and airfields with squadrons of fighter jets. The fence also ended the migration route of the reindeer and divided the community of the Sami in Norway from their brethren in Russia.

Before the chapel, the sea comes into view and the air is so clear; one can see so far the curve of the earth is there and the clouds look to be floating in the water. The chapel sits at the base of a steep hill. A large cross is in the Arctic grass field in front of it.[135] It is here as a symbol of the flag of Norway. A statement saying: "This is our side of the border." I went in alone and was alone. I had not thought of cremation before, but it struck me that this is where a few of my ashes should one day rest. I signed the visitors book and marked the date.

WHAT TO DO ABOUT THE DEATH CLOUD OF NIKEL?

Bob Dyer is back in town and that means Russian border here we come again. This time it is arranged by the Norwegian consul in Murmansk for us to be driven to the border to cross at the new checkpoint and go on to "observe" the giant Nikel smelter just five miles east of the Norwegian border.

The occasion, in September 1996, was the official opening of the third International Barents Symposium, "Environment in the Region," in Kirkenes. This is a meeting of Norway and Russia, the two countries that border that shallow part of the Arctic Ocean called the Barents Sea.

The U.S. is a member and other Nordic countries are invited. A meeting of experts.

I will speak at the opening and leave, while Bob will hang around to wax eloquent on the technical issues regarding nuclear waste.

The crews on the Kirkenes flights are getting to know me or getting suspicious. Maybe both. On Thursday morning, September 13, 1996, at 7 a.m. we leave Kirkenes by car for the border crossing. This state-of-the-art facility financed by Norway is the first-ever official border entry into Russia at this point. I flash my diplomatic passport to the raised eyebrows of the agents on the Russian side, and we are off.

There are people on the roadsides with small tin buckets picking berries. The wooden road signs may or may not tell the way, as many are there to misdirect invading NATO forces.

We are in the region that was once part of Finland and known then as Petsamo. Just north of Nikel is the port where on August 6, 1940, the *SS American Legion* docked to rescue Crown Princess Märtha and her three children—the Princesses Ragnhild and Astrid, and Crown Prince Harald—and the American ambassador to Norway, Florence Jaffray Harriman.

Nikel is the name of the nearby small town. Norilsk Nikel is the enterprise of the smelter. Not far over the border we see yellow haze and then belching smokestacks and soon experience the smell of sulfur, like the smell in your high school chemistry lab when the teacher did that experiment with eggs. The giant plant sits amid a thick cloud that fans out to produce a dead zone of land.

The ore is smashed into concentrate, then to dust that is soaked to make a slurry. Then 2,500-degree furnaces heat this and the result is nickel—and a cloud of toxic sulfur dioxide that wafts its way to Norway by the prevailing winds.

The Cold War may be over, but nothing has changed here. Whether the Soviet Union or Russia, those with the purse strings in Moscow will not spend a nickel on pollution control on Nikel. Norway's protests of the health hazard are not heard.

What am I going to do about it? There is a reason I am getting a firsthand look at the Nikel smelter hosted by the Norwegian Foreign Ministry: Because this is an important issue to Norway. I had sent a personal letter to President Bill Clinton as background for his scheduled 1994 trip to Norway and included the smelter as an item for him to know about. Although the trip was canceled, the smelter lives in the briefing papers for a subsequent trip.

Back in Oslo, we send a cable looping in Vice President Al Gore. Ron Klain is his chief of staff, and we know each other from the campaign, so it will get noted. The suggestion is to add this to the agenda of a Gore-Chernomyrdin Commission meeting.[136]

MEETING IN BERGEN TO STEM THE NUCLEAR THREAT

In the early 1990s, Sherri Goodman was on the staff of the Senate Armed Services Committee working for Chairman Sam Nunn. She was responsible for oversight of the nuclear weapons accounts.

With the election of Bill Clinton and Al Gore and their promise of environmental leadership, a new position in the Department of Defense was created: deputy undersecretary for environmental security. Sherri was chosen to be the head.

Her task was to cajole, charm, and shame the Russians and her own colleagues in the U.S. military to ignore their past mistrust and work together to get control of nuclear hazards in the Arctic. "I recall several memorable evenings when, being pregnant with my second child, I asked a military member of the U.S. delegation to be my 'designated drinker' as our Russian counterparts hosted one of their 80-proof 'trust-building' sessions."[137] My guess is this duty was snapped to with a sharp salute and a "Yes ma'am."

We had met several times in D.C. but this trip, in September 1996, was her first to Norway. We joined up in Bergen to meet Secretary of Defense William Perry for a NATO meeting, and then a separate event later in the day with the Russian minister of defense for the signing of a cooperative agreement between the U.S., Norwegian, and Russian defense ministers on environmental cooperation in the Arctic.

Almost three years earlier—November 28-29, 1993—then-Deputy Secretary of Defense Perry had come to Oslo to get to know Norwegian Minister of Defense Jørgen Kosmo. Secretary of Defense Les Aspin had asked Perry to take this job for good reason: Perry was the expert on Soviet nuclear weaponry.

During that visit, Kosmo hosted a dinner for Perry, Foreign Minister Johan Jørgen Holst hosted a breakfast, we met with Prime Minister Brundtland, and I hosted a working lunch for Perry and Kosmo.

By the end of the intense two-day schedule, that elusive thing in diplomacy was archived: clarity. U.S. assistance in engaging Russia on the cleanup of the nuclear hazard of the decommissioned Soviet-era nuclear submarines near Murmansk was the priority for Norway in the Norwegian-U.S. defense relationship. Deputy Secretary Perry and Minister Kosmo became Bill and Jørgen. Their backgrounds couldn't be more different—Perry actually was a rocket scientist with a Ph.D. in mathematics, and Kosmo started as a union leader and small-town mayor. They shared the essential quality for the jobs they held: They were calm.

At his confirmation hearing in the Senate for secretary of defense, Sen. Robert Byrd had this advice for Perry: "I hope you will not be overly apologetic about being soft-spoken. Some of our illustrious predecessors on this planet were soft-spoken. George Washington, Abraham Lincoln, and Jesus. You stay what you are." Perry was confirmed by unanimous vote.[138]

Dear reader: A high government official is a different person when out of Washington. They are the guest. They become that person they once were. The ambassador is their protector and instant friend. Count up the number of hours I spent with Perry in cars together, the two of us at meetings, breakfasts, lunches, and dinners and we end up finishing each other's sentences. What became apparent to me was that Perry felt he was in this post at this time to end the threat of nuclear war and that this was his purpose.

HISTORIC "ARCTIC MILITARY ENVIRONMENTAL COOPERATION" AGREEMENT—IT'S PARTLY ABOUT COD

Secretary of Defense William Perry and the defense ministers of Norway and Russia met on September 26, 1996, in Bergen, Norway, to sign the Arctic Military Environmental Cooperation declaration (AMEC), beginning an unprecedented cooperative effort. For the first time, the Russian military is working directly with the American and Norwegian militaries on projects intended to help clean up massive amounts of radiological and other pollution in northwest Russia.[139]

The projects deal with rescuing the decommissioned Soviet/Russian submarines from their current fate—a Chernobyl happening in slow motion. There are 52 submarines no longer in service that sit at the docks of the naval bases around Murmansk with their reactors and fuel still onboard. The used liquid reactor coolant is stored in a ghost ship moored to the dock in the civilian harbor.

Safe transport to safe storage of the radioactive material is the purpose of the projects.

The AMEC projects are to be done "without increasing the Russian Navy's operational capabilities." All the credit for this section of the agreement—a deal-breaker without it—goes to the remarkable juggling of the interests of the three navies by my Assistant Naval Attaché Al Nadolski.

As I witnessed this signing ceremony, I thought about how far we have come from hiding under our desks in grade school to this. And I thought of cod. The world's largest cod fishery is in Norway. The decommissioned Russian submarines float in it—the waters of the Barents Sea.

"Every winter, a miracle happens in the northern part of Norway. The skrei—prime Norwegian Atlantic cod—returns from the ice-cold waters of the Barents Sea to their original spawning grounds off the northern Norwegian coast. This heroic journey means the Norwegian Arctic cod develops strong muscles and incredibly firm flesh, unsurpassed in taste and texture."[140]

Dried cod was the staple of the larder of the Viking longships that allowed their journeys. Dried and salted cod was the first Norwegian commodity traded. When the Catholic Church imposed meatless Fridays, it was Norwegian dried cod made into the dish bacalao that became the substitute.

When you visit the doctor regardless of the diagnosis or prescription, it is added to take a daily capsule of cod liver oil. I was scolded by my doctor when I did not faithfully follow this regimen.

The stomachs of Norwegian immigrants would not let go the need for cod. No matter if they were in a sod hut in the middle of North Dakota. The other staple was the Lutheran Church. So the two got together.

Lutefisk is the rehydrated dried cod that had been preserved in lye shipped to America from Norway in wood barrels. At Christmas time in Norwegian Lutheran churches in America, there are lutefisk dinners in the church basement. It is a rite of the season.

There are even men's eating societies called Torske Klubben—the cod club.[141]

The lunch features flat bread, steamed cod, and boiled potatoes topped with a sprig of parsley. Generous amounts of melted butter are available. A shot of Linie Aquavit accompanies every meal. The Klubben sings both the American and the Norwegian national anthems. After singing all members and guests are asked to raise their glasses of aquavit and pound the table three times followed by the full-throated instruction to the wait staff to 'Bring on the Torske,' whereupon the meal is served. The history of the Atlantic cod is the history of Norway.[142]

The safeguarding of the cod fishery is a promise of AMEC.

REPORT TO THE PARLIAMENT ON CHERNOBYL OF THE NORTH

On October 29, 1996, Foreign Minister Bjørn Tore Godal presented to the Parliament a very detailed report on nuclear safety initiatives in Northwest Russia that involved Norway. He pointed to the Arctic Military Environmental Cooperation deal as a breakthrough with the U.S., Norwegian, and Russian militaries working together for the first time. Norway had budgeted $33 million for projects dealing with decommissioned submarines in 1995, 1996, and 1997, with $10 million spent so far. The news to me was that there was an ongoing Norway-Russia program budgeted at $6 million to buy for the Kola nuclear power plant an emergency generator, emergency communications equipment, computers, vibration detectors, and equipment to upgrade safety functions in the control room. None of this was to in any way prolong the operation lifetime of the reactors. Norway's position was that the Kola plant was not safe and should be shut down. Godal reminded all that when Chernobyl happened the radioactive cloud drifted over northern Norway. The prevailing winds would send a similar disastrous cloud if the Kola plant failed.[143]

RETURN TO MURMANSK

On March 10, 1997, it is cold in Murmansk—the high temperature around 28 degrees and the low hovering around zero. The days are getting longer, with sunrise at 8:45 and sunset at 5:30. But it is a rare day when it is not overcast or does not snow.

We were to drive from Kirkenes, Norway, to Murmansk, Russia, in two minivans, one a backup with survival gear. The 150-mile trip was estimated to take four hours. The road this time of year was a path of snow kept open by continuous plowing.

The event was a program arranged by the Norwegian consul general in Murmansk for me, Alan Hecht, EPA deputy director of international affairs, and Marshall Adair, assistant secretary for European affairs in the State Department.

Alan and Marshall flew in from D.C. to Oslo on March 10, arriving in the morning. We then took the afternoon flight to Kirkenes. Four hours later, we were at a dinner hosted by the Barents Council. The council was formed in 1993 to foster cooperation—business and cultural—among Russia, Norway, Finland, and Sweden in the Arctic.[144] The U.S. had observer status.

Marshall and Alan were on the program as speakers and I observed—such was my status.

On March 11, we met Knut Hauge, who had been the first-ever consul general for Norway in Murmansk, at the Norway-Russia border crossing at Storskog. Knut was now director for European Affairs in the Ministry of Foreign Affairs. He was driving one of the vans. A translator from the Foreign Ministry would be in the other van with the driver. The route would take us past Nikel, Zapolyarny, Pechenga, and Litsa.

To call what we embarked on a road was being kind. A winter's worth of snow had been banked up ten to twenty feet on each side by the plows. Marshall started to recite *The Charge of the Light Brigade: Forward the Light Brigade! Charge for the guns—into the Valley of Death.*

Little did he know. Soon we came upon a marker that commemorated the several hundred thousand Russian and German soldiers who had died in the WWII battle here that lasted over four years. Then near Pechenga, we were attacked by tanks. Out of the snow burst several tanks; the commander's head could be seen sticking up through the top of the turrets. The steel tracks of the tanks were churning up clouds of snow, making things seem even more ominous. And then we were driving across the edge of the tarmac of a military airfield with planes parked everywhere. It was part of the road. The tanks and the airport were east of Pechenga in a place only identified on the map as Np Sputnik.

Presumably the tanks were on a practice maneuver. But if it was done for my benefit, bravo!

After five hours, we were in Murmansk, drinks in hand at a reception for us given by the consul general. *Oh when can their glory fade? O the wild charge they made!*

In the morning, we started on a schedule that Consul General Odd Skagestad and the mayor of Murmansk had arranged.

A long meeting with officers from the Northern Fleet Command took most of the morning. The translator got a workout as Marshall and Alan and the officer heading the Northern Fleet delegation had a substantive discussion on whether the U.S. and Russia were in sync on the understanding of the cooperative agreements regarding safe transport and storage of nuclear waste from decommissioned submarines.

And then lunch aboard one of Atomflot's nuclear-powered icebreakers hosted by the county governor, where I was reunited with my old pal, the CEO of the Murmansk Shipping Company, Vyacheslav Ruksha. The lunch was a highlight for all of us. The dining room is high up in the superstructure with windows all around. It was a sunny day. The view of the harbor and the city was postcard perfect. Alan and Marshall stayed the course on the toasts of vodka.

At 4 p.m. we left Murmansk airport on a flight to Kirkenes and caught the connecting flight to Oslo. Back at 11 p.m.

1997 UPDATE ON NUCLEAR WASTE PROGRESS

My May 23, 1997, letter to Tom Still of the *Wisconsin State Journal*: a promised update on nuclear waste progress since his visit to Oslo:

> Hi Tom,
>
> We had quite a success here in Oslo last week. We (U.S. & Norway) negotiated the last details and signed agreements with the Russians on perhaps the three most important projects dealing with nuclear safety for the Russian submarine fleet in Murmansk. The first is the development and manufacture of a prototype container for spent nuclear fuel; the second for design and construction of a treatment system for solid radioactive wastes generated during decommissioning of Russian nuclear submarines; and, those two follow on our first project which expanded a facility for processing low-level liquid radioactive waste (the contaminated cooling liquid for the reactors on submarines)...

The commitment the Russians have is to stop dumping nuclear waste at sea. And the agreements are essential to keep the ongoing disarmament of nuclear weapons programs on track, which is the overriding goal of all this.

These projects, by the way, do not increase the Russian Navy's operational capabilities. I have worked on these projects for three years ... it will likely take me one more trip to Murmansk this summer to do a little retail politics to make sure all is well but that probably will be enough...

Thanks again for helping with our press-to-press program by coming to Norway and engagingly engaging your Norwegian counterparts in Oslo and Bergen.

Ambassador Tom

CHAPTER 25
1996 NOTABLE DIARY ENTRIES

Collected here are short and sweet versions of some of the most important events of 1996, from my diary.

APRIL 18, 1996:
PM (Gro Brundtland) again shows her flair for the right words to silence critics of NATO expansion...quote from cable from embassy Vilnius on remarks she made on trip to Lithuania: "It was not for Norway, a net importer of NATO security, to tell other democracies they cannot enjoy the same type of security."

APRIL 24, 1996:
50th anniversary celebration of Fulbright Program at University of Oslo Aula (concert hall). My birthday. The Queen gave me flowers. His Majesty wishes happy birthday.

JUNE 4, 1996:
(Richard) Holbrooke called last night responding to my note that he should visit me after his scheduled trip to Stockholm. Siebert (U.S. Amb. to Sweden) has been encouraging him to campaign for Nobel Prize and H asked me if this was appropriate. Of course you should come. Jimmy Carter just left so the field is open. You have a chance, I

told him, as it was a timely prize after Dayton.[145] He said, "It would be just prior to former Yugoslavia elections. Humbled by this incredible thing to be considered for peace prize, etc."

JUNE 6, 1996:

Informed Norwegian Navy north command had plans for one of our special rescue/mapping subs to operate for three days at 28 degrees east (very close to Murmansk)—we said no way one week before Russian elections. And, Shalikashvili (chairman of the Joint Chiefs of Staff) arrives the 9th with visits to PM and His Majesty scheduled and a big hoopla dinner hosted by Gen. Solli, chief of Defense, and boat trip with Kosmo.

JUNE 7, 1996:

Win some, lose some. *Aftenposten* wine critic recommends California wine Fetzer Chardonnay as suitable for dishes with whale meat.

AUGUST 3, 1996:

Told Mike Scanlon (press attaché) to take a photo of the used heroin needle disposal box at the statue of FDR in the harbor. I want to send a letter of complaint. He said he will call mayor's PR person and get it taken care of. "Nothing in writing is needed on this!"

AUGUST 19, 1996:

Arne Olav Brundtland (the PM's husband and a scholar at the Norwegian Institute of International Affairs, or NUPI) lunch. He arrives on bicycle and we eat in cafeteria. He had double hamburger, fries and lettøl, a low-alcohol beer. Had a new beard—all men want to be Hemingway? I thought it made him look younger and told him. Subject was planning for a NUPI NATO meeting: "Could I get (Deputy Secretary of State) Strobe Talbott?"

SEPTEMBER 1996:

The future king of Norway, Crown Prince Haakon, starts undergraduate studies at UC Berkeley. Political science. I had been informed some time ago. Kept very quiet. His father HM King Harald graduated from the Norwegian Military Academy in 1959 and then studied history at Oxford University in London for two years. Independent

Norway's first king—Crown Prince Haakon's grandfather—HM King Haakon—was trained at the Naval Academy in Denmark, graduating in 1893.[146]

OCTOBER 23, 1996:

After hearing news of (PM Gro) Brundtland's resignation start to get ball rolling on Jagland (head of the Labour Party and a member of Parliament) visit to White House after election. Call Morten and say I will see Jagland Monday night at the Arafat dinner and will mention.

OCTOBER 24, 1996:

(Donna) Shalala (head of U.S. DHHS) calls, asks if it is OK to put Brundtland on the U.S. list to head the World Health Organization. Call Morten and he says: "She didn't say no."

(Note: The head of the World Health Organization has to be a medical doctor and it was Europe's turn to have the post. Brundtland is an M.D.)

NOVEMBER 27, 1996:

Private meeting with Gro in her small office in the Parliament building...Told her what a joy it was to write my book[147] and encouraged her to get going on autobiography. She outlined her ideas of making it a personal story—her husband also writing a book. "I haven't seen a page of it." But they have to agree on what is said about the children, especially their late son Jorgen (who committed suicide in 1992). We watch Prime Minister Jagland on television on the 1 p.m. news announce that Terje Rød-Larsen would be leaving his government. Gro said Rød-Larsen had never been in her government. "A premonition that he was too big for his britches." (Note: Terje Rød-Larsen, one of the chief architects of the Oslo accords, was appointed a deputy prime minister by Jagland but had to resign after a brief tenure when a discrepancy involving his taxes became public.) Gro noted that when I came it was great that I was "a real politician" of the Democratic Party. "Someone like us to talk to."

CHAPTER 26
JANUARY 1996

NORWEGIANS "BEWILDERED AND SHOCKED" AS U.S. BUDGET SHUTDOWN CLOSES EMBASSY

"...day twenty or so of the shutdown, I have $200 on hand in the embassy, hadn't paid half the staff, and I was asking our heating oil supplier for forbearance. I wrote my congressman, one of the few political activities I am allowed under State Department rules." (From a letter from me to Jim Holperin, a former colleague in the Wisconsin Legislature)

When Speaker Newt Gingrich caused the federal government to be shut down for 21 days starting on December 16, 1995, by preventing the passage of an operating budget, U.S. embassies were made Potemkin villages.

It was as if day had turned to night, and suddenly, I couldn't find the light switch.

Most of the 129-person staff,[148] 55 Americans and 74 Norwegians, had to leave the embassy. Go home. Visa and passport services stopped. Presumably the Americans would one day get their back pay for this "furlough" period. The Norwegian staff had to leave immediately as under Norwegian labor law they could not work under the promise of someday being paid.

The Marines and the defense attachés could stay. They were under the Pentagon budget, which was mostly exempted from the shutdown.

The staff at the Residence were considered employees of the ambassador and were not affected. Entertaining at the Residence also OK, as technically I paid for this expense. I was to carry on—a smile, a car, a driver, and a flag.

Mike Scanlon, the press attaché, and I were busy. He was fielding questions from the press and scheduling me for the constant requests for TV interviews. Each day we would do a briefing for the staff with a note. A frequent question from the American families was, "Will our kids' school tuition be paid in time?"

On January 8, the first day of operation after the shutdown, I served coffee to those in the long line out on the sidewalk waiting for visas. This was carried on every TV station.

A State Department assessment of the embassy's performance during this period was very complimentary, but this line was added: "...the sympathetic Norwegian public was bewildered and shocked..."[149] The image of America had changed.

FORMER AMBASSADOR ROBERT STUART JR., "MR. QUAKER OATS," LOOKS BACK ON TENURE IN OSLO

Robert Stuart Jr. was ambassador to Norway from 1985 until 1989, appointed by President Reagan.[150] At the time he was chairman of the Quaker Oats Company, the Stuart family business headquartered in Illinois.

His very-welcome visits to my office became more frequent after his marriage in October 1995 to Ingegjerd Ebba Dagmar Løvenskiold— known as Lillan—the Mistress of the Robes to Queen Sonja, the highest-ranking female member of the royal court.[151]

Bob and Lillan's marriage was embraced by the society pages. You can write the headline: "American millionaire diplomat marries wealthy Norwegian royal. Widow and widower find love again." A lot of photos. Bob had a full head of silver hair, dark suit, broad smile, and bad knees. When he sat down for a visit, he was not getting up for a while.

Our visit in mid-January 1996 was the first time I was able to thank Bob for inviting Barbara and me to his and Lillan's julebord (Christmas party) and get him talking about what stuck with him about his time in Norway looking back. (Dear reader, Here I am adding context and condensing a number of discussions with Bob.)

Three interrelated events involving nuclear war, which promised a new and safer world, were significant during his tenure—important to him and to Norwegians. The Reagan-Gorbachev Summit in Iceland in 1986, where the dream of nuclear weapon disarmament had come close and resulted in the Intermediate Range Nuclear Forces Treaty limiting some weapons; Gorbachev's Murmansk Initiative in 1987, where in a stunning and wide-ranging speech Gorbachev proposed eliminating nuclear weapons from the Arctic and laid out several policy changes on nuclear weapons specifically relating to Norway;[152] and "Star Wars," the derogatory moniker hung on Reagan's proposal for a missile defense shield—incoming ICBMs would be destroyed before they could reach a target, thus rendering nuclear weapons useless. Bob was an advocate but found a very skeptical reception to this idea of Star Wars in Norway. It was, shall we say, hard to explain.

It was not until years later that I happened to learn that Bob went to the Los Alamos Ranch School, a private college preparatory school in New Mexico. The school and its land were procured in 1942 for the site of developing the atomic bomb.[153]

Postscript: Bob Stuart died at age 98 of a heart attack on May 8, 2014.[154] He was on a plane with Lillan returning to the U.S. from Paris.

We kept in touch all those years.

CHAPTER 27
A STOP IN BRUSSELS AND HOORAY FOR HOLLYWOOD

On the way back to Oslo from a three-day conference of U.S. ambassadors to NATO countries in Stuttgart, I stopped in Brussels to visit our ambassador to Belgium, Alan Blinken, and his wife Melinda. Barbara and I counted them among our best friends. They visited us in Oslo, and we visited them in Brussels. And we traveled together on a vacation to St. Petersburg.

Alan's brother, Don, was the U.S. ambassador to Hungary. Their father was a Jewish immigrant from Kyiv and here they were back in Europe. Truly American stories. Clinton had a knack for picking ambassadors with a history like this.

Melinda was Hollywood. Her father Howard Koch had been the head of film production at Paramount Pictures and was a Hollywood icon. Just like the glamorous old days they had parties and showed new-release movies that were flown over tucked in the diplomatic pouch. Now that's diplomacy.

Alan had once run for the state Assembly in New York. He lost, but it was the experience of his life, he said. He loved the campaigning. He shook hands at the subway entrances. We had this experience in common, although I shook hands at the entrance to Friday night high school football games.

While in Brussels, I met with the Norwegian ambassador to the EU and had lunch with Norway's ambassador to NATO. And squeezed in a briefing at the U.S. mission to the EU.

CHAPTER 28
MARCH 1996

I SKI AND SHOOT IN THE MINNESOTA NATIONAL GUARD BIATHLON AND LIVE TO TELL ABOUT IT

When I was asked to bring my cross-country skis along to Camp Torpo to visit the Minnesota National Guard's winter training exercise, I was not expecting it was for the purpose of competing in a biathlon with the troops.

Every even-numbered year, the Minnesota Guard, about 100 of them, come to Norway for winter skills training. The Norwegian Home Guard goes to Minnesota for the same purpose in the odd-numbered years. The exchange, which began in 1974, is the longest-running military exchange partnership between any two nations.[155] And 1996 was a special year as it was the 50th anniversary of the founding of the Home Guard.

The Home Guard in Norway[156] is like the U.S. National Guard, but there is a distinction: Norway has mandatory military service for men starting at age 19. Most spend their time at bases in northern Norway near the Russian border.

About 40,000 of these veterans are enlisted in a Home Guard rapid-reaction force strategically dispersed throughout the country. They could be quickly mobilized if war broke out. An invasion by Russia was the planned-for scenario. The tasks could be to guard a railroad station, an airport or other potential enemy target, or active duty.

I was very much looking forward to the arrival of the Minnesota Guard, as the point man who would come in advance was none other than my old pal Harry "Tex" Sieben, who was the Speaker of the Minnesota House when I was the Speaker in Wisconsin. Colonel Harry Sieben had a long and very distinguished career in the Reserves and the Guard and was bucking for a promotion to general.

Tex and I left Oslo for Camp Torpo at 7 a.m. March 4, 1996, and arrived at 10:45. It was cold but sunny. Good snow conditions.

Another familiar face greeted me. Major General Eugene Andreotti, the adjutant general for the state of Minnesota. I last saw the gregarious general in Minneapolis at the send-off bash in 1993 that Tex, Walter Mondale, and my dear friend Senate Majority Leader Roger Moe hosted for Barbara and me.

Right away, I was told to strap on my skis, as the biathlon was about to get underway, and yours truly was expected to join in. (Dear Mr. President, was this anywhere on my list of official duties?)

We were to ski for two miles on a winding track with .22-caliber rifles strapped to our backs. There are targets along the way, and you drop down to a prone position and shoot. Miss the target and you have to ski a 100-yard penalty lap.

I finished in the top 25 percent. I had been skiing a lot since arriving in Norway. And my army training kicked in, just like knowing how to ride a bicycle never leaves you. Hitting a target is all about the breathing.

The score was a combination of the targets hit and the time it took to ski the course. Ski slow and make it up by hitting more targets was my plan. I couldn't ski very fast anyway. Most tried to ski as fast as possible and were breathing heavily when they reached the targets. If you are breathing like a bellows, you can't hold the rifle steady enough to squeeze off an accurate shot.

Well, I was a hail-fellow-well-met, but things could have gone wrong. I imagined a scene in the Oval Office where President Clinton is told: "Loftus shot himself in the back of the head with a rifle while skiing with the Minnesota National Guard."

(Note: I happily became one of the many who wrote a letter in support of Tex's promotion to general. A year later he phoned me: "Mr. Ambassador, this is General Sieben calling.")

COLD WAR IS OVER, BUT COLD-WEATHER MILITARY EXERCISES CARRY ON

It was not a surprise that Russian Ambassador Juri Fokine was joining me on the plane to Harstad in northern Norway to observe U.S. Marines in their winter warfare training Exercise Battle Griffin on March 7-8, 1996. The Cold War was over but not the cold-weather war games.

In this exercise, the Marines fly into Norway with not too much more than their guns and the packs on their backs, marry up with their pre-positioned materiel of Humvees, artillery, etc. and join Norwegian and certain NATO forces for winter warfare training.[157]

Norway runs this show, so off I went at the invitation of the Norwegian Ministry of Defense with my fellow NATO country ambassadors along with our colleagues from Russia, Sweden, and Finland.

How far north is Harstad? It was the northernmost Viking power center in Norway. Even they weren't going any farther north. A local landmark is four "Adolf Guns" left by the Germans. They are the large guns used on battleships but were placed on land here to guard the harbor and airfield.

I was briefed at the Marine's HQ compound of tents, and the colonel drove me in his Humvee out into the snow-covered field at the base of a mountain to observe Marines in combat action using live fire. The heater did not work.

Dinner that night was hosted by Defense Minister Kosmo. Russian Ambassador Juri Fokine offered a toast to the troops. The next day we all gathered and had lunch with the men and some women from units participating (U.S., Norwegian, Dutch, German, and French).

AMERICA'S FIRST BLACK AMBASSADOR FROM THE FOREIGN SERVICE

At the Tuesday Country Team meeting on March 9, someone mentioned that Clifton Wharton Sr., whose photograph was on the wall in our meeting room with all the other former ambassadors to Norway, was the first Black Foreign Service officer to rise to the rank of ambassador.

There was some confusion because Clifton Wharton was the deputy secretary of state before Strobe Talbott took over this post. That was his son, Clifton Jr. When JFK sent Clifton Wharton Sr. to

Norway in March of 1961, he was only the sixth U.S. ambassador in Norway's young history as a country.

Note: Early Black ambassadors were political appointees sent to either Haiti or Liberia starting in 1869, including Frederick Douglass (Haiti 1899). Not until Clifton Wharton Sr., was there a Black ambassador appointed to a country other than in Africa or to Haiti.[158]

Clifton Wharton Sr.'s first posting was as vice consul in Liberia in the 1920s. Liberia, a tiny enclave on the west coast of Africa, founded by freed slaves from America, was then the only secure source of rubber for the Firestone Tire and Rubber Company. The twentieth-century history of Liberia and the politics of American presidents appointing Black ambassadors is found in the history of Firestone.[159]

BRINGING THE BALTICS INTO THE WESTERN FOLD

It was a feat of scheduling. All seven American ambassadors were present: Ed Elson, Denmark; Larry Taylor, Estonia; Derek Shearer, Finland; Larry Napper, Latvia; Jim Swihart Jr., Lithuania; yours truly, Norway; and Tom Siebert, Sweden.

We were gathered in London to pitch U.S. businesses on opportunities in our respective countries. We all stayed at The Churchill Hotel on Portman Square and came together the first night to have what was (I'm not kidding) listed on the agenda as a "working cocktail" with the sponsors: 3M, IBM, HP, and Manpower.

It is just a five-minute walk from Portman Square to the U.S. Embassy on Grosvenor Square where our meetings were held.

When I walked up to this grand building, there was a familiarity I couldn't quite grasp until I learned the architect was Eero Saarinen, the same architect as the embassy in Oslo.

Our host was our ambassador to the Court of St. James's, William J. Crowe Jr., known as Mickey to his friends.[160] Admiral Crowe had been chairman of the Joint Chiefs of Staff under both Presidents Reagan and George H.W. Bush. He was Clinton's defense advisor during the campaign and was lauded as an excellent ambassador pick by the new president. He knew Norway, as he had been the head of the Navy Command for Europe, also a NATO post.

We gave our talks, and we each hosted a table for lunch. Joining me at my table was Tom Vraalsen, Norway's ambassador to the Court of St. James's. A pleasant surprise. Very thoughtful for him to be invited. Good for me to have this important connection.

Business representatives could ask for private meetings, and I had one taker. Slipping into the room was the fellow from Philip Morris.

In my campaign for governor in 1990, I had run a TV ad proposing a cigarette tax hike of a dime to pay for health insurance for children. As Speaker several times when I needed a few million to get to the budget number I would, in the middle of the night, add a penny to the cigarette tax, which raised $10 million.

Philip Morris spent a gazillion dollars trying to defeat me. In the most diplomatic way, I told him I would not lift a finger to help American cigarette companies. Letting bygones be bygones is a vastly overrated sentiment.

TEA WITH BETTY BOOTHROYD, FIRST WOMAN SPEAKER OF THE BRITISH PARLIAMENT

It was the high point in my quest to meet the Speaker or president of Parliament on my travels.

A query was made by our embassy in London as to whether the Speaker would be available to meet me. The response was quick, and I was to come over to the Parliament for tea. To have tea with Speaker Betty Boothroyd, the first woman in history to hold this position, was an honor.

Her small office behind the chambers of the House of Commons was all oak of a hue gained by a few centuries of pipe and cigar smoke. The dark leather Chesterfield sofa had hosted the bottoms of many a maker of history.

Speaker Boothroyd was as casual as could be: She poured tea, we both took milk, and we had a nice chat with our tea and chocolate-chip biscuits. I was gobsmacked when she told me right off she went to America in 1960 to observe the Kennedy campaign and ended up staying for two years working as a legislative assistant to congressman Silvio Conte of Massachusetts.

Her background was the Labour Party in microcosm. Her parents were factory workers. She did not go to private schools. She was one of the Tiller Girls, a dance troupe that appeared in music halls. She left show business, went into Labour Party politics and soon went to work as a secretary to a Labour member of Parliament.

She ran for Parliament four times before being elected and rose through the ranks. She was elected Speaker in 1992, the choice of both the Conservative Party, which was in the majority, and Labour. She told me being the first woman Speaker was one thing. Her next hurdle was whether she would wear a wig like every Speaker before her. She would not, but ruled this would not constitute a precedent for those who followed. She had beautifully coiffed gray hair and in the photo of her in her official garb she was quite magisterial.

Madame Speaker was quite keen to hear about how the Labour Party in Norway was doing under Gro Harlem Brundtland from the American point of view. Quite well, I assured her, and said I would mention our meeting to her.

One certainty was that when she was no longer the Speaker, the shoes she wore while presiding, black patent leather with a silver buckle, were to go to the historical collection of the Women's Library.

CHAPTER 29
APRIL 1996

VACATIONING IN BERMUDA WITH TED KENNEDY, DON SHULA, AND BOB FARMER

The call from Bob Farmer, a friend from the Dukakis and Clinton campaigns and now the U.S. consul general in Bermuda, inviting our family to stay with him for Easter break, April 1-6, was welcome indeed. As the boys said, "We won't be forced to go skiing!"[161]

Norwegians are serious about the Easter break. No business. Go to the mountains or someplace warm. This was a good time for me to be away.

The other guests would be Sen. Ted Kennedy and a couple of his children, his wife Victoria Reggie, and Don Shula, the former coach of the Miami Dolphins, only recently retired, and his wife Mary Anne Stephens.

The adults drank scotch, enjoyed seafood, and told stories: Ted regaled on both JFK's and his presidential campaigns, and Don Shula told of freezing on the sidelines when playing the Green Bay Packers at Lambeau Field. The kids played ping-pong, shot baskets, and ate hot dogs.

There was a secluded beach by Chelston, the consul's residence, and we walked on the beach and swam in the cold Atlantic Ocean. Ted organized a swimming competition for the kids and had our

9-year-old son Karl racing for the gold, exhorting him in his booming Irish brogue: "Swim faster, Karl." When one race was done, he would tell the exhausted kids, "OK, let's do it again."

When the other guests left, Bob put me to work. It was pleasant duty. A tour of Parliament and meeting the Speaker; a speech to the Hamilton Rotary Club where there was amazement that Norway was the third-largest exporter of oil in the world; a tour of the renowned aquarium for the boys by the director. And a dinner in my honor.

The Right Honorable Lord David Waddington, the governor of the British overseas territory of Bermuda, was kind enough to join us at dinner. One of Bob's bridge partners.

Bob had been busy with the ceremonial and practical details of the closing down of the U.S. Naval Air Station that had been in Bermuda since 1941.

This air base was used to track Soviet submarines operating near the East Coast of the United States—the same special planes with radar and sonar tracking equipment that frequented the bases in north Norway.

By the 1990s, the advancement in technology of the missiles launched from Soviet submarines had increased their range so much that the subs no longer needed to be near the East Coast. They now operated beyond the flying radius of Bermuda patrol aircraft. The Naval Air Station was now a relic of the Cold War and no longer needed.

REVISITING THE SCENE OF THE CRIMES IN NYC

We thanked Bob for his gracious hospitality, left Bermuda in his care, and headed for New York to meet my mother Margaret, the boys' doting grandmother, and my sister Jerry, the boys' even-more-doting and beloved aunt.

Jerry's son Bret, my nephew, who was working as an artist at a design studio in New York, would be joining us for dinner and a play. We took rooms at The Sherry-Netherland on Fifth Avenue and the boys were in heaven. Their grandmother and aunt, American TV shows for kids, and room service hamburgers, described as "real hamburgers."

Norway did not allow American beef to be imported—even the new McDonald's wasn't the real thing—and they were promoting the "McLaks," a ground-salmon burger meant more to address the glut of salmon than any demand. Kids—Norwegian, American, or otherwise—were not happy with this meal.[162]

We took the boys to the American Museum Natural History to see the dinosaur skeleton, but Alec insisted that only Jerry could take him and Karl to the FAO Schwarz toy store. He wanted to show her the scene of the crimes.

In 1992, Barbara and I had taken Alec with us to NYC to the Democratic Convention where Clinton was nominated. I took Alec, then age 9, to FAO Schwartz while Barbara roller-bladed on 5th Avenue—a photo of her in the Wisconsin papers the next day.

Outside FAO were a dozen men selling knock-off Rolexes, among other items. They would open a briefcase to show the stuff when a tourist came by. All of a sudden four plainclothes cops shouted, "NYC PD. You're under arrest." Men ran, watches scattered on the sidewalk. It was operatic.

If that wasn't enough for Alec's wide-open-with-amazement eyes, minutes later a half-block away we stumbled upon a three-card-monte operation. We watched a bit and bam, the person next to us grabbed the mark's money and ran. The dealer ran the other way. The shill melted away into the streets. And, what an adventure.

Barbara, Bret, my mother, and I went to the Broadway play *Victor Victoria* starring Julie Andrews. This play, based on the 1982 film, also starring Julie Andrews, had rave reviews, and it delivered.

I confess, I would have given Julie Andrews a standing ovation for reading the telephone book. I was smitten with her after seeing her in the 1964 film *The Americanization of Emily*.

Julie Andrews would win a Tony for her performance.

STILL AT ODDS ON WHALING

Talked to the PM (Gro Brundtland) on whaling when she came to sign the condolence book for Ron Brown April 11, 1996, in Oslo. I observed she had a good tan on her face and asked about her Easter break. "The best I ever had." Followed up on the call she had received from VP (Al) Gore to not increase the whale kill numbers. Noted this was an election year and another muted reaction could not be expected. PM said it was "reasonable to wait." Send cable reporting.

(Note: Ron Brown was the Secretary of Commerce and former chair of the Democratic Party who died in a plane crash in Croatia on April 3, 1996.)

A VISIT FROM UN AMBASSADOR MADELEINE ALBRIGHT

The visit of the United States ambassador to the UN is important to Norway. And, given that Clinton's ambassador to the UN was the illustrious Madeleine Albright, all the more so, as her visit to Oslo was an opportunity for the Norwegian prime minister.

Norway is one of the ten most-important countries in the UN, essential to its operation by contributions to the budget and sending talented people. Belief in and support of the UN is part of the Norwegian national character. Norway was a founding member of the UN and Norway's wartime foreign minister, Trygve Lie, was the first secretary general of the UN, guiding the organization from 1946 to 1952.

I picked up Madeleine Albright at the airport at noon April 26 for the start of an event-packed 24-hour visit. It was reminiscent of the fall of 1988 when we met the first time. Then, I had picked up Madeleine at the Madison airport, and we drove to Janesville. She was the foreign policy advisor to the Dukakis for President campaign. and I was the Wisconsin chair of the campaign.

We were going to a meeting of the leaders of the United Auto Workers, the union representing the workers at the Janesville General Motors plant. The UAW had endorsed Dukakis, and we were to give not a rousing speech but rousing reasons why the leaders needed to rally their fellow union members, families, and the people of Janesville to vote for the Democrats.

She gave a brilliant talk about democracy and the role of unions. She said it was the union leader Lech Wałęsa and the shipyard workers at Gdańsk who freed Poland from the Communist puppet government of the Soviet Union. In America, it was UAW President Walter Reuther who made organized labor a force for civil rights and worker rights. "You stand on their shoulders," she said, and there was a rousing cheer when she said, "Solidarity means that you get out the vote." Dukakis won Wisconsin.

Madeleine knew life without democracy as a girl growing up under the Nazis and then the Communists in Czechoslovakia. In 1948, her father, a diplomat, managed to get the family to America and asked for political asylum: "I cannot, of course, return to the Communist Czechoslovakia as I would be arrested for my faithful adherence to the ideals of democracy. I would be most obliged to you if you could kindly convey to his Excellency the Secretary of State that I beg of him to be granted the right to stay in the United States, the same right to be given to my wife and three children."

The saying is the rest is history, but for Madeleine the rest was her making history. In the 1992 Clinton for President campaign we met again. She was a foreign policy advisor and I was the campaign chair in Wisconsin. In 1993, Madeleine was appointed by President Clinton to be ambassador to the United Nations.

In my briefing to her in the car from the Oslo airport, I summed up the Norwegian position on the expansion of NATO. I mentioned France always had an alternative to how the enlargement process should work that was always opposed by us. Madeleine said, "I know. But they can't always be wrong. Tom, I have a good idea. Let's accept every fifth idea France has regardless of what it is." This was said not totally tongue in cheek.

Madeleine would stay at the Residence. Already at 12:45, there was scheduled a private lunch with Foreign Minister Bjørn Tore Godal and his UN team leader Jan Egeland. Madeleine and I got to the Residence just in time to greet them at the door.

Then a dash to Ministry of Defense HQ for a meeting with Minister of Defense Jørgen Kosmo. The gist of this discussion dealt with UN peacekeepers and Norway's change in policy. After a long history of providing soldiers for UN peacekeeping missions, personnel would now be devoted to NATO peacekeeping operations. No surprise here.

Just months earlier, on December 20, 1995, the Dayton Accords ending the war in Bosnia came into force. The accords, negotiated by Richard Holbrooke, who was then assistant secretary of state for European affairs, stipulated that 60,000 NATO troops would be deployed to take over from the 25,000 UN peacekeepers who had been there three years and had been unable to stop the fighting. This was a bitter pill for the combatants to swallow but Holbrooke insisted, and NATO was now in the peacekeeping business.

Next was a press conference at the embassy. Then a one-hour lull.

It was 5 p.m., and she had yet to unpack. She arrived with one suitcase. Her tutorial on how to pack was a delight. Knits, wraps, and scarves that didn't wrinkle, a simple necklace but a prominent pin to draw the attention. An eagle with a pearl in its talons was a favorite.

The guest list for dinner was a who's who of those who cared about the UN, including members from each party on both the

Parliamentary Committee on Foreign Affairs and the Finance Committee, and every newspaper and broadcast journalist in Oslo covering foreign affairs, including *The New York Times* editor with responsibility for Scandinavia.

In my briefing to Madeleine on the dinner guests, I had to explain a familiar name among the Norwegian journalists. Linn Ullmann was the daughter of the Norwegian Actress Liv Ullmann and the Swedish film director Ingmar Bergman. Linn was a respected journalist and word in the publishing world was that her soon-to-be-released first novel[163] would make her a celebrated author.

This got us talking about the Bergman/Ullmann films and wondering out loud if we had really seen all these films or did our familiarity come from reading the reviews by Pauline Kael in *The New Yorker*.[164]

The day and dinner achieved the goal of Madeleine being heard and the Norwegians getting to talk to her without a filter.

"Remember she is allergic to shellfish." This was in the briefing and mentioned to the chef. So that night I woke up recalling that there was a garnish on the plate—a small puff pastry with a mussel tucked inside. Was she now dead in the bed in the guest room down the hall? Not the case. The next morning, she assured me that she was very careful at this stage in life, and a mussel was not a shellfish she was allergic to.

The underlying purpose of the trip was for Madeleine to achieve a closer personal relationship with the Prime Minister Gro Harlem Brundtland. Gro had the same goal and invited Madeleine to her home for breakfast. Just the two of them. Gro made scrambled eggs.

Back to the airport for wheels up at noon.

Loftus family photo after arriving in America in 1885. Ambassador's grandfather Edward is the blond boy on left in first row. Photo credit: Author's personal collection.

Oval Office February 1993. The handshake that will lead to the nomination to become the ambassador to Norway. Photo credit: Official White House photograph.

Ambassador Loftus, First Lady Hillary Rodham Clinton and Florence "Flo Jo" Joyner at Lillehammer Olympics, February 1994. Photo credit: USIA, U.S. Embassy Oslo, Norway.

With PLO Chairman Yasser Arafat at dinner in honor of Oslo Accords, November 25, 1993. Photo credit: USIA, U.S. Embassy, Oslo, Norway.

Barbara and Karl Loftus at swearing in at the Capitol in Madison on
November 10, 1993—Karl blowing a bubble gum bubble.
Photo credit: *Milwaukee Sentinel.*

The author dancing with HM Queen Sonja in the ballroom of the Waldorf Astoria, New York City, on the State Visit of Their Majesties, October 1995. Photo credit: Anita and Steve Shevett, courtesy American Scandinavian Foundation.

Touring liquid radioactive waste storage facility in Murmansk, Russia, with chief of Atomflot nuclear icebreaker fleet Vyacheslav Ruksha, August 16, 1995. Photo credit: USIA, U.S. Embassy, Oslo, Norway.

Skiing with Alec Loftus, age 12, on the downhill run at the Olympics, February 1994.
Photo credit: Author's personal collection.

With Prime Minister Gro Harlem Brundtland at 4th of July celebration, 1995, at
Ambassador's Residence. Photo credit: USIA, Embassy Oslo.

American diplomat Richard Holbrooke with Ambassador Loftus, September 5, 1996, in Oslo at the Norwegian Atlantic Committee's conference on "The Baltics and Balkans." Photo credit: NTB The Norwegian News Agency.

With HM Queen Sonja in front of American flag. Photo credit: Johnny Seversen, Scan Foto, Oslo, Norway.

With sister Wendy Loftus. Photo credit: Author's personal collection.

Photo left to right: Norwegian Minister of Defense Jørgen Kosmo, Ambassador Tom Loftus, U.S. Secretary of Defense William Perry. Photo credit: USIA, U.S. Embassy, Oslo, Norway.

Barbara and Tom Loftus in front of Ambassador's Residence, Oslo, Norway.
Photo credit: Tom Still, "Diplomacy, Loftus Style." Courtesy, *Wisconsin State Journal*

Prime Minister Gro Harlem Brundtland and Arne Olav Brundtland. Photo credit: Alamay Images.

His Majesty King Harald V. Photo credit: Getty images.

The Royal Norwegian Order of Merit
Cross of St. Olav
Awarded to Ambassador Loftus by King Harald V
for "outstanding service in the interest of Norway"

Photo credit: Author's personal collection.

CHAPTER 30
MAY 1996

GOVERNORS HAWK AMERICA IN OSLO

A visit by a governor is prized by an ambassador. Governors come with a delegation of businesspeople from their state. The embassy's Commerce Department attaché helps organize a meeting schedule for the group. The ambassador hosts a dinner which is pretty much a guarantee the guest list will include the leaders of the businesses they are targeting.

Governors, when in a foreign country, shed their partisanship and portray their state as God's gift to humankind—their government the best since Pericles ruled Athens. I had sent a letter to every governor inviting him or her to bring a trade mission to Norway, explaining in it the services that were offered through the embassy, and that I would host a dinner in their honor. Governors love things done in their honor. Four governors visited during my tenure, from Maryland, Minnesota, North Dakota, and Wisconsin.[165]

The governor of Maryland, Parris Glendening, came to Oslo May 5 on a trade mission promoting the Port of Baltimore, tourism, and Maryland-based defense contractors. The governor's focus was to urge Norwegian shipping companies and shipowners to make more use of the Port of Baltimore. He understood that the rail connection to the port was an issue, but it was being resolved. The Maryland ports administrator was along to fill in the details. It was quite cozy but we managed 42 for dinner for Gov. Glendening.

Among the guests were the head of the Norwegian Shipbrokers Association and several from the Norwegian military, including the chiefs of staff and the heads of procurement of both the Navy and Air Force. Baltimore was the home of Westinghouse Electronic Systems Group, serving both commercial and military shipping. The company's vice president was in the governor's delegation.

Gov. Glendening was also promoting the Icelandic Air flights to and from Baltimore (with a stop in Reykjavik) as a gateway for Norwegian tourists planning to visit Washington, D.C. The head of Icelandic Air in Oslo and the director of a major Norwegian tour company were at the dinner.

The dinner was on the last day of the meeting schedule, so it allowed a social occasion to help cement new business relationships. The invitations included spouses, as did all like events at the Residence. There were seven tables, each hosted by a member of the embassy staff or a spouse. Barbara had the Air Force chief of staff, Major General Einar Smedsvig, at her table. The embassy protocol officer knew from experience that a valued guest would be charmed if seated next to Barbara; part of this was how pleased the guests at her table were that she was learning Norwegian and was already quite proficient.

The governor of North Dakota, Ed Schafer, also took me up on my invitation to each state's governor and came in 1995 with only the state's tourism director in tow. He was promoting Norsk Høstfest: The Norwegian Autumn Festival, North America's largest Scandinavian festival. The governor was highlighting the festival to get Norwegians to think about including his state when they vacationed in America.

Some background here: Norwegians traversed the United States by car. They embraced the freedom of the great American road trip. Fly to New York City, see the sights, rent a big American car with a V8 engine, hit the Interstate, and drive it like it was the Thunder Chariot of Thor. Then Chicago and eat steaks, visit a relative in Wisconsin, Minnesota, Iowa, or the Dakotas. Off to Las Vegas, Yellowstone, Hollywood, Disneyland, the Grand Canyon, Denver, St. Louis.

Some of my relatives had driven coast-to coast-more times than Jack Kerouac.

TWO QUEENS

"It is a good thing I am young," I told my press attaché Mike Scanlon, when he added another whirl to my whirlwind schedule. He replied, "You get the big salary, and you asked for the job." Mike was plainspoken.

On May 8, 1996, HM Queen Sonja was to celebrate the first anniversary of the Red Cross United World College at Fjaler near Bergen. She was a patron of this college and her guest would be Queen Noor of Jordan, also a patron of the Red Cross colleges. She called the college "mitt hjertebarn"—the child of my heart. I had accepted the invitation to be at this event some time ago. The American ambassador should be nowhere else on this day.

We had to be in Bergen a day early in order to get to the college the morning of May 8, as it would take two hours by ferry, leaving early in the morning. To avoid idling away valuable time Mike had added me to a seminar in Bergen on May 7 that the United States Information Service was holding for the press on the 1996 presidential election—a task USIS was charged with under their public diplomacy mission. I was to talk about the differences in farm policy in the two campaigns. Mike surmised that since I had been a politician in "America's Dairyland" I could probably plow this furrow.

The ferry docked right at the campus. It was a small compound of brightly painted buildings designed to resemble an idyllic Norwegian village in the countryside. The students were from dozens of countries, many of them from places torn by war or cursed by poverty.

I had coffee with the mayor and the head of the county government, and a question-and-answer session with an inquisitive group of students still shocked that there were two queens and an American ambassador in their midst.

Mike gave a presentation to interested students, and the college counselor walked them through the university admission process in the United States. There are only two years instruction here, then the students transfer elsewhere. Mike also met with the librarian about providing material for the new library.

After the ceremony, HM introduced me to Queen Noor. In taking my leave, I mentioned to HM that the next day I would visit Lofthus. Her charming smile known to all in Norway became even more so and she said, "Lofthus is a wonderful place. The Hotel Ullensvang is there."

Mike and I caught the last ferry and arrived back in Bergen at 8 p.m.

LOFTUS GOES TO LOFTHUS

There had been a long-standing invitation from the fine people at the village of Lofthus for me to visit. The correspondence was always addressed to Ambassador Lofthus.[166] Mike had added this trip for May 9, as to get to Lofthus you start at Bergen.

We left Bergen in the morning in a rental car for the two-hour drive to Norheimsund to catch the catamaran ferry trip of 45 minutes to Lofthus and arrived at 1 p.m. We were met by Edmund Harris Utne, the owner and manager of the Hotel Ullensvang.[167]

Coming into the bay of a split of sea off the Hardangerfjord, there is a vision: verdant fields that appear to be vineyards at the base of a snow-capped mountain. The long, low, 170-room hotel, perhaps the winery, even the silo-like tower that juts above the roof, has a pyramid of glass over it and glints in the sun like a lighthouse guiding you to safe harbor.

What comes into focus is row after row of cherry trees that march from the base of the mountain down to the water. They were in full blossom and there was a sweet aroma in the air. The annual Cherry Festival is in May, which is the month with the most sunshine in Norway, and on this day, sunrise is at 5 a.m. and sunset at 10 p.m.

The population of Lofthus is 500. Mr. Utne has arranged for lunch with the mayor and the council president at the hotel in Grieg's dining room. The composer came to Lofthus for inspiration.

I tell them of all the people who assumed my Norwegian roots were from Lofthus, which they should be proud of as these people knew of Lofthus as a special and beautiful place.

The high point of the tour of the modern hotel is the glass enclosure at the top of the tower with "panoramic views of fabulous fjords, the Folgefonna glacier and Hardanger plateau."

The hotel is quite different from the 1846 original, when 17-year-old Hans Utne started an inn for coach travelers that consisted of two straw beds in the loft over the shipping office.

Next on the printed schedule Mr. Utne had sent to the embassy in advance was, "A slow drive to Ullensvang Fruit Research Station. We will drive on the smaller roads, along the lanes of trees, showing the ambassador as much as possible of the village, to include the places where the composer Grieg worked."

This national research station supporting the fruit industry functioned just like a research station of an Agricultural Extension Department of a U.S. university. I had a large UW Extension station in my legislative district.[168]

I thanked my gracious host Mr. Utne, and it was back to the ferry dock for the reverse journey, where we arrived in Bergen at 8:30 p.m.

A YOUNG WOMAN NAVY SUB COMMANDER, AND THE HOME OF A FAMOUS VIOLINIST

Mike left Bergen May 10 and our Air Force Attaché Colonel Dan Penny arrived. The rental car keys were handed off at the airport. A changing of the guard.

It was about time I visited Haakonsvern, the main base of the Royal Norwegian Navy located about 12 miles south of the city of Bergen. Minister of Defense Kosmo would politely inquire on occasion if I had yet been to Haakonsvern.

Since I had been piped aboard dozens of Norwegian and U.S. Navy ships of every size and British, French, and Dutch ships during NATO exercises, I requested a visit to a Norwegian Navy submarine as part of the tour.

My other request was a visit to Lysøen, the home on a nearby island of the violinist Ole Bull, the most famous Norwegian of the 19th century. This would be a sort of pilgrimage for me.

The naval base is tucked in an inlet of the Grimstadfjord and protected from the open sea by a string of islands.

There was a tour and briefing on the Royal Norwegian Navy's present and potential business with the United States. This was Dan Penny's bailiwick as his job was to facilitate defense procurements.

Norway had six Ula-class diesel-electric submarines made in Germany. Well known for their stealth, they are tough to detect and highly maneuverable. Perfect for coastal use and intelligence gathering for NATO. There is a crew of 21 on the 200-foot-long sub, and it carries eight torpedoes. The Navy's first submarines were built in Norway from an American design and entered service in 1922.

As I embarked, the captain greeted me, asking first if I was OK, because I had hit my head on the low ceiling. She was in her late 20s, I guessed. Hers was a very prestigious assignment, as the Ula was considered the most effective weapon in the Royal Norwegian Navy. Most interesting was the captain's explanation of how the air-supply system worked when the sub was underwater for long periods. I ducked my head on disembarking.

It was thirty minutes to Lysøen from Haakonsvern by launch.

The house appears, and what is this? My first thought was that this large wooden house with an onion-domed tower and adorned with filigree could be in Istanbul on the banks of the Bosporus. I was there to further my education on Ole Bull, world-famous violinist, who vied with Paganini as the virtuoso of all time, founded a Utopian Norwegian colony in Ohio, ended up later in life in Madison, Wisconsin, and married the daughter of a lumber baron.

A portrait of Bull, violin on his shoulder, was owned by the Wisconsin Historical Society and hung in my office the eight years I was Assembly Speaker. It came to Oslo as part of the Arts in the Embassies program.

His biography, published in 1993, was the last book I read before leaving for Norway. The subtitle is *Norway's Romantic Musician and Cosmopolitan Patriot.*[169]

Colonel Penny and I were back in Oslo by 7 p.m.

A VISIT FROM JIMMY CARTER

I met former President Jimmy Carter at the airport May 28, and we went directly to the Parliament to meet with Kjell Magne Bondevik, the leader of the Christian Democratic Party. After the meeting, the three of us walked the short distance to the Grand Hotel for a lunch hosted by Bondevik.

Bondevik has described himself as a '68er—one of those young people throughout the world moved by the student strikes in Paris and Vietnam war protests in America in 1968. The '68 movement brought a change to the Christian Democrats, spearheaded by the party's youth arm—notably Bondevik—to become more activist and move peace and human rights to the fore.

Bondevik is more than likable. His smile is understated and genuine. A Lutheran minister, he was elected to Parliament at age 26 and served as minister of education and church affairs (June 1983-May 1986) and then foreign minister (October 1989-November 1990) in the two Conservative Party-led governments of the 1980s. The Christian Democratic Party was the coalition partner that gave the Conservatives the numbers to form a government.

The party's platform doesn't diverge much from the Social Democrats on labor unions, economics, and support of NATO. Defending the monarchy, preservation of the state religion, regulation of alcohol, limits on abortion but paired with support of the wide availability of contraceptives, set them apart.

It is a small party, with its strength with voters along the southwest coast Bible Belt, but always held enough seats in Parliament to be a deal-maker and end up in coalition governments with influence beyond its numbers.

The party in Parliament was a stalwart supporter of development aid, pushing for a set percentage of the total national budget to be devoted to development programs in poor countries. Bondevik's support was important to the Carter Center programs in Africa, and he felt a kinship with Jimmy Carter himself. Bondevik and Carter were a rare duo: two political leaders still finding time to teach Sunday school.

President Carter was staying with us at the Residence for the night but the host of his visit was Kari Nordheim Larsen, the minister of international development. This department of the Foreign Ministry was created in 1983 by the coalition Conservative Government, and the first minister was from the Christian Democratic Party.

We met Kari at the venerable Hotel Bristol for the dinner she was hosting, and as we walked through the bar to the private dining room, the bartender gave me a nod.

What to say about the Bristol? Opened in 1920. The first hotel with hot and cold running water in all its 100 rooms. It is where jazz was introduced and took hold in Norway. There was an in-house jazz band. Eartha Kitt performed in the ballroom. The restaurant is of Moorish style architecture with a thirty-foot-high ceiling. It is where a hotel guest, an anti-Nazi German engineer, in 1939 wrote the Oslo Report, a description of Nazi weapons systems that was then secretly delivered to the British ambassador in Oslo. "Going to the Bristol" became a phrase of the in crowd.

A note: For President Carter's 20-hour visit to Oslo, the embassy's schedule for moving the delegation, the secret service, myself, and the president was six single-spaced typed pages of ten-minute intervals and took three vans, my Chevy, seven embassy staff, and a dedicated unit of the Oslo police. It went off without a hitch.

From my diary notes:

May 28, President Carter and I blithely wander around the field above Akershus Fortress looking for the sculpture that is supposed to be there, given to Norway by the Carter Center to memorialize the Oslo Accords. We zigzag and there is no sign of it. Secret service agents uninterested in helping. Found it. Called *Marriage,* an L shape of black steel.[170]

Better luck at the meetings with PM and others. A big pledge of money for Carter Center programs on river blindness, etc., in Africa.

Dinner in honor of Carter and Rosalynn at Residence...dessert interrupted by son Karl wailing on his battery-powered toy guitar on the upstairs landing. Rosalynn says, "This makes the dinner memorable."

May 29, with President Carter in the VIP room at airport waiting for his plane and Dalai Lama walks in. Carter greets him with a big hug. He asked Carter to help with Chinese on setting up meeting. Carter said yes, when he saw a change in China, meaning when Deng dies. Noted to DL we met at dinner in his honor given by Donna Shalala at the chancellor's house at UW in Madison in late '80s. Send cable reporting DL meeting.

MEETING THE MARINE CORPS COMMANDANT

From my diary of May 31, 1996: Meeting with General Charles C. Krulak, commandant of the Marine Corps. My briefing memo from Lee Wakefield (Major Lee Wakefield, Marine Corps attaché) notes Krulak's father was a distinguished Marine Corps leader who served in WWII, Korea, and Vietnam and helped design the landing craft used on D-Day. The navy PT (patrol torpedo boat), captained by John F. Kennedy, helped evacuate Krulak's force from the Choiseul Raid in 1943 in a surprise diversionary attack on the Japanese in the Solomon Islands. To repay Kennedy, Krulak promised a bottle of whiskey, which he delivered when Kennedy was president of the United States. I enjoyed dinner at Oslo's Government Guest House, hosted by General Solli, Norway's chief of defense.

CHAPTER 31
JUNE 1996

DINNER ON THE ROYAL YACHT WITH HIS MAJESTY

The most special event with His Majesty was a summer evening reception June 4 for ambassadors on the royal yacht, *Norge*.[171] I wore my double-breasted blue wool blazer and yellow tie patterned with small sailboats. I was going for the jaunty nautical look.

We were tendered out to the gleaming, white-hulled yacht, which is anchored in the Oslo harbor, and greeted by The King with a big smile and a handshake. Standing by were cadets of the Norwegian Navy offering champagne. A tour of the ship introduced a grand vessel, brass shined, the teak deck buffed to a mirror, and technically up to date, its age belied as it was completely rebuilt after a fire in 1985.

The 265-foot yacht was built in 1937 in England and used as a convoy escort during WWII. In 1947, it was purchased through donations from the Norwegian people and presented to King Haakon on his 75th birthday—certainly a gesture of gratitude for his valiant leadership of Norway through the war and occupation, but also as a very practical way of bringing The King to the people, as 90 percent of the population lives near a fjord with a harbor. And it is a unifying symbol of the shared history of a people, much like the *USS Constitution* in Boston harbor.

THE CHAIRMAN OF THE JOINT CHIEFS OF STAFF PAYS A VISIT

I had been practicing pronouncing "Shalikashvili." When I met the chairman of the Joint Chiefs of Staff at the airport June 10, the general's name tripped off my tongue and there was a big smile.

John Shalikashvili was born "stateless" on June 27, 1936. His parents were both refugees—his father, Dmitri Shalikashvili, was an aristocratic Georgian nationalist who fought the Soviets and emigrated to Poland. There he met Maria, a refugee from St. Petersburg, Russia. In 1944, the family fled to Germany in a cattle car as the Soviet Army advanced. After the war, the family came to the United States and settled in Peoria, Ill.

"I've never been a citizen of any other country except the United States," the general said in an interview in 1995.[172] He was the first foreign-born and first draftee to become chairman of the Joint Chiefs.

The first night, Barbara and I hosted a dinner at the Residence for the general and his wife, Joan. It was a rare intimate gathering as it was only the five senior embassy staff and spouses. Informal, no program, laughing. In my welcoming toast, I noted the general and I had the same start to our Army careers—we were both drafted.

During a packed three-day schedule, I was with him to meet the PM and the foreign minister at a lunch hosted by the minister of defense, escorted him to an audience with His Majesty at the Palace, and a half-day briefing on the Norwegian Army's vaunted Telemark Battalion. The chief of defense, General Solli, hosted a dinner that included Barbara and Joan. The last afternoon there was a three-hour boat tour of the Oslo Fjord, a chatty wine-sipping excursion enlivened by Barbara and Joan, with dinner onboard.

On the boat, John Shalikashvili was a happy guy—ebullient and mellow from the elixir that is a sunny summer day in Oslo, Norway. After three days together we were like long-lost friends reunited.

June 12, I said goodbye at the airport, and it was wheels up at 4 p.m.

CIA DIRECTOR IS A BULL IN A CHINA SHOP

From my diary notes: June 12, called John Deutch (head of CIA) last night with concerns of Siri Bjerke (deputy foreign minister) with the way his upcoming trip had evolved into "a big show like some head of state visit." Deutch was miffed. "I don't have to come at all. Not my priority. If Kosmo doesn't want his money I've been fighting for, fine." ("Money" refers to U.S financial support for Norwegian intelligence operations.) I said, he wants you to come, be successful, form a personal relationship. Deutch an arrogant type. He expressed no sense that he was to be a guest.

June 17, went to see Morten about the Deutch visit to make sure he knew details and that it was to be low profile and make sure he knew itinerary and potential for Russian reaction. Told FM (Foreign Minister Godal) about it last week. Have ascertained that Kosmo gave personal OK for CIA plane to land at Kirkenes on the Russian border. But it would be a small jet, not the airliner with CIA on it in huge letters sitting on the runway in Oslo.

Deutch arrived with a full entourage of agents and attendants. He insisted on bringing people without the right security clearance into his briefing by Norwegian intelligence, so they limited the briefing and held back on the top-secret stuff. I stayed out of the briefing. Let Kosmo tell me the story. He did.

When later there was talk in Washington that Deutch was being considered for Sec. Defense if Perry left, Kosmo called me and said, "If this becomes serious, I want you to call the president and tell him we can't work with this [person]." (The historical record need not be burdened with the actual colorful words used by Kosmo to characterize Deutch.)

On December 6, at the 50th anniversary of the Home Guard, there was a large banquet at Akershus. Yesterday, the president announced new Cabinet members for his second term. He nominated Madeleine Albright for Sec. State and (Republican senator from Maine) William Cohen for Sec. Defense. General Solli (chief of defense) and Kosmo cornered me and made a point of telling me how happy they were that Deutch didn't get the Defense job or "anything else."[173]

THE AMBASSADOR GETS A REPORT CARD

I did not know an ambassador got a report card. It is called an Inspector's Evaluation Report, which is part of an in-depth look at an embassy's operations by the State Department Office of Inspector General.

Embassy Oslo's took place from June 17 to June 28, 1996. Retired State Department veteran Ambassador Robert E. Barbour led the inspection team.

I must have bamboozled Bob because he gave me an evaluation that made my mother blush. Here it is:

Ambassador Loftus has the presence that comes from public life. He projects confidence in himself, in his abilities, and knowing where he wants his mission to go, how it should go about getting there, and what the public dimensions are.

His manner is a mixture of seriousness, warmth, wit, and of command of his subject, a command that comes from doing his homework. I have not heard him deliver a speech, which he does often, but I suspect that if I did, it would be short and purposeful, sprinkled with homely examples and delivered with a captivating casualness that would sound extemporaneous but whose polishing might have kept him up much of the night before.

This 129-person mission has two agendas. The first is synthesized in a well-focused Mission Program Plan that has drawn praise from the State Department and which was used by the Ambassador as the basis for a town meeting, which is a meeting with all staff.

The second is the protection and support of a large, unusual and very important security relationship. Unlike the sections and agencies, which are driven by one or the other of these agendas, Ambassador Loftus is driven by both, and he and the Deputy Chief of Mission are the only two in the Mission who bring both agendas together. Like other skiers, he is sometimes on one ski and sometime on the other, but usually he is working to keep both together and in parallel.

How? He has a busy schedule, does a lot of travel around the country (much of it military), sees a lot of Norwegians, hosts many visitors, entertains a good deal, and is active in public diplomacy. He has good civil and military contacts in the government, can see the Prime Minister when he needs to, and is in touch with party politicians. Embassy officers say it was his personal intervention with people like these that persuaded Norway to pick up several multi-million-dollar tabs.

He uses his staff well and invites them to use him, be it substantially or ceremonially. He lets the staff use his residence to entertain or roll Easter eggs. Relations with his DCM are close, cordial, and informal. In both personal and professional contexts. Ambassador Loftus describes himself as his DCM's mentor. He is also a mentor to his officers. When this year's budget dust had settled, he showed this care for his people by going through the embassy to thank all, especially the Norwegian staff, for their patience and understanding.

And, he uses his contacts. When Value Added Tax refunds ran into a Norwegian Government snag, Ambassador Loftus issued a friendly ultimatum directly to the Ministers of Finance and Foreign Affairs. 'It's our money,' he said, 'and we want it back.'

Public diplomacy comes naturally. Interviews, speeches, visits with students, and delegations are on almost every page of his calendar. Like Americans, the sympathetic Norwegian public was bewildered and shocked when the U.S. Government went out of business last winter. Norway wanted reassurance. Ambassador Loftus provided it—on radio, on TV, and in print. And, when at last the embassy reopened and visa lines re-formed, there he was serving coffee to those in the queue.

Charged by the President to go and sell, Ambassador Loftus took up residence in a country rich in oil income and thirsty for big ticket defense items. Leading an energetic high-profile multi-agency sales effort, he has pushed millions of dollars of sales in the right direction. But possibilities are more than military. Every governor in the U.S. has received a letter from him describing a range of business possibilities in Norway and inviting him or her to visit Oslo, where the embassy will introduce them, provide assistance, and offer hospitality.

Nuclear-waste clean-up in northern Russia, 'all those rusting submarines' brings together a whole basket of public and private U.S. interests in several large projects he was instrumental in creating.

The inspection finds little to take exception to in Ambassador Loftus's way, goals or management. He has town meetings, he participates in events organized by the embassy recreation association, and he eats in the cafeteria, but it would still be well for him to visit more with lower-ranking embassy staff, American and Norwegian, and, when he can, to include them and the Marines in events at his residence.

He should write more, for no one else sees the people he sees or has his perspective, and he should have more ruminative, non-operational exchanges with Norwegians who think about the future.

But when it comes to doing his job, his sureness of purpose, self-confidence, command of his subject and his ability to project are powerful tools. He uses them well.

Relations with Norway are in good hands.[174]

WALKING THE PATH WITH A SABOTEUR WHO BLEW UP HITLER'S ATOMIC DREAM

On February 27, 1943, nine Norwegians saboteurs skied from their hideout on the Hardangervidda, the wild mountain plateau covering much of Telemark, to the hydroelectric plant at Vemork where the heavy water needed for a Nazi atomic bomb was produced, climbed down an ice-covered cliff, crossed a small river, crawled up another cliff, snuck in the plant like cat burglars, placed explosives at the tank of heavy water, set the timer and got out.

Behind them as they skied away, they heard the explosion. Hitler's bomb water was now a big puddle on the plant floor. Some made it to Sweden, some back to the mountains to hide out, but one of them, Claus Helberg, decided to go to Oslo to be hidden by the Norwegian Resistance.

When he thought the coast was clear, he went back to the commandos' hideout on the plateau, but as he arrived at this cabin, he was ambushed by a German ski patrol. He out-skied all of them except one he shot in a gunfight. Then he skied off a small cliff and broke his shoulder. He made it to the town of Dalen. He convinced the Germans there he was working for them, and they took him to a doctor and then to a hotel where, of all people, Josef Terboven, the head of the German occupation, came that day for lunch and sat down near Helberg.

Terboven asked a pretty Norwegian girl to join him. She wouldn't and said her father was in the Resistance, and she was proud of it. Terboven ordered every Norwegian in the hotel arrested and sent to Grini prison camp.

On the bus to the camp, Helberg smashed through the door, fell out on to the road, broke the same shoulder again, got up and ran, and was hit in the back by a thrown grenade. But it did not explode. He made it to Sweden.

Barbara and I had been invited to the hydro plant to walk the path taken the night the heavy water was destroyed.[175] Claus Helberg would be our guide. Claus was 77. Still leading-man handsome. Chiseled cheekbones and a full head of wavy silver-gray hair. I had met Claus before, as he was a guest at the Residence for a few receptions, but we never got to talk much, and on the invitation list, he would be identified as the former head of the Norwegian Trekking Association.[176] Founded in 1866, the association's more than 200,000 members pay a small fee to keep up the trails and mountain cabins for hikers and to promote tourism.

After college in Bergen, Claus returned to Telemark where he was born and grew up and became a mountain guide and ski instructor. In 1938, the association enlisted him in its efforts to promote tourism in Telemark.

For most Norwegians, he was the living symbol of outdoor life: the architect of the nationwide system of hiking trails marked with the small pyramids of smooth stones with one painted red on top. Claus was always pictured in the mountains, with a pack on his back, slim and fit, the horizon clear—perhaps on Gaustatoppen, the highest mountain in Telemark, which is very close to Rjukan, where Claus was born. Vemork, the hydroelectric plant where Hitler's heavy water was being produced, is 4 miles up the road from Rjukan.

We met on June 21 at the museum at the hydroelectric plant still owned and operated by Norsk Hydro. When this plant opened in 1911, its main purpose being to fix nitrogen for the production of fertilizer, it was the world's largest power plant. Norsk Hydro, now one of the world's largest producers of aluminum and fertilizer, was our host.[177]

Norsk Hydro is a publicly traded company, with the Norwegian government being the major shareholder, ensuring that control of this strategic company would never be in foreign hands.

It was a clear day, and now in June 1996, the sun could reach the bottom of the steep-sided, very narrow valley which becomes a gorge at the plant site. The plant is at the bottom of a waterfall that is no longer there. It has been channeled into dozens of large pipes to force the water to fall at an accelerated speed.

Before we started our walk along the marked trail, Claus wanted to make clear to us who they were that night: Under their white coveralls, they wore British Army uniforms. They were part of the Allied forces. Because of his local knowledge, Claus had determined the route they would use to get to the plant from the hideout and the way out.

On our walk, he pointed out the spot where they took off their skis to proceed on foot. The place of the final check to see if all had their cyanide pills. The conduit opening for cables into the building where the three who would plant the explosives squeezed through. He listed who went in and who watched guard. And he described where they were when they heard the muffled explosion as they skied away.

At the end, after I told him my grandfather came to the United States from Telemark, from a farm on the road between Dalen and Rjukan, he wanted to know that history. And when I told him Barbara and I had hiked on the association trails on the Hardangervidda, he started right in telling me things that I, almost a native son, needed to know about Telemark today.[178] Claus was a one-man chamber of commerce for Telemark.

For the last stop of the day, we traveled the short distance to Gaustatoppen to go to the top. Inside the mountain, there is a tram that runs through a tunnel to the summit. This tramway, once imagined to transport skiers to the top and promote tourism, was built by NATO.[179]

It was used for NATO radio communications for 40 years. No longer needed, the tram was fulfilling the original dream of carrying hikers and skiers. Another boon for tourism in Telemark.

I left Claus feeling that I now had some real responsibility to sing the praises of my grandfather's place of birth and come back to Telemark many more times.

THE WEDDING OF AMBASSADOR PETER GALBRAITH AT THE RESIDENCE, WITH HOUSE GUESTS PROFESSOR JOHN KENNETH AND CATHERINE GALBRAITH

Peter Galbraith, America's first ambassador to the newly independent Croatia, was getting kudos for his hands-on help in ending post-independence ethnic strife with the Serb minority.[180] He was already well known before this posting for spiriting out of northern Iraq 14 tons of captured Iraqi secret police documents detailing the atrocities that Saddam Hussein had committed against the Kurds. This swashbuckling happened in 1992 when he was senior staff on the Senate Foreign Relations Committee.

We had become fast friends. He had his eye on running for office in Massachusetts one day, and since I was the only one in the ambassador group that had been elected (nine campaigns and eight wins) and was handy, we had tutorials.

Peter called me in early June and said he would be coming to Norway to be married on June 29. He had met a Norwegian aid worker during the Balkan wars and...

"Say no more. You must have the wedding at the Residence. You'd have to hock your Harvard class ring and get a second mortgage to afford the champagne and a dinner and reception at a hotel in Oslo."

"OK, can my parents stay with you?"

Peter Galbraith was 10 in 1961 when President Kennedy sent his father, Harvard economics Professor John Kenneth Galbraith, to India as the United States ambassador. Young Peter wasn't enthused and in a conversation between Professor Galbraith with the president this was mentioned. JFK wrote a letter to Peter:

The White House, March 28, 1961

Dear Peter,

I learn from your father you are not very anxious to give up your school and friends for India. I think I know a little about how you feel. More than twenty years ago our family was similarly uprooted when we went to London where my father was ambassador. My younger brothers and sisters were about your age. They had, like you, to exchange old friends for new friends.... I think of the children of the people I am sending to other countries as my junior peace corps. You and your brothers will be helping your parents do a good job for our country and you will be helping yourself by making many friends. I think this is perhaps what you will enjoy most of all.

My best wishes.

Sincerely yours,
John Kennedy

I a little wish I were going also[181]

Apparently, Peter got over this youthful reluctance to explore foreign lands.

Right after I hung up the phone, I faxed the invitation to his father and his mother Catherine (Kitty) to stay at the Residence. The acceptance arrived shortly and JKG asked what he could bring. "Please bring your book *Ambassador's Journal.* I will give you a copy of my book."[182]

I had read JKG's *The Affluent Society* (1958) and *The New Industrial State* (1967). I pondered on the spot (where else would one ponder) if I had also read his *Ambassador's Journal* (1969). I couldn't remember. What I remembered was the wit with which he wrote.

I had met JKG when a fellow at the Institute for Politics at the Kennedy School in 1991. He came to one of our Tuesday lunches, and after our opening glass of sherry, he talked on the subject of the day with such erudition that I can no longer remember the subject.

Fleetingly, I thought about the bed in the guest room. JKG was 6'7". Would he fit? He must have this figured out by now.

What did we talk about? The Residence of course. JKG: "Don't let the bean counters at State try to pull a fast one and try to sell this icon of America." Barbara and Kitty compared experiences on running a household where they were hostess, staff director, and mother.

Barbara was known for her mastery of the dinner party. Close friends addressed her as the ambassadress.

Kitty had written of her experience as ambassador's wife in India in *Atlantic Monthly*. In this piece, she recounts the list of guests as a remarkable parade of the fabled and the glamorous (Angie Dickinson!).[183]

We talked a lot about the experience of hosting first ladies— Hillary Clinton in Norway and Jackie Kennedy's famous trip to India in March 1962. JKG and I learned we both worried most of the time about what could go wrong during the trips.[184]

We exchanged books. JKG had signed my copy and gone through it to mark for me the places where he had observations on being an American ambassador and his dim view of the State Department: "I had no instructions but one should use what freedom he has." "An embassy is rather like a state government—it is organized to function with good leadership, in the absence of leadership and in spite of it." The State Department is "a leader of the status quo."

On Secretary of State Dean Rusk, JKG wrote: "He is a traditionalist and thinks because foreign policy was bad under Truman and bad under Eisenhower it should be at least mediocre under Kennedy."

When I read, or reread, the *Ambassador's Journal* it was with hindsight. The subheading *A Personal Account of the Kennedy Years*, tells the tale. It was to be a collection of letters to the president from India, but it needed more context and explanation of these years when there was turmoil seemingly everywhere: India's border war with China in the Himalayas, the Bay of Pigs, the Cuban Missile Crisis, and the birth pangs of Vietnam.

On Vietnam, JKG in his letters to the president urged him not to enter into a war; he did not carry the day. It is hard to read the book knowing of the bright light and brief life of JFK and of the war that would come.

Shortly after he returned from Oslo, JKG wrote a thank you letter that I will always cherish. (Kitty wrote a separate letter to Barbara.)

> *Our time in Oslo was the beginning of a friendship that I am sure will endure...I am writing you Tom particularly because I want to say a special word about the book (*The Art of Legislative Politics*)...I have now read it through and I am better informed on Wisconsin politics than anyone outside the State and I judge many therein. You should not doubt that it is well written and exceedingly well informed as to history (the detail is marvelous)... there is your marvelous memory of incident, agreement and*

conflict and the good lessons you draw therefrom. All this brings me to your next book....

The letter went on to urge me to write another book with my advantage of not being from Washington: "There has been little expression of this sort from the mid-west and almost none from the La Follette and Wisconsin purview which we are reminded once dominated the American political scene..." He added that he would open doors to secure a national publisher.

What can I say other than thank you, Peter, for bringing your mother and dad into our life.

CHAPTER 32
AUGUST 1996

A GARDEN ADVENTURE IN DINING, CALIFORNIA STYLE

The invitation was to the ambassador's Residence for a "Summer Garden Adventure in Dining, California Style." "Some of Norway's finest chefs have composed a typical California wine country menu inspired by superb California wine and the best of Norwegian ingredients."

Music by Hot Club de Norvège. (Dear reader, FYI the hottest jazz quartet in the kingdom.) The distributors of California wines in Norway would contribute to the expenses and provide the wine. The chefs' talents would be sponsored by their restaurants.

The organizing of this August 20 gala was magnificently done by Barbara, my assistant Sue Meyer, and the director of protocol May-Britt Ivarson. The management of the chefs and the serving was conducted maestro-like by Anne-Lise, the Residence chef. Not an easy task given the small kitchen with no warming drawers. Extra help and more wine glasses were needed. Purchased from IKEA: 75 red wine glasses and 75 white wine glasses.

The food and wine writers from the daily newspapers would be guests and write about the event. *Aftenposten* would send its own photographer. A reporter for the national television network, NRK, would film a segment for their cooking show. *Mat & Drikke* (Food and

Drink) magazine would do a photo feature with recipes.

Seventy-five guests in all from the leading restaurants and hotels. There were the big players—Radisson SAS hotels—and the small, including the idyllic hotel Hardanger Gjestegard on the Hardanger Fjord near Bergen, only an inlet away from Lofthus.

The smartly dressed guests arrived and each seemed in their own spotlight in the sun-splashed evening. There was a table candelabra at each of the ten tables graciously loaned for the event by Blom restaurant. There were five courses, each paired with an American wine. Before each course, I introduced the chef and he or she then described the food they had prepared.

The menu:

Grilled Aurland Saltwater Crayfish with Ginger and Lime paired with Mondavi Coastal Sauvignon Blanc 1994

Boudin of Lobster, Scallops, and Prawns served with Lobster Fumet and Beurre Blanc paired with Grgich Hills Chardonnay 1994

Grilled Tenderloin of Rabbit with Gorgonzola Cream and Roast Polenta paired with Clos du Val Zinfandel 1992

Lightly Cured Breast of Duck paired with Beringer Cabernet Sauvignon 1993

Peach and Vanilla Cobbler with Hazelnut Ice Cream paired with Far Niente Dolce 1992

Total wine glasses used 400. Breakage zero.

Barbara and I tried to dress in a California glam style. She succeeded. One of the many photos in the press was of her in a sunshine-yellow pantsuit with the chefs in their whites lined up behind.

Note to future ambassadors: You want to sell wine? Serve it with class to those in the business of serving it. And you will get a thank you note like this:

August 29, 1996

Mrs. & Mr. Loftus,

Thank you very much for the fantastic experience it was to be your guests. We appreciate it immensely! We have already purchased American wine! It was a great event with a good director. We got to know many nice people, and we thoroughly enjoyed ourselves the entire time. It was also amazing that you could remember our names among all the people you meet constantly.

It was really great!

You are welcome to visit us!

Sincerely, Torild and Per Mælen, Hardanger Gjestegard[185]

VISITING A RUSSIAN RESEARCH SHIP IN SVALBARD

We left Oslo at 2:30 p.m. in bright sunshine August 22 and at 9:30 p.m., still in bright sunshine, started the approach to the Longyearbyen Airport on Spitsbergen. Out of the window, I marveled again at the shoreline of cliffs of sheer ice and the snow-capped mountains. On the descent to the runway the plane passed low over the harbor.[186]

There, anchored close in, was a small ship painted bright blue and flying the Russian flag. This is the Arctic research vessel *Professor Logachev*. I had been invited to visit this ship on a trip organized by our new defense attaché, Captain Bob Paleck. A Naval officer who was a submariner. Bob was the continuation of the practice of posting a submariner as the attaché in Oslo. This was also a chance for Bob and me to get to know each other and for me to introduce him to the life of the ambassador.

We were staying at the historic Funken Lodge Hotel. My practice was to learn the history of a hotel in Norway—I was in enough of them—and to my pleasant surprise this hotel started as the housing built in 1906 for the miners of the Boston-based Arctic Coal Company. The company was owned by American John Munro Longyear; thus comes the name Longyearbyen (byen means city). The company had American administration, but mostly Norwegian laborers.

Coal was transported the three-fourths of a mile from the mine to the port using an aerial tram. The structure is still there, a historic marker. This company was bought from Longyear by a coal company started and owned by the Norwegian government in 1916.

Eighty years later, here we are. The history of the hotel is a cultural and sociological chronicle of how men and women workers over the decades were both separated and accommodated. The rebuilding after it was flattened by an avalanche in 1953. And the lodge's evolution from housing for coal miners to a first-class hotel 78 degrees north of the equator.[187]

The *Professor Logachev* had been contracted for by a consortium of American academics for some specific research on the seabed. The captain explained that leasing the ship to researchers was one of the purposes of this quite new and sophisticated ship. With a shrug and a bit of a sad face, he offered that this was almost all of the business since after the Cold War, when money from Moscow had dried up.

The ship is 337-feet long, carried a crew of 29, and could accommodate up to 12 scientists. The information brochure offered in English was best read between the lines. "...the ship carries out searches for different types of minerals and raw materials, as well as sunken objects, on continental shelves and abyssal zones (depths of 10,000 to 20,000 feet). The undertaking of marine seismic investigations is one of the main activities."

The captain said it was an honor to have the American ambassador on board and to have this wonderful cooperation with scientists from the United States. "Please report our availability." I asked Bob if he had ever been to Svalbard before. He said, "Only in a sub."

NORWAY IN THE BIG LEAGUE AT OFFSHORE NORTHERN SEAS

You can say about Norway that the planes run on time. After hosting a lunch August 26 at the Residence for famous U.S. economist Lester Thurow of MIT, I was at the airport and on the plane to Stavanger by 4 p.m. for a packed schedule at Offshore Northern Seas.

This large international conference, which included a trade show, started as a meeting place for the oil and gas companies that pioneered exploration and the development of the North Sea basin.

The important American event would be a dinner in honor of Lucio A. Noto, chairman and CEO of Mobil Oil. I would give the "takk for maten" (thanks for the meal speech).

The next day HM King Harald and PM Gro Brundtland would stop at the American pavilion in the convention hall and I would be there to greet them. And then a lunch hosted by the mayor of Stavanger with HM the guest of honor.

Mobil Norway was headed by Maury Devine, a real friend and ally of the embassy. She was a presence in Oslo, with her own diplomatic duties, the big event being Mobil's sponsorship of the Bislett Games, one of the Golden Four meets in track and field (Berlin, Brussels, Oslo, and Zurich).

Track and field had become a premier summer sport for Norwegian athletes after Grete Waitz took track and field by storm, winning and setting the world record at the 1979 New York City Marathon, which she went on to win nine times; in 1984, she won an Olympic silver medal and five times she was the world cross-country champion. The list goes on and on.

Maury called to give me the scoop on Mr. Noto. "After the first handshake he will say, 'Call me Lou.' He was my mentor, and I was his protege. His trust in me made me the highest-ranking woman in the company."

Maury sent me the profile of Lou in *The New York Times* when he took over Mobile Norway.[188] "He's the Brooklyn-born son of the leader of a union local comprising mostly Italian immigrants. He rose through the ranks at Mobil in planning and marketing, rather than winning acclaim with big finds in the exploration division. And he made his reputation not in this country but overseas."

We shared a birthday, April 24. His ideal escape: "Driving an Italian sports car on the autostrada to lunch at a restaurant in a small Italian city." He played golf. Drove a 1958 Lancia. Went to Notre Dame. We shook hands and he said, "Call me Lou."

In my "takk for maten," I praised Maury, telling the story of sitting with her at the finish line at the Bislett games, and noted how Italian immigrants and Norwegian immigrants had helped make America America.

When His Majesty came by the American stand to greet me and shake hands he was beaming. Many times I had seen his smile, and this was a record-breaker.

Perhaps it was that now so many Norwegian companies were represented—engineering, consulting, insurance, and Statoil, the Norwegian State oil company, now the big player. Not at all like this event as it was at the start when there were so many Texas companies in Stavanger that the conference was like a meeting of the Houston Chamber of Commerce.

CHAPTER 33
SEPTEMBER 1996

RICHARD HOLBROOKE COMES TO OSLO

The guests were the feast at the dinner for Richard Holbrooke. I'll get to that.

Richard Holbrooke was back in Oslo September 4-6, 1996, and was very welcome. Now a private citizen, he had left his post as assistant secretary for European affairs at the State Department in February, a few weeks after Madeleine Albright had been named secretary of state. Holbrooke would give a speech to the Norwegian Atlantic Committee on the Baltics and the Balkans at the Nobel Peace Prize Center.

Had Ernest Hemingway lived during the Vietnam War and been there as a journalist, he would have known Holbrooke at the start of his career—a 26-year-old Foreign Service officer alone in the jungle running a pacification operation in a garrisoned village—and writing at night in his diary that this was madness. He would have made Richard Holbrooke the protagonist of a novel. War, wives, writing—it was all there.

The first time I met Holbrooke was in Bonn at a NATO ambassadors meeting in early 1994. He was the American ambassador to Germany. His real job was being Richard Holbrooke; it showed, and I loved this about him on the spot.

It was after dinner at the ambassador's Residence and he was sitting on a couch with Kati Marton, who was introduced as a foreign correspondent and biographer. They were enamored with each other.[189]

He knew I was on the FOB list (Friend of Bill's). He said to me, "I hear Clinton said you were one of the six people who made him president." The one mystery to Holbrooke was what it was like to be the candidate in a campaign. What did it take to do this stuff? And he asked the inevitable: "What was Clinton like?" Perhaps he was already drafting the letter in his head for my signature recommending him for secretary of state.

After his ambassadorship in Germany, Holbrooke took charge of the European section at State. First thing, he called a Nordic ambassadors meeting in Stockholm (April 21-23, 1995).

We had never before met in this grouping: Norway, Sweden, Finland, Denmark, and Iceland. He said, "This is so you know each other, visit each other, and when someone is on vacation, take your family to their place for your vacation."

Get support from your governments for expansion of NATO for Poland, Hungary, and Czechoslovakia. Work to get the Baltics in any Western institution you can. How to do it? "You're smart. You got this far. You'll figure it out." This all happened at the hotel bar.

He spoke free of jargon in measured words honed over decades.

He came to Oslo often, and like many others, he had dreams of the Nobel Peace Prize. There were other Americans dreaming of the prize who also often found a reason to be in Oslo.

I would explain to all that neither the prime minister, the foreign minister, nor His Majesty had a say in the matter, even though the members of the Prize Committee each represented one of the political parties.

But I did my best for them all by making sure they met socially with Geir Lundestad, the director of the Nobel Institute. Geir did not have a vote but he did set the agenda.

Geir was a Ph.D. historian whose publications included *Empire by Invitation?* and *Beyond the Cold War.* He delighted in talking to Holbrooke. A historian is like a journalist with more complex questions—looking for the footnote, not the quote.

I took my cues from Holbrooke on the newly independent Baltic States. By 1996, the Dayton Accords a year in the rear-view mirror, he had thought things through, and in his speech in Oslo in September 1996, he talked about the Baltics.[190]

He claimed to the audience, "Our wonderful Ambassador Tom Loftus suggested that I throw away the text and talk from my own experiences and from my heart about the Baltics and the Balkans." Now, it is one of the older tricks in the book to say you are throwing away your prepared remarks, get the audience thinking they are going to hear something special, and then proceed to give the prepared remarks.

True, I said a rehash of NATO expansion would be a waste of his time; his view on the Baltics would be the item of great interest in Norway.

"The end of the Cold War at this point looks more like the interwar period or even the 19th century at times. The challenge is to deal with the old problems that have returned. Settle them so we can deal with the new problems."

He noted he had reorganized the European Bureau at State, creating a Nordic/Baltic Bureau taking Estonia, Latvia, and Lithuania out of the grouping of former Soviet satellites. "(F)unction ends up following form. So a small bureaucratic change over time can create new ways of thinking...and that was my hope."[191]

Norway, Sweden, and Finland need to take the lead in helping the economies of the Baltics, he said, and, "to bring the values of free enterprise, democracy and human rights..."

"We look of course to Oslo for a leadership position." Sounded like a policy that would work for me.

After his talk, we met with Foreign Minister Bjørn Tore Godal and Minister of Defense Jørgen Kosmo, who was so gracious as to come to the Foreign Ministry to help our tight schedule, then we met with Prime Minister Gro Harlem Brundtland and the speech was history. It was time for the dinner.

The guests included: Geir Lundestad, director of the Nobel Institute; the leaders of three of the political parties: Labour, Progress, and Socialist Left; the youth party leaders of the Labour, Center, and Conservative parties; the head of the most prominent publishing house in Norway; the senior foreign affairs journalists; the ambassador of Lithuania, Kornelija Jurgaitienė; Chargé D'Affaires of Estonia Tiit Naber; and three polar explorers: Liv Arnesen, Erling Kagge, and Børge Ousland.[192]

At my table were Holbrooke; Geir Lundestad; Deputy Foreign Minister Siri Bjerke; Ambassador Jurgaitienė; Carl I. Hagen, leader of the Progress Party and bad boy of Norwegian politics;[193] and publisher William Nygaard, who published Salman Rushdie's novel *The Satanic Verses*, was subjected to the Ayatollah Khomeini's fatwa and was shot three times outside his house in Oslo in October 1993.

The before-dinner, dinner, and after-dinner conversations? I mean how many times do you get to chat with someone who has skied to the South Pole, North Pole, and climbed Mount Everest? The person who makes the list of possibles for the Nobel Peace Prize? The person who had the courage to publish Salman Rushdie and was shot because of it? The politician who questioned the comfortable status quo? And the ambassador from recently independent Lithuania who had a Ph.D. in American women writers from the South, subject chosen so her Soviet minders had to let her out of the country to study in Mississippi?

Holbrooke was in someone else's element, and he loved it. He wasn't the most interesting person in the room for a welcome change. Nobel Peace Prize? Certainly, some notes in the files.

The Foreign Ministry of Lithuania and Estonia received cables recounting the night with Holbrooke and his reassuring words on the Baltics' future.

Holbrooke and I found out we shared a birth date: April 24.

A LITTLE DANCE FOR BALTIC FREEDOM?

Mid-September is the time of the autumn equinox when temperatures start a steady decline, as do the hours of sunshine in a day. But fall is still only hinting. Sunrise is at 6:45 and sunset 7:40. On Bygdøy alle, the main avenue from downtown through the west side of Oslo, the famous horse chestnut trees that flower in springtime still have every leaf of their green canopy.

The weather in Oslo is quite pleasant. Of which I am thankful, because from September 15 straight through until October 1 there are important, some historic, events hosted by Embassy Oslo with yours truly the maître d'.

On the 15th and 16th, the American ambassadors of the Nordic and Baltic countries meet in Oslo—my colleagues from Finland, Lithuania, Latvia, Denmark, Estonia, and Iceland attend.[194] Time flies. I have been in country longer than any of the others.

Most of our time together is at the Residence. All want a look at the kitchen and to meet the chef. Thank her in advance. Size up the silverware (how many settings, not to take home as swag). Inspect the inventory of the wine cellar. And, given the size of the Residence, one or two would like to see the furnaces.

We have dinner together, lunch together, and sit around drinking coffee and discussing our view of the lay of the land in the region. Looking at my many pages of notes after the meeting, it was a freewheeling discussion but assumed Russia was gone from the Baltics and their membership in the EU and NATO were no longer pipe dreams but dreams to be realized.[195] (Sweden and Finland became members of the EU on January 1, 1995.)

The only program was at lunch the second day with Kjeld Vibe, the former longtime Norwegian ambassador to the U.S. (1989 to 1996) and Arne Olav Brundtland, the PM's husband, here with us as an expert on the political history of relations between Finland and Russia. Both insightful and delightful.

TO BERGENHUS FORTRESS AND
THE MANOR HOUSE IN ROSE VALLEY

After a press briefing on the Arctic Military Environmental Cooperation declaration by U.S. Secretary of Defense William Perry the morning of September 27, he left and Sherri Goodman, staff of the Senate Armed Services Committee, and I stayed in Bergen for briefings on Norwegian military environmental programs.

The venue for our environmental briefing was Bergenhus Fortress. A castle is inside the fortress surrounded by ramparts; the fortress has defended Bergen harbor since the 1600s. It was the Germans' western headquarters during the occupation. It houses both a museum and offices of the Norwegian military.

Our introductory session was in the castle's breathtaking Håkon's Hall, built between 1247 and 1261 by Håkon Håkonsson. It was the largest of the royal residencies in the 13th century, when Bergen was the political center of Norway.

The hall has curving ribs of oak beams that support a peaked roof, giving one the sensation of standing upside down in a Viking ship. Or, if you prefer, standing right side up inside a Viking ship turned upside down.

Adjacent to the hall is Rosenkrantz Tower (not named after the pal of Guildenstern). The tower was built in the 1560s by the governor of Bergen Castle, Erik Rosenkrantz. We climbed the narrow stone stairs to the rooftop. This is the view of Bergen that will stick with you.

The castle and the hall are not to be missed in Bergen. Another thing not to be missed is Bergen fish soup. Don't try to make this at home, but if you must, try this recipe.[196]

Sherri was in Norway to learn, not advise. And when that became clear our hosts relaxed and were very enthusiastic about telling their story.

Ending ozone-depleting chlorinated fluorocarbons (CFCs) from fire-fighting systems onboard naval vessels was well under way. And, after a short boat trip to the nearby Coast Guard squadron base, we were given a demonstration of the special oil-pollution-cleanup equipment onboard Coast Guard vessels.

The good people of Bergen were not letting the American ambassador and a high-ranking official from the Pentagon get out of town without seeing Rosendal—the Rose Valley.

So, the next morning we boarded the express ferry with our guide to sail up the Hardangerfjord past waterfalls coming down the steep mountainsides. There are red barns and white farmhouses perched on the plateaus. The round-trip ticket is good for fourteen days and our guide explained that when some come here, they can't leave, as this is the place on earth to stop and smell the roses.

The grandeur of Norway just cannot be captured in words or photos, only in paintings, especially those of Johan Christian Dahl and the duo of Hans Gude and Adolph Tidemand. A print of their painting *Bridal Procession on the Hardangerfjord* hangs in many a home of Americans of Norwegian descent. My favorite is *Midsummer Eve Bonfire* by Nicolai Astrup.

Then we are among the roses in the renaissance garden of the Barionet Rosendal, "the Manor House from 1665 between fjord, mountains, glaciers and waterfalls," where we had lunch.

"Our chef serves coffee and cake in the Tea Room, light lunches in Rosendal Greenhouse, and three- or five-course gourmet dinners in the Blue Dining Room," its website reads. "All menus are based on fresh ingredients from the newly restored Kitchen and Herb Garden in Rosendal Garden. Fresh ingredients are harvested daily throughout the season."[197]

The Manor House has been left as it was in 1927—a home expecting the return of the family. The library of books from the 17th century are all there, and the sitting room with walls painted red patiently waits to receive callers on the baron.

PLANES, TRAINS, AND DINNER WITH DEFENSE MINISTER KOSMO

The morning of September 30 Sherri Goodman, the American undersecretary of defense for environmental security, and I were off to Gardermoen, the site of the new airport to serve Oslo that would open in a year. It was to be environmentally state-of-the-art in everything from aircraft pollution control to the material comprising the coffee cups.

The big deal was the big tunnel that was being bored through a solid rock stretch of hilly terrain in the countryside to allow a direct rail link to arrive inside the new airport from Central Station in downtown Oslo. The goal was that 70 percent of traffic to and from the airport would be by this train, other connecting interurban trains, and express bus routes.

Gardermoen was the first military airport and was the main airport for the Germans during the occupation. It was then small, with a control tower and a few hangers and barracks. It had been built up over the years to such an extent that when international flights started to use planes too big for Fornebu this became their airport.

The Norwegian Air Force squadron of C-130s was now there and would share the new airport with civilian operations. Fornebu would close and the prize real estate it sat on that jutted out into the Oslo Fjord would be converted to housing and an office park.

As we were dazzled by the slide shows, maps, and animated video of the train going through the tunnel, my thoughts turned to how much Fornebu was a part of my life and the U.S. Embassy's connection with all of Norway.

I would miss the VIP room with the hard seats and bad coffee, which was the family's first stop upon arrival in Norway. Hundreds of times had Edmund driven me the fifteen minutes to Fornebu in the Chevy to fly out, meet visitors, and drop off guests. I have a pass to flash, and the first time my mother came I was out on the runway at the bottom of the departure ramp to greet her.

Three times Her Majesty had been on my flights, escorted on as the last passenger to be ushered to her seat in the first row. Both of us off to do our day jobs.

And, the cocktail flight. When we had friends come to visit in the summers when Oslo was quiet and the government on holiday schedule, the routine was to assemble for cocktails on the terrace of the Residence at five o'clock. Promptly at 5:15, a plane would appear, ascending from Fornebu and flying west to east trailing a white plume against the clear blue sky.

Minutes before the plane came into view, I would announce that a flyover had been arranged to honor their visit. Always a good line that brightened faces and that some took for real—just for a moment.

Anyway, my thoughts as we finished at Gardermoen were back in Oslo, where it was another all-hands-on-deck day. The new head of the Nordic and Baltic Bureau, Carol van Voorst, was making her first visit to Oslo, so DCM Sharon Mercurio (DCM McCahill had left his Oslo position in January 1996) was taking her to meet those she would be working with in the government: Jonas Gahr Støre, now director of international relations in the PM's office, and Ambassador Finn Fostervoll, director for North America in the Foreign Ministry.

And I was thinking of the dinner in honor of Sherri that night with Norwegian Defense Minister Kosmo and that I must remember to have one of the maids put ashtrays on the terrace so Kosmo would know that even though there was no smoking in the Residence it was OK outside.

The guest list focused on those in and out of government with interest in nuclear waste issues surrounding the decommissioned submarines. This included Frederic Hauge, the leader of the environmental group Bellona. Not one of Kosmo's favorite dinner chums.

Sherri and Kosmo were naturals together. A working friendship was formed. Sherri had the mandate to deal with the Russians and Kosmo had the wherewithal to help her out on the social niceties in Russia through the very savvy Norwegian Consul in Murmansk.

CHAPTER 34
OCTOBER 1996

THE ROLE OF THE EMBASSY IN THE
U.S. PRESIDENTIAL CAMPAIGN

In presidential election years, U.S. embassies are charged with helping Americans living abroad to vote absentee using the Federal Voting Assistance Program[198] and hosting congressionally authorized programs designed to educate the press on such mysteries unique to the American system as the nominating process and the electoral college. The ambassador is expected to be out and about speaking to any and all interested audiences.

The Democrats Abroad and the Republicans Abroad are very helpful in all this, running their own "how to vote" campaigns. They are official arms of the political parties and send delegates to the conventions.

I had been an elector, and a delegate to four Democratic Party nominating conventions, so my value was explaining things by telling stories of the foibles of the political animal. Named names did I.

U.S. PRESIDENTIAL ELECTION IN NORWAY IS
ALL ABOUT MINNESOTA AND ROGER MOE

Not since FDR had an American president been so involved with Norway: the Oslo Accords, Hillary at the Olympics, the dinner at the

White House for the first State Visit of Their Majesties, engaging Russia on the Norwegian border to end the Cold War.

So, no surprise the press coverage of the '96 election had a very pro-Clinton bent, and there seemed no doubt about the outcome. It was a bit boring.

What would the average Norwegian reader be interested in? A legislative race in Minnesota of course. The week before the election I opened the paper and find a full-page story in *Aftenposten* featuring my dear friend state Sen. Roger Moe, who was running for reelection in his rural district.

I translated it myself—adequate at this if I knew the subject matter—and faxed it to Roger. Some excerpts:

> Roger Moe, Norwegian descended senator in Minnesota, has his strongest voter support among Indians on the reservation...Northern Minnesota has pine forests, lakes, cornfields, and a couple of Indian reservations. The Chippewa 'voted 93 percent for our party last time,' said Moe ...

> Moe is the leader of the Democratic majority in the state Senate. His grandparents immigrated from Harpefoss, Leikanger, Tjotta, and Voss ...

> The state's Governor, Arne Carlson, is Swedish...

> When Moe visits the elderly home in the little town of Clearbrook, the names in the entry are the same as those in a Norwegian telephone book ...

> In the small town of Bagley, Senator Moe faces all the questions young Americans are concerned about: what is your view on the right to abortion, should the drinking age be raised, do you support homosexual marriages, the death penalty, legalizing marijuana ...

> The mayor of Bagley, Clayton Stenersen, with family from Gudbrandsdalen, wants money for a new jail ...

> On the Indian Reservation, there is a new central point— the gambling casino. Indians have a monopoly to run casinos...

Moe says 'As history's losers the Indians have not had it easy. Our hope is that the casinos will give them an economic base'...

(Note: Roger won handily.)

SWINGING THE CLUBS IN NORWAY

What a welcome surprise. The Ministry of Foreign Affairs was hosting a golf outing October 8 for members of the diplomatic corps at the Oslo Golf Club.[199] Sign me up.

I started playing golf at age 12 when my dad bought me a set of clubs, Tommy Armour brand: a driver with a persimmon wood head, three irons, and a putter.

In our high school, it was decided to have a golf team since all the other area schools were having golf teams, and the Lions Club had spearheaded a campaign to build a Sun Prairie golf course, to open in 1962. Since I had a set of clubs, one of the criteria for trying out since the school had no clubs, I ended up on the five-man team as number five. We learned to play golf better by playing practice rounds. (In golf, they are all practice rounds.)

George Conom, our brilliant economics teacher, was pegged to be the coach. He didn't play, but was a master at coaching kids and drove us to the matches in his 1956 cream-on-brown, four-door, hardtop Buick Roadmaster.

Most of the area courses were nine holes and Monona Grove, just a few miles away, became our home course. Future two-time U.S. Open Champ Andy North would play on their team starting the year I left high school, so I never had the opportunity to be beaten by him.

We won the Madison Suburban League championship my last year. I shot a 9 over par, even bogey.

When the Sun Prairie course opened it was a big day for the town. The nine holes followed the contours of the two farm fields that were cleared, and the fairways were separated by former fence lines now studded with young oak trees. The old farmhouse was the clubhouse, where you paid Howie Knodt for your round. He ran the course, rented clubs, sold clubs, and was the pro.

Then I took golf lessons from Arnold Palmer via a 1963 *Sports Illustrated* that had a five-part series by Arnold Palmer called "My Game and Yours." It was not how to play golf but how *he* played. I adopted the full Monty right down to the knock-kneed, elbows-out putting stance.[200]

It was the same year Arnie started his own golf club company, and I bought a set from Howie. Leather grips, a driver, a two and four wood, a set of irons—2, 3, 4, 5, 6, 7, 8, 9—but no wedge.

And these were the clubs I still had that Edmund took out of the trunk of the Chevy the day of the Foreign Ministry's golf outing at the Oslo Golf Club.

This course played along the shore of Lake Bogstad on top of Holmenkollen. Drive up the mountain until the ski jump is on your right and take a left and soon there you are.

"Established 1924, it is the oldest golf club in Norway. The first golf shots were hit one autumn day in 1924. Except for the 2nd World War period, when people grew potatoes and other vegetables on the course, we have been playing golf here ever since."[201] I shot even bogey.

It had been a golf summer. My son Alec had good friends at the International School, and the fathers of two of the friends and I took our sons to Malaga, Spain, to play golf.

(I had my first-ever golf lesson at one course. He said, "Widen your stance," and charged me 50 bucks.)

And noted golf-course architect Robert Trent Jones Jr. came to Oslo to explore for a Norwegian entrepreneur the building of a destination golf course in the seaside vacation area around Kristiansand on the southern tip of Norway. I invited the two, Jones and the prospective builder of the course, for lunch, and I had an agenda.

Jones was very casual. A guy who might give you a five-foot putt in a round of friends. My interest was in the course he designed for the Sentry Insurance Company in Stevens Point, Wisconsin. It was somewhat notorious as it was uniformly concluded that it was the ego of the CEO represented in 18 holes. The signature hole was a man-made island of white flowers with a small green in the middle. It looked like a white-walled tire with a grass hubcap.

I had played the course the year it opened in 1983 with my dear friends Bill Kraus and Chan McKelvey, who had come to Madison when the chancellor of the University of Wisconsin at Stevens Point, Lee Sherman Dreyfus, was elected governor in 1978.

They were Sentry Insurance stalwarts—Bill ran the place and took care of politics and Chan ran the international business. This whole Sentry gang took over state government with a cavalier touch. "We're here now. We'll be going soon. Don't get excited." Visigoths of niceness.

I knew the CEO. In his top-floor office, three sides of which were large windows, he had a large telescope on a tripod to look out over the course.

Jones said I had the whole thing pegged right. But it was an easy course to build because the land was quite malleable. (Portage County, where Stevens Point is the county seat, is sand covered by a thin layer of topsoil. It was the potato-growing center of the Midwest because of this.)

HELSINKI: MUSTARD ON YOUR HERRING?

Derek Shearer, ambassador to Finland, said to hop over to Helsinki October 11-13. "Mr. NATO enlargement" Ron Asmus, at the time a special consultant working for the State Department, will be there, and he is keen to catch up with his fellow Badger (we were both alumni of UW-Madison).

There was a lunch followed by a round table with Asmus holding court before an assemblage from Finland's foreign ministry, ministry of defense, academia, and think-tank types interested in NATO enlargement.

Foreign Affairs had just published an article by Asmus, "NATO and the Have-Nots: Reassurance After Enlargement."[202] A cleaned-up version of the Rand draft papers focused on the Baltics that had held my fax machine hostage earlier in the year.

Derek told me there was a rumor going around that Asmus would be appointed to a State Department position so he could officially guide the NATO enlargement policy. Since Derek was the one spreading the rumor, it was from a reliable source.

Derek had brought his hometown of LA to his diplomatic cuisine and served a California-Finland fusion menu which, dear reader, you will just have to imagine. Derek's mother had been mailing over a steady supply of Starbucks coffee beans and Toll House milk chocolate chips, essential to get the American chocolate chip cookie flavor and texture. Coffee and a cookie at the ambassador's was becoming legendary.

To my great delight, it was the weekend of the Baltic Sea Herring Festival. The harbor was filled with wooden fishing boats, the flag of

Finland fluttering in the brisk breeze from every mast and yardarm. The flag, a lake-blue cross with a snow-white background, dated only from 1918 when it was adopted upon independence from Russia.

The boardwalk was a long string of vendor tents with herring prepared every way probable. A veritable midway of herring hawkers. Pickled herring, plain or in sour cream, was a staple in our house around Christmas. But I had never had fresh herring. Grilled with a mustard sauce my winner.

PRIME MINISTER BRUNDTLAND WILL STEP ASIDE

It was a fax. "Tom, for your information. Morten."

The header on the October 23 press release was, "Change of Prime Minister in Norway." "Prime Minister Gro Harlem Brundtland announced today that as of Friday October 25, she would be succeeded as Head of the Norwegian Labour Government by the incumbent Leader of the Norwegian Labour Party, Mr. Thorbjørn Jagland."

The reason: The head of the party and the head of government should be the same person heading into the party's convention in November and the election in September 1997. "There are no other reasons, neither personal, nor political, why I have decided that the time for a change is now."

The time is now for a drink with Morten.

CHAPTER 35
NOVEMBER 1996

WE ARE ON OUR TOES HERE!

The furniture was removed. The ambassador's Residence was awash in light and beautiful people on November 16—in this case ballet dancers.

Glen Tetley, the celebrated American ballet dancer, choreographer, and teacher, was in Oslo to perform his dance interpretation of *The Tempest*, a ballet based on the Shakespearean play with music by Sibelius. Tetley was an Oslo favorite.[203]

Cultural attaché JoDell's eyes had been sparkling for weeks. This was a cultural attaché's dream. She had pirouetted from a small reception for Mr. Tetley to what was now the plan. Every member of the Norwegian National Ballet would be invited to a reception, and we could charge it to my wine cellar. Every future Nureyev and Fonteyn in town would grace the place.

Barbara and I were in our VIP seats at the Opera House at 6 p.m. for the stunningly good performance. After the standing ovation, we dashed through the rain out to the Chevy. Edmund had the doors open and the engine running, so we could quickly get back to the Residence and greet the guests.

By 8:45 the first of the 75 dancers, musicians, set designers, and choreographers arrived. Mr. Tetley and the cast came soon after.

Glen Tetley was 70 years old but fluid: He seemed to glide among the young dancers and others all evening listening and offering encouragement. No staid dark suits or cocktail dresses in this crowd. Chic, swish, hip—garb only the lithe and young can wear.

When the last guest had left JoDell looked at me and took a bow.

PM JAGLAND VISITS ESTONIA

Prime Minister Thorbjørn Jagland made his first official visit out of the country to Estonia November 19. This quote from his remarks at the dinner in his honor on November 19, hosted by Estonian Prime Minister Tiit Vähi: "NATO will continue to change with the circumstances. The Alliance remains open to democratic countries. No doors will be closed. No outside power will have a veto over NATO's own decisions."[204]

CHAPTER 36
HOSTING CELLIST AND HUMAN RIGHTS CHAMPION MSTISLAV ROSTROPOVICH

I had rushed back to the Residence from the December 9 cello performance of Mstislav Rostropovich at the Oslo Concert House immediately after the 20-minute standing ovation to be at the door to greet him.

He entered, took my hand and said, "Mr. Ambassador, vodka." And, he went right to Barbara, kissing her on one cheek, then the other and back again to the first. He entered and the room was brighter. Teeth were whiter. The guests glittered from his reflected light. Every woman would report he kissed their hand—perhaps he did.

Glasses of Russian vodka appeared. Toasts were offered. The table was a smorgasbord—a cornucopia of meats, cheeses, herring, dark breads, sliced eggs with red salmon caviar, gravlax, champagne.

The world's greatest cellist, champion of human rights in the Soviet Union, once an exile, awarded the Presidential Medal of Freedom by President Reagan, for seven years a director of the U.S. National Symphony Orchestra, and supporter of Yeltsin's democracy,[205] was quite at home in America's house in Oslo.

All the American staff and spouses at the embassy were invited to honor this friend of America, personification of civilization, and hope for the world in one beating heart.

Juri Fokine, the Russian ambassador, was my guest. He and his wife were beaming.

JoDell Shields, our wonderful cultural attaché who had put this night together, was over the moon.

Here was one of those few humans who are comets that fly above us, a streak of white light tailing them, and they make mortals look to the sky in wonderment. They come once in a lifetime. But for me this was the second time I came into the orbit of Rostropovich.

Gingerly interrupting him, daring only to take him away for a few minutes from the adoring, I told him that I was there that memorable night in West Berlin in 1985 at the concert hall when he conducted the Berlin symphony orchestra. He knew the night.

Here is that story from 1985:

Three Soviet generals, unsmiling, chests of their uniforms a confetti of ribbons and medals, walked in and took their seats in the front row just minutes before Rostropovich lifted his baton.

In 1978, Rostropovich's Russian citizenship was taken away because of his actions in support of freedom in the Soviet Union. The generals glowered at this most famous exile.[206] I'm sure they were music lovers too.

I could witness this in 1985 because in this concert hall the audience can see each other since the seats are organized in five sections that surround the stage.

My two escorts told me the symphony was about the Red Army's liberation of Berlin in 1945. It was the 40th anniversary year of this time marking the end of Hitler and Nazi Germany. Triumph for the Soviets. A horrific period for the civilian population still left in Berlin, I was to learn.[207]

If this wasn't drama enough, there was an incident during the 1985 performance. Actually, the same incident twice. The trumpet player's mute fell out after a solo. A thud. An accident. Near the end it happened again. A gasp. The concert was over and Rostropovich pointed his baton to the trumpet player and motioned he should rise. We held our breath. Rostropovich started to applaud him. The proper Berliners in the audience shed all inhibition and stood and cheered and the applause rose to a crescendo.

We had witnessed a great moment.

I had come to Berlin in 1985, when I was Speaker of the Wisconsin Assembly, on a trip organized for me by the press section of the Foreign Ministry of West Germany. Their purpose was to show me, a political leader with a future (this was good to know), the Germany of today.

I visited the parliaments of a few of the 10 West German states, met with leaders of the party factions, usually then went to a lingering lunch at a stube (a tavern serving food) where friendships would be made. Gemütlichkeit is the German word describing this type of conviviality.

Wisconsin was the most German state by immigration in America. Our sister state was Hessen, and the relationship was quite robust with exchanges and trade offices. The dairy cow—about 95 percent German Holsteins—is Wisconsin's state animal.

My tour called for me to travel to Frankfurt, Munich, Hamburg, and a farm in Schleswig-Holstein on the border with Denmark. I would then be put on an American Airlines plane to fly the air corridor to Berlin, an island inside East Germany divided into West Berlin—the American, British, and French sectors—and East Berlin—the Soviet sector behind the Berlin Wall.

My escort on the first part of the trip was a vibrant woman my age whose father had died on the Eastern Front. What I learned about Germans I learned not in the meetings but from conversations with her. The guilt and need for atonement, the blessing that it was the Americans who had saved and protected West Germany, and the passion of the belief that the European Union must succeed and replace the nationalism that had plagued Europe before the war.

The governor of Hesse gave us his driver and car, an armored Mercedes, to make the scheduled rounds in Frankfurt and the capital of Wiesbaden. Upon return to his official residence, with the governor standing in the driveway to greet me, the driver got out to open the door for me and my escort. I accidentally hit the alarm in the back seat, which set off a siren and locked us in the car. Quite an entrance.

In Munich in 1985 I had lunch with Petra Kelly, the most notable young political leader in Germany of this time. She was a founding member of the national Green Party and was in the first small group of Greens elected to the West German Bundestag.[208] She was now a member of the Bavarian State Parliament. She had lived in America, graduated from American University in Washington, D.C., and had campaigned for Robert Kennedy.

Petra Kelly was a leader in the protests against nuclear weapons and protests for women's rights; she was OK with the label "eco-feminist."[209] I knew of her from following the news of the large anti-nuclear weapons protest in Germany in 1981. She was pleased to learn when I told her that in September 1982 a statewide vote in Wisconsin advocating a nuclear weapons freeze had passed by a wide margin. (In June of 1982, one million people demonstrated against nuclear weapons in New York City.)

A sunny day, we were at an outdoor cafe. Some men on the street were wearing lederhosen. She ordered for us the traditional Bavarian Weiss beer and a plate of sausages that came with a small glazed pot of brown mustard and red cabbage slaw. Most of the beer on the menu would have been offered in Milwaukee: Hofbräu, Hacker-Pschorr, Löwenbräu.

In West Berlin, there was a tour of the empty Reichstag, silently waiting for a reunited Germany when the capital would move from Bonn to be once again in Berlin, and a visit to the small building where those officers who tried to kill Hitler by placing a bomb under his desk were tortured and hung up on meat hooks.

The second day I was met at my hotel by a U.S. army corporal and driven to Checkpoint Charlie to cross into East Berlin, the Soviet sector. "Keep the window rolled up and just flash your passport to the guard."

First thing on the other side, the corporal asked me if I wanted to buy some Cuban cigars. This was not an odd question, as Cuban cigars were outlawed in the U.S. and several Americans he had given the tour wanted once again to experience the sweet aroma of this contraband.

We stopped at Humboldt University and stood over the glass plate in the sidewalk to look down on a room full of shelves but no books. This is the spot where the books of 20,000 "degenerate" authors were taken from Humbolt's library and burned in a great bonfire by the Nazis in 1933.

After a briefing by a political officer at the embassy of the United States to East Germany, it was back to West Berlin.[210] Then came the concert of the Berlin Symphony conducted by Rostropovich that I describe above.

CHAPTER 37
A NEW NATO IS BORN

A DELICATE DANCE WITH NATO

Aldri Mer ("never again") are the two words every Norwegian knows refer to the surprise invasion of neutral Norway in April 1941 by Nazi Germany and the five-year occupation that followed. Never again would this happen. It helps explain why Norway became a founding member in 1949 of NATO (North Atlantic Treaty Organization). This alliance was directed at defense against the Soviet Union and pledged each member country to be defended by all the others. In reality, this meant the defense of Western Europe by the United States.

Norway at that time was the only NATO country with a border with the Soviet Union—a border that had been defended and re-established by soldiers of the Red Army. The German war machine, from bases in north Norway, had tried for five bloody years to cross this border and take the port of Murmansk. A successful effort would choke off the only entry point in all of Russia for the war materiel that arrived in convoys of ships from America and Britain to resupply Soviet forces on the Eastern front.

When the Germans failed and retreated, burning the towns of north Norway behind them with Soviet forces in hot pursuit, it was natural to assume the Soviets would stay as occupiers. Never again, the Soviets could have declared.

But they did not. After the war they went home and closed the border, not to open it for 50 years. Thus, the Soviet Union was none too happy when Norway joined NATO. This was tacitly acknowledged by restrictions Norway put on NATO activities and infrastructure. No troops. No air bases. And no nuclear weapons on Norwegian soil.[211]

When I arrived in Norway in late 1993, the situation among the U.S., Norway, and the Soviet Union could be accurately described as this: "U.S. relations with Norway are cordial and unusually close... they have a greater depth and complexity than is generally realized. A strong NATO member, Norway sees the United States as the main guarantor of its security and does not welcome any ideas that could either dilute this guarantee or provoke Russia, with which Norway shares a common border."[212]

EXPAND NATO AND/OR A PARTNERSHIP FOR PEACE?

When the expansion of NATO to include Poland, Hungary, and the Czech Republic was getting real traction in the lead-up to the January 1994 NATO summit in Brussels, followed by the first Clinton/Yeltsin summit, the real Russian reaction started to emerge. Despite President Boris Yeltsin's kind words and proclamation of a "new Russian-Polish relationship," with Poland's President Lech Wałęsa stating that Poland had a "sovereign right" to join NATO, the word from Moscow was: "Don't do it. It will blow up the circuits of U.S.-Russian relations."

This was pretty much the view as well in the Clinton foreign policy brain trust: "(T)he Pentagon was overwhelming opposed...Les Aspin, the Secretary of Defense was opposed...his Deputy William Perry was opposed, arguing our goal should be the demilitarization of the Russian economy and the denuclearization of Ukraine." The military advisor to the State Department, Lt. General Barry McCaffrey, said, "We will get ourselves sucked into some godforsaken Eurasian quagmire."[213]

The Norwegian attitude was, and I paraphrase, "You want us to be pledged to the defense of Poland, which has no army and no money, irritate the hell out of Russia, and we will be expected to pay."

Deputy Secretary of State Strobe Talbott, a rare combination of academic, journalist, and diplomat, and a friend of Bill Clinton's from their time together as Rhodes scholars at Oxford, suggested playing down the expansion at the summit and focusing on the Partnership for Peace, Secretary of Defense Les Aspin's approach that would allow military and peacekeeping cooperation with Russia as an equal participant. OK, that was the plan.[214]

I became a champion of Partnership for Peace because it was Les' baby. As a Wisconsin congressman and chair of the Defense Committee, Aspin was a longtime friend and along with the irascible, lovable, powerful sage from northern Wisconsin, Congressman David Obey. We had been a team through many a political war. My enthusiasm for Les' plan was abetted by the fact that David was now chair of the U.S. House Appropriations Committee and had jurisdiction over the State Department's budget.

The Norwegians, especially the politician's politician Jørgen Kosmo, the defense minister, liked this a lot, as the first cooperative effort would be a naval exercise with a ship from the Russian Northern Fleet—a chance to form a relationship with the Russians on the other side of the border. He was good with the plan. An impish smile from under his mustache. He came from the ranks of union members, unlike the other political leaders of the Labour Party. He rolled his own cigarettes.

NAVAL OPERATION POMOR AND THE HISTORIC SHOT OF VODKA. NOSTROVIA!

A diary entry from March 18-22, 1994: I flew to Bodø and soon was in an orange survival suit for the helicopter ride across Vestfjorden to land with a bang on the flat patch of the aft deck of the *USS Thorn*, a Navy destroyer with a crew of 300, around nightfall. A wave was violent enough during dinner to clear the table of dishes. ...I stayed late on the darkened bridge talking to the captain...at daybreak we were at the entrance of the fjord and sailed three hours to the south before we saw the city of Tromsø and the Arctic Cathedral, a tall white A-frame structure, a Lutheran church, that can be seen from miles away. The purpose of this was a naval exercise of NATO countries that would for the first time include a Russian ship, a frigate from the Northern Fleet. ...The Russian frigate came south on water like a mirror and turned full around to tie up to the *Thorn*. ...I stood on the deck with the Russian ambassador. We had to shade our eyes from the bright sun and squint to see on the deck of the frigate. There stood a band, 20 sailors in cream-colored blouses and black sashes with accordions and brass horns, and there was Vice Admiral

Kasatonov, the No. 2 in Russia's Northern Fleet. When the ships were secured and a boarding bridge in place, the Russian ambassador was piped aboard the frigate and then I followed. Soon the American and Russian sailors were throwing snowballs and trading pins and T-shirts...the other ships were Dutch, Norwegian, and British. At lunch on the frigate, the first toast of ice-cold vodka was from the admiral to the memory of (the late foreign minister) Johan Jørgen Holst. On the table were plates of thinly sliced sausage, liver pâté, and circles of white bread heaped high with orange salmon eggs, the caviar of Norway. ...More toasts. ...I said of Holst that he was 'a believer that warm relations could be fostered in cold climates.' Then it was lemon-flavored vodka in a new glass to wake the palate and then it was strong coffee, as black as licorice, made drinkable by three cubes of Cuban sugar.

The next day the ships would sail north to Kirkenes and along the way execute the first-ever naval exercise with a frigate from the Russian Navy as a partner rather than an adversary.

EUROPEAN AMBASSADORS CONSIDER NATO

During the April 1994 meeting of all European ambassadors in Brussels, Bob Hunter, U.S. ambassador to NATO stated: "EU only a fledgling capacity for security actions. France accepts U.S. leadership. PfP (Partnership for Peace) announced by president signals U.S. is going to lead. Enlargement yes. Need for militaries to de-communize. We have one Greece and one Turkey and that is enough for any alliance. Russia welcomed to PfP and could have a special relationship to NATO. We have a tremendous stake in seeing PfP work. NATO expansion will go 100 percent with EU expansion."

When I spoke, I quoted Norwegian Prime Minister Gro Brundtland from her January 10, 1994, statement at the meeting of NATO Heads of State and Government in Brussels. "We are embarking on an evolutionary process toward a future expansion of NATO...The U.S. Partnership for Peace proposal provides a brilliant answer. ...PfP membership could function as preparation for NATO membership."

I added that the immediate problem is Russian policy, on hold for the moment, of dumping in the Barents Sea the low-level radioactive liquid that is used to cool sub reactors. I am making it my priority to focus U.S. Embassy, especially our Navy team, on helping and leading the effort to get a deal on no dumping of the sub reactor coolant.

NATO DEBATE: BABY BOOMERS VERSUS COLD WARRIORS

In 1995, I took every opportunity to give speeches, press interviews, and informal chats stressing three reasons to explain American policy as to why NATO should add Hungary, Poland, and the Czech Republic.

Before NATO membership would be considered, these countries would have to settle any border disputes with neighbors, establish civilian control of the military, and recognize the rights of minorities. These were the basic building blocks of democracy and a peaceful Europe to come.

I felt the government and pro-enlargement policy leaders could use these democracy reasons to make the case to the Norwegian people, counter the charge that enlargement was a threat to the new Russia, and, perhaps, help dampen the grumbling in the Norwegian Ministry of Defense that militarily these countries could add little to the defense of Europe. Plus, that they would add nothing to the defense of Norway.

Reading of the enlargement debate occurring in the U.S., I noticed that the baby boomers now in power were all in on the goal of enlargement, but the previous generations, the Cold War warriors, most notably George Kennan, the architect of the policy of containment, were opposed. Kennan, called enlargement "the most fateful error of American policy in the entire post-Cold War era."

President Clinton was pretty good at gently countering the opposition to expanding NATO by pointing to the eventual democratic results of previous NATO enlargements to support U.S. policy. Warren Christopher made this part of his talking points.[215]

"West Germany's admission contributed to the reconciliation of France and Germany and, eventually, to the formation of the European Union. The admission of Greece and Turkey moved their dispute over Cyprus from the brink of war to the mediation table. And NATO's embrace of Spain ensured that the Spanish military would remain under civilian control in the uncertain times following the death of Francisco Franco," Christopher wrote.[216]

He would add that to leave Poland, Hungary, and the Czech Republic out of NATO would enshrine the dividing line of Europe imposed by Stalin. This was the punch-in-the-gut argument—visceral and potent. Understood by ordinary people.

When Henry Kissinger visited the embassy in January 1995, he made a strong case for expanding NATO in remarks at the embassy and at a private lunch with Foreign Minister Godal that included Arne Olav Brundtland and other Norwegians who would form Norway's stance on NATO.

THE "STRONG RESOLVE" NATO WAR GAMES IN TRONDHEIM

The NATO war games are called Strong Resolve, which pretty much describes what I will need to get through this seven-day schedule in late February 1995. Rob Garverick, our newest and youngest political officer, will shepherd me. The DCM told him it would build character—his, not mine. Once we get below the Arctic Circle, Rob is to be relieved by a more senior political officer.

I will recount two events: the visit to the Sami Parliament and the NATO war games, which involve 22,000 troops, including 2,500 U.S. Marines who will secure the beachhead—in this case a rocky shore in the dead of winter.

Ensconced in Trondheim's Britania Hotel, "the city's most influential meeting place for the past 125 years" according to the hotel brochure I find in the lobby, I meet my NATO ambassador colleagues from Oslo in the bar, where each signature cocktail comes with a story. Before we could get to the one that promised to tell "the role of fish in bringing an end to Norwegian prohibition," it was time for dinner, hosted by British Air Chief Marshal Sir Richard Johns, commander of the exercise forces.

After breakfast, we were welcomed and briefed by General George Joulwan, the Supreme Allied Commander of U.S forces in Europe (SACEUR). I knew General Joulwan quite well as he was a frequent visitor to Oslo, and I had been with him in Brussels for our NATO ambassador meetings.

He is "dual-hatted" as commander of the U.S. European Command and one of two NATO commanders. He had his NATO hat on this day.

This was a "cold weather exercise, not a Cold War exercise," we were informed.

We were to note that France was participating in the exercise not as a NATO member but as "part of the normal training relations with their allies." (I hoped they were bringing the food.)

It was stressed that on Norwegian territory a Norwegian would be in charge: That would be Vice Admiral Bjørnar Kibsgaard.

The invasion force, the Greens, will have 12,221 troops, 66 ships, and 170 planes and helicopters. The defense force, the Whites, will have 8,000 troops, 36 ships, and 150 planes and helicopters. (Smart money is on the Greens.)

We are bused to the helicopters. "There will be four groups with escort officers arranged: Please try to remember your group." We spend the day helicoptering from briefing to briefing: logistics support, the field hospital, the UK Fighter Squadron, the land forces HQ.

The special side briefings given to me are on the role of the 2,500 U.S. Marines, who have been flown here from their bases in the U.S. Except for the Marine Guards at the embassy, there are no Marines permanently stationed in Norway. There are stocks of pre-positioned equipment for the Marines, including near Trondheim. This materiel ranges from battle tanks to field rations, from Humvees to a field hospital.[217]

None of this is secret and is even publicized by the Marines in their press releases regarding their cold-weather training exercises in Norway. I had been well briefed on this before, but it is important that I have the specifics on this particular exercise. Norway has a keen interest in the role of the U.S. Marines as they have a specific role in the defense of Norway. The other backdrop is that the Oslo press and many politicians are questioning not just this exercise but the need for NATO to expand or even to exist since the end of the Cold War.

Dinner is at the archbishop's palace. "Aperitif served (short historical talk will be given)." The archbishop is not in. He has not been in since 1537, the year Olav Engelbrektsson, the last Catholic archbishop of Norway, was chased into exile by the Reformationists. The Grand Palace is now a museum.

Dinner in the Grand Salon is hosted by General Joulwan and Marine General John Sheehan, the Supreme Allied Commander, Atlantic, NATO's western military arm. At 6'5" General Sheehan, "call me Jack," is hard to miss. He had also been to Norway several times and was quite well known even in non-military circles as a Marine is historically not a supreme allied commander. Both Joulwan and Sheehan are polished diplomats and well versed in politics.

Day Two is spent at the Værnes Military Airport, lunch is at the Combined All Ranks Mess with the base commander, and then there is a briefing and tour while walking about the parked planes of the UK Fighter Squadron.

That night is free, and we repair to the Britannia Bar and the signature cocktails. The mystery of how fish helped end prohibition is solved.[218]

Day Three is a tour of the command ship, the *USS Mt. Whitney*. It is a unique-looking ship with a flat deck, except for just a bump of a bridge and a transmitting tower. It is stuffed with communications equipment that can process large amounts of secure data. The flat deck basically clears the way for the transmitting signal. From this ship the land, air, and sea forces of the exercise can be commanded. With a million gallons of fuel, the *Mt. Whitney* can stay at sea a long time and operate in any theater of war.

The Greens prevailed. I returned to Oslo.

GRO FOR NATO?

From my diary November 18, 1995: Yesterday urgent request from Peter Tarnoff (undersecretary of state for political affairs) asking my personal view on Gro's qualifications for NATO's top job. Respond: "real leader with long experience...would lead organization rather than see role as forging consensus...definition of NATO is in her gut...NATO is U.S. commitment to defend Norway and Europe...she would demand U.S. lead...well known among important members of Congress...I could see her lecturing them...she is a Social Democrat from her nose to her toes ...supports Clinton and Hillary...she starts with the assumption she has the moral high ground...her style would appeal to Americans...English is American not British...will have Russia on her mind...geography is history...would she accept? Arne Olav would like it...children are gone...EU vote was the last unclimbed mountain...UN would be her dream job...she is not going to hang around as PM too much longer...

From my diary November 30, 1995: Ambassador Hunter (U.S. ambassador to NATO) called late last night. 'Gro was acceptable to us but Spanish Foreign Minister will be chosen tomorrow.' Sounds like Gro never got to first base.

MEET, EAT, AND TALK WITH
NATO AMBASSADOR ROBERT HUNTER

Robert Hunter, the U.S. ambassador to NATO, arrived at the Residence from Brussels the evening of February 4, 1996, just in time to go to bed.

We had him scheduled the next day nonstop. Breakfast was with the NATO country ambassadors, plus those from the Baltics, Finland, Sweden, Russia, and every Eastern European country that was once in the Soviet bloc. And Switzerland.

Lunch was with journalists. Dinner with Morten Wetland, representing the PM's office, and parliamentary party leaders. The chef and staff at the Residence fed 66 guests that day.

We met with the members of the Parliament's Foreign Affairs Committee, and the two of us met privately with Minister of Defense Kosmo and then with the prime minister. In between breakfast and lunch, Bob spoke on NATO expansion at the Norwegian Atlantic Committee's annual security conference held at the Nobel Institute.[219] This was a big-deal event.

The purpose of this conference was to engage with the "media, opinion-formers, politicians, diplomats, civil servants, academics, military personnel, and the successor generation on current and emerging international and transatlantic issues." Every opinion leader who cared about NATO was there. Quite handy for our purposes.

Bob Hunter introduced me with a line good enough to steal, which I did. "We have a greeting card company in the United States called Hallmark. Let me borrow their slogan: The United States cares enough about Norway to send our very best."

Bob laid out the U.S. position on NATO at this stage after the end of the Cold War:

> (O)ur security in the West will not be sufficient unless we help take responsibility for the security of countries that have emerged from the dark night of communism and of Soviet oppression....

> (I)t is a purpose of NATO to help the success of the great Russian experiment in democracy and...in Russia playing a full and active and legitimate and necessary part in the security of the rest of Europe...

> (O)ur security depends, in large part, on what the Russians are able to do positively with us...

NATO will enlarge. And we will do so in a way that increases the security for all and diminishes it for none...

Partnership for Peace now with 27 members...will provide for permanent association with NATO...

(W)e are employing a direct relationship with Russia. The Russians have joined Partnership for Peace....

(H)istory is an exacting judge...we need to get this right.

U.S. MILITARY BRIEFS NATO AMBASSADORS IN STUTTGART

The three-day conference February 26-28, 1996, of U.S. ambassadors to NATO countries in Stuttgart at the headquarters of U.S. forces in Europe gave us all a chance for an update from General George Joulwan. He had visited Norway several times, so I knew him well. He was the commander of U.S. forces in Europe, and the commander of all NATO forces. A two-hatter, in the jargon.

This was a military briefing on current operations. Mostly about the Balkans. It was necessary because our usual diet of NATO issues was all on the political side of things.

An important part of this gathering was that I could finally meet Marc Grossman, our ambassador to Turkey. And talk turkey with him as to why the Norwegians were just not going to sell their Penguin anti-ship missiles to Turkey. (The human rights behavior of Turkey and the likelihood the missiles would be used against Greece—things better said than written down in the leaky cable traffic.)

Marc probably had the toughest post in Europe.

RON ASMUS: THE UW MAN WITH A PLAN TO EXPAND NATO

There arrived throughout August 1996 draft papers on how to expand NATO. One hundred faxed pages in all flopped on the floor from the machine next to Sue's desk. She had stacks of ink, toner, and paper because if any one of these was used up the fax transmission stopped. The other American ambassadors in Europe also found the papers in their inbox. They came from Ron Asmus, a researcher at the Rand Corporation, a well-regarded nonpartisan think tank that promises "objective analysis and effective solutions."[220]

Ron Asmus was born in Milwaukee on June 29, 1957. His parents had immigrated there after surviving WWII in Germany. He went to public schools. He enrolled at UW-Madison upon graduation from high school. While an undergraduate he visited Berlin to look for the house where his grandmother had lived during the 1930s. (This trip to divided Berlin must have made quite an impression on him.) He graduated from the University of Wisconsin in political science and went on to earn a Ph.D. in European studies from John Hopkins.

We were both alumni of the century-old UW political science department.[221] Noted in Ron's bio was that he was a lifelong fan of the Green Bay Packers. UW and the Packers. Good enough for me. Let's go with his plan.

Asmus had written several relevant papers: "What Will NATO Enlargement Cost?" Priced out in different scenarios. "NATO's Three Way Divide." An analysis of the positions of the current member countries' positions. The "Have-Not Problem." After the addition of Poland, Hungary, and the Czech Republic, how to position our position so that the Baltics[222] are in the queue to eventually join. And Russia: "Keeping the door open to more members and not allowing the Russians to have real or shadow veto over the enlargement process."

I recognized the method from state budget papers. There were options but one always stood out as the choice. This from a Ron Asmus paper with the title "The Imperative for a Baltic Strategy: Why Not the Baltic States in NATO?"

> Baltic airspace should be integrated with that of the West in a fashion akin to the Central European Regional Airspace Initiative. Such steps would lead over time to the state of affairs where the Baltic States start to approach the defense status currently enjoyed by Sweden or Finland, countries with modern militaries with a heavy emphasis on a national self-sufficiency doctrine—but also countries enjoying very close relations with NATO and which are capable of being integrated in to NATO on relatively short notice if and when that political decision is taken.

The obvious option to choose.

Mr. Asmus' approach was like the assembly instructions for a piece of IKEA furniture. This Swedish company is noted for its instructions using diagrams. Sweden and Finland, both new members of the European Union, would champion EU membership for the Baltics, starting with Estonia. They both became EU members for national security reasons. Given their history, Russia was as likely to stop being the neighborhood bully as the sun coming up in the west.

The United States and Denmark would champion the Baltics within NATO by ensuring the members were all singing out of the same hymn book: "Independent countries of course are eligible to join NATO one day." (Norway could be counted on to hold the hymnal open to the right page.)

The U.S. never recognized the Baltics as part of the Soviet Union, so giving any indication that Russia would have some say over whether they could join NATO was off the table. President George H.W. Bush recognized the Baltics as independent on September 2, 1991, during the chaotic breakup of the Soviet Union, right in the middle of Gorbachev being ousted and Yeltsin's rise to power.[223]

Denmark had historical ties to Estonia. It had been a duchy in the Danish Baltic empire. Denmark implied their support for other Eastern European countries to join NATO would hinge on not closing the door for the Baltics. Denmark's navy was a Baltic fleet designed for defense against the Soviets.

Asmus: "The fact that the Baltic States are unlikely to be in the first tranche of NATO enlargement, however, does not negate the imperative for the Alliance to have a Baltic strategy. On the contrary, it magnifies the need for a credible Alliance strategy as an alternative to enlargement to sustain their independence and security and integrate them into the West by other means."

The "other means." Next three pages of instructions "the interim package."

1. Foster a "joint defense" effort between the three countries. "The most promising model for the Baltic Defense is the Finnish national model a la IKEA."

2. NATO should announce an expanded program of Partnership for Peace activities in the Baltic region to expand cooperation between NATO and non-NATO members—to also include Russia.

3. Estonian membership in the EU would represent the crossing of a symbolically important Rubicon—a former part of the Soviet Union will have joined the West. This is the key to Baltic membership in NATO.

4. Assemble and tighten the screws.

TO ESTONIA AND SOVIET REACTOR SARCOPHAGI

Imre Lipping, the chargé of the American Embassy in Estonia, met me at the airport in Tallinn October 9, 1996. (Ambassador Larry Taylor was out of the country.)

We talked and walked about the stunning mix of the city's medieval, baroque, and Rococo architecture and along the top of the city wall, dating from the 16th century.

Imre Lipping's father was Elmar Lipping, who was an officer in the Estonian army during that period of freedom from Russian rule starting in 1918 until the Soviets occupied the country in June 1940. When the Germans came in June 1941 to drive the Soviets out as part of the invasion of the Soviet Union (Operation Barbarossa), Elmar Lipping fought alongside the Germans in a special Estonian corps.

He was seriously wounded, and the end of the war found him in West Germany, where he worked for the U.S. military. He emigrated to America and joined an Estonian exile group, the Voice of Estonian Freedom. Elmar Lipping was the foreign minister of the Estonian government in exile from 1982 to 1990.

My host, Imre Lipping, went to the Virginia Military Institute, and on to graduate school at the University of Maryland, where he wrote his Ph.D. thesis on events in Estonia between 1919 and 1939. After a stint as an officer in the U.S. Army, Imre joined the State Department and now here he was in the Estonia that was once again free from the Soviets. An American story.

My trip memo gave me all the background information I needed in one sentence. Strobe Talbott had reported that on his visit to Estonia in 1996, President Lennart Meri summed things up for him. "Meri couldn't have been more forthright: Russia was a malignancy in remission; the Yeltsin era was at best a fleeting opportunity to be seized before Russia relapsed into authoritarianism at home and expansionism abroad."[224]

My meeting with Foreign Minister Siim Kallas was like chatting with an old friend, as my friend Tiit Naber, the Estonian chargé in Oslo, had sent a briefing memo in advance praising me as a real friend of Estonia.

Siim Kallas was named president of the national bank of Estonia when independence was gained. Sort of the Alexander Hamilton job. He founded the free-market Estonian Reform Party. For some reason, unable for me to comprehend although he tried his best, the party is nicknamed the "Squirrel Party."

His grandfather was one of the founders of the Republic of Estonia in 1918 and was the commander of the Estonian Defense League (similar to our National Guard) in the War of Independence.

The talk turned to American participation in the recent Partnership for Peace joint exercise called Baltic Challenge, held in Latvia in July 1996, which consisted of troops from the three Baltics and U.S. Marines.[225]

Russian President Boris Yeltsin was only slightly miffed. But the leader of the Communist Party, renamed the Liberal Democratic Party, Vladimir Zhirinovsky, was quoted as saying, "For the first time since 1918 an American soldier tramples on Russian soil."[226]

I would be attending the next Baltic Challenge in 1997. 2,800 military personnel from nine nations—Estonia, Latvia, Lithuania, Norway, Sweden, Finland, Denmark, Ukraine, and the United States— would conduct an exercise to "demonstrate a range of capabilities that support operational objectives in Europe."[227] Zhirinovsky might have a heart attack.

The former Soviet submarine training base at Paldiski is a short drive west of Tallinn.[228] It is in a bay on that part of the Baltic Sea known as the Gulf of Finland. Helsinki is just two hours from Tallinn by ferry. Thirty minutes by commercial air.

I was expecting a harbor where submarines docked and crews were trained on them. Not the case. There was a big, long building that held two submarine mock-ups with nuclear reactors in place. The Russians had removed the submarine hulls but not the reactors. They were encased in concrete. Cold War mummies.

The Estonians were left with the task of cleaning up the hazards and rebuilding to state-of-the-art standards the concrete sarcophagi. (A perfect word used in the explanation material.)

A large stone sculpture of a hammer and sickle still stands.

Hara was a Soviet submarine base east of Tallinn dating from 1953 that was abandoned some time ago. We did not go there as there was nothing to see. The site is now part of Lahemaa National Park. This base was used to de-magnetize submarines so they were hard to detect and would not attract floating mines.[229] Who knew?

Kai Lie, the Norwegian ambassador to Estonia, had invited Imre and me to lunch.

On our walk to the restaurant, we stopped at a big flea market in a vacant lot. Mostly Russian speakers selling cheap household items. Times were tough and this brought it out.

Talk at lunch was about the language law and the problems it was causing Estonia with the West and Russia. The large number of Soviet citizens who had lived in Estonia for years, perhaps their whole lives, were not granted Estonian citizenship unless they passed a test showing knowledge of the language and the constitution and signed a loyalty oath. The Estonian language is close to Finnish, and it does not even have a nodding acquaintance with the Russian language.

The shoe was now on the other foot. During the Soviet occupation, thousands of Estonians were deported to Siberia; huge numbers of Soviet citizens were given incentives to settle in Estonia, especially in parts where whole populations had been cleansed of native Estonians; the Russian population grew from 25,000 in 1945 to 475,000 in 1991. Along with Russian speakers this was 35 percent of the population.

The wife of Foreign Minister Kallas when she was six months old was deported with her mother and grandmother and didn't make it back to Estonia for ten years. Still, we all concluded something had to be done to get the Russians and Russian speakers inside the tent if the Estonian democracy was to succeed this time. EU membership requirements would certainly force some change in the language law before Estonia could join.

I had a Saku brand porter beer and the grilled venison. They were out of the wild boar.

RUSSIA'S NORTHERN FLEET ADMIRAL: "THE SAILORS ARE SELLING THEIR BLOOD"

As the 300th anniversary of the Russian Navy approached, Admiral Oleg Yerofeyev, commander of the Northern Fleet, gave an interview November 5, 1996, to *Country and Navy*, a publication covering news of the Russian Navy akin to our *Navy Times*.

The intended audience was the Yeltsin government and the Ministry of Defense in Moscow. It was both a best-face-forward report and a stark assessment of the dire straits of the Northern Fleet. It was a document of a time and place after the end of the Cold War and those who were holding on at the front lines of an uncertain future. And a plea that the Russian Navy not be forgotten.

We will celebrate the 300th anniversary. A large reception will be held in the officer's club...1,000 officers will be invited...their wives are invited for the first time. So this will be a family affair. Many officers will be honored with gilded dirks (swords). There will be dancing with music by the Northern Fleet song and dance ensemble...

In spite of our troubles we have not had a bad year if we go by results. For the first time in about a decade we have carried out large-scale exercises in the Norwegian Sea and live weapons firing was done for the first time in many years...

In spite of the continual decrease in Anti Submarine Warfare ships, the number of contacts with foreign submarines and time spent shadowing them has increased...

In spite of all the successes the Fleet is experiencing enormous financial strain. The Fleet's entire personnel has not yet been paid for July...we settled up for June only a week ago...the troops go off base and sell their blood for money...and forage for mushrooms and fish to feed their family...

Those working in our ship repair yards haven't been paid since April...

A day does not go by without my appealing to someone for money... Moscow promises but it does not happen...

We owe money to the towns where our people live for gas, electricity, and water...the district heating plant at Severomors[230] only has 48 hours supply...we cannot pay for cooking gas for our apartments...because of these debts the utility workers are threatening to cut off our supplies...[231]

The Navy is needed not so we are seen as a great naval power but to protect our interests. The military success of NATO in the Persian Gulf and Yugoslavia show that their policy of "strikes from the sea" works. The first strikes were delivered by cruise missiles from submarines and surface ships. Only after air defense systems have been neutralized do aircraft take to the air and ground forces begin to operate...

(The admiral notes that Russia's one aircraft carrier, the *Kuznetsov*, did make it to the Mediterranean Sea for a few weeks of exercises and fighter pilots made successful test flights from the deck of the carrier.)

Incidentally, the Norwegian government has revoked the moratorium on holding exercises east of the 24th meridian, that is to say NATO can operate right next to our border...

I do not want to end on a pessimistic note. I believe in the common sense of our people and that the Ministry of Defense will come through...

On the eve of the Navy's 300th anniversary, I would like to congratulate all the sailors and the entire Russian people on this great and important event and ask the government once more to not to turn its back on the Navy.

RON ASMUS STUMPS IN OSLO FOR NATO ENLARGEMENT

Ron Asmus arrived in Oslo early the morning of November 20, 1996, for a packed schedule the U.S. Embassy had arranged. He was now a consultant to the State Department. His plan on NATO enlargement was now understood to be the blueprint. I would brief him and he would brief me. Then an hour-long discussion with the Country Team in the same format.

Lunch with 30 guests at the Residence from the Ministry of Defense, the party leaders on the Parliament's Foreign Affairs and Defense committees, former PM Kåre Willoch, former Chief of Defense Fredrik Bull-Hansen, and former ambassador to the U.S. Kjeld Vibe— éminence grise all (a kinder phrase than elder statesmen)— several from the Norwegian Institute of International Affairs (NUPI), including Arne Olav Brundtland, who would be our host at a NUPI roundtable for Asmus after lunch, and all the influential journalists.

One thing that unites University of Wisconsin alumni is the fudge-bottom pie that is served at the student union in Madison. My plan was to serve this for dessert at lunch and build a whole introduction of Ron around it. I called the UW Union and they faxed the recipe, but one look at what it took to prepare this masterpiece of confection and the chef said not for 30 people. Oh well, here in the footnote you can find the recipe and the history of the legendary chef that brought dreams of this sweet to generations of Wisconsin students.[232]

My brief to Ron was that for the Norwegian Labour Party government and most of the other political parties it was "yes" on Poland, Hungary, and the Czech Republic, and that the NATO-joining requirements of getting their institutions in order to build a democracy was a selling point for Norway.[233]

They understood the historical reason that expansion of NATO to these three countries would "keep Germany in and Russia out." For the military, in which one should include the Home Guard and just about every family in Norway because of the mandatory service requirement for males, most of whom served their time on bases near the Russian border, there were a lot of questions.

Our team of Defense, Air Force, Army, and Marine attachés and CIA station chief gave Ron an excellent summary of the issues.

1. Would this threaten the American commitment to the defense of Norway through NATO, such as a movement elsewhere of pre-positioned equipment or a dilution of the special Norway mission of U.S. Marines?

2. The Norwegian military defense posture is directed at a defense of Norway from Russian threats on the border. Adding to this orientation would take time and money.

3. Poland, Hungary, and the Czech Republic do not have functioning militaries and Germany has a desultory military they are not willing to use outside the country. They offer little to NATO.

This was all good background for Ron and he noted the general issues in his remarks after lunch. He addressed them at the Norwegian Institute for International Affairs discussion, more fully going into his cost estimates based on different scenarios. His pitch for the Baltics to be in the NATO queue seemed still abstract to the Norwegians. Arne Olaf Brundtland was quite good at summarizing to Ron the Nordic dimension of Norwegian policy on NATO expansion.

By 4 p.m. we were back at the airport, and Ron said he had learned a lot more information than he had imparted, which would serve him well. Fudge-bottom pie together the next time we are in Madison.

AMERICA'S "MR. GERMANY"

After more than three years on the job, my observation was that Germany was Norway's most important relationship after the United States. It was the main trading partner, most tourists came from Germany, and the port of Emden on Germany's North Sea coast was the destination of the undersea pipelines for Norwegian oil and natural gas.

It was the essential diplomatic relationship in Europe. The most experienced Norwegian diplomats were posted there. Morten Wetland, Prime Minister Brundtland's top assistant, was named ambassador in 1998.

German Chancellor Helmut Kohl was a big part of the reason. He had been chancellor since 1982, brilliantly handling reunification with East Germany; he was the mainstay of the European Union. He was the champion of Norway joining the EU, and although that effort failed, his strong advocacy for Norway and sympathy with the reasons of those who opposed joining was not forgotten.

Prime Minister Gro Harlem Brundtland's pitch in the November 1994 referendum on Norway joining the EU that Norway, a NATO member, would be the first EU member to have a border with Russia didn't influence many voters, but the promise of this was not lost on Kohl. Norway's membership in the EU would have made a positive difference in Russia, the EU, and NATO. (Norway voted no, 52 percent to 48 percent.)

So it was not much of a surprise that there was great interest when it was announced that America's "Mr. Germany" was to be the keynote speaker at the annual Norwegian Atlantic Committee's two-day conference on security issues in Oslo, February 3-4, 1997.[234]

"Mr. Germany," James D. Bindenagel, always called J.D., was the chargé d'affaires at the U.S. Embassy in Bonn. J.D. had served as deputy chief of mission or chargé in three different Germanys: West, East, unified. He was in East Germany in 1989-90 and reported brilliantly on the democratic revolution, the fall of the Berlin Wall, and the unification of Germany.[235]

J.D. was staying at the Residence. We had become fast friends at the first NATO ambassadors meeting in early '94. He was Ambassador

Richard Holbrooke's DCM then. He was at the University of Illinois getting a B.A. and master's in political science the same years I was at the UW-Madison doing the same thing.

J.D. delivered the goods on what people came to hear: How was Kohl maneuvering with Russia through NATO expansion? He outlined a history of the issue and Kohl's position on NATO expansion at our small private lunch at the Residence with Deputy Foreign Minister Siri Bjerke; Jonas Gahr Støre, lead foreign policy advisor to the prime minister; and Martin Kolberg, state secretary of the ministry of defense.

From my notes:

(German) Defense Minister Volker Rühe pushed NATO membership for Poland, Hungary, and the Czech Republic... Chancellor Kohl and Foreign Minister Genscher were cautious and reluctant...Rühe found a willing partner in Richard Holbrooke...they agreed informally to advocate opening NATO to new members...Partnership for Peace would be the start...September 1994 Berlin New Traditions Conference organized by the U.S. Embassy[236] ...Holbrooke and Rühe and J.D. choreographed conference....Holbrooke asked Vice President Gore to speak and suggest Gore propose a debate begin on opening NATO...(Al Gore had torn his Achilles...spoke via interactive video and called for the opening of the NATO debate)...Rühe publicly joined in the call by Gore...the perplexed U.S. Secretary of Defense William Perry, who also attended the conference, disagreed and noted NATO military chiefs' reluctance to take new NATO members from the Warsaw Pact just three years after the Warsaw Pact dissolved...after Holbrooke left and became assistant secretary for Europe (September '94-February '96) he pushed Clinton for immediate membership of Poland, Czech, Hungary, and the Baltics...Perry asked for a meeting to make his case for a delay of two or three years[237] ...Gore was forceful...Clinton agreed to Poland, Czech, and Hungary but delay for the Baltics...Kohl adopted position that if NATO could find a consensus limited to the U.S. preference for only three new members—Poland, Hungary, and the Czech Republic, he would support.[238]

On our way to the airport, J.D. urged me to come to Germany as soon as possible, certainly before I went again to the Baltics. He would organize a two-day schedule. I agreed, and by the time I got back to the office, his assistant had called my assistant Sue; a date for the visit was set for February 25, three weeks away.

BONN WITH J.D.: OYSTERS AND MUSCADET

The schedule for my February 25-26, 1997, trip to Bonn was set up by J.D. and was all about the Baltics.

The first meeting was with Ambassador Andris Kesteris, the Latvian ambassador to Germany. He was very interested in my impression of Latvia after my trip there in 1994. What did I think of the people I met? What was Norway's thinking on the Baltics joining NATO? The ambassador noted his main task was working with Germany on the steps Latvia would have to take to gain EU membership.

Then on to the Estonian Embassy to meet with Ambassador Margus Laidre. His task was also working to gain EU membership. He had pretty much the same questions of me as Ambassador Kesteris. What was my impression of Estonia after my trip there in 1995? He was very pleased to learn that Imre Lipping, the U.S. chargé, was my host on that visit. "That someone from this family, lauded in Estonian history, was posted to Tallinn was very appreciated."

Ambassador Laidre was a noted historian. We talked about an area of his expertise that I recognized from my work with emerging parliaments, including Latvia. This was the need for small countries with a history of occupation to find a time when they were independent, with functioning democratic institutions, and highlight this period as the norm.

He explained Estonia's phases like this: emergence (1918-1939), oblivion (1940-1991), and rebirth (1992-present)—a phase that Estonia will be in for a long time. The 1919-1939 period was the norm.

The meatier part of the chat was my upcoming trip to Estonia in the summer to observe Baltic Challenge '97, the Partnership for Peace joint military exercises. The U.S. Marines would have a big presence. NATO member Norway would participate, which was in itself a signal to the Baltics.

As a historian, Ambassador Laidre had lectured and written in English and had a collection of sayings from American movies and TV shows he used to punctuate his points—including from the

1980's television series *Miami Vice*: "Drop that gun or you're history!"

Lunch with the Norwegian ambassador to Germany Kjell Eliassen. Kjell was another example of the best the Norwegians had to offer being posted in Germany. He was ambassador in the United States from 1984 to 1988, United Kingdom 1989 to 1994, and Germany since 1994. (Morten Wetland succeeded Kjell as ambassador to Germany in 1998.)

After I told him that his Estonian and Latvian colleagues mentioned as their priority EU membership, Kjell said "that was once my priority." We both found that humorous. (Norway voted "no" on joining the EU in November 1994).

It was hard to categorize the cozy bistro-type restaurant we visited—French with a German twist or vice versa. From the "menu plaisir" (plates of small pleasures): Half-dozen oysters (Belons) and winter vegetable salad with sautéed mushrooms. Bottle of Muscadet (shared).

J.D. continued the Baltic theme at the dinner he hosted for me with members of the Federal Parliament (Bundestag), German-Scandinavia Parliamentary Group, and German-Baltic Parliamentary Group as guests. (These groups are like subcommittees). The Christian Democrats, the ruling party, and the Social Democrats, the main opposition party, were represented.

I gave brief comments on my time as Wisconsin's Assembly Speaker to establish I was a fellow politician; mentioned Wisconsin, through immigration, was the most German state in America; and that our sister state was the German state of Hessen.

J.D. focused his remarks on his recent trip to Oslo and the support he found there for NATO expansion for Poland, Hungary, and the Czech Republic, and the widely held opinion that there was no reason to exclude the Baltics from future membership. Then he looked at me so I could nod. I nodded vigorously.

We had decided it made more sense for him to deliver this message than me. After all, he was America's Mr. Germany.

TO POLAND TO HEAR ABOUT NATO

President Clinton did not send me 4,000 miles away from home to forget where I came from.

And where I came from had a special relationship with Poland. There was a large Polish immigration to Wisconsin that concentrated on the South Side of Milwaukee.

St. Stanislaus was the first Polish parish in Milwaukee and the St. Stanislaus Catholic Church, "a towering twin-spire church topped by golden domes" dating from 1872, is the landmark of Milwaukee's South Side.[239]

The Poles were factory workers, union members who often voted Socialist, but in 1932 in the midst of the Depression the Polish wards gave FDR 93 percent of the vote. The vote stayed heavily Democratic. There was a unifying political outlook among Milwaukee's Polish population that did not change over the decades: freedom for Poland and anti-Communism.

The personification of this was their congressman, Clement J. Zablocki, who served in the House from 1949 to 1983. A staunch supporter of Social Security and Medicare, and an advocate of a strong U.S. military and freedom for Poland from Communism and the Soviets. And he had a thing or two to say about it, as from 1977 to 1983 he was the chair of the House Foreign Affairs Committee.

I knew Clem as a friend and political ally. He was one of the reasons I felt that I must do what I could as ambassador to get Poland into NATO. There were others from Milwaukee's South Side trusting me to do what was right by Poland. Clem's successor was Gerald Kleczka, my colleague in the Wisconsin Legislature, and Wally Kunicki from the South Side succeeded me as Speaker. And my dearest friend in the Assembly, the stylish Joe Czerwinski, nicknamed the Polish Prince. (His name was pronounced Sir-Winski).

So when the suggestion bubbled up that May 8 and 9, 1997, I escort to Poland a delegation of influential political leaders and Sverre Lodgaard, the new head of NUPI (the Norwegian Institute of International Affairs)[240] to meet counterparts and hear firsthand what NATO membership would mean to Poland, I said, "Let's go."[241]

Sverre Lodgaard was the new head of NUPI but he had been an important voice in Norwegian foreign policy for a long time. There was a thick file of clips on him in the embassy press office. Sverre was a student leader in the '60s at the University of Oslo, gaining fame for conducting Saturday debates that challenged convention wisdom on Norwegian foreign policy. Think of the Oxford Union, the debating society associated with the University of Oxford.

The newspapers loved him. Making news on a Saturday for the Sunday papers. He was Gregory Peck handsome. The perfect public intellectual. Adding to his allure was that he refused military service in protest of nuclear weapons and spent four months in jail for it.

Eventually Sverre earned a Ph.D. in political science leading to a career as a researcher at the Peace Research Institute of Oslo (PRIO),[242] the United Nations Institute for Disarmament Research, and then NUPI. His intellect and clear writing established him as a notable in the field of nuclear arms control. He gained notoriety when in 1978 he published a paper revealing that Israel had obtained the heavy water for their nuclear program from Norway.

We were both born in 1945, and at age 52, we had lived the history of the Cold War. What was it like for someone our age to have lived these same fifty-some years in Poland?

Our schedule was arranged by our host, U.S. ambassador to Poland Nicholas Rey.[243]

Nick was born in 1938 in Warsaw. His family fled to the U.S. to escape the Nazi invasion in 1939. His parents were not diplomats but of a stature such that they would be hunted by the Nazis.

The U.S. ambassador to Poland at the time, Anthony J. Drexel Biddle Jr., arranged for 20-month-old Nicholas Rey and his parents to join the convoy of diplomats leaving Poland, which was bombed and strafed by Nazi planes several times along the way.

Ambassador Rey had a photo of Ambassador Biddle prominently placed in the Residence. I recognized this photo, as I saw it every time we had a Country Team meeting in our conference room at the embassy in Oslo. Ambassador Biddle was one of my predecessors.

Appointed by FDR to Norway, Biddle served from 1935 to 1937, when FDR sent him to Poland as ambassador.

Ambassador Biddle followed the government of Poland, first to France, then to London where they organized as the government of Poland in exile. Whereupon President Roosevelt added to his portfolio, naming Biddle the ambassador to several other European governments in exile in London, including Norway.[244]

Nick was a veteran of Democratic presidential campaigns. Important to candidates and the Democratic Party in these campaigns was his prominence in the Polish-American community. Nick was the head of the Polish-American Freedom Foundation, which had been established by Congress in 1989 to support freedom in Poland.[245] Our paths had not crossed in the presidential campaigns. We met the first time at the all-Europe ambassadors meeting in Germany in 1994.

"The Residence of the U.S. Ambassador in Warsaw occupies an attractive one-acre tract of land on a hill overlooking the southern approaches to the city. The red brick house, designed in the Williamsburg style was constructed in 1963."[246]

I noted to Nick that my fellow UW alumnus Ambassador John Gronouski from Green Bay, Wisconsin, appointed to Poland by President Lyndon Baines Johnson, would have lived in this residence. Nick had known John and of his spirited representation of America during a period of harsh Communist rule when the Catholic Church was under attack (1963-68).

As we sat around the table in the Residence, Sverre and the others were quite taken with Nick's story and of my mention of Ambassador Biddle's connection to Norway. Nick was doing everything he could to advance the day Poland would become a member of NATO. But he told the group: "You didn't come to Warsaw to hear my pitch." They would hear the views on this best from the members of the Polish Parliament they would meet. (I had been in Warsaw in 1991 after the first free parliamentary elections for discussions with the new parliamentary leaders.)

The discussions on NATO expansion had nothing to do with process or treaties or anything to do with the positions of Germany or Russia. Instead, they were a passionate recounting of what it was like living under Soviet-controlled Communist bosses. The cramped lives. The paranoia fostered by the Secret Police. Schools that taught lies. The Catholic Church as the enemy.

The message was: We are an independent country once again after more than 50 years but will never be free to develop unless we are under NATO protection—either Germany or Russia or both will seek as they always have to dominate us. The Russians just left. We are helpless if they come back.

For Sverre and the others, gone was the abstraction of NATO expansion in the conferences, the policy papers, and those who had a blithe disregard for the former Soviet states, claiming the world was now about America and the "new" Russia. Not new. A bear in sheep's clothing. Don't be fooled—it is the same Russia of the Soviets and the czars.

I took a long walk in the center of Warsaw early in the morning of the day we left. I bought an amber brooch for my mother from a guy on the street. He said it was the real thing, thousands of years old from the Baltic Sea. Maybe it was.

Back in Oslo I sent a thank you note to Nick, adding that Sverre would be an important voice in Norway's foreign policy for a long time and this trip would have an impact on his thinking.

BALTIC CHALLENGE '97 IN ESTONIA

The Partnership for Peace exercise in Estonia, "Baltic Challenge '97," which occurred July 21-23, 1997, was like opening night on Broadway.

Permission was granted by Norway to take a significant amount of the Marine's pre-positioned stocks of war-fighting materiel out of Norway and transport it to Estonia for the Baltic Challenge.

Norway and the U.S. were sending guns, not butter. I was the only U.S. ambassador to a NATO country who would be present. Important to Norway.

Moving the very large amount of equipment from the tunnels in western Norway to Estonia was done by rail though Sweden and by ferry to Estonia. Some was airlifted.

When this deal was made earlier in the year, I told our defense attaché to work with the Ministry of Defense to make this known in a matter-of-fact way. There should be no surprises like the press "discovering" it would go through Sweden.

The ambassador to Estonia's historic residence

Embassy Oslo's dashing Marine Attaché Major Lee Wakefield met me at the airport in Tallinn.

Lee is fluent in Norwegian. Skis in Wisconsin's Birkebeiner. He and his wife Kim dazzle at the Marine Ball by dancing the tango.

"Did the equipment arrive OK? Does it work?

"Yes sir. And, yes sir."

The Marines had issued this description of the exercise to the media:

> Baltic Challenge '97 is a multinational exercise conducted in the spirit of NATO's Partnership for Peace (PfP) initiative. More than 2,600 military personnel from Denmark, Estonia, Finland, Latvia, Lithuania, Norway, Sweden, and the USA will participate in the second PfP land exercise conducted in the Baltic region. While this exercise will conduct training along peacekeeping/humanitarian assistance

mission standards, significant U.S. Navy and Marine Corps capabilities never exercised in Europe will be performed including the use of equipment from the U.S. Marine Corps Norway Air-Landed Marine Expeditionary Brigade (NALMEB) Prepositioning Program.[247]

That first night Ambassador Larry Napper (Latvia) and I stayed with Larry Taylor, U.S. ambassador to Estonia, in his residence, a historic house in downtown Tallinn.

We had all been together in London and Oslo at the meetings of Nordic and Baltic ambassadors and had become friends. We had all gone to noted public universities—UW, Ohio (Larry T) and Texas A&M (Larry N)—and knew each other's stories, so we told stories.

Larry Taylor gave us a tour of the house and its history. It had once been the home of General Johan Laidoner, the George Washington of Estonia.[248] He was the general in command during the 1918-1920 war of independence from Russia. He later resumed the command and in 1939 led Estonian forces in the fight against the invading Soviets. Upon the Soviet occupation in 1940, General Laidoner was sent to a prison near Moscow, where he died in 1953.

Ambassador Taylor said he would not be showing us the basement of this old house. "Even our cat won't go down there."

Larry Taylor's hobby was collecting British colonial maps—he had a room full, completely in keeping with those who have traveled the globe. (My collection of old maps of the Arctic stood at three.)

Larry had introduced me to his hobby when we were together in London. He had been the economic counselor from 1984 to 1989 at our embassy in London and knew the town. He took me on a walking tour of shops that sold such things and then to one of his regular haunts, an Indian restaurant in Covent Garden. A memorable evening.

Larry told the tale. "The owner insisted on taking us downstairs to show us the tandoor oven. It turned out to be much more than a basement. It was a series of large rooms connected through tunnels that even, he said, extended to other buildings. There was a sketchy group of men there, and they weren't baking bread. Given their threatening glares it appeared they were not pleased to see us. I doubt that we would survive that trip downstairs if we were foolish enough to do it again."

Larry T. also told of meeting JFK and Bobby when campaigning for JFK in the West Virginia primary in 1960 and being inspired to join the Peace Corps after college, where he served in Columbia.

Before dinner the house manager said there was a telephone call for me. It was Esther from the Lands' End catalog in Dodgeville, Wisconsin: "On the khaki pants you ordered, did you want cuffs or no cuffs?"

She had called the embassy in Oslo. My assistant gave her the number in Estonia.

Estonia's president: We need NATO

The three of us were briefed on the PfP exercise by the officers of II Marine Expeditionary Force (MEF) from Camp Lejeune in North Carolina. "We have used the equipment from Norway and the integration of it into the operation is successful." (First, they explained what a MEF was. It's a combined arms force consisting of ground, air, and logistics units that has the capability for projecting offensive combat power ashore while sustaining itself in combat without external assistance for a period of 60 days.)

By early afternoon July 22, we were in the VIP section for the closing ceremony at Paldiski. It was my second visit to this former Soviet submarine base.

The ships used in the exercise were just offshore, each flying the flag of its respective country. A parachute drop from a clear blue sky started things off. The band in the center of the field played the national anthem of each participating nation (this took a while). Then the troops of the nations, men and women, marched by the reviewing stand in uniforms of many different colors. A roar in the near distance, then a flyover of fighter jets.

The president of Estonia, Lennart Meri, gave a speech. It was translated into English as he spoke. Larry Taylor said it was a variation of the short speech the president had given at the recent NATO summit in Madrid where Poland, Hungary, and the Czech Republic were formally invited to become members.[249]

The main point: "I believe that it is fair to say that the Cold War will only finally be over when the Baltic countries have assumed their place behind the NATO Council table."

After the ceremony at the reception hosted by the Estonian Ministry of Defense, the three of us noted the crowd seemed quite pleased with the event. They were standing tall, to use the U.S. Army expression.

The foreign minister and a shipboard lunch

Ambassador Napper returned to Latvia July 23.

Back at Paldiski, Larry Taylor and I were ferried out to the Military Prepositioning Ship (MPS). This support ship for the Marines has supplies and ammunition for thirty days of operation.[250] These ships are deployed to strategic places around the globe to wait—ready to meet the Marines when the Marines land. As we get closer to the ship the cranes for offloading equipment come into focus. The Baltic Sea here is calm. Just lazy waves today.

Lunch is hosted by the captain, and we are joined by officers and some of the crew, who explain how the equipment is speedily offloaded to be there when the Marines need it.

Late afternoon, Ambassador Taylor and I meet with the foreign minister, Toomas Hendrik Ilves. He grew up in New Jersey and attended Columbia University.[251] He has only recently returned to Estonia after three years as the Estonian ambassador to the United States.[252] The foreign minister is delighted with the PfP exercise. Another step toward NATO membership for Estonia.

It was a good assumption, as just a few weeks earlier (June 27, 1997), Mr. NATO expansion, Ron Asmus, official title deputy assistant secretary of state for European affairs, had been in Tallinn and had flatly stated that the Baltics' membership in NATO was now the administration's official policy. This was not to be announced, but it was decided.[253]

The next morning, I said goodbye and thank you to Larry, and promised upon return to Oslo I would forage the antiquarian shops to look for British Empire colonial maps. Not a likely place to find them but you never know.

WE SEND NATO EXPANDER ASMUS TO RUSSIA

The two-day visit, August 14-15, 1997, of Ron Asmus, deputy assistant secretary for European affairs, had him moving like a balloon with the air going out.

Asmus' charge was to develop the plan for Estonia, Latvia, and Lithuania to eventually join NATO—a plan that was to accommodate the needs of Russia. (Put a call in to the undersecretary of alchemy!)

August 14: From 9 a.m. until 4 p.m. there was a meeting every hour. A get-to-know-you meeting for the embassy staff. Then Foreign Minister Bjørn Tore Godal and a briefing with the Ministry of Foreign Affairs senior staff; lunch meeting. Back to the embassy to meet the Country Team to brief on NATO expansion, and off to the airport for the flight to Kirkenes with Jonas Gahr Støre, the head of international relations for the prime minister (Due to other pressing business, I did not accompany Ron on this trip).

August 15: Asmus is driven to Murmansk. The Norwegians are not missing any opportunity to give American decision makers the lay of the land. Only by driving through it can one grasp the Arctic terrain, the sulfur smell of the yellow cloud from the nickel smelter, see the Barents Sea inlets where the nuclear submarines lurk, and experience Murmansk, a city of 400,000 and Russia's only ice-free port on the Atlantic.

At 4 p.m. there is a meeting with officers of the Northern Fleet, then dinner aboard the nuclear-powered icebreaker *Artika* hosted by the CEO of the Murmansk Shipping Company, Vyacheslav Ruksha, my by-now old friend.

At 8 p.m. was a reception for Asmus aboard the Norwegian Coast Guard vessel *KV Tromsø* with local dignitaries. The ship is there because Norway and Russia are holding a month-long border exercise.

August 16: Asmus leaves Murmansk for Helsinki on a Finnair direct flight.

THE LIST OF NATO EXPANDERS EXPANDS
AS RON ASMUS RETURNS

On September 3, 1997, I flew to Bergen to meet Marc Grossman, assistant secretary of state for European affairs (formerly ambassador to Turkey) and Ron Asmus, deputy assistant secretary for European affairs—aka Mr. NATO expansion in the State Department.

The event is billed as Nordic/Baltic/U.S. discussions. That evening there is a meeting with the foreign minister of Estonia, Latvia, and Lithuania and then a dinner. Norwegian Foreign Minister Bjørn Tore Godal is the host.

The meetings continue the morning of the 4th and a somewhat notional paper on NATO membership for the Baltics in the future is presented and labeled "The Way Ahead." Back in Oslo in the afternoon for a meeting with Prime Minister Jagland. Then Ron Asmus leaves. I host a "working dinner" at the Residence for Ambassador Grossman with a select guest list from the Parliament, Foreign Ministry, Ministry of Defense, and Jonas Gahr Støre, head of international affairs for the prime minister.

Jonas has been a dinner guest so often lately I have asked the chef to check the back menus to try to make sure he is fed something new each time.

STROBE TALBOTT ON RUSSIA, BALTICS, AND NATO EXPANSION

Deputy Secretary of State Strobe Talbott's speech on NATO expansion at Stanford University on September 19, 1997, was distributed widely. At Embassy Oslo, we circulated it to the Country Team and forwarded it to the foreign minister and prime minister.[254]

As a speechwriter, as I was and am, one reads a speech differently than others. Strobe wrote this himself. It would have taken an hour to deliver.

The opener: He "courted" his now-wife when she was at Stanford in the 1960s. He was there researching early 20th century Russian history at the Hoover Institute (part of Stanford). She is in the audience. Smiles and nods guaranteed.

Strobe is known as the "Russia hand." A scholar of Russian history. A veteran journalist: over 20 years in Moscow with *Time* magazine. He became friends with Bill Clinton when they were both Rhodes Scholars at the University of Oxford. During his time there Talbot translated Nikita Khrushchev's memoirs.[255]

He was once against NATO expansion—now he sings in the choir that praises the idea.

In the audience were former Secretary of Defense William Perry and former Secretary of State Warren Christopher. Perry was a skeptic on NATO expansion and the decision to go ahead quickly and include the Baltics was one of the reasons he had left. They were "Bill" and "Chris" in the written text.

Strobe has a mastery of the subject and gives a travelogue of the centuries of Russian history in building up to the first point. "Internally Russia long ago adopted an autocratic order. Along the way, it missed the advent of the modern nation state in the 16th century, the Enlightenment in the 18th, and the Industrial Revolution of the 19th. The Bolshevik's coup d'état plunged Russia into misery, brutality, isolation, and confrontation with the outside world."

(Coup d'état? The Bolsheviks in the October Revolution in 1917 overthrew the short-lived Russian Republic headed by Alexander Kerensky. Kerensky spent many of his 50 years in exile teaching at the Hoover Institute at Stanford. Strobe would have known him.)

"Now that Russia is again Russia rather than a metropole of an empire or headquarters of a global movement, the old debate rages anew: 'What is Russia?'" Strobe asks. Strobe says it is up to Russians to decide whether they return to the norm of autocracy or throw that baggage on the dust heap of history and choose to make their fledgling democracy last.

"Which brings me to the most salient issue of Russian foreign policy for Russia and the rest of the world alike, which is how Russia relates to those new independent states that were, until only six years ago, part of the Soviet Union and, as such, subject to Russia's domination."

On the Baltics: "(I)n our diplomacy we need to balance two factors. One is the Balt's anxieties about Russian motivations and their desire to join the EU and NATO...the other factor is Russia's fear and loathing at the Balt's fulfilling those aspirations."

"Quite bluntly, Russians need to get over their neuralgia on this subject...stop looking at the Baltic region as a pathway for foreign armies...or a buffer zone...such old-think offends and menaces the Balts...and doesn't make sense, there are no would-be aggressors to rebuff."

It would be undiplomatic to just say it, but he gets the message across that getting Eastern Europe and the Baltics inside NATO would take away any temptation for Russians to revisit their imperialist DNA. It would help answer the question of whether Russia "will be a big neighbor, or a good neighbor."

Other than using the confusing and likely untranslatable word "neuralgia," it is a very good tutorial on what makes Russia tick, and why NATO has a role to play in the post-Cold War world. It is especially helpful for United States embassies in Europe.

"MR. NATO EXPANSION" ASMUS IN OSLO—AGAIN

The plane was late on Nov 3, 1997. I met Ron Asmus at the door of the Residence at 11 p.m. A few words of welcome and then off to the guest bedroom. I told him I was thinking of a plaque for the room that said, "Ron Asmus slept here, and not just once."

The occasion for this visit in early November was U.S.-Norway bilateral talks on NATO enlargement and the Baltic States. Two words help explain why Ron Asmus so passionately works to get Eastern Europe and the Baltics into NATO: divided Berlin.

There were few surprises on my first trip to divided Berlin in 1985. I had been there before dozens of times in the movies. The classics: *The Third Man* (1949), *The Spy Who Came in From the Cold* (1965), *Cabaret* (1972).

Ron Asmus had a different experience. His parents and grandmother left Germany at the war's end to start a new life in Milwaukee. His grandmother told him stories about what life was like in Berlin before the war.

He enrolled in the University of Wisconsin at Madison to study engineering. Like many other students he went to Europe on a study abroad program. He searched for his grandmother's house in Berlin but didn't find it. He visited battlefields, concentration camps, traveled to East Berlin passing through the barbed wire and the guards, with snarling dogs, who would shoot to kill if anyone tried to escape to the West.

"The reality of this was a pivotal experience...it horrified me."[256]

He came back, changed majors, and graduated with a degree in political science. In graduate school at Johns Hopkins, he researched his dissertation on the division of Germany at the Free University of West Berlin.

On October 3, 1990, he traveled to Berlin just so he could be in the crowd standing in front of the Reichstag on the day Germany was officially reunited.

Later when he wrote a book about NATO enlargement, which he dedicated to his son Erik, he got his feelings down on paper.[257]

MEETING THE NEW PRIME MINISTER AND NEW GOVERNMENT

After the Labour Party's defeat in the September 1997 election, a new coalition government was formed and took office October 17. Kjell Magne Bondevik, leader of the Christian People's Party, became prime minister.

My briefing to Ron on Bondevik and the new government: There was no change in policy on NATO expansion; the priority remains continuing to build post-Cold War relations with Russia on the northern border; and, development aid, important to the Christian People's Party, will be more in the forefront.

The prime minister was a Lutheran minister. He could have easily been a politically active, progressive pastor in St. Paul, Minn.

Bondevik described himself as a '68er—influenced by the student strikes in Europe and the anti-Vietnam War protests in America of that year. He had a relationship with Jimmy Carter and had advocated for Norwegian help in financing the Carter Center programs in Africa.

It was no surprise Bondevik was the consensus choice for PM by the coalition, as he was a trusted hand with experience in earlier coalition governments, including a stint as foreign minister.

On the Baltics, my personal take was that support for Baltic membership in NATO was about geography. Norway, now the only NATO member bordering Russia, would feel more secure if there were other NATO members with such a border. And, like the commitment to Norway, this would mean the United States would be pledged to the defense of the Baltics.

The new foreign minister, Knut Vollebaek, whom I had just met on my courtesy call, was a career diplomat and had been the deputy director general. He was associated with the Christian People's Party. His smile of all teeth and dimples made everyone feel like he was very happy to meet you. Vollebaek had spent some time studying at the University of California-Santa Barbara.

This bilateral meeting was important and meant that along with Asmus came the top two leaders dealing with Nordic and Baltic Affairs from both the State Department and the Department of Defense.

The guest list for the lunch I hosted on November 3, the only day Asmus was in Oslo, was indicative of the need to take this opportunity to establish relations with the new government—eight from the Foreign Ministry, three from the Ministry of Defense, and the prime minister's new international advisor, all of whom needed a social occasion to get to know their American counterparts. The seating arrangement accomplished this.

At 7 p.m., I left Ron at the airport. He and the others were off for stops in Sweden, Finland, Estonia, Latvia, and Lithuania.

CHAPTER 38
THE 1997 CAMPAIGN FOR GRO TO HEAD WHO

Dr. Gro Harlem Brundtland was now an official candidate to be the director general of the World Health Organization.

She was the candidate of the United States and the other donor countries—Scandinavia, Western Europe, Canada, Japan, Australia, and New Zealand. Most of the funding of WHO came from these countries and most of the money was spent on infectious diseases in the developing world—Africa and parts of Asia. The U.S. was by far the largest funder of WHO.[258]

WHO is headquartered in Geneva with regional offices in Africa, the Americas, Europe and Southeast Asia.

The agency has a laudatory history. Formed after WWII to rebuild the health systems of war-ravaged Europe, it had performed well. It led a brilliant campaign to eradicate smallpox in 1977. The WHO-led effort to eradicate polio was near the finish line. And after decades of trying to eradicate malaria, the mosquito won, but a robust malaria control program was getting results.

In 1997, it needed reinvigoration and new management.

The donor countries had been withholding part of their dues in an effort to force more transparency in how their money was spent. The retirement of the current director general, whose management was not thought of at all highly, was the opening that was needed.

Gro, the former prime minister of Norway, a political leader known and respected, someone who would not put up with the petty graft that plagued WHO in certain regions, was the ideal candidate.

WHO is a "specialized agency" of the United Nations but is independent. Countries have to join WHO. They are not automatically members because of their membership in the United Nations. The WHO member countries elect the director general. The secretary-general of the UN, Kofi Annan, would have no say in this decision.

Officially, the health ministers of the 194 countries belonging to WHO make the decision when they meet in the annual Health Assembly, WHO's governing body. In practice, and certainly in the case of Gro with her stature and backing by the U.S. and Western Europe, this would be a decision made by heads of government.

U.S. Secretary of Health and Human Services Donna Shalala would spearhead the campaign for the U.S. and travel the globe to collect votes. Secretary of State Madeleine Albright and First Lady Hillary Clinton would be on the team behind the scenes.

Yours truly would be the liaison with the Gro campaign team in Oslo, which was headed by old friend and confidant Morten Wetland. Jonas Gahr Støre, now an adept tactician, would be directing strategy in the prime minister's office and counting votes. And putting pins on a map to determine where Gro should travel to next.

Norway had over 70 embassies worldwide that were brought to the task. This was a big diplomatic footprint for a country with a population of five million.

The U.S. plan was straightforward: Donna directed each of the over 190 embassies for a démarche (i.e., instructions) to ask the government of the country they were in if they would be voting for Gro. This would be a delicate ask in many countries and would be handled by the ambassador meeting with the head of government or foreign minister.

The results and comments would be sent by cable to Donna and to me, and a very few others. A number of cables relating to the reasons for a "no" vote or still being uncommitted discussed the personalities and Palace intrigues involved in this decision and there were a few reports of a hinted quid quo pro on an unrelated matter. And some candid comments about Gro. She wasn't liked everywhere!

I would then meet with Morten or Jonas, sometimes with Gro, or I would call them, to tell them what was in the cables they needed to know.

For meetings of this import, Morten and I decided lunches at the Bristol Hotel and the Theater Cafe would be fitting venues. Nothing in writing, not even a handwritten note. Too much risk of embarrassing an official in some country or causing a public statement of denial of some faux pas or duplicity found in a cable that would cost Gro support.

Now, dear reader, you ask why Gro Harlem Brundtland would have any opposition?

First, there were four other candidates: the heads of the WHO Africa, the Americas, and Southeast Asia regions, and a respected UN program leader in New York.[259] Each had some localized support.

Second, there was that speech to the UN Population Conference in Cairo in September 1994. A section of her speech was used by the Holy See in countries with large Catholic populations to label her as anti-Catholic and pro-abortion and by a number of countries with large Muslim populations to label her as an affront to Islam:

> Women will not be empowered because we want them to be...(the population action plan) must promise access to education and basic reproductive health services, including family planning as a universal human right... sometimes religion is a major obstacle but morality becomes hypocrisy if it means accepting mothers suffering or dying in connection with unwanted pregnancies and illegal abortions.[260]

Third, cigarette companies, alcohol producers, infant formula makers, and Western pharmaceuticals companies feared her like the plague. Cigarette taxes were a prime source of revenue for countries worldwide and there were several state-owned tobacco companies, including China, that were big parts of the economy. Of the private brands, Philip Morris was disputing every study there was showing the dangers of tobacco, including secondhand smoke, with shrouded and obliquely paid researchers ready to challenge the research methodology.

If WHO started to also emphasize non-infectious diseases like cancer and heart disease, then the inevitable result would be to put tobacco against the wall without a last cigarette. This could be recommendations against advertising, high taxes to reduce consumption, and ending tobacco grower subsidies.

However, the bigger threat would be Gro attacking the tobacco companies' intense advertising campaign to get more poor women to smoke. The only growth market left worldwide was young women. Over 60 percent of men in China smoked, but less than 10 percent of women. Smoking rates of women worldwide were very low.

Alcohol producers feared the Scandinavian mindset of Gro. Curb the advertising of alcohol, tax it to the hilt, and link it clearly to chronic diseases and as a risk in pregnancies.

Infant formula-makers, Nestlé being the big one, were targeting child-bearing-age girls in poor countries with slick promotions on how bottle feeding was the hip modern way and was healthy. Formula requires clean water and refrigeration and the lack of this was glossed over.

Gro would certainly stress that breastfeeding was essential for the health of children, especially necessary in poor countries, and would shame formula companies for marketing this costly product in countries where people were living on a dollar a day.

Western pharmaceutical companies had a lot at stake. Their goal was that their very expensive and profitable drugs continue to be protected by patents. There was already a movement to bring the same drugs in generic brands, mostly manufactured in India, into poor countries, especially in the fight against HIV. Gro would likely pressure for both lower prices, even free supplies, of patented drugs, and pave the way for generics.

The opposition to Gro fizzled. The desire of the donor countries to bring new leadership to WHO and the widespread demand for transparent budgeting and spending proved the winning ticket. The votes were well in hand by Christmas of 1997.

Dr. Gro Harlem Brundtland was nominated by WHO's executive board on January 27, 1998, and elected to the post on May 13 by the member states meeting in the Health Assembly. She took office as director-general of the World Health Organization on July 21, 1998.[261]

CHAPTER 39
A WHIRLWIND VISIT TO D.C.

A mbassadors are expected to show up in Washington once in a while to check in—sort of like a newsy letter home but delivered in person.

When I saw my final D.C. schedule for February 18-23, 1997, a marathon of 23 meetings, three lunches and five dinners in six days, I thought of the runner in the first-ever marathon who brought the news of victory at the battle of Marathon to Athens. Then he dropped over dead.

First stop, the Norwegian Embassy on the corner of 34th Street and Massachusetts Avenue just across the avenue from the vice president's house, which is on the grounds of the U.S. Naval Observatory. This embassy has the most staff of any Norwegian embassy in the world.

After being introduced to the Country Team, and doing my best to answer questions, Ambassador Tom Vraalsen invited me upstairs to the living quarters for a private lunch. This is the principal floor of this three-story mansion of Georgian architecture built originally as a private residence.

It housed all the offices and the ambassador's residence until 1941, when a new administrative wing was added for the increased staff needed to coordinate the WWII relations between the Norwegian government in exile in London and the Roosevelt White House, the State Department, and the U.S. War Department.

The Norwegian government, The King, and the Crown Prince were conducting the war effort while in exile in London, and Princess Märtha and the three children were living in Washington.

Tom recounted the friendly visit when he presented his credentials to President Clinton. The president told him about his trip to Norway as a student and what a good night it was when Their Majesties came to the White House for the State Dinner in 1994.

I noted that the steady stream of high-level officials from the State Department and the Pentagon coming to Oslo all dealt with NATO expansion or nuclear issues in northwest Russia. My schedule in D.C. demonstrated these two priorities.

Meeting with Donna Shalala

My meeting with Secretary of Health and Human Services Secretary Donna Shalala focused on the effort to elect former Norwegian Prime Minister Gro Brundtland the next director general of the World Health Organization.

I had just met with Gro in her office in the Norwegian Parliament one week before to get her take on where things stood and mentioned I would see Donna in Washington to give her an update on the campaign.

Donna was optimistic and enthusiastic about traveling to corral votes where needed. She would be at the World Health Assembly in Geneva in May and was scheduling meetings to talk about Gro. She expected to leave there with a count of the firm votes she could pass on to Oslo.

I had first met Donna when she was named chancellor of the University of Wisconsin at Madison in 1988 ten years before, almost exactly to the date. Her office in the federal Health and Human Services Building had one wall with bookshelves that were stacked with UW Badger swag—footballs, jerseys, and a stuffed Bucky Badger.

Chatting with Martin Olav Sabo

A stop to see Martin Olav Sabo, the head of the Norwegian Caucus in the Congress, was a must. Marty, whose parents had immigrated from Norway, was a longtime friend and political ally.

I last saw him when he was the host for the Norwegian Caucus lunch for His Majesty during the State Visit in 1994. He was chairman of the House Budget Committee then.

We first met in 1975 when he was the Speaker of the House in the Minnesota Legislature—the first Democrat to serve as House Speaker in state history. I was then the assistant to the Speaker in Wisconsin, Norman Anderson, and Marty came to visit. He was then the president of the National Conference of State Legislatures.

The only Minnesota-related news I had was that the head of the Minnesota National Guard, our mutual friend Major General Andreotti, was on my schedule for lunch at the end of the month. He was coming for the Norwegian Home Guard's March training exercise. I would go with him. (The Minnesota Guard and the Home Guard have had a training partnership since 1974.

To Sherri Goodman at the Pentagon

The Pentagon is not a place you just show up even if you are an ambassador. In bold letters, my assistant Sue had put on my schedule, "Take a taxi to the Mall Entrance of the Pentagon—your escort will meet you there and take you to Undersecretary for Environmental Security Sherri Goodman's office."

It was good to see Sherri on her home turf. Brass at her service. I gave my update to Sherri on AMEC (Arctic Military Environmental Cooperation). I had just met with the Department of Defense AMEC technical team before I left Oslo. They reported all good on that front.

The meeting with Sherri was in the late afternoon. When it was over, I dashed to a meeting with Sandy Vershbow, the head of European Affairs at the National Security Council.

And then a taxi downtown to meet Sherri at one of those see-and-be-seen D.C. restaurants for a dinner with her team. A happy bunch, aware they were doing something meaningful. Martini with a twist. Ribeye medium rare.

To the Environmental Protection Agency

On to the Environmental Protection Agency to reunite with Bob Dyer; Bill Nitze, head of international affairs; and Alan Hecht, the deputy. The team in charge of the northwestern Russia nuclear waste initiatives.

Bill was world-wise and well known for his family pedigree.[262] Like Bob Dyer, Alan was a scientist determined to make a difference and was in the right place at the right time.

Alan and Marshall Adair, assistant secretary for European affairs in the State Department, were coming to Oslo in March for a Norway, U.S., and Russia meeting in Kirkenes. Then the three of us would go on to Murmansk for a conference hosted by the Russians. (Marshall and I had already met for lunch at Cafe La Ruche in Georgetown. My very favorite and near the State Department. I had my usual: liver and onions, glass of house red.)

Bob drove me to the White House in his Corvette, where I checked in with Bruce Lindsey, the president's alter ego, ostensibly the deputy legal counsel.[263] We had been in the Clinton campaign at the beginning and now there was a second term. "Congratulations on the election victory, impressive winning margin in Wisconsin, tell the president all's well in Norway," and I was out of there.

I did the rest of the schedule. Safe now from the fate of the first marathon runner.

Then it was catching up with friends. A get-together with the staff I had started with in the embassy in Oslo who were now living in D.C. was organized by former political officer Hal Meinheit; and dinners with old friends including Brady Williamson, who happened to be in town.

Brady was a fountain of stories including tales from the Clinton-Yeltsin meetings. He had negotiated the locations and the staging for several of the Clinton-Yeltsin summits. Setting the October 1995 summit at Hyde Park his masterpiece.

CHAPTER 40
VACATION AT A FRENCH CHÂTEAU AND ARMAGNAC FOR PRESIDENT CLINTON

On March 24, my family and I flew to Bordeaux, picked up the small Renault van we had reserved, and drove southeast toward the foothills of the Pyrenees past vineyards and farms and small villages to the County of Armagnac. It was spring and green and the perfume of first crop of hay was in the air. It was Easter break from school for the boys.

In two hours, we were at our destination to meet our friend Endre Røsjø at his not-so-small country house, the Château de Lisse. Endre Røsjø, who lived near the Residence in Oslo, was a friend of our family and of the embassy.

We had started to rely on the kindness of Norwegian friends to help with the dinners and receptions at the Residence for the steady stream of VIPs, generals, and admirals visiting Oslo. This was partly to relieve the spouses of the embassy's staff, who were starting to wonder when they would have a life of their own. Endre, with his natural charm, always made himself available.

The château was 500 years old and showing its age. It would remind you of the Sleeping Beauty castle at Disney World. Endre was restoring it to preserve what the French called its patrimony (heritage). On the second floor, there were six bedrooms. Each had a full-size coat of armor outside the door. Meals were prepared on a spit turned by hand, or in iron pots hung on hooks, in the wood-burning hearth.

The caretaker couple lived nearby and shopped in the local town early in the morning, bringing back baguettes, bakery, butter, and jam before we were up.

There was a good restaurant in the nearby village of Jegun that served food of the season. Al fresco in a tiled courtyard when the weather allowed.

Endre had a dog named Ivre, and that dog attached himself to Karl. The boy and dog explored the estate, finding a pond where there were frogs and other things boys love to catch and dogs will bark at. The château's blue-feathered peacock screeched if they came near.

Barbara could rest and swim in the pool. There was no one to entertain or any schedule at all.

This very rural part of France of tree-lined country roads with tractors being the usual traffic was the perfect place for me to teach Alec, soon to be 16, how to drive and learn with a stick shift. (Kids in Norway can't get a license to drive until age 18.)

Endre and I were the same age and had the same interests. We went off to the local golf course. A relaxed place. Endre took the dog along and Alec came and took lessons. When he got his already-pretty-good swing down and learned the rules, he would be set for life.

Lunch in the stone house at the family-run golf course was the focus. A fashionable crowd lingering over wine. Definitely not the American game, where lunch is a hot dog wrapped in tin foil and a can of beer grabbed to-go between the first and second nine.

After golf the first day, Endre took me to visit the local wine cooperative, where farmers brought their grapes, and when it was wine, collected their share in bottles for home consumption and local sales. Endre bought wine here and put a label on the bottles of a drawing of the Château de Lisse. (He once shipped me 60 cases of this wine.)

At night, we all went outside to look up in the clearest of clear skies to see the Hale-Bopp Comet. A bright circle of light trailing white and blue tails. The whole world was watching this in wonderment.

We were in one of the best places in the world to see it. There were no streetlights, no haze, and silence. This comet would next come around in 4380.

Armagnac is the area in France where Armagnac brandy is distilled. Cognac is better known, as its regions of production are near seaports and thus it could be distributed widely. Armagnac has its devoted connoisseurs who think it much better than cognac. I was about to join this camp.

One of Endre's friendly neighbors, Mr. Patrick Maurer, was a producer of Armagnac, and he invited us to a tasting fresh out of the barrel. Mr. Maurer had left Paris, where he had worked as a stockbroker, to come home and run his family's business.

In a long shed were several rows of large oak barrels resting on their sides in wooden cradles. Mr. Maurer, who was not a small man, hopped up onto a plank ledge to be standing above the chosen barrel. He pried out the large stopper and inserted a plastic tube, then putting his thumb over the end, and pulled up to siphon a flow of the liquid. Endre and I were standing below holding our snifters high, like baby birds with open mouths in a nest waiting to be fed. Barbara took a more refined stance. The liquid was a new taste, very smooth.

Mr. Maurer was pleased that an American ambassador had tasted his Armagnac. The next day, when Endre had invited him to be our guest for lunch at the golf course, he presented me with a bottle of Armagnac in a gift box. "Mr. Ambassador, would you please deliver this to President Clinton?" The customs forms were all filled out and were in an envelope fastened to the box with a red ribbon. I was trapped. "Of course I will," I said.

Fortune was with Mr. Maurer. The next day, April 1, we returned to Oslo. I left for Washington on April 2, to meet the Norwegian foreign minister, Bjørn Tore Godal, to escort him on two days of meetings including with Secretary of State Madeleine Albright.

No time to waste. A diplomatic mission to deliver to the president of the United States a bottle of Armagnac in order to further relations with France, our oldest ally, required the utmost discretion. Certainly, too important to put anything in writing.

I called my old friend Jim Bailey, who had been an assistant to the president's chief of staff, to negotiate the handover. He called our mutual friend Debi Schiff, the president's secretary, who presides over the lobby of the West Wing where people who have appointments with the president check in and wait to be escorted to their meeting.

I arrived early the morning of April 3rd, before my schedule with the foreign minister was to begin, and handed over the gift box to Debi, with a note suggesting the staff test the gift from the land of Lafayette to check the quality before informing the president. Also in the note was that Mr. Maurer should receive a thank you letter on White House stationary signed by the president. On April 22, 1997, the letter was mailed.

> *Dear Mr. Maurer,*
>
> *Thank you for the bottle of Armagnac, which Ambassador Loftus forwarded to me. I was delighted to receive this special treat from France, and I appreciate your thoughtfulness.*
>
> *Mrs. Clinton joins me in sending best wishes.*
>
> *Sincerely,*
> *Bill Clinton*

In my thank you note to Jim and Debi, I noted: "Your quick actions in this diplomatic mission have enhanced the relations between the United States and the Armagnac-producing area of France. And, once again Norway, although they didn't know it, played the role of the honest broker..."

CHAPTER 41
APRIL 1997

PRESS MEETS PRESS IN OSLO

Tom Still, *Wisconsin State Journal*

The State Department regularly sponsors programs where American journalists are invited to visit their counterparts in a foreign country.

1n 1997, there was a Pew Foundation Civic Journalism Program. (The press is not just to inform but also is to engage citizens to create public debate.)

Mike Scanlon, our press attaché, signed us up at Embassy Oslo. Nothing the Norwegian press liked better than to talk to their American brethren, especially when it would include wine on the ambassador's nickel. I asked Mike to get Tom Still of the *Wisconsin State Journal* invited as he was involved in the civic journalism project.

Tom Still as a reporter covered the Wisconsin Legislature, then was promoted to an editor of the *State Journal*, the morning daily in Madison, and was a member of the National Association of Editorial Writers. Tom was joined for the April 13-15 event by an editor and a publisher from elsewhere in the U.S.

They were a hit and did programs in Oslo and Bergen. The dinner I hosted for the group was a great opportunity to bring the Norwegian journalists on the daily beat to the Residence. Usually, it was only those writing on foreign affairs.

James Fallows, *U.S. News and World Report* and Carter's speech-writer

The other outstanding guest in 1997 on a press-to-press program was James Fallows, a former editor of *U.S. News and World Report*, who had been President Jimmy Carter's chief speech-writer. He came to Oslo November 17-18.

Jim Fallows' was a memorable performance. He had laryngitis and would whisper his remarks and answers to questions to his wife, Deborah, who was standing beside him and she would then respond. "Which was the ventriloquist?" one wag in the Norwegian press corps asked me later.

"TOM, IT'S TOMMY. CAN I COME UP AND SEE YOU?"

On April 10, I received a phone call:

"Tom, it's Tommy. Can I come up and see you? I am in Germany."

"Sure, what are you doing there?"

"A trade mission. Norway is not on the agenda so I need something to do when I get there."

"OK. Come up and by the time you get here I will have arranged something. Just bring your cheerleading self and the Irish smile."

Wisconsin Gov. Tommy Thompson and I had been friendly adversaries in the Assembly, and continued as such when he was governor and I was Speaker. Then an interlude of the not-so-friendly variety when I ran against him for governor in 1990. Now just friends. Tommy was in his tenth year as governor, well liked, with a well-deserved reputation as Wisconsin's foremost booster.

A quick message went out to the staff and at the Country Team meeting the next day Commerce Department counselor Burt Engelhardt said he had found a large Norwegian wood products company that was looking to set up a wood-flooring factory in the U.S. Wisconsin was one of four states under consideration. Enough said.

Tommy arrived at the Residence with the young Bill McCoshen, the Wisconsin Commerce secretary and a Tommy protege; Mary Regal, the head of international development at the Wisconsin Department of Commerce, who had been arranging trips for governors for decades; and Jerry Baumbach, Tommy's State Patrol security.

Bill and Jerry were hauling enough luggage for a trip by an English lord embarking on the Orient Express for a two-month stay in Istanbul.

All l had to do was let Bill and Burt get the details on what a deal would look like with the wood products company. Bill then could explain the sweeteners for the company the state could offer. Tommy, only thing to do is to get him in front of the decision makers, and I am there to introduce him. I give him the cue, and it is showtime.

Thirty-eight guests for dinner April 16, plus a piano player.

The head table is me, Tommy, the company vice president who will make the decision on the plant location, and the VP's wife.

The others are polar explorer Liv Arnesen (first woman to ski to the South Pole alone); and the charming, talented, and famous Ellen Horn, the director of the National Theater.

Burt Engelhardt and his wife Lynn host the table with the executive vice president of the wood products company and his wife.

At her table, Barbara is hosting Gudmund Hernes, minister of health, who dropped everything to help us out on short notice as we needed someone from the Cabinet representing the prime minister.

Our two interns from the University of Wisconsin, Wendy Green and Emily Fleckner, are each hosting a table.

The menu included marinated salmon with mustard sauce and dilled potatoes; filet of reindeer with game sauce, vegetables, and lingonberries; dessert of cloudberries and ice cream. The wines were Beautour sauvignon blanc and Beringer cabernet sauvignon.

I introduced Gov. Thompson for the traditional "takk for maten" (thanks for the meal)—a brief talk the guest of honor gives. Dessert was on the tables.

By the time Tommy got through extolling his best friend Tom Loftus, the business climate in Wisconsin (different than the climate in winter), the University of Wisconsin (we are both alumni), pointing to the two interns, saying it is likely they are running the show here in Oslo, complimenting each person at his table such that they blush, and saying how impressed he is with the obvious business acumen of the vice president and the vivaciousness of his lovely wife, the ice cream had melted.

The wood-flooring factory ended up in Wisconsin.

CHAPTER 42
MAY 1997 DIARY NOTES

MAY 15, 1997:

Sherri Goodman, the U.S. undersecretary for Environmental Security at the Pentagon, arrives in Oslo for an Arctic Military Environmental Cooperation meeting with a major general and a rear admiral in tow. Russian delegation is a rear admiral and three others. Embassy Oslo arranges schedule. I host dinner at Residence. Russian vodka. California wine. Arctic cod from the Barents Sea. The second night we go to the opera (*Don Giovanni*).

MAY 21, 1997:

Barbara and I attend Bergen Music Festival opening. Music from *Tales of Hoffman.* A small reception with Their Majesties in VIP room during intermission.

MAY 23, 1997:

After a call two weeks ago from the White House personnel office informing me that it is likely political appointee ambassadors will be asked to resign end of summer, a call today: Can you stay? Don't make any plans to leave. We can't get a successor vetted anytime soon and with Jesse Helms (Republican from North Carolina) as chair of Senate Foreign Relations it will be a struggle to get anyone confirmed for months.

Word is that to avoid reappointing certain big-name ambassadors to other posts, Clinton will say his policy is that all first-term political appointees will go. I send a note to Brady Williamson: "Looks like I can determine my own time for exit and conditions thereof." He responds: "Of course. They will be relieved to not have to make the decision."

MAY 23, 1997:

Goodbye intern Emily Fleckner, hello intern Karen Febey.

MAY 29-30, 1997:

Helsinki. Conference hosted by U.S. and Russian embassies re: business opportunities in Russia. Train to Finland's historic 700-year-old Turku Castle: dinner and Russian dancers. Honeywell, J.P. Morgan, Motorola, United Technologies are U.S. participants.

CHAPTER 43
JUNE 1997

50TH ANNIVERSARY OF THE MARSHALL PLAN IN NORWAY

In honor of the 50th anniversary of the Marshall Plan in Norway, there would be a two-day celebration on June 5 and 6, 1997.

On June 5, the Norwegian Atlantic Committee and the Nobel Institute would host an event at the Nobel Institute where I would speak to open the program. In the evening at the Residence, a reception and a talk by Jo Benkow, former president of the Parliament—a lion of post-war Norway, a man of letters, and the first person I asked for advice when I arrived in Norway.

On June 6 in Stavanger, I would be the host of a program at a lunch with Ambassador Richard Holbrooke the speaker.[264] Then a reception at the art museum in Stavanger. In the evening, the mayor of Stavanger, Leif Johan Sevland, would host a dinner.

There were hundreds of guests over the two days—almost one hundred at the Residence reception to hear Jo Benkow.[265] This was yet another all-hands-on-deck event handled superbly by the embassy staff.[266]

For background, it was fortunate that my friend Geir Lundestad, head of the Nobel Institute, non-voting chair of the committee that awards the Peace Prize, and a historian, had written a book published in 1980 on the Cold War in Norway, with a section on the Marshall Plan.[267]

The Marshall Plan was a program the United States launched in 1948 to rebuild European economies after WWII. It would give grants, not loans, and how the money was spent was up to those who joined the plan.[268] The German economy was to be rebuilt. Quite different from the reparations regime in the Treaty of Versailles meant to cripple Germany economically after WWI. It was understood that countries that decided to participate in the plan were choosing to be with America and the West. They would be bound to limit the influence of Communist parties in their governments and expected to join NATO.

Norway joined early on without much debate. There was consensus both in the government and among the public that the only way to secure Norway's defense and democracy was to align with the United States.[269]

The anti-Communist position of the Labour government was strong and became entrenched when the Norwegian Communist Party supported the Soviet-backed Communist Party coup in Czechoslovakia in 1948.

American Ambassador Charles Ulrick Bay worked hard to get the labor unions to forcefully and publicly support the plan among their members, wanting there to be no doubt among workers in Norway that the Marshall Plan had union support. He was successful.[270-271]

RICHARD HOLBROOKE IS BACK IN TOWN, THE NOBEL ON HIS MIND

In 1997, President Clinton named Richard Holbrooke a special envoy to Cyprus and the Balkans on a pro-bono basis as a private citizen.

Holbrooke's numerous press interviews and talks on the Marshall Plan in Oslo and Stavanger focused on the still-tense situation in the Balkans after the Dayton Accords. When I picked him up from the airport June 5, 1997, he asked, "What's new?"

"Throwing down shots of vodka for my country in Murmansk and travel related to the Baltics. You?"

"Still on the war and peace circuit. How am I doing?"

On June 5 was a meeting with Foreign Ministry State Secretary Jan Egeland, the government's peace process facilitator. Egeland was one of the participants in the secret meetings that led to the Oslo Accords; he also managed the successful Guatemalan Civil War reconciliation talks. He was currently negotiating the final details of an international treaty to ban land mines.

The tall, fair-haired Egeland still had the California look from his days as a Fulbright scholar at UC Berkeley.

On June 6, breakfast at the Residence with Foreign Minister Bjørn Tore Godal and Jonas Gahr Støre, head of foreign relations for the prime minister. Prior to the breakfast, I updated Holbrooke on the recent meeting Godal and I had with the secretary of state in D.C.[272]

Then a flight to Stavanger for the Marshall Plan events. I had him at the airport late afternoon. Stavanger to London to catch the Concorde to New York.

We spent a lot of time together. He certainly was in the mix for the Nobel Peace Prize, and my mission was to give him my take on who gets the prize and how the decision is made.

Choosing the winner of the Nobel Peace Prize is pretty much like choosing the pope, absent the white smoke from the Sistine Chapel.

As Tip O'Neil said, "All politics is local." The members of the Nobel Committee have risen to this august position from a start as local politicians.

They are chosen by the political parties in the Parliament. Because it is based on the number of members a party has in the Parliament, the Labour Party had two appointments to the five-member committee.[273]

The decision on who is awarded the prize does not have to be unanimous. Two members resigned over awarding the prize to Henry Kissinger. One resigned over the prize going to Yasser Arafat. Two resigned in 1935 over the award to the German pacifist Carl von Ossietzky.

The prize is a subject of lobbying. Considering the political party pedigrees of the committee members, it is safe to assume the party leaders are not silent. Jagland and Brundtland were both party leader and prime minister.

The international arms of the parties would weigh in. Sweden is pushing for Carl Bildt, their former prime minister, for his role in bringing about peace in the Balkans. The Lutheran Church prays for their favorites. And there is the influential Jan Egeland, who sees the prize as leverage to bring to the recipient added power to foster the resolution of ongoing conflicts.

A big part of the decision is how it fits with the image Norwegians have of themselves. Which goes back to just why Norway and not Sweden was chosen in Alfred Nobel's will to give the Peace Prize. Nobel thought Norway was more interested in facilitating peace.[274]

What are the odds Richard Holbrooke gets the prize in 1997? Maybe if Carl Bildt is a co-awardee. Probably not because the recent trend is to influence future events—1996 to help the transition of East Timor to an independent country, 1994 to give credence to the Oslo Accords, 1993 to help Mandela when he took over as president of South Africa, 1990 to help Gorbachev stay in power.

(Proof of this for me was my involvement in the discussions held on the margins of the 1996 prize.)[275]

When I left Holbrooke at the gate in the airport, I said no one is denied the prize because he, she, or it lobbied for it. There is constant lobbying of these committee members. Everyone on the committee is a politician.[276]

UW HEALTH ECONOMICS PROFESSOR AND WHO ADVISOR RALPH ANDREANO STOPS BY

Diary note. I had asked my friend UW health economics professor Ralph Andreano to stop by Oslo on his way to WHO headquarters in Geneva. He makes it June 10. Lunch with Morten Wetland, former top aide to PM Brundtland who is now running the WHO campaign for Gro, at the Grand Hotel. Ralph has been a policy advisor for WHO for 20 years and knows all the players. He gives Morten a frank assessment of the senior staff at WHO and notes people Gro can rely on if she gets the post. I learn Ralph was Fulbright scholar at the University of Oslo 1952-1953, and that he writes assessments of WHO programs, several of which have been published as books by the UW Press.

THE PARIS AIR SHOW

Our Paris hotel was the St. James and Albany on the north side of the Tuileries Garden. The Louvre was across the way. A few steps from the hotel was our Metro station, the Pyramides. The name commemorates Napoleon's victory in Egypt in the battle of the Pyramids in 1798.

The line runs north past the stop La Courneuve-8 Mai 1945—VE Day in Europe—and soon we are at Le Bourget Airport, the site of the 42nd Paris Air Show.

Over 200,000 will attend the June 15-19 show, with 1,800 exhibitors and delegations from 97 countries. It was to open to the public on the weekend. Colonel Dan Penny, chief of the Office of Defense Cooperation, and I are escorting the top officers from the Norwegian Air Force and the head of procurement for the Ministry of Defense to the show for a program hosted by American military contractors Lockheed Martin, Sikorsky Helicopter, Northrop Grumman, Bell Helicopter and Boeing.

Le Bourget Airport is where Charles Lindbergh, a UW alumnus, landed at 10:24 p.m. on May 21, 1927, completing the first-ever solo flight across the Atlantic. He was greeted by a crowd of 100,000.

There was a grandstand like the one at the Kentucky Derby with the runway in front. Lockheed Martin had a glassed-in suite on the second level with food and drinks, where we watched. The planes paraded much like racehorses with a slow taxi down the runway, then a pivot and take-off like bats out of hell.

There was real *Top Gun* stuff. Both the F-16 and the Russian fighter jet, in turn, screamed by and then lifted their noses and shot straight up like rockets. The full-throttle roar rattled the glass in our suite. Then silence. They cut their engines, stood still for a moment, then gravity took hold and they dropped like rocks toward earth. At what seemed the last possible moment they hit the engine, pulled out of the dive, and swooped past the grandstand.

The U.S. Apache helicopter did barrel rolls the length of the runway and had the crowd gasping, and then applauding. The toga-clad fans at the gladiator games in the Coliseum perhaps had such a visceral experience.

It is largely military aircraft for sale, most of which is from the U.S., Europe, Russia, and Ukraine. Sweden with their Saab fighter jets is in the arms business. Finland is not in the fighter jet market. They were the last big buyer ordering a number of Boeing F-18s. (Good job, Ambassador Shearer!)[277] Tough times for arms merchants. The end of the Cold War—a lot of arms, and not much market for them.

For Lockheed, maker of the F-16, the Norwegians were perhaps the only buyers on the horizon, as the Norwegian Air Force fleet of F-16s was a bit outdated.

Dinner the first night (June 15) was hosted by Sikorsky Helicopters at the L'Opera Garnier. The walk from our hotel to the Paris Opera House took Colonel Penny and me past Harry's New York Bar. No stopping—we had both been there in an earlier life.

I had not been inside the Opera House before. A tour for our group had been arranged.

We walked up the outside steps and into "the Grand Escalier with its magnificent thirty-meter-high vault. Built of marble of various colours, it is home to the double staircase leading to the foyers and the various floors of the theatre..."

Then into the hall to see the 2,000 red-velvet seats on four tiers "horseshoe-shaped...so-called for the way it was designed for the audience to see and to be seen...there hangs a 8-ton bronze and crystal chandelier with its 340 lights...The ceiling painted by Marc Chagall..."[278]

The private dining room off a foyer was adorned with frescoes framed in gold leaf, most of a Roman motif. An idyll with a woman slightly draped playing a lyre would be an example.

The food and wine were sublime. They were French.

The demand for helicopters was steady and Sikorsky had opportunities other than military buyers. My many flights on rescue and commercial helicopters in Norway were proof, including a 200-mile flight from Stavanger out to the Ekofisk oil platform in the North Sea in a two-rotor passenger helicopter. This ferry of the sky brought a shift of 30 workers and supplies to the platform and returned with workers ending their three-week shift. When we landed, I was given a tour of this small city and then whisked away on a small four-seat helicopter to visit two other platforms.

In the early mornings of the air show, I walked about Paris like a flâneur, along the streets of the six-story Hausmann buildings of Parisian limestone, taking in what is fondly called "the capital of the 19th century." One morning crossing at a busy intersection my name is called out. It is Paul Fanlund, who covered the Legislature for Madison's morning newspaper, the *Wisconsin State Journal*. Here on a family vacation.[279]

The second night (June 16) there is first a reception at the American ambassador's residence for U.S. Sen. Tom Harkin of Iowa hosted by the Deputy Chief of Mission Donald Bandler.

Alas, Ambassador Pamela Harriman is gone. She died on February 5, 1997, after suffering a stroke while swimming in the pool at the Paris Ritz. She was given all the honor she so rightly deserved by both America and France. I have cherished memories of being with Pamela as her guest on prior trips to Paris. I had previously stayed with her at the American ambassador's residence at 41, rue du Faubourg Saint-Honoré. *The New York Times* obituary could only summarize her eventful life. Her life could not be contained in words.[280]

Harkin was a former Navy pilot. I knew him quite well. He ran for president in the 1992 Democratic primary and came to Wisconsin a lot to campaign. He had won the Iowa caucuses and primaries in Idaho and Minnesota, but his message of Midwest populism didn't travel. He dropped out and was the first of that '92 primary field to endorse Clinton. We in the Clinton primary campaign owed him a lot.

We chatted and caught up, but I had to leave for the Eiffel Tower. The Northrop Grumman reception was in the Gustave Eiffel Room, which is a glass-enclosed restaurant 100 feet up the tower. From this vantage point the rooftops of Paris spread out before you at eye level.

I had read Charles De Gaulle's memoirs, Jean-Paul Sartre, and Simone de Beauvoir. But what I knew about France since the 1960s was what I knew about Paris, and what I knew about Paris was the Paris of the French New Wave films of the '60s, especially those of Jean-Luc Godard and his masterpiece, *Breathless*.

Maybe I was looking down on the street of the last scene where Jean-Paul Belmondo is gunned down by the cops after being ratted out by Jean Seberg. Finis.

The food and the wine were sublime. They were French.

The next day (June 17) we were all at the Boeing Chalet on airfield grounds for lunch. Then Colonel Penny and I left our group of Norwegians to meet with Norm Augustine, the CEO of Lockheed Martin. Norm was a regular in Oslo and a frequent dinner guest at the Residence.

Lockheed Martin had pending business with the Norwegian armed forces, including the Navy, for sales that required offsets. Offset means that if we buy what you are selling, we expect you to buy something relevant to the deal that we manufacture.

It is a negotiation with explicit rules for the U.S. contractor governed by the Bureau of Industry and Security in the Commerce Department. Minute attention is paid to any proposed technology transfers that could conceivably risk United States' national security.[281]

Our military attaché cadre in the embassy facilitated the meetings on offsets and brought me in when a smile, a dinner, and a nudge were needed to lubricate the negotiations.

The evening reception was hosted by the chairman of Bell Helicopter at the Carnavalet Museum.[282]

The Huey emblematic of the Vietnam War was a Bell helicopter. Traffic helicopters and just about anything used for commercial purposes are Bells. At this air show the Bell Tilt Rotor, known militarily as the Osprey, was being showcased for commercial use.

On Wednesday (June 18), a private evening of drinks and then dinner for just the Norwegian delegation hosted by Lockheed Martin. I am the co-host with the Lockheed executive with the Norwegian account. The two of us and the head of procurement of the Ministry of Defense will have a private lunch tomorrow (June 19). After lunch, Colonel Penny and I would take the airport train to Charles De Gaulle and catch the direct flight to Oslo.

Dinner is at a Michelin Star restaurant on Île Saint-Louis. It was a modest place, not one of those white-tablecloth establishment with hovering waiters. This eatery was all about the food.

I looked at the paper menu in English, meant to be a souvenir, and was shocked at the prices. Quite a bit lower than a similar place in Oslo. I kept the menu and underlined my choice: Turbot with watercress, saffron butternut squash, cockles, in a creamy barley sauce.

GOODBYE DINNER FOR THE RUSSIAN AMBASSADOR

From my diary, June 23, 1997: Ambassador Juri Fokine (the Russian ambassador) is leaving to be Russian ambassador to the United Kingdom. We host a going-away dinner for him and his wife Maia. Juri has been my closest colleague for three years. We may have had thirty lunches together. A reformer aligned with Yeltsin and Kozyrev (former Russian foreign minister). He will be missed.

"DIPLOMACY, LOFTUS STYLE"

"OSLO–'Diplomacy,' deadpanned U.S. Ambassador Tom Loftus, the former Assembly Speaker from Sun Prairie, 'is just local politics with better food.'" That was the first line of the June 29, 1997, newspaper story. The headline was "Diplomacy, Loftus Style."

When Tom Still, the associate editor of the *Wisconsin State Journal*, Madison's morning paper, came to Oslo in April to participate in a United States Information Agency program with Norwegian journalists, he followed me for two days for a story he would write on my experience.

In the June 29th Sunday *Wisconsin State Journal*, he delivered. A photo above the fold of Barbara and me with the Residence in the background. Given the perspective the house looks enormous. (Well, it is not small.)

An experienced journalist, Tom accurately captured my three-and-a-half years in Norway. He knew to start with the stuff interesting to the Sunday paper reader sitting at the breakfast table in a bathrobe with a cup of coffee and a piece of toast.

Second paragraph: "Take the April evening Barbara Loftus hosted a charity fashion show at the American ambassador's Residence in Oslo, Norway's captivating capital. The show was nearly over when her husband took a seat in the front row—just as a tall blonde modeling a see-through dress strolled by." (He must have eyes like Superman. I don't remember this dress!)

"Loftus had just come straight from a wine tasting reception at the U.S. Embassy, where three California wineries tried to catch the eye of Norway's top sommeliers and the product director of the state-run 'Vinmonopolet,' which translates quite literally to 'wine monopoly.'

"The California wineries paid all the bills for the reception at the embassy, which is in sight of the Royal Palace.

"He explains alcohol is not allowed to be advertised in Norway, and has to be purchased at the state-owned stores, so these wine tastings are one way to get California wine in the noses and on the lips of the buyers. This is one of several examples given of the embassy's effort to promote American business."

The entire second page of the article is devoted to the efforts in Murmansk of the U.S.-Norway-Russia cooperative programs to secure nuclear waste from the Russian Navy's submarine fleet.

In a sidebar, Tom features the newly organized sixty member UW Madison Alumni Club that had its first meeting in March at the Residence. Header: "Can 'Varsity' be sung in Norwegian?" ("Varsity" is an ode sung in praise of the UW, including at football games.)

Tom pegs me this way: "There was a time when most ambassadors were independently wealthy socialites who were rarely heard or seen outside diplomatic circles...Clinton expects his ambassadors to do more, explained Loftus, the son of a farm implement dealer who brought neither wealth nor a white-tablecloth upbringing to the job."

My mother said, commenting on the story: "You tell him we had a white tablecloth on the table every Easter!"

CHAPTER 44
DIARY NOTES JULY 1997

HONG KONG GONE

On July 2, 1997, I attended a reception at the Chinese ambassador's residence: "Celebration of Resumption of Sovereignty over Hong Kong." First time I have ever been to anything hosted by the Chinese ambassador, my diary notes.

A HOLE IN ONE FOR A VISITING BADGER?

Dave Travis, a friend from the Wisconsin Legislature, visits July 30. On a golf course near Oslo, we are at a par 3 hole, where you shoot from a hill over a gorge down to the green. Dave's iron shot hit the green, rolled to the flag and disappeared. Hooray! Alas, it is behind the hole, hidden in the shadow of the pin. After golf, Dave, noting that the walk-in refrigerator in the kitchen is stocked with lettøl, asks the chef what that means. She accurately translates the word as "light beer." Ah hah! Like his favorite American quaff, Miller Lite. Dave concludes that this Norwegian beer "doesn't have much of kick but tastes good."

CHAPTER 45

A NOTE TO RICHARD HOLBROOKE, A LITTLE FAVOR FOR GRO

From my diary dated August 22, 1997: *Aftenposten*[283] has today a long interview with Holbrooke (currently special envoy to Cyprus) at his apartment in Manhattan overlooking Central Park. It is all about Bosnia, etc. "The core of the problem is the Serb republic within Bosnia. The Bosnian Serb republic is run by a group of criminals who still control the media...war criminals and old-fashioned crooks...the Serbs are the worst...their media spreads racist and fascist agitation... it would be as if Goebbels or the Ku Klux Klan were in charge of a TV station."

I have it translated and fax it to him so he will have it mid-morning East Coast time. It notes in the article that although a private citizen, President Clinton has appointed him special envoy to the divided island of Cyprus.

I write a note on the fax cover sheet. "Dick, for your information Cyprus has a vote on the WHO committee that will choose the next Director. As you know, Gro Harlem Brundtland is our candidate."

CHAPTER 46
SEPTEMBER 1997

TEDDY BEARS, DOLLS, AND FLOWERS FOR PRINCESS DIANA

Diary note September 2: 10 a.m.: Signed the condolence book for Princess Diana on behalf of the president, first lady, and Americans.[284] Thought a lot about what to write and practiced writing it. My mother would think this important. She was taught the Palmer method and had beautiful handwriting. There were teddy bears, dolls, and flowers wrapped in cellophane, most with notes pinned to them, in neat piles covering the sidewalk in front of the British Embassy. My assistant Sue left flowers. Sparkles of reflected light from the cellophane on this sunny morning. A steady stream of mostly young girls waited for their turn to place flowers. Perhaps they believed the notes would be collected and given to angels to read to the princess in heaven. Perhaps they were right.

RECEPTION HOSTED BY THEIR MAJESTIES KING HARALD AND QUEEN SONJA AT SKAUGUM

The Skaugum Estate is the residence and private home of Their Majesties, so the invitation to the autumn reception for the Diplomatic Corps for September 2, noting it would be held at their private home, Skaugum Estate, set things abuzz at the embassy.[285] May-Britt, the embassy's director of protocol, who has now kept me faux-pas free for over three years, had marked on my schedule in capital letters in bold print "Dark Dress!" Meaning not a tuxedo but almost.

When Crown Prince Olav married Princess Märtha in 1929[286], this farm with its large wooden manor house and expanse of land was secured for their official residence and home. It burned down the next year.

A new house was built of brick and ready for Crown Prince Olav and Princess Märtha in 1932. It was here on February 21, 1937, that King Harald was born.

In WWII, it was expropriated by the Nazi occupation regime and the head of the occupation, Reichs Kommissar (Governor) Josef Terboven, lived there until his suicide in a bunker on the grounds in 1945 when the war was lost.[287]

This house was featured in the PBS Masterpiece Theater series *Atlantic Crossing* in 2020.[288] Skaugum is an easy half-hour drive south of Oslo along the fjord and Edmund (my driver) pulled the Chevy onto the gravel drive leading to the house exactly in time to be exactly on time.

"Skaugum farm is situated high above the town of Asker, with Skaugum Hill behind it. The main house rises above cultivated farmland on one side with the beautiful garden and park stretching westwards from the back of the building."[289]

Sunset was hours away and with the sun and the smiles of Their Majesties the reception room was brightly lit. The living area was devoid of trappings and comfortable. It would not be proper for me to describe their private home beyond this.

His Majesty and Her Majesty became quite relaxed when they saw me, a friendly face of several years. I was an ambassador with one of the longest tenures now. I did slip in during the chatting that I would be leaving at the end of the year. His Majesty said these years had gone by too fast.

PARLIAMENTARY ELECTIONS ARE A BUST
FOR THE LABOUR PARTY

The ruling Labour Party under Prime Minister Thorbjørn Jagland (also the party chairman) made it their platform for the September parliamentary elections that if they did not get 36.9 percent of the vote on September 15 they would resign.

I thought I knew a thing or two about campaigns, and this seemed the surest way to lose. Added to this was the rationale (a different word than rational) that Labour under Gro Harlem Brundtland had received 36.9 percent of the vote in 1993.

This Brundtland versus Jagland comparison was more like a plotline from a Shakespearean play about palace intrigue than a vote-getting strategy. It also allowed the other parties to concentrate on picking off traditional Labour Party voters. Three parties formed a united front in opposition, sending a signal that they would be able to form a coalition government if Labour lost.

A winning strategy. Labour received 35.1 percent of the vote. They would leave government in mid-October. They had only lost two parliamentary seats and were still the largest party in Parliament, with 65 seats out of 165.

Kjell Magne Bondevik, the leader of the Christian People's Party, which had made impressive gains from the last election, getting 13.7 percent of the vote and growing to 25 seats, was chosen prime minister by the coalition. The Cabinet posts would be distributed among the other two parties.

The new government would take over on October 17. The people I had worked with for near to four years, whom I had come to know well and were friends, would be gone: PM Jagland, Foreign Minister Bjørn Tore Godal, Minister of Defense Jørgen Kosmo, and head of international relations for the PM, Jonas Gahr Støre, would be replaced by a new team.

The embassy got busy scheduling me to say goodbyes to the outgoing and hellos to the incoming.

U.S. SUPREME COURT JUSTICE ANTONIN SCALIA TALKS ABOUT THE DEATH PENALTY IN OSLO

When, on September 24, U.S. Supreme Court Justice Scalia came to speak to the Oslo University Law School on "originalism," he stated that in his legal philosophy, because the death penalty was common when the Constitution was adopted in 1789 and is not singled out as "cruel and unusual punishment" in the Eighth Amendment adopted in 1791, it can't be outlawed by the court. He went on to say, with the glibness that only someone with a lifetime appointment could venture, that he may be able to uphold cutting someone's ear off as a penalty.[290]

Did I hear that correctly? Yes, I did, and so did the students. Back to them in a moment.

I escorted the justice on a tour of Oslo, and he wanted to buy a souvenir. Because he didn't want to change any money, he asked if I would pay and then let him know the next time I was in Washington and he would buy lunch at the court. Which I did. No reply.

Back to the law students. The law students would have studied the death penalty trial for the Norwegian traitor Vidkun Quisling, who headed the puppet government for the Nazis during their occupation of Norway in WWII. This trial was followed throughout the world.

After the end of occupation in Norway, when the Labour government and members of Parliament were back in Oslo, the question of the treatment of those thousands of Norwegians who had been traitors, collaborators, henchmen, double agents, enablers of the Nazi regime, and Norwegians who had joined the war as soldiers on the German side required original thinking about the death penalty.[291]

The charges against Quisling were his formation of a "government"— he claimed he was a head of state and should be treated as such—his complicity in the deportation of Jews; his responsibility for death sentences for Norwegian patriots; and, "even before the invasion in 1940 he had been an accomplice of the Germans, received financial support from them, and assisted them in their planning of an attack on Norway."[292]

Part of the proof for this latter charge came from notes taken of a 1939 meeting between Quisling and Hitler by one of those in the meeting. This came out at the Nazi war crimes trials in Nuremberg. "At the end of the meeting we all shook hands and probably will not meet again until the action has been successfully completed, and the name of Norway's Ministerial President is Quisling."[293]

Quisling was sentenced to death. There was no death penalty under Norwegian law. There was the death penalty in the code governing the Norwegian military for treason. This was clarified by a law enacted by the government-in-exile in London during the war to include acts of treason by civilians. Quisling was executed for his many treasonous acts.

The law students would have studied how their country grappled with and resolved such questions as: How could be there be assistance to the enemy when Norway was not at war with Germany? It had capitulated. Furthermore, the occupation was over and how could penalties be applied retroactively? Something that is prohibited in the Norwegian Constitution. Did the Norwegian government-in-exile in London have the power to legislate when they made treason a civilian crime? Few knew this had ever happened, so how can they be prosecuted under a law they did not know existed?

In the end, there were death sentences of 30 Norwegian collaborators, including Quisling and two of his deputies, and 15 German war criminals. Ten of the Norwegians were members of the Rinnan gang, undercover Gestapo agents who exposed more than 1,000 members of the Norwegian Resistance, causing hundreds to be tortured and shot.[294]

The other case the law students must have been fascinated by was the trial of Knut Hamsun, Norway's most famous and prestigious author, who had won the Nobel Prize for literature in 1920. His well-documented and public support of the Nazis, before and during the war, including meeting with Hitler, was treason.

The death penalty wasn't in question, but a long prison term was. Hamsun was 80 when the Germans invaded, and 87 when he stood trial. Did he know what he was doing? Was there a stroke during the war that caused brain damage? A psychiatric report said he was incompetent.

He was brought to trial in a civil case, charged with collaboration and convicted. His fine was calculated to take most of his wealth but not leave him destitute.[295]

CHAPTER 47
NOVEMBER 1997

REUNITING WITH JEAN KENNEDY SMITH AND
MEETING U.S. AMBASSADOR TO THE VATICAN

The all-Europe ambassadors meeting at the headquarters of U.S. Army Europe in Wiesbaden, Germany on November 4 and 5 was an opportunity to get to know and be briefed by the leaders of other embassies I had little contact with. My meetings were mostly with ambassadors to other NATO countries, and with my Nordic and Baltic colleagues.[296]

There had been quite a few departures since the second Clinton administration had started. My friend Alan Blinken (Belgium) and his brother Donald (Hungary) were still in country, and it would be great to see them again before I left.[297]

I had not seen Ambassador Jean Kennedy Smith (Ireland's ambassador and JFK's youngest sister) since our friendship was sealed at the last all-Europe meeting in 1994. We quickly took up where we left off. After the program and an observable interval at the reception in the Officer's Club, we left and found a booth in the relaxed bar of the nearby Non-Commissioned Officer's Club (sergeants), which also served as pool hall and burger grill, complete with pinball machines.

We decided that since I was leaving Norway soon and she was thinking about making it in Ireland until St. Patrick's Day in March 1998 but didn't know for sure, we would form a club and only meet when chance brought us together. We clinked glasses and it was the official first meeting. Talk about exclusive.

The schedule of briefings was packed and only non-NATO-country ambassadors spoke. A thought-provoking session was on property restitution in the former Soviet states of Eastern Europe and the Baltics. All the property, including art, that had been stolen by the Nazis or expropriated by the Communists had to be accounted for and some settlement with the rightful owners was needed. This was one of the conditions that countries joining the EU or NATO had to agree to.

The Army, always a good host, had arranged for our dinner at the historic spa in Wiesbaden, the Kurhaus (cure house). "The Wiesbaden Kurhaus, landmark of an elegant city, is surrounded by a lot of green, and splendid historical buildings. Twelve rooms and parlors of varying size and style, several restaurants and the Casino are all assembled under one roof, adjacent to the theater colonnades with the State Theater of Hesse built in the baroque style. The Colonnades opposite running over 129 m, are the longest columned hall in Europe providing additional space for further events, special fairs, and exhibitions. Besides, it's there, where you find the so-called 'Petty Gamble' of the Casino."[298]

On the free afternoon there were short excursions offered, touring the base or a driving tour of historic Wiesbaden. There was a trip by minivan up the Rhine River to a vineyard and a sampling in its cellar. None of my continental European colleagues chose this, likely having had their fill of vineyard visits.

Norway having no vineyards and all the wine served at the Residence being from California, I chose this outing and was joined by Lindy Boggs, the United States ambassador to the Vatican (officially the ambassador to the Holy See).

I knew of Lindy. Her husband, Hale Boggs, was in the House representing a district in New Orleans and had risen to the post of majority leader before he died in a plane crash in Alaska in 1972 while campaigning for the re-election of a colleague. Lindy was elected to fill his seat in a special election and served in the House for almost 20 years.

On the trip up the Rhine, we found a lot of things in common, including me telling her that her son Tommy Boggs, a lawyer in D.C., had helped me in my campaign for governor in 1990. Also, I was a delegate for Morris Udall at the Democratic Convention in Madison Square Garden in 1976 when she was chair of the convention. (She was the first woman to preside over a major party convention.)

The keeper of the wine cellar was so pleased that two U.S. ambassadors were there to taste the vineyard's wine that he took us to the cellar below the cellar where the good stuff was kept. Bottles from historic years going back more than two centuries.

This dark and damp treasure vault was accessed by going down a narrow stairway of stone steps and pulling back a curtain of cobwebs. The uncorking was a ritual of patience on his part. As for us, we wondered what a bottle from this old vintage would taste like. Not bad! We were complimented as being the most appreciative samplers in recent memory.

ME? IN HARLEY DAVIDSON MOTORCYCLES' NEW AD CAMPAIGN?

Early on the morning of November 6, Dr. John Gatto, the head of the Wisconsin trade office in Frankfurt, only a 30-minute drive from Wiesbaden, picked me up after I had checked out of the hotel.

First, a visit to the trade office to meet the staff, and then to the Harley Davidson Motorcycle dealer to see the latest made-in-Milwaukee model on sale in Europe and take photos of me on the bike. Unlikely, but possible, that a slim man in a double-breasted Savile Row bespoke light gray suit could spur sales.

Lunch was hosted by the "Friends of the Hessen-Wisconsin Partnership," representatives of several Wisconsin corporations with operations in Europe, along with some familiar faces from the Hesse Parliament.

Then off to Berlin.

PELIKAN PENS AND PARKER PENS IN BERLIN

Richard Holbrooke had insisted that I visit Berlin before I left Norway. Berlin had a spell on me. I was there in divided Berlin in 1985. The Rostropovich concert I attended then left an indelible memory.

In November 1989, on a Wisconsin-Hessen sister state trip, the West German consul general in Chicago arranged an onward trip to

Berlin for Barbara and me not knowing that it would be only a few days after the border between East and West Berlin was opened.

I have a photo of me from that trip with a small sledgehammer pounding on the wall. We walked through the checkpoint with thousands of West Berliners into the mysterious East. Walking into the West were thousands of East Berliners, singing and crying.

Holbrooke had founded The American Academy in Berlin in 1994, and it now had a director and the first class of fellows. Its purpose was "an effort to replace soldiers with scholars ...and enhance the long-term intellectual, cultural, and political ties between the United States and Germany."[299]

It is privately funded and housed in the Hans Arnold Center, a 40-room villa on the Wannsee, a lakeside area in the Berlin suburbs—a facility made possible by the city of Berlin.

I met Dr. Gary Smith, the first director of the academy, still in his office in nearby Potsdam readying to leave his current position as the director of the Einstein Forum. "Underlying the Einstein Forum is an abiding belief that thinking has a purpose besides advancing scholarly and scientific knowledge. It must provide orientation, foster curiosity, and inspire creativity...like Albert Einstein himself, it must be committed to social responsibility ..."[300]

Next at Holbrooke's suggestion was a meeting with the director of the Aspen Institute of Berlin. "The Aspen Institute Germany promotes dialog among conflicting parties, and Euro-Atlantic cooperation by convening decision makers and experts from the fields of politics, business, academia, media, culture, and civil society in five programs."[301]

On my list was a meeting with the president of the Berlin State Parliament (Abgeordnetenhaus). Like Hesse, Berlin is one the 16 states of Germany.

The American diplomatic presence in Berlin started in 1797, then the capital of Prussia, with the first ambassador being John Quincy Adams, appointed by President John Adams, his father.

During the Cold War, the U.S. had embassies and ambassadors in West Germany in Bonn and East Germany in East Berlin. There was also a U.S. mission in West Berlin, diplomatically attached to the Bonn Embassy but on certain topics answering to the commanding U.S. general in the American zone. With Germany and Berlin reunited, the American Embassy would now move back to Berlin (scheduled for 1998).

In my briefing on Dr. Herwig Haase, president of the Berlin State Parliament, he was described as "amiable, well-educated, and polished."[302] President Haase had just one month ago hosted a dinner for a visiting delegation of American state legislators.

Haase was an economist with a Ph.D. and told me his academic training helped, but when the goal was to get money to the former East Berlin for roads, schools, and health care as fast as possible, there was no textbook to consult. The delegates representing former East Berlin were fitting in and the Parliament had no problems functioning.

Then the gift. He presented me with one of the famous German-made Pelikan Souverän Fountain Pens in a box with a bottle of ink nestled inside. The lettering on the barrel of the pen was "Abgeordnetenhaus of Berlin. Der Präsident."[303]

This led to a delightful discussion. I informed him that Parker Pens, which he was very familiar with, were made in Janesville, Wisconsin. President Clinton used them for signing legislation and then giving as gifts.

When back in Oslo, I called my friend Roger Axtell, who handled international relations for Parker, and learned that starting with JFK, all U.S. presidents used Parker pens for bill signings. LBJ once ordered 60,000 Parker pens and used up to 70 of them to sign a bill and then give as souvenirs.

I included these details in my thank-you note written with my Pelikan to President Haase.

SUNDAY TEA WITH PRINCESS RAGNHILD

Princess Ragnhild and her husband Erling Lorentzen invited Barbara and me to their home in Oslo for Sunday tea November 9. The Princess is the eldest sister of His Majesty.[304] They were not often in Oslo as they lived in Rio de Janeiro. Mr. Lorentzen had substantial business holdings in Brazil.

This was a very gracious gesture by the Palace to acknowledge I was leaving Norway soon. (Their Majesties do not entertain ambassadors socially.)

My protocol officer prepared a briefing. The princess is addressed as Your Highness. (Official title: Her Highness Princess Ragnhild Mrs. Lorentzen.)

Mr. Lorentzen was a member of the Linge Company during the war. These were the commandos engaged in sabotage, including the disabling of the heavy water plant at Rjukan, although Mr. Lorentzen was not in this group.

After the war, he was in the Royal Police Escort, a special unit responsible for safeguarding The King and the royal family, including Princess Ragnhild.

There was nothing formal about our visit at all. We had coffee and cakes.

Both the princess and Mr. Lorentzen had questions about President Clinton—"What is he like?"—and the State Visit to the White House by Their Majesties in 1995. I told the story of the president inviting His Majesty to the Truman Balcony, where Clinton was to produce a cigar and light it so it was a clear signal to The King it was OK to have a cigarette.

Princess Ragnhild had vivid memories of FDR, the White House, and the years she and her mother (Crown Princess Märtha) and two siblings (Prince Harald and Princess Astrid) lived in Maryland during WWII. She was a teenager by the war's end and their return to Norway.

"How did First Lady Hillary Clinton enjoy the Winter Olympics in Lillehammer?" Princess Ragnhild opened the 1952 Winter Olympics in Oslo as her grandfather King Haakon and father Crown Prince Olav were in London for the funeral of King George VI.

Mr. Lorentzen is tall with broad shoulders and her highness is charming and has captivating eyes. They are both quick to laugh. There was controversy over their marriage as she was the first of the royal family to marry non-royalty. Their smiles indicated it was meant to be.

CHAPTER 48
DECEMBER 1997

ANNE BROWN, THE ORIGINAL BESS OF *PORGY AND BESS*— SAYING GOODBYE AND THANK YOU

The soprano Anne Brown, the original Bess of *Porgy and Bess,* was a special friend of the embassy and our personal friend.[305] Anne was very often a guest at the Residence. An American icon and a Norwegian institution. A legend.

After George Gershwin was captivated by her singing of Bess in early rehearsals of his opera—it was a minor part—he rewrote the part for Anne Brown to be one of the two main characters. She would sing the lead role of Bess.

The opera debuted in 1935 and was a sensation. However, her career was a constant fight against racism. In 1936, along with the other Black performers, she refused to perform *Porgy and Bess* at the National Theater in Washington, D.C., unless the audience was integrated. The management relented but segregation returned when the show closed.

Brown toured Europe from 1942 to 1948, leaving the United States because of the ongoing racial prejudice. She sang with operas and symphony orchestras. Her voice became compromised by asthma, and she stopped singing.

In 1948, she married a Norwegian Olympian, ski jumper Thorleif

Schjelderup, and settled in Oslo. They eventually divorced. Anne became a Norwegian citizen and continued teaching singing and staging operas in Norway. [306]

When we met in 1994, she was 82 and still beautiful. Always dressed as if ready for the photographers on opening night. Her soft brownish hair wonderfully coiffed. In the photos of her through the years you will see it was a look that was hers alone.

She was a regular at the Steinway in the Residence, which was available to her anytime she wanted. She became Barbara's singing teacher and dear friend. When she was guest at a dinner there was an excitement among the Norwegians to meet her.

One of our greatest days in our four years in Oslo was when Anne invited us to lunch at her small apartment and we had cheese sandwiches, red grapes, and coffee on the sunny balcony, which barely fit the three of us given the many pots of geraniums.

In 1998, Anne would receive the Peabody Award for her outstanding contribution to music in America. When she was 16, her application to study voice at the Peabody Institute, in her hometown of Baltimore, was rejected because of her race.

THE NOBEL PEACE PRIZE GOES TO AN AMERICAN

The announcement

It is a great honor for an American to be awarded the Peace Prize, which was announced October 11, 1997 and this meant the embassy had a special task: to welcome and help host the prize recipients. It was a joint prize, awarded to the International Campaign to Ban Landmines and American Jody Williams, who coordinated the campaign. The ceremony will be December 10. [307]

I know Jody Williams and consider her a friend. We met in Nicaragua in 1987. [308] The prizes are in recognition of the advocacy that helped bring about the 1997 Convention on the Prohibition of the Use, Stockpiling, Production and Transfer of Anti-Personnel Mines and on their Destruction. It is the international agreement that bans anti-personnel land mines. A United Nations treaty that Norway was instrumental in negotiating. [309]

The final document was worked out at a meeting in Oslo on September 26. Norwegian Foreign Minister Bjørn Tore Godal and the Canadian minister of foreign affairs of Canada, Lloyd Axworthy, representing the two countries that led the negotiations, presented the agreed-upon document, with UN Secretary General Kofi Annan looking on.

It has a great deal of support, with more than one hundred nations set to support the treaty on December 3, the first day open for signing. Norway will sign on this day.[310] This prize brings with it some controversy for President Clinton that will need attention. As my press attaché Mike Scanlon often tells me, this is why I get the big salary.

The United States is not signing on to the treaty. The president has said he wants to be able to sign, but his condition was rejected: an exemption for the mines in South Korea on the border with North Korea. Absent these mines there would be no slowing of invading North Korean forces getting to Seoul.

The pressure on Clinton is pretty intense. Add to this is the recent death of Princess Diana, who was a champion of ridding the world of land mines. This treaty is part of her legacy. The president is criticized by Democrats, the press, former members of his administration, and General Schwarzkopf, the hero of Desert Storm, which pushed Iran out of Kuwait in 1991.

America's allies are urging that an international treaty requiring signing nations to stop deploying mines—and to clean up those in the ground within 10 years—also include the world's largest military power.

Jody Williams called the president a coward, addressed him as Billy, and said he was a "weenie," adding, "He has time to call the winners of the Super Bowl, but the winner of the Nobel Peace Prize he can't call?" She adds that he probably had not called because, "If he calls me, he knows I'm going to say, 'What's your problem?'"[311]

Did I mention I consider her a friend?

The next day after the prize was announced, October 12, we had a special Country Team meeting to plan the way forward. A few minutes of grumbling about the disrespect for the president, then down to work. Congratulations from me go out to the laureates immediately. There will be a lunch hosted by the ambassador at the Residence and the Nobel Prize awardees are to invite most of the guests. We will take out all the furniture, fit in every table possible, and make it a gala affair. There will be a point person at the embassy to call day or night.

Here is a summary of our brief. Finland, Estonia, Latvia, and Lithuania will not be signing—call that a vote of no confidence in the future of a "new" Russia. The new members of NATO, Poland, Hungary, and the Czech Republic, will be signing—call that a vote of confidence in NATO protection.

There are 100 million live anti-personnel mines buried in 60 countries left from wars. Civilian populations are most at risk; 25,000 people are injured or die every year. Bobby Muller, a Marine officer who when in Vietnam in 1969 was crippled from the waist down from a bullet that hit his spinal cord, will be with us. He founded Vietnam Veterans of America, which in turn co-founded the International Campaign to Ban Landmines.

To be clear, we will be hosting Jody Williams for her prize, and Bobby Muller for the prize representing the campaign. We know there is some resentment toward Jody Williams getting a separate prize (not her decision). The point being there should have been just one for the campaign. Our brilliant protocol officer May-Britt Ivarson will have her work cut out for her to put together this seating chart.

The awards ceremony

I am seated in the City Hall December 10 with the other ambassadors and invited guests for the awards ceremony. This year I am in the front row because the laureate is an American.

The chair of the five-member Prize Committee, Professor Francis Sejersted, gives the reasons why the campaign and Jody Williams were chosen. He makes a point of noting the first Nobel Peace Prize was awarded to a woman, Bertha von Suttner, and goes on to say: "With her self-sacrificing, untiring, and fruitful service to humanity and peace, Jody Williams is a worthy successor to Bertha von Suttner, who inspired the Peace Prize and brought Alfred Nobel to the realization that peace must be rooted in the human mind."[312]

Jody Williams gives the lecture on behalf of herself and the campaign but handles it this way: "It is a privilege to be here today, together with other representatives of the International Campaign to Ban Landmines, to receive jointly the 1997 Nobel Peace Prize."

She then covers the history of the effort to ban mines, singling out the early efforts of the International Committee of the Red Cross, lists countries where the mines are, notes that 121 countries have signed the treaty since December 3, and gives the U.S. Congress credit for "the early lead taken in the United States, with the first legislated moratorium on land mine exports in 1992."[313]

The banquet

This is my first peace prize banquet, as only the ambassador and spouse representing the country the laureates are from are invited. It is a black-tie affair held December 10 in the Grand Hotel's blue-themed ballroom, the Rococo room.

The Rococo is considered one of the most beautiful and unique banquet halls in Norway, with its classic ceiling painting, authentic Italian silk tapestry, and shimmering Venetian chandeliers.

At the Nobel Banquet, some 250 guests are welcomed by the Nobel Committee before in due course finding their places at the round tables in the banqueting hall—laid for the occasion with the special Nobel dinner service—to enjoy a five-course gourmet meal.

The laureate's table is right in the middle of the hall. Seated with the laureate are the members of the Nobel Committee, the president of the Parliament, and the prime minister.[314]

Next day, lunch at the Residence

It was a bright sunny day, rare for Oslo in December. Sixty-five guests at round tables. A record for this venerable house.

At the head table, Jody Williams is on my right and Bobby Muller is on my left. Former Prime Minister Gro Harlem Brundtland, the president of the International Federation of Red Cross and Red Crescent Societies Astrid Nøklebye Heiberg, the chair of the Nobel Prize Committee Professor Francis Sejersted, and Canadian Ambassador to Norway Marie-Lucie Morin fill out the table.

My welcome is short: I bring greetings and congratulations from the president and first lady. I say how pleased Barbara and I are to host the family and friends of the laureates. And I note that we are honored to have with us today Geir Lundestad, director of the Nobel Institute; Arne Olav Brundtland (Gro's husband), a scholar at the Norwegian Institute of Foreign Affairs; Professor Lucy Smith, president of the University of Oslo; and (her husband) Carsten Smith, the chief justice of the Norwegian Supreme Court.

After lunch, I introduce the head table, noting the key role Canada played in managing the treaty negotiations. I then explain to the American guests the wonderful Norwegian custom of "takk for maten" (thanks for the meal). A short talk by the guest of honor. In this case we had two honored guests. Bobby Muller spoke first and then Jody Williams. They were good at this. Both were eloquent, humorous and brief.

Jody referred to me as Tom.

RECEIVING THE GRAND CROSS OF THE NORWEGIAN ORDER OF MERIT

At my official farewell luncheon on December 15, 1997, held at the Hotel Continental, the chief of protocol of the Foreign Ministry presented me with a wrapped package. Inside was a hinged blue velvet box lined with white silk holding a golden star-shaped medal.

I was awarded the Grand Cross, conferred on me by His Majesty. It is the highest order of the Norwegian Order of Merit. "It is conferred on foreign and Norwegian nationals as a reward for their outstanding service in the interest of Norway."

I was touched. I felt great responsibility. Was it the hand of St. Olaf himself I felt on my shoulder? I wasn't speechless. I said this was a great honor I will cherish and please inform His Majesty of my appreciation and gratitude.

My protocol advisor had only said I would receive something to commemorate my time in Norway. I am sure she knew, but it was not her place to tip me off.[315]

COUNTING THE SILVERWARE

There is a list of things to do in preparation for leaving a post. Some to do in Norway and some to do at the State Department in D.C.

And, I kid you not, counting the silverware is one of them. Along with the dishes, linens, wine, ketchup—anything needed for an inventory of items in the Residence. The baseline for the next ambassador.

A physical is required, with a series of tests that replicate the tests when I was nominated four years ago. I had aged well. Must be the daily capsule of fish oil. Barbara and the boys are also required to have physicals.

My papers need to be labeled and boxed. There are guidelines. Except for cables and anything marked classified, I can sift through the rest. This has already been prepared for by my assistant, Sue Meyer, who did this same task when I left the Speaker's office with instructions from the Wisconsin Historical Society on how to label.

The essential documents for me are copies of my schedules. Every day of the four years in Norway was accounted for in a detailed daily schedule. Hour by hour is recorded. Every trip I made. Every flight, including the airline and flight number. Every meeting I had, names and titles. Every dinner with the menu, the guest list, and seating chart. Every reception with the guest list whether ten or one hundred present.

These were marked "sensitive" and were distributed to twelve others who then knew what they would need to do—Barbara, the deputy chief of mission, my driver, the chef and maids, the Residence guards, the political officers, and the protocol director.

There is paperwork to complete to update my account in the Federal Employees Retirement System. It is like an IRA account with an employer and employee contribution. It is invested in a dedicated bond and stock fund called the Thrift Savings Plan. This pot of money follows me, and I manage it and must draw payments from it at retirement age. This plus Social Security is the retirement plan for civilian federal employees.

Alas, my diplomatic passport the day I exit will have a corner of the front cover clipped off, no longer valid. Now a souvenir. I am issued a new regular passport and an ID card given former ambassadors for access to the State Department building and which, among other things, establishes eligibility for the State Department Employees Credit Union. I will always be a member of the State Department family and the title of ambassador is mine for life.

The Norwegian Foreign Ministry has a book of instructions I will follow titled "Protocol Procedure for the Commencement and Termination of a Diplomatic Mission to Norway." There will be a private farewell audience with The King. "The dress for gentlemen: Dark suit. For ladies: Afternoon dress. Gloves. Hat not obligatory."

There will be a farewell luncheon. "Eighteen persons will normally be invited. Apart from the ambassador and his or her spouse, the deputy chief of mission and his or her spouse, there will be the secretary general of the Foreign Ministry, and the chief of protocol with their spouses, and ten persons proposed by the ambassador." (This was at the Hotel Continental.) "A representative of the Protocol Department will be present at the departure from Oslo of the ambassador."

GOODBYES

November 21, 1997:

Pop in on Terje Rød-Larsen (one of the secret negotiators of the Oslo Accords) at his 50th birthday party. He is one of the first people who sought me out when I arrived. A gracious man.

November 27, 1997:

Lunch with Gudmund Hernes, secretary of education in Brundtland's government. He really educated me—that is his job. A special person.

December 4, 1997:

Finland National Day. Say goodbye to Finland's ambassador, Jorma Inki. We've been in Oslo together my whole four years. He has kept me from going soft on Russia. A pro. (Only Jorma and Lithuanian Ambassador Kornelija Jurgaitienė remain of the group I started with.)

December 8, 1997:

I call on Jørgen Kosmo in his office in the Parliament. Minister of defense up until the change of government in October. It is his birthday. He has been my closest associate in the government, and we became good friends. A bit of an alter ego as we were small town pols that made it big.

December 12, 1997:

1 p.m.: The final interview with Nils Morten Udgaard, foreign affairs editor of *Aftenposten*. The reporting on the policies of President Clinton have been learned, insightful, and without bias. I was lucky to have him on my beat.

3 p.m.: Farewell call on Foreign Minister Knut Vollebæk. He mentions I will be missed around the ministry, as I was always available.

4:30 p.m.: Say goodbye to Oslo Police Chief Ingelin Killengreen. I thank her for keeping me safe.

December 15, 1997:

10 a.m.: A fond farewell to Arne Olav Brundtland and the staff at the Norwegian Institute of International Affairs (NUPI). Their conferences and policy papers had a role in my thinking and the

cables sent to Washington informed by their analyses made us look pretty smart.

Noon: Met with former Prime Minister Thorbjørn Jagland in his office in Parliament. I looked forward to this in order to tell him that I had read all his foreign policy speeches when he was PM and they were good. We quoted them in cables quite often when he spoke on NATO expansion and the Baltics.

1 p.m.: The official farewell luncheon hosted by the secretary general of the Foreign Ministry at the Hotel Continental.

December 16, 1997:

Farewell call on Prime Minister Bondevik. We note our meeting early in his tenure when I arrived and me telling him, several times actually, that I had some understanding of those from the Bible Belt of Norway who voted for his party (the Christian People's Party—Bondevik is a Lutheran minister). My grandmother's family immigrated from this area when she was a girl, and she fit the voter profile. Alcohol is evil, gambling bad, Lutheran Church every Sunday without fail, and not too much good to say about Catholics. This always brought a smile to his face. I mentioned that one of my best memories was his talk with Jimmy Carter on the obligation of wealthy Norway to help the sick and poor with development aid, especially in Africa.

FAREWELL MEETING WITH HIS MAJESTY

My farewell meeting on December 17 at the Palace with His Majesty was at 11 a.m. It is the Bird Room (Fugleværelset) where one waits for an audience with His Majesty. This large room has a sky-blue trompe l'oeil ceiling with a few puffy clouds and an eagle in flight. The door to His Majesty's office opened at 11:01.

HM was standing and smiling. We shook hands. I said "takk for sist" (thanks for the last time we were together) and he replied "i lige made" (same here). I mentioned he looked pretty much the same as when we first met four years ago. This brought a laugh and a bigger smile.

We reminisced about the dinner in the White House on the State Visit. I thanked him for his friendship with America. We sat down, chatted about 20 minutes, and at the end he said something to me he had said before: "These years have gone too fast." He asked if I enjoyed myself in Norway. And said in parting: "We will see each other again." Although curious as to why HM said this, it would not have been polite to inquire further. And, with no instructions from my protocol officer, I did not mention the great honor of the Grand Cross bestowed on me by HM. It didn't seem appropriate.

Upon leaving, I used the common Norwegian phrase: "Ha det...vi sees." A goodbye and a foretelling of seeing each other again.

HONORARY DOCTORATE OF HUMANE LETTERS CONFERRED BY SCHILLER INTERNATIONAL UNIVERSITY, LONDON

I was pleasantly surprised when invited by Schiller International University in London to receive an honorary doctorate and be the speaker at the winter graduation ceremony on December 19, 1997.

Schiller is a U.S.-accredited university with several campuses in Europe and offers both bachelor's and master's degrees in international relations and diplomacy.[316]

"Ambassador Loftus has distinguished himself as a legislator, political leader, and advocate for children, a mentor to parliamentary leaders in new democracies, an author, and a diplomat...

"He has also been a 'public scholar' seeking opportunities to teach young people who hope to pursue careers in public service." This sentence explained why they had me on their radar. Interns. One of the six interns at Embassy Oslo, Christopher McGovern, had been their star pupil.

My speech to the students, who had already decided to pursue a life outside the comfort zone of most, encouraged them to look for an opportunity with perhaps little pay but a lot of responsibility. And I told the stories of the interns of Oslo, who were given a lot of responsibility—new graduates just like today, and every one of them rose to the occasion. "So too will you."

The State Department's internship program for college students was a godsend for the embassy. Because the intern would have a security clearance, he or she could be a regular member of the staff. Given our loss of people and a position freeze, the intern could plug holes in the political, economic, and consular sections.

Most important, after accompanying the others on a démarche or two and being introduced around the Foreign Ministry, an intern could be sent off on their own to do this essential task, which had to be done in person. The Foreign Ministry was a five-block walk down the street from the embassy.

Not to be underestimated, the intern could be a table host at a dinner; represent the embassy at the unrelenting receptions and national days; meet the harpsichord player sent on a cultural outing; be someone's dance partner at the Marine Ball and mingle aperitif in hand.

Political officer Russ Trowbridge took the interns into his care to show them the ropes, help find housing, and scrounge up some money for their expenses. There was no pay or housing provided in State's intern program.

THE EMBASSY INTERNS

Emily Fleckner's story: The intern and the billionaire

Intern Emily Fleckner arrived in Oslo in January 1997 and introduced herself to me the day she arrived.

Emily had just graduated from the UW in the winter of 1996 and had the choice between going to Washington to work at State in D.C. or overseas. Oslo was her dream and her parents were relieved of imagining her being sent to some fever-ridden terrorist haven halfway around the world.

It turned out Emily could mingle. She had no relevant experience, but she had pluck, and was motivated by the goal of to one day be in the Foreign Service. Emily ended up in the small apartment above the garage at the Residence. Her three-month internship was extended to six months.

She went quickly from intern to diplomat, spending many afternoons with the junior officers in the Foreign Ministry chatting, drinking coffee, standing outside with the smokers for the cigarette breaks, and coming back with the response to a démarche.

One day the American pilot of the private jet of one the richest men in Norway telephoned the embassy wanting to hire a flight attendant who did not speak Norwegian—someone who would not understand the conversations in Norwegian that took place on the plane.

As this interesting request made the rounds in the embassy, it eventually found Emily.

Emily took off, so to speak. A new haute wardrobe was part of the deal. She flew all over Europe and to the French Riviera, a regular haunt of the businessman.

The pilot soon realized she could do much more than not speak Norwegian and wear Dior. She became the expediter for the entire flight team, oversaw the maintenance of the company's helicopter, and started the process to buy another private plane.

Emily saved enough to go on to graduate school at the London School of Economics. Then she joined the State Department. With her experiences and drive she rose quickly through the ranks.

As of this writing she is representing America with wisdom and style as the chargé d'affaires at the U.S. Embassy in the Sultanate of Brunei.

Wendy Green: The intern who eloped on her lunch break

Wendy Green told me when she arrived at the embassy to start her internship that she was not there by chance.

In May 1994 when I escorted Prime Minister Brundtland to UW-Madison for her to receive an honorary degree, one of the events was a reception hosted by the Scandinavian Studies Department.

Wendy was an undergraduate studying Norwegian. "I bought a new outfit, came to the reception, met Brundtland, and hit you up on the spot for an internship in Oslo." My response, she said, was "Sure, we will make it happen." Leaving nothing to chance, or my memory, she had a friend take a photo of the asking.

The end of her junior year abroad at the University of Oslo in 1995, her security clearance in hand, still in her student apartment near the embassy, proficient in Norwegian, she started as an intern in the political section and made herself indispensable.

She stayed past her summer internship, through December, because of the unexpected departure of the junior foreign service officer due to a family emergency. This was when the government shut down twice and, because of her status as "intern" I gave the OK for her to be one of the staff members who was allowed to continue working. She answered the phone, delivered démarches to the Foreign Ministry, and turned off the lights at closing time.

She went back to school in December 1995 to finish her degree and graduated in December '96. Whereupon the head of personnel, Jorunn Nesset, called Wendy and said, "We need you back here in two weeks if possible."

Jorunn explained that the stalwart Hal Meinheit, head of the Political Section, had moved on, the new head, Mike Butler, had just arrived, and our political section secretary left unexpectedly. "You have the clearance and you know the work..." Wendy's security clearance was still good. An intern emeritus returned to the fold.

Back in Oslo some money was found to pay her. Her housing plan was a musical chairs series of moves to temporarily empty apartments and houses we had on long-term leases. One of the houses she moved into, a huge place overlooking the fjord just vacated by a senior embassy official, had no furniture. Our warehouse contained an ensemble of 1970s-era office furniture. Wendy picked out desks, chairs, lamps, and a couch that had once been in the embassy lobby. She used an old door on a makeshift stand as a dining table. And someone found two twin beds.

She fell in love with Ole Morten Orset. They had met when they were students at the University of Oslo. He was now a journalist. Wendy asked her friends in the consular section to arrange for a fiancé visa for her husband-to-be so they could go to the United States and get married. Her friends—she also worked in the consular section when needed—kindly informed her this was a lot of paperwork and required proof, which was quite a bother to assemble, of intent to marry within 90 days. Their suggestion: "Why don't you get married here, then no problem getting to the U.S. and your husband has a legal status."[317]

So, they made an appointment with the Oslo Courthouse and eloped on her lunch break, September 5, 1997. Intern Emily Fleckner tagged along to take photos, and they all went to lunch afterwards, splurging on a glass of wine.

The new bride returned to work—a little tipsy.

Christopher McGovern's story

Christopher McGovern, from Green Bay, Wisconsin, had received his BA in international relations in 1996 from Schiller's campus in Heidelberg, Germany.

He was the valedictorian, editor of the school newspaper, and received an award for academic excellence plus an award for excellence in German language and literature studies.

Chris came to the embassy while still in school. Found a place to live with a Norwegian family. Learned Norwegian so fast we started to send him to events asking for a Norwegian speaker. Filled a spot in doubles tennis with the Canadian ambassador.

Schiller strives to place students and graduates in a diplomatic setting. This is not easy to do. The State Department Interns Program is one of those ways. Chris's internship was under the auspices of the State Department's Advisory Commission on Public Diplomacy, from May 1995 to June 1996.[318-319]

DINNER IN LONDON WITH MY FRIEND THE RUSSIAN AMBASSADOR

My old friend Ambassador Juri Fokine, the former Russian ambassador to Norway now posted in the United Kingdom, met me at the door of Harrington House all smiles, grasped my hand tightly and said, "Tom." His wife Maia had that seeing-a-friendly-face smile.

Built in 1853 in the Gothic style as the home of the 5th Earl of Harrington, the Russian ambassador's residence is called Harrington House. It is a three-minute walk from Kensington Palace.

The dinner was a private affair. Juri had sent me a note saying to invite my friends. With me were Endre Røsjø, a friend from Oslo who had a house in London, and Stephanie and John Riley. Stephanie started as an unpaid intern for me in the Wisconsin Speaker's office and rose to be an administrative assistant. John, a charming Brit, had the good luck to find her and whisked her off to London to get married.

After introductions, a glass of champagne in our hands, Juri said, "Tom and Endre, Stephanie and John, I must excuse myself briefly as the British government has just announced a few of my embassy staff would be expelled on the ridiculous charge that they were spies. Some papers to sign. I'll be right back. Please have another glass of champagne."

The reception room of Harrington House, called the saloon, could have been the set of a black-and-white movie with Boris Karloff and Bela Lugosi. Ringed with statuary and walls covered with paintings of the dearly departed (one presumes). There is a grand marble staircase.

Our dinner in the private dining room was lively. Juri, who was once a personal assistant to Andrei Gromyko, the Soviet foreign secretary, regaled us with spy stories. During a dessert of apple pie and vanilla ice cream, he said he was sure that right now there were those in Moscow leafing through the staff roster of the British Embassy to see who they could classify as spies.

Only one toast with vodka. Nostrovia and cheers!

PRESIDENT CLINTON ACCEPTS MY RESIGNATION

President Clinton's letter accepting my resignation arrived six weeks after I had left my post on December 22, 1997:

January 30, 1998
The White House

Dear Mr. Ambassador,

I have received your letter of November 12, 1997, and it is with deep regret that I accept your resignation as Ambassador to Norway.

America has been well represented during your tenure, and I commend you for your dedicated work. By advocating the democratic values that have always made our nation strong, and by working closely with local officials, you have promoted our important U.S. foreign policy objectives in Norway. During your service as Ambassador, you demonstrated an unwavering commitment both to advancing our interests and to assisting the government and people of Norway.

I salute you for the important role you have played in strengthening U.S. ties in the region, in particular the Arctic. I have relied on your diplomatic skill and wise counsel on a wide range of issues of importance to both the United States and Norway.

Along with my gratitude, please accept my very best wishes for every future success and happiness for you, Barbara, Alec, and Karl.

Sincerely
Bill Clinton

UW'S LA FOLLETTE SCHOOL SUMS IT UP

From the Robert M. La Follette School's "La Follette Alumni Notes," Spring 1998:

Tom Loftus (1972) returned to Madison following the official end of his term as ambassador to Norway. Tom's final days as ambassador were filled, and we mean filled, with honors, awards, and visits with royalty. On Monday, December 15, he was presented the Grand Cross, the highest order of the Royal Norwegian Order of Merit, given by His Majesty King Harald. The next day, Loftus attended a farewell visit with Prime Minister Kjeld Magne Bondevik. Also that day, General Per Mathisen, the Commander of the Norwegian Home Guard, presented the ambassador with the Norwegian Home Guard National Service Medal. On Wednesday, December 17, there was a farewell audience with His Majesty King Harald. After a day off, Ambassador Loftus gave the graduation address on Friday, December 19, and received an honorary degree, Doctor of Humane Letters, from Schiller International University in London. The university noted that he had distinguished himself as a legislator, political leader, an advocate for children, a mentor to parliamentary leaders in new democracies, an author and a diplomat. ... He has also been a public scholar, seeking opportunities to teach and encourage young people who hope to pursue careers in public service. That night, the Russian ambassador to the United Kingdom, Juri Fokine, gave a dinner in honor of Loftus. Ambassador Fokine was formerly the Russian ambassador to Norway and worked closely with Ambassador Loftus on efforts to control nuclear military waste in Northwest Russia. On Saturday, December 20, Loftus returned to Oslo, and on Monday, December 22, he left Norway and returned to Madison.

WHEW![320]

ABOUT THE AUTHOR

Tom Loftus served as U.S. ambassador to the Kingdom of Norway from 1993 through 1997. A member of the Wisconsin Legislature from 1977 to 1991, he was the longest-serving Democratic Speaker of the Assembly, from 1983 to 1991. In 1990, he was the Democratic candidate for governor. Tom was special advisor to the director general of the World Health Organization from 1998 to 2005. He was a member of the University of Wisconsin System Board of Regents from 2005 to 2011, and in 2020 and 2021 was senior policy advisor to the UW System president. Tom is on the board of the Outrider Foundation. A U.S. Army veteran, he is a UW-Whitewater graduate and earned a master's degree from UW-Madison's La Follette School of Public Affairs.

ACKNOWLEDGMENTS

For four years the talented Lynn Danielson edited, collated, and became the historian of this book. This allowed me to write. LuAnn Sorenson, my former Norwegian tutor, did the translations, including HM King Harald's speech marking the 50th anniversary of the end of Nazi Germany's occupation of Norway in 1995. Michael and JoAnn Youngman continued their support of books that tell the story of people who shaped Wisconsin political history and the University of Wisconsin–Madison. A special thank you to my wife, JoAnn Loftus, for her support and encouragement over the four years of writing the book.

The advance readers. Their enthusiasm for the book and the storytelling chronicle format kept me going. Invaluable.

Ambassador Derek Shearer, former ambassador to Finland and professor of diplomacy at Occidental College. Morten Wetland, top aide to Prime Minister Gro Harlem Brundtland and former Norwegian ambassador to Germany. Ambassador Larry Taylor, former ambassador to Estonia. Ambassador Daniel Speckhard, former ambassador to Greece and Belarus and former deputy assistant secretary general at NATO. Parker Borg, former ambassador to Iceland. James D. Bindenagel, chargé d'affaires to Germany 1996-1997. Fred DuVal, former deputy chief of protocol, U.S. State Department.

Dennis Dresang, professor emeritus of public affairs and political science at the University of Wisconsin–Madison. Odd S. Lovoll, Ph.D., professor emeritus of history at St. Olaf College, Northfield, Minnesota, and University of Oslo. Katharine Lyall, president of the University of Wisconsin System 1992-2004.

Journalist and author Doug Moe. George Hesselberg, journalist and writer about Norway. Peter Ross Range, author and journalist who covered international affairs for *Time* and *U.S. News & World Report*. Dave Iverson, journalist, filmmaker, and author. Steve Hannah, journalist and former CEO of *The Onion*. Neil Heinen, veteran political commentator and TV host.

Thanks to Tracy Will for all his help collecting and crediting the photos.

I am very grateful that my friend Jody Williams, 1997 Nobel Peace Prize laureate, read the draft on the politics inside embassy Oslo on the controversy surrounding her selection and pronounced it accurate.

A special thank you to Hillary Rodham Clinton for reading the draft recounting her trip to the 1994 Lillehammer Olympics when she was first lady and her encouraging words: "Well done Tom!"

APPENDIX A
NORWAY AND AMERICA,
A SHORT HISTORY

"AMERICA FEVER"

Norwegian immigration to America started in 1825 with the arrival of the sloop *Restauration* in New York harbor. It sailed from Stavanger on July 4 with a small number of Quakers and Haugeans fleeing religious persecution. The U.S. Post Office noted the centennial with a stamp, with the small sloop portrayed as a Viking ship in full regalia.

The immigration that was caused by the collapse of the Norwegian farm economy began in the 1850s, and there was a steady stream that followed. By the onset of World War II, 800,000 Norwegians had immigrated to North America—about one-third of Norway's population.

It was not just hard times in rural Norway, it was also primogeniture—only the first-born son inherited the farm. I suppose one could muse that Norwegian-Americans are the descendants of second sons and their sisters.

The letters of these settlers to those relatives still "over across" describing the bounty of the American land—well, it almost seeded and harvested itself—brought more and more. And the Civil War awakened a great patriotism, with Norwegian regiments from Minnesota and Wisconsin joining the fight.

In 1862, the bonuses offered to those who would come and join the Union Army caused a great rush of young men to immigrate. Bersven Nelson was one who came and joined the Wisconsin 15th "Norwegian Regiment." He wrote home that he had received $100 for enlisting, was paid $13 a month and after the war he would get $50 and 160 acres of land. The enlistment bonuses soon grew to $300.[321]

Every time I walked into the state Capitol building in Madison there would be standing proud the statue of Colonel Hans Christian Heg. Born in Norway, the abolitionist and soldier led the 15th Wisconsin Volunteer Regiment and died at the battle of Chickamauga. That regiment of Norwegian speakers, along with the First Minnesota Volunteers, saw a lot of action and casualties.[322]

It was easy to immigrate, as the shipping lines offered cheap passage. It was a good business. My grandfather Edward and his family left from Oslo on July 4, 1885, on the steamship *SS Kristiania* headed to Gothenburg, Sweden. There they boarded the *SS Katie* on July 7, and arrived in New York at Castle Garden, America's first official immigration center, on July 25, 1885. Their ultimate destination was Stoughton, Wisconsin.

IMMIGRANTS SHAPED WISCONSIN WHILE IT SHAPED THEM

In this memoir are many references to Wisconsin people and history as they relate to Norway, the Norwegian Lutheran Church, and the University of Wisconsin.

When the massive wave of Norwegians immigrated beginning in the 1840s, they came through the Port of Quebec and the destination was Wisconsin. They were mostly farmers and they wrote letters home extolling America and the bountiful land of their farms. The America referred to was the fertile prairies of Dane County in Wisconsin and LaSalle County in northern Illinois.

The first Norwegian Lutheran Church and Norwegian language newspaper, the *Nordlyset,* were founded in Muskego in 1845, a tiny town near Milwaukee. The state of Wisconsin had an agent in Quebec as early as the 1850s to greet and direct immigrants.

The transport of Norwegian immigrants to America gave birth to the Norwegian shipping industry that today constitutes half the merchant and cruise lines in the world.

The Lutheran Church of Norway was the state church headed by the king from 1637 to 2012. The church not only followed the immigrants, sending pastors to set up congregations, it also founded universities—Luther in Iowa; Augustana in Sioux Falls; and Concordia, Augsburg and St. Olaf in Minnesota. Each of the names of these colleges symbolizes an expression of a tenet of Lutheranism found in the Augsburg Confession from the year 1530: "... the unanimous consensus and exposition of our Christian faith, particularly against the false worship, idolatry, and superstition of the papacy ..." The pope remains an issue.

Martin Luther was very influential in his writings on the role of government, which helps explain the DNA of Norwegian and Norwegian-American political thinking today: "A man who would venture to govern an entire community or the world with the gospel would be like a shepherd who should place in one fold wolves, lions, eagles, and sheep," he said. "The sheep would keep the peace, but they would not last long."

The University of Wisconsin-Madison has over 400,000 living alumni and they are everywhere around the globe. It has been the No. 1 source of Peace Corps volunteers since the beginning. The UW has for decades educated and trained Norwegians in special programs promoted and often funded by Norwegian-Americans. UW was a destination for Marshall Plan students brought from Norway. Professor Einar Haugen was the leading academic of the first Scandinavian Studies Department in the U.S., which became the Center for the Teaching of Norwegian Language and Literature. He wrote *The Norwegian-English Dictionary: A Pronouncing and Translating Dictionary of Modern Norwegian.* A seminal work.

Wisconsin's most famous political leader, Robert M. La Follette, rode to victory with the solid support of Norwegian-Americans. Not to be outdone, there is a front-page picture of me raising the Norwegian flag above the Capitol building in Madison one Syttende Mai (17th of May), Norwegian constitution day. The MacDonald's in Stoughton, the town in which I was born, has rosemåling as the motif.

Minnesota has as deep of connections, but they one up Wisconsin as they have former Vice President Walter Mondale. He explained the relation between Norwegians and Norwegian-Americans when during his time as vice president, he visited Mundal, the small town from which his ancestors emigrated. There he famously said: "I don't know many of you, but your faces are familiar."

THOSE WHO STAYED SHAPED A NEW NORWAY

While this mass exodus from rural Norway helped shape America's development and politics, especially in the Midwest, and the bond between those who left and those who stayed was strong for two generations, it was those who did not entertain the idea of going to America—the intellectuals, the politicians, and the urban middle-class—who were shaping a new Norway.

It was during this period that Henrik Ibsen wrote *A Doll's House*, Edvard Munch painted *The Scream*, Edvard Grieg composed, and Roald Amundsen was the first to reach the South Pole.

An agreed-upon unifying Norwegian language called Bokmål was adopted—best described as how they spoke in Oslo. Gone was the Danish and the many dialects of the countryside. It took three extra letters to the alphabet to accomplish: å, ø and ae. The sounds are: Ah, Er, Oar.

It was also the time of agitation for Norwegian independence from Sweden.

Norway lived in a union with Denmark under the Danish king and had little say in its trade or foreign affairs until 1814. That year, on May 17, the day now celebrated as Syttende Mai—like our Fourth of July—a constitution was adopted at a meeting in Eidsvoll. It was also the year the union with Denmark suddenly ended.

The Danes chose to back Napoleon when he invaded Russia. In one of history's most notable blunders, Napoleon unwisely decided to invade in the fall. When the harsh Russian winter came, the army was forced to retreat, and Napoleon had lost. Sweden had joined Britain and Russia. They ended up on the winning side and the price Denmark paid for backing Napoleon was they were required to cede control of Norway to Sweden. That was 1814.

This new Norway-Sweden union was less formal, as Sweden recognized the Eidsvoll constitution and the Norwegian Parliament (the Storting) had powers but again, not over foreign relations, and this finally was the foundation of the demand for dissolution of the union. On June 7, 1905, the Parliament voted for unilateral declaration of independence, with the Swedish king bowing to reality and accepting the union's dissolution. To finalize the independence and create the new nation, a question was put to the voters as to whether to have a constitutional monarchy. Did they really need a king after being under first the Danish and then Swedish kings in the unions with those countries? Yes—by a landslide.

The Norwegian Parliament then offered Danish Prince Carl the post. Prince Carl asked for popular support before accepting and voters then approved the question: "Do you agree with the Storting's authorization to the government to invite Prince Carl of Denmark to become King of Norway?"

Important to the new country and the Norwegian narrative ever since is that Carl, who would take the Norwegian name Haakon, was elected king of Norway.

Smart people, these Norwegian voters. Prince Carl was married to Princess Maud, the daughter of King Edward VII and Queen Alexandra of the United Kingdom. They already had a son, thereby assuring succession. Also important were the instant connections to the royal families of Europe, which offered the newly independent, very small nation of Norway some protection from invasion and being handed back to Sweden or Denmark after the next round of wars.

King Haakon, Queen Maud, and their son, who was given the Norwegian name Olav, arrived in Norway on November 25, 1905.

In 1929 Crown Prince Olav married his cousin Princess Märtha of Sweden. They had three children: Princess Ragnhild, Princess Astrid and Prince Harald (the future King Harald V).

WORLD WAR II:
THE NORWEGIAN-AMERICAN ALLIANCE DEEPENS

The invasion of neutral Norway by Nazi Germany occurred on April 9, 1940. It was spearheaded by the German heavy cruiser *Blücher*. The cruiser was to sail at high speed up the Oslo Fjord with 1,000 men aboard to land at dawn and secure the capital city, and, most importantly, capture King Haakon VII, so he could not escape and form a government in exile.

Control of the Norwegian fjords would give Hitler harbors from which German submarines could attack the British fleet and disrupt supply ships in the North Atlantic.

Blücher was spotted and the garrison at Oscarsborg, a small island fortress at the narrowest part of the fjord, was alerted. At 4:30 a.m.,

Blücher came into range and 65-year-old Col. Birger Eriksen ordered his shore guns to fire, and then ordered the launch of two 40-year-old torpedoes, hoping they would work. All were direct hits at close range. *Blücher* rolled over and sank at 7:30 a.m.—210 feet to the bottom where she remains today. Oslo was only 28 miles away. The sinking of *Blücher* delayed the taking of Oslo by only a few days. It was enough.

In 1937, President Franklin Roosevelt had appointed Florence Jaffray Harriman ambassador to Norway (then called "envoy").[323] She was only the second woman ambassador in U.S history. Her life in Norway at Nobels Gate 28, the ambassador's Residence, was at first uneventful. She was noted for embracing the Norwegian outdoors culture of "friluftsliv." Photos of her cross-country skiing, salmon fishing, and eating like a Viking were prominent in the newspapers.

All this changed dramatically. On April 5, 1940, the diplomatic delegations in Oslo were invited and expected to attend the showing of a "peace film" at the German Embassy. It was a newsreel propaganda film glorifying the invasion of Poland. The "peace" part was if you did not help Britain there would be peace.

Norwegian Foreign Minister Halvdan Koht did not attend the event but was still late for a dinner hosted by Ambassador Harriman in honor of the newly arrived French ambassador. The foreign minister did not arrive until 7:30 and given the Norwegian DNA, much like a bird's instinct to migrate, which directs one to be on time, he apologized and explained. First the German ambassador had visited him and then the French and British ambassadors came to call. Norway and the United States were neutral at this time. Britain and France were at war with Nazi Germany.

Like many dinners where diplomats gather, the talk was of rumors. It was known by Harriman that several German warships sailing west had passed through the Skagerrak, the narrow passage between Denmark and Norway that leads from the Baltic Sea to the North Sea and the Atlantic. A coded cable from Copenhagen relayed this news but nothing else. Where were they headed? Certainly, this was an action against Britain.

On April 8, the now-routine air raid sirens in Oslo sounded but it was thought that, as in the past, there was no need for real alarm. No need to go to the newly built bomb-proof room in the basement of the ambassador's Residence (now a sauna).

At 3 a.m. April 9, Ambassador Harriman was awakened by a

telephone call from the British ambassador. Would she take over his embassy? There was an invasion under way. Next a call from the French. The same request. She said yes. No time to consult Washington. Members of the U.S. Embassy staff were sent immediately to take over.

By 7 a.m., Harriman was ready to follow her orders in case of an invasion, which were to stay with the Norwegian government. Her trusty Ford car, an American flag draped on the roof, was in the motorcade heading toward Lillehammer by 9:45 a.m. "It was one of those lovely northern spring days which made you feel as if the whole world were young again. I was aware only of the contrasts of the earth itself and the ill will and crimes among men."[324]

The ambassador took the code book used for encrypting secret cables out of the embassy safe and tucked it under her coat, confident no German officer would dare search her. She fled in a motorcade with the Norwegian government during the several-day retreat. It turned quickly into a race to neutral Sweden. Then Crown Princess Märtha and her three children, including Harald the future king, separated from The King and Crown Prince—who fled to Tromsø and eventually to London to form a government in exile—and joined the group with Harriman.

It was a harrowing, multi-day journey, with the Luftwaffe bombing the route. Once over the border (it was April 12), Harriman was able to telephone a report to the American Embassy in Stockholm and was informed that U.S. Army Captain Losey, a military attaché, would meet them and be her escort to Stockholm. "'The new military attaché is a nice, spare young man in a flying corps uniform', Harriman said."[325] Photos show a dashing figure in a trench coat.

In Stockholm, Capt. Losey made plans for himself and Ambassador Harriman to drive to Lillehammer to find American refugees. It was April 18. He did not want her to go with him. "You might be bombed," he said. "But so might you," Harriman replied, "and that would be worse for you are young and have your life before you, while I have had a wonderful life and nearly all of it behind me."

She didn't go to Lillehammer. On April 22, she was informed in a call from the U.S. Embassy in Stockholm that Captain Losey was killed the day before by a German bomb. The body was returned by the chauffeur. The American flag from atop the trusty Ford was draped over the coffin.

Captain Robert Losey was from Iowa, attended West Point, and had a master's degree in meteorology from Cal Tech. He was 33, married, and the first American military casualty of WWII.

Ambassador Harriman marked time in Sweden with the crown princess and her children at the Grand Hotel in Stockholm waiting to be given the all-clear to go back to Norway to join The King and government, then waited in Tromsø, which was not yet under German control. The situation became hopeless, and the decision was made that The King and government would be removed to London. King Haakon and Crown Prince Olav made it to England after a month on the run, protected by a valiant but futile resistance to the German invaders from the remnants of the Norwegian military and Allied help. A daring rescue by a British destroyer saved them. They became the government in exile in London along with Prime Minister Nygaardsvold and the Labour Government. Hitler was denied his goal of capturing King Haakon and Crown Prince Olav and setting up a puppet government.

"I was disappointed that I had been unable to complete my mission and accompany the Norwegian Government to the British Isles...but I was completely reconciled when Crown Prince Olav sent confidential word from London asking that I accompany Princess Märtha and their children to the United States."[326] They had been invited to come as guests of the president. A transport ship, the *American Legion*, would be waiting for them in the Arctic Ocean port of Petsamo in Finland, 20 hours north of Stockholm by train. They set sail for America on August 16 with 1,000 other fleeing people crammed on board.

Crown Princess Märtha, the two girls, and future King Harald went to live in the White House. President Roosevelt helped the children with their homework. In time, they found another place to live near Washington, D.C., called Pooks Hill.

On D-Day, June 6, 1944, FDR's schedule said "fishing," and he was. He took Prince Harald with him on the *Sequoia*, the presidential yacht.[327]

Ambassador Harriman returned to Washington. She remained a tireless campaigner for reform and peace. At age 92, she received the Citation of Merit for Distinguished Service from President John F. Kennedy.

THE LABOUR PARTY AND THE WELFARE STATE

The modern Norwegian Labour Party formed and had great success by addressing the needs of the unemployed and fostering trade unions during the Depression. They gained power and remained the dominant party, with policies providing old-age pensions, health insurance, unemployment compensation, and much else that became the welfare state. And there was one other important reason why Labour thrived.

The Norwegian Communist Party was a political force after the WWII, with support built from the fact that the Soviets had liberated northern Norway. Labour tolerated the Communists, but when in 1948 a Soviet-backed coup installed the Communist Party as the government in Czechoslovakia and the Norwegian Communist Party supported Moscow, the Labour Party became anti-Communist. This was cemented by a famous speech by Labour Party Prime Minister Einar Gerhardsen: "There is a threat to the Norwegian people's freedom and democracy—that is the danger that the Norwegian Communist Party forever represents...the most important task in the fight for Norway's independence, for democracy and the rule of law is to reduce Communist Party and Communist influence...we will fight against communism with democratic means and spiritual weapons...."[328]

The existential threat that Labour saw in the Communists was a reason that when the opportunity came in 1949 to join NATO, Norway signed up.

The Communist party in Norway withered away. Labour, through the welfare state and aligning with America and the West, gave Norway the foundation for the strong democracy it is today.

APPENDIX B
A SHORT HISTORY OF NORWEGIAN WHALING

The whaling industry—which processed whale oil for fuel for city lights and lubricant for guns and sewing machines, whale fat for margarine, and whale bones for stays in corsets—greased the machinery of the industrial revolution.

In Janesville, Wisconsin, is the Tallman House, a mansion built by a wealthy land speculator who was an abolitionist. He went to hear Illinois Congressman Abraham Lincoln speak on the ills of slavery in nearby Beloit on October 1, 1859, and invited him to spend the night at his house. Dinner was under a chandelier glowing with a soft light created by whale oil.

After the Civil War, the price of a 35-gallon barrel of whale oil was $1,200 in today's dollars. It was the oil industry of the 17th, 18th, and 19th centuries. Fortunes were made by the shipowners, brokers, distributors, and commodity traders. As a comparison, think of the cattle in Texas, the cattle drive to the railhead, the stockyards of Chicago, the butchers, the futures markets, and the fortunes of the cattle barons and the meat packers Cudahy, Hormel, and Oscar Mayer.

The invention of the harpoon cannon by Norwegian Svend Foyn in 1863, which killed by a gun powder grenade exploding in the whale's head, was the first technological advancement. Svend Foyn is called the "father of modern whaling." Then Peter Sørlie's invention of the slipway "allowed whales to be hauled up on the deck of the factory ship to be processed. Weather was no longer a factor."[329] Heretofore the whale was lashed to the side of the ship, the blubber sliced away and rendered in boiling vats onboard the ship.

As a result of the cannon and the slipway ship, and with the whale population decimated elsewhere, the whales near Antarctica became the target. In the winter of 1930-1931, Norway produced 2,316,962 barrels of whale oil, the best-ever Antarctic season.

Soon the whale population of the Southern Hemisphere was depleted. In 1946, the International Whaling Commission was established "to provide for the proper conservation of whale stocks and thus make possible the orderly development of the whaling industry." This voluntary-membership organization had no enforcement and seemed to exist to bring some order to the extinction of whales. Non-whaling nations joined and gained a majority and adopted more stringent rules.

When the environmental movement worldwide and the Save the Whales campaign became a politically powerful force in the 1970s, it led the U.S. Congress to pass legislation that allowed the president to sanction nations that did not abide by the stringent IWC regulations. The threat of the U.S. prohibiting fish imports from the bad actors among the whaling nations resulted in a de-facto moratorium on whaling.

By the 1990s, Norway had become a pariah because of its insistence that it would commercially harvest the minke whale in its waters but abide by all other IWC rules. The sanctions may have been popular among anti-whaling groups but was not a realistic policy when it came to Norway, our staunch ally and beacon of democracy worldwide. Diplomacy was the tool to use.

APPENDIX C
WHAT DID I KNOW OF RUSSIAN HISTORY AND WHEN DID I KNOW IT?

I learned most of what I knew about Russian history by listening to the radio. After the launch of Sputnik in 1957, there was a flood of federal money sent to universities to educate students about the Soviet Union. The Soviet Union got the atomic bomb in 1949, the hydrogen bomb in 1953, and with the launch of Sputnik, they were beating us in the space race with the first satellite.

The UW's philosophy declared that the people of the state would also be students through the broadcast of lectures by faculty on public radio and television. This is the Wisconsin Idea.

Russian history professor Michael Petrovich, a former officer in the Office of Strategic Services, America's WWII intelligence arm, organized lectures on the Soviet Union, Communism, and Russian history for broadcast in the late 1950s.

Petrovich was a rock-star professor, with his classes overflowing as his lectures delivered in declarative sentences gave students historical context from Peter the Great to Khrushchev. This was the always-expecting-the-atomic-bomb generation. An explanation of their world was what Petrovich provided.

His voice was made for radio and his lectures were replayed in the mid-1980s on public radio starting at 6 p.m. I would adjourn the state Assembly at 5:50 p.m. in order to get to my car to listen to the lecture, which lasted exactly the 30 minutes it took me to drive home. His TV lectures are still used in courses in how to teach history.

I had read essential literature with Dostoyevsky's *Crime and Punishment* and Solzhenitsyn's *One Day in the Life of Ivan Denisovich*, leaving a lasting impression of Russia. And, in the 1960s among college students, Sergei Eisenstein's silent film from 1924, *Battleship Potemkin*, was a must see. The scene of the massacre on the Odessa Steps will not be forgotten.

I had once tried to read through the classic *Ten Days That Shook the World*, American journalist John Reed's chronicle of the October 1917 Bolshevik revolution. There were a lot of meetings reported on and I soon knew what Oscar Wilde meant when he said he might have been a socialist but "it would take too many evenings." Much better was the great film of Reed's book *Reds* from 1981 starring Warren Beatty, Diane Keaton, and Jack Nicholson.[330]

And, when Ambassador Fokine of Russia told me over lunch that his big event coming up would be the 300th anniversary of the founding of the Russian Navy by Peter the Great, I read Robert Massie's 1981 biography of Peter the Great, which had won the Pulitzer.[331]

The eye-opener for me was that this book was about the Swedish empire ending and the Russian empire being born.[332] The history of the fights for control of Finland and the lands of the eastern littoral of the Baltic Sea, what is now the Baltic states, is a history that helped me see in new light my colleagues from Latvia, Lithuania, and Estonia. My grasp of their history was quite restricted to World War I and the World War II Nazi and then Soviet brutal occupations. My view of the Baltic states and Finland was going from black and white to technicolor.

APPENDIX D
THE NORWEGIAN RESISTANCE

For this short briefing on the Norwegian Resistance, I relied on a series of short books from the 1980s written by Norwegian historians and the memoir of one of the saboteurs, all published in English.

There was a resistance through stubbornness by the populace, an organized Resistance movement inside the country, and a more official military arm (Milorg) in Sweden and the UK. This group was officially recognized by the Norwegian government in exile in London.

The paper clip was invented in Norway and it became a mark of resistance when displayed on one's clothing during efforts at "Nazification" early in the occupation. Nazification was a strategy to enlist teachers, the church, and professional associations to become agents in indoctrinating Nazi ideology to create a society like that in Germany under Hitler. This was directed by the occupiers with the veneer of legitimacy of the puppet government of the Norwegian traitor Vidkun Quisling.

Nazification failed. When teachers were instructed to pledge loyalty to the regime there was organized a uniform response: "I will remain faithful to my teacher's calling and my conscience, and on this basis to follow, now as before, the directives of my work justly given by my superiors." All the bishops and 645 of the 699 clergy of the state church resigned rather than answer to Quisling.

The Nazis left the labor unions alone for fear of a general strike that would halt factory production needed for the German war machine. Especially necessary were the fish-oil factories, where a byproduct was glycerin needed for the manufacture of ammunition. (These were regularly bombed by the British.)

Britain and the U.S. first discouraged an active resistance meant to prepare the way for the imminent liberation of Norway. That was not going to happen. However, when Nazification failed and acts of sabotage increased there came a harsh response—teachers arrested and sent to prison camps in the Arctic, summary executions of resisters, towns burned to the ground when items of help to the clandestine movement such as shortwave radios were discovered.

Soon all radios of any type were confiscated, resulting in the rapid growth of an underground press, 300 different newspapers with thousands of people involved. The value of these papers with titles such as *Whispering Press* and *London Radio* can hardly be overestimated.

And it had become clear to the Allies that "despite what his military advisors said, Hitler was quite sure the Allied invasion would come in Norway." Why else were there 300,000 well-trained soldiers, an unnecessarily large force for occupation? "Fortress Norway" was continually being strengthened with even more coastal defense installations. To keep these troops in Norway became a strategy and more sabotage helped in this cause.[333]

APPENDIX E
NORWAY AND NATO: THE BACKGROUND

A CHANGE OF POLICY DURING WWII

When the Labour Party-led government in London during World War II got to the point where it was realistic to plan for a post-war security structure, the options debated were three: return to neutrality, create a Scandinavian military alliance with Sweden, or firmly cast their lot with the United States and Great Britain.

The first two options were quickly dismissed. Trygve Lie, the foreign minister and strongest proponent of a future alliance with the Western democracies, started to outline this change as early as April 1941 in a message to the British legation from the Norwegian government.

He repeated the proposed change in policy in Washington that same month, before the United States had entered the war, by telling the U.S. ambassador assigned to Norway that "the nations bordering on the North Atlantic should seek a plan for the future security of the North Atlantic area."[334]

Lie went public in London in November 1941, in a piece in the *London Times* calling for a post-war "community of nations." The sub-heading was "The Bankruptcy of Neutrality." That there would be use of Norwegian harbors was a significant part of this policy change, as it meant some part of Norwegian sovereignty would be subject to an alliance or even some powerful League of Nations-type international organization.

The question of how to handle the Soviet Union came in 1944 when it was clear that the Red Army would push the Germans out of northern Norway and pursue them south, thus creating a de-facto occupying force. There was already a liberation agreement with the Western Allies should they liberate Norway. An identical but separate liberation agreement was proposed to the Soviet Union and was agreed to and signed in May 1944.[335] These agreements outlined when the liberating troops would leave Norway.

THE UN, MARSHALL PLAN, AND COUP IN CZECHOSLOVAKIA

In June 1945, the United Nations Charter was adopted. Norway had been firmly on the side of the final deal on the powers of the Security Council. Each member would have a veto. Simply explained: "(W)ithout the power of the veto the Soviet Union would stay out of the UN and take care of its security interests by other means."[336]

Trygve Lie had chaired the commission that drafted the Security Council provision of the charter. In 1946, he was chosen as the UN's first secretary general.

Norway kept its head down in the early UN debates among the great powers. The Atlantic alliance idea had faded in hopes the UN was now the answer to security. The U.S. ambassador to Norway summed up Norwegian foreign policy this way: "1. Pro-UK-US to the greatest extent she dares. 2. Pro-Soviet to the extent she must. 3. Pro-UN to the extent she can."[337]

The fence-sitting ended when realpolitik entered. In the spring of 1948, the Marshall Plan was proposed. Norway's joining was debated, but it was soon accepted since Norway needed the aid. This was tantamount to joining the West as the Soviets were against this U.S.-led recovery plan.

The Soviet-backed Communist coup takeover of Czechoslovakia in February 1948 left no choice. Norway was with the democracies. No turning back. It was now clear there was no real alternative such as a Scandinavian defense alliance that would guarantee Norway's security and independence.

After the agreement was reached that there would be no foreign military permanently based in Norway and no nuclear weapons on Norwegian soil, Foreign Minister Halvard Lange on April 4, 1949, signed the North Atlantic Treaty in Washington, D.C.

The United States and Great Britain were now committed to the defense of Norway.

ENDNOTES

1   I was in Stockholm, Sweden, from May 23-June 5, 1993, invited by the Swedish Parliament to learn how they operate. I had unfettered access to the Speaker and members, a stipend, and a very small flat. It was a special program of The Bicentennial Swedish-American Exchange Fund. From my notes: "Expecting the president to call any day. May 28 a call from Brady Williamson. He will be with Clinton in Milwaukee June 1, and will try to confirm my nomination is imminent. I call the mayor of Milwaukee, John Norquist (a close friend from our days together in the Legislature) and tell him to say something to Clinton on the Norway job. The last night in Stockholm Brady called at 2:30 a.m. and after telling Barbara that Walter Mondale had been appointed ambassador to Norway, laughed, and told us the president had signed the papers for my nomination. And, the White House had tried to reach me in Sweden. At Boston airport on the way to Madison called Jim Bailey in the White House. He said he couldn't tell me "the good news," but the president would call in the next few days. (Bailey: an old friend from Wisconsin politics, now an assistant to Mack McLarty, the president's chief of staff). The president called on June 12 when I was at home. "I am calling to ask if you will accept my nomination to be the ambassador to Norway."

2   Brady Williamson was my political advisor and confidant throughout my career. He is a constitutional lawyer at a Madison law firm. That is his day job. In Democratic presidential campaigns, he is the adult in the room. He negotiated the debate format for Clinton in 1992 and 1996, and the locations and settings for the Clinton-Yeltsin summits.

3   3 PN579—103rd Congress (1993-1994) Senate Roll Call votes Nov. 3, 1993. This documents the hold on my nomination. It is the vote on cloture, which failed, and shortly after that the objection was removed and I and the others were approved on a voice vote. www.congress.gov/nomination/103rd-congress/579

4   *Sun Prairie Star* newspaper, Nov. 18, 1993

5   One of the reasons my name brought recognition, good will, and was often spelled "Lofthus" in the press was that in 1786 Christian Jensen Lofthus led a farmers' revolt against Denmark, the colonial ruler. It became known in Norwegian history as the Lofthus uprising: "Lofthusreisingen." A natural leader, Lofthus had been selected by his village of Risør to present a list of what were considered unfair taxes on farmers and ask for a repeal of the monopoly Denmark held on grain and the trade in timber. Lofthus was granted an audience with the regent, Crown Prince Frederick. Upon his return Lofthus reported that the crown prince sympathized with the farmers and started a petition to collect names to bolster the demands of the farmers. Apparently, there was some miscommunication, as the local Danish-controlled authorities sought his arrest. The farmers, armed with shotguns and hunting rifles, stopped the arrest. But not for long. Arrested and convicted after a sensational trial where his famous defense attorney vilified the Danes, Lofthus was thrown in jail and died in prison of a heart attack on June 13, 1797, at age 47. The ideas of the American Revolution and the French Revolution were sweeping Scandinavia at this time and Lofthus and the farmers' revolt were credited as part of the movement that led to Norway's own peaceful revolution: the Eidsvoll Constitution adopted in 1814. There is a modest statue of Lofthus on his farm in Vestre Moland. It is in the middle of a field. I went there to pay my respects. I had a hat on, and I tipped it.

6   www.nytimes.com/1989/06/02/world/john-paul-begins-scandinavian-tour.html

7   www.youtube.com/watch?v=TfcKQcGg_sM

8   https://madison.com/1992-democratic-winner-bill-clinton/article_fee4e3c3-7ddd-5183-8879-8dcf8596c333.html

9   Ambassador Laurits Selmer Swenson, in a telegram to the State Department, 1923

10   Sweden, Finland, Denmark, and Iceland

11   The Northern Fleet is the largest part of the Russian Navy. It is mainly a submarine force headquartered near Murmansk near the Norwegian border. This year-round ice-free port is the Russian Navy's only access to the Atlantic.

12   Ibsen's apartment is on the next block down the hill from the embassy. This is where he walked from each day, checking his pocket watch against the time on the clock on the University Aula and then to his table at the cafe of the Grand Hotel. He sat alone.

13   A debate among some, but I conclude this parallelogram is a rhombus.

14   In 1994-1995, the three large houses were sold for $1.7 million and two apartments were bought for $477,000. The deal with State was to be we could use the gain to construct six townhouses for staff. Something new, not more money pits. We were still fighting with State for our money when I left.

15   Julia Child writes quite a bit about life in Norway (very pithy) in *As Always, Julia: The Letters of Julia Child and Avis DeVoto* (Houghton, Mifflin, Harcourt, January 2010) such as: "December 29, 1960: The great thing around here for Christmastime is the julebord, or groaning Christmas table, filled with cold meats, pickled herring etc. We have been to numerous ones, and even had one ourselves. I got a half of a smoked pig's head, which you cook just like ham, and then glaze. That was fun."

16   "Skål" has come to mean cheers or to your health, but the origination is from Viking times when the skål was the communal wooden bowl from which the beer was drunk.

17   *Mission to the North*, Ambassador Florence Jaffray Harriman, Lippincott, 1941, p. 48

18   https://en.wikipedia.org/wiki/Per_Egil_Hegge

19   *History of Norway*, John A. Yilek, Wasteland Press, Aug. 7, 2018

20   https://www.royalcourt.no/

21   I was well versed on the historical backdrop of The Oslo Accords, having met David Fromkin at Harvard in 1991 and then reading his just-published book which became a classic, *A Peace to End All Peace: The Fall of the Ottoman Empire and the Creation of the Modern Middle East*, David Fromkin, Henry Holt, 1989.

22   This was not the first Nobel ceremony I attended. In 1990, I was in Oslo and American Ambassador Loret Miller Ruppe invited me to go with her. That year Mikhail Gorbachev was awarded the prize but did not come to Oslo for fear there would be a coup or some action that might prevent him returning to Moscow.

23   GATT was the precursor to the World Trade Organization. Divestment was the movement in legislatures to pass state laws to require that state employee pension funds eliminate from their portfolios stock of companies doing business in apartheid South Africa.

24   On the first day, there was a staff person in the suite with Mandela but not a person involved in GATT. On the second day the deputy chief of mission came with me to be the notetaker.

25   I felt well versed on what exactly apartheid was in South Africa as I had read the 1979 "Study Commission on U.S. Policy toward South Africa," which had a great influence on U.S. opinion leaders. www. bridgespan.org/insights/audacious-philanthropy-case-studies/anti-apartheid-movement

26   One event was held Dec. 6, 1993. A second julebord hosted by the chief of station was Dec. 11. From my notes, it is unclear which night the Holst meeting took place.

27   www.presidency.ucsb.edu/documents/statement-the-press-secretary-the-death-foreign-minister-johan-jurgen-holst-norway

28   On the trip to Israel, we also met the U.S. ambassador to Israel, Tom Pickering, a brilliant career ambassador, who briefed us on the U.S. policy toward Israel and the Palestinians and hosted a reception. (At the time of the Holst funeral, he was Clinton's ambassador to Russia.) It was a trade mission but the trip was promoted by the Milwaukee Jewish community and the Israeli Foreign Ministry, one of the type of trips that countries organize for American political leaders who are influential and likely to become more important. We were scheduled so tightly that Tommy Thompson took some meetings and I took others. I met with the Speaker of the Knesset and had tea with the mayor of Jerusalem, a Christian.

29   White paint was expensive and showed the owner's wealth.

30   The idea of a helicopter taking Hillary from Oslo to Lillehammer and back each day was dismissed quickly because of weather and image. One draft schedule had her landing at the base of the downhill run during an event.

31   Ms. Joyner and Mr. McMillen were the co-chairs of the President's Council on Physical Fitness and Sports.

32   It is little known that Odin, in addition to being the Norse God of wisdom, poetry and death, also handled hotel reservations.

33   Political officer Rodger Deuerlein took charge of the hotel updates. A West Point graduate who as an Army officer was a platoon leader and piloted AH-1F Cobra attack helicopters.

34   Melanne's son Mike was alder for downtown Madison.

35   Fred and I met in 1975 during the Morris "Mo" Udall for President campaign, my first presidential campaign. Fred was from Tucson, Udall's district in the House, and did advance work. For Udall the Wisconsin primary in 1976 was a must-win. A great campaign with such icons in the making as Mark Shields as the "of course we're winning" sidekick to Mo. And, Julie McCarthy, then a college student at UW-Madison who went on to a brilliant career as a foreign correspondent for NPR and currently the Manila Bureau chief. A real bond was formed by the veterans of this campaign as Mo was declared the winner the night of the Wisconsin primary when the polls closed only to lose to Carter when the paper ballots from rural areas trickled in the next day. We went to bed winners and woke up losers.

36   I had met Liv Ullmann in Madison when I introduced her at an event at the Union Theater.

37   Traditional costumes are bunads.

38   All I could think of was Grace Kelly and the picnic scene in *To Catch a Thief* and the car, a blue 1955 Sunbeam Alpine roadster.

39   The reputation Holbrooke had as arrogant? Compared to some of the pettifoggers and mummers I dealt with, he was Mr. Rogers. Holbrooke had only been ambassador to Germany since September of '93—his first diplomatic posting since 1981.

40   I had met Pamela Harriman before. Her PAC gave $10,000 to my campaign for governor in 1990. She seated me next to her at her fundraising event in D.C. featuring Paul Simon and some of the singers from the *Graceland* album. Pamela charming. Paul very nice. Interested in us. I would stay with Pamela in Paris later.

41   I had met Tom Pickering in Israel in 1988 when he was the ambassador there. He so impressed me. I never went wrong by following his cue.

42   Nicholas Rey was born in Poland in 1938 and left when his family fled to the U.S. on the eve of WWII. I visited him in Warsaw later.

43   I was invited to Harvard's Institute of Politics at the urging of Pat Lucey after my loss for governor in 1990. This was the spring semester of 1991. There were only six of us that semester and we each taught a seminar. Doris Kearns Goodwin was in our group and researching the book that would become *No Ordinary Time*, published in 1994. This is where she chronicled the stay at the White House of Princess Märtha and the three children, the future King Harald and his two sisters. She would read excerpts to us at lunch from her handwritten draft on a yellow legal pad. John Kenneth Galbraith was a guest at one of our every Tuesday lunches (prefaced by a glass of sherry). Galbraith and his wife would be our house guests in Oslo, a most memorable event detailed in these pages. We were available to any student. We had an office. We had a faculty ID, a membership in the Faculty Club (had coffee there with Gore Vidal. Good timing as I had just read his novel *Burr*). We could audit any course we wished. There was a stipend and housing. So, we all packed up and moved to Cambridge. I started to write my book *The Art of Legislative Politics* in my office, learning as I wrote how to use a PC. We had a budget to bring speakers to our seminars. There was not a speaking fee offered but they could stay in John F. Kennedy's dorm room, which was controlled by the institute. I was a guest speaker when my former colleague in the Wisconsin Assembly Mary Lou Munts was a fellow (Fall 1984) and stayed in this two-bedroom suite (JFK had a roommate) with a sitting room and a fireplace. There is a guest book. The person staying there before me was Pierre Trudeau. The governing board of this enclave within Harvard included Sen. Edward Kennedy, John Kennedy Jr., Caroline Kennedy, and Ron Brown, the former head of the Democratic Party. He

was chair when I ran for governor in 1990 and campaigned for me in Wisconsin a few times. A board meeting was held at lunch, with the fellows telling a bit of their experience and a goodly number of stories by Ted. John Jr. and Caroline took a real interest in our experiences. The IOP's purpose is to recognize and value the political life. It is a living legacy to their father. Pat Lucey, Paul Soglin, Mary Lou Munts, Jim Doyle, and Jim Moody are among the list of fellows from Wisconsin.

44   *Patrick J. Lucey: A Lasting Legacy*, Dennis L. Dresang, Wisconsin Historical Society Press, Sept. 15, 2020

45   Joseph Kennedy was ambassador to the UK from 1938-1940.

46   There were very public protestations by the State Department, the American Embassy in London, within her own embassy, and the British government about her role in the January 1994 granting of a visa to attend a meeting in New York by President Clinton to Gerry Adams, the head of Sinn Fein in Northern Ireland.

47   Jean was not dissuaded. Four months after our meeting in Brussels on Aug. 31, 1994, a cease-fire was declared. At the urging of Ambassador Smith, her brother Sen. Edward Kennedy, and others, President Clinton met with Mr. Adams at the White House in 1995. www.nytimes.com/2020/06/18/us/politics/jean-kennedy-smith-dead.html

48   Loret Miller Ruppe was from Milwaukee, a Marquette graduate, and her grandfather founded the Miller Brewing Company. She married Phil Ruppe, who represented a House district in Michigan. Loret was the campaign chair for George H.W. Bush in the 1980 Michigan primary. He won but dropped out soon after as Ronald Reagan had locked in a path to the nomination in other primaries. Before being named ambassador to Norway by President Bush in 1989, Loret Ruppe had served as director of the Peace Corps, appointed by President Reagan, promising a return to an "independent Peace Corps." And she delivered. Kudos all around for her tenure. When I told her that her mother had sent me a check for my campaign for governor she laughed and said she could have guessed it. Daughters know mothers.

49   Excerpt from Gorbachev's acceptance speech: "1990 represents a turning point. It marks the end of the unnatural division of Europe.

Germany has been reunited. We have begun resolutely to tear down the material foundations of a military, political and ideological confrontation...I do not regard the 1990 Nobel Peace Prize as an award to me personally, but as a recognition of what we call perestroika and innovative political thinking, which is of vital significance for human destinies all over the world." www.nobelprize.org/prizes/peace/1990/gorbachev/acceptance-speech/

50   Gro was trained as a medical doctor and her first job was as a public health doctor in elementary schools.

51   Presumably the Holy Father did not mention the state religion of Norway was Lutheran and there had been a rocky relationship with popes since Martin Luther nailed his objections to the church doors on Oct. 31, 1517.

52   When I came to Oslo in October 1993, Dick Norland was finishing up closing a "listening post" of the embassy in an office in Tromsø. He gathered valuable information from newspapers and by talking to people. His charm helped. A brilliant member of the Foreign Service who I was lucky to have on the desk at State. He went on to hold several ambassadorial posts. We had a bond, as his first real job was as an analyst in the Iowa House of Representatives.

53   Not as long as *War and Peace* but with more characters, St. Olaf College Professor Odd S. Lovoll's *A Century of Urban Life: The Norwegians in Chicago before 1930*, Norwegian-American Historical Association, July 1, 1988, is more a cultural anthropology written as history.

54   After more than 125 years, Norwegian-American Hospital changed its name in 2021 to Humboldt Park Health to better reflect the diverse community it serves.

55   https://gns.wisc.edu/person/harald-naess/

56   *Wisconsin State Journal*, May 21, 1994

57   The Quisling Clinic was a renowned example of Art Moderne architecture, as was the Edgewater Hotel, built by the Quislings as a place for visiting patients.

58   *Wisconsin State Journal*, May 21, 1994

59   https://seniorclass.students.wisc.edu/wp-content/uploads/
sites/372/2021/06/Historical-Record-of-UW-Madison-Commencement-
Speakers-Sheet1-1.pdf

60   In WWII, the Germans tried but failed to bomb the weather
station, which was then aiding the Allies. Although the Germans
occupied Norway, the weather station remained under the control of
the Norwegian government in London.

61   www.unfpa.org/sites/default/files/resource-pdf/94-09-05_
Statement_of_Norway_H.E._Mrs.pdf

62   A biography of Hillary Rodham Clinton states: "Perhaps the
most important speech First Lady Hillary Clinton delivered was her
September 5, 1995, address on global gender equality violations at the
United Nations Fourth World Conference on Women in Beijing, China.
It was a gathering of women from the globe's diverse national cultures
united in their belief that, as Mrs. Clinton famously put it, "women's
rights are human rights." In doing so, she became the first American
dignitary to address China's violations on Chinese soil." http://archive.
firstladies.org/biographies/firstladies.aspx?biography=43; www.
youtube.com/watch?v=xXM4E23Efvk

63   Cliff told of his long history with Wisconsin and the Experimental
Aircraft Association in Oshkosh, flying his personal plane to the annual
air show in July, rarely missing a year. He had just in 1993 established
an internship at EAA in Oshkosh where 16- and 17-year-olds get to
work in the hangers, get room and board, earn some money, and
take free flying lessons. His love of flying came about by working at a
single runway, very small airport in his hometown of La Jolla cleaning
the hangars when he was a teen and getting flying lessons as his pay.
http://airportjournals.com/cliff-robertson-time-must-have-a-stop/

64   1972 vote: 53.5 percent no, 46.5 percent yes. 1994 vote: 52.2 percent
no, 47.8 percent yes. After the loss in 1972, the Labour Government
headed by Trygve Bratteli resigned.

65   Kissinger received the Nobel Peace Prize in 1973 for negotiating
a ceasefire in Vietnam. He did not go to Oslo to accept the prize. His
acceptance speech was read by the American ambassador, Thomas R.
Byrne.

66   Rob went on to a distinguished career, becoming an ambassador, and is still in the State Department as of this writing.

67   https://www.sofn.com/

68   The eight-gun salute is still a mystery. Ambassadors and other special guests are traditionally piped aboard by the boatswain using his whistle. I was piped aboard ships of every Navy, including the Russian, as long as it was in Norwegian waters.

69   The offshore Ekofisk oil field in Norwegian waters in the North Sea was announced Christmas Eve 1969 by the American company Phillips Petroleum.

70   The director of the rocket range is Kolbjørn Adolfsen. He informs me his two sons, Roger and Kristian, are UW alumni.

71   Andøya is a civilian commercial operation. In 1962, Norway joined the space age with the launch of Ferdinand, named after the peaceful bull. Improving long-range radio communications and study of the northern lights through measurements in the ionosphere was the purpose. Launching satellites for polar orbit was becoming important. In polar orbit, a satellite passes over the earth's poles at each orbit and thus can get 24 hours of sun for its solar cells. This is important to Norway as these satellites provide good communication and sea monitoring in the north.

72   Adapted from an op/ed that originally appeared in *The Capital Times*, Madison, Wisconsin, Jan. 19, 2015.

73   The Norway-America Association's mission is to strengthen the ties between Norway and North America through educational exchange. NORAM's goal is to provide funding to encourage more students, researchers, and professionals to study in the U.S. and gain important experience. NORAM contributes in this way to strengthening competence, international exchange, networking, and mutual understanding.

74   A snorkel truck boasts a long lift mounted on a turntable on the firetruck body, enabling firefighters to reach locations difficult to reach with conventional ladders.

75   Svalbard is under Norwegian administration and legislation. Citizens of all signatory nations have free access and the right of economic activities. Spitsbergen remains demilitarized. No nation, including Norway, is allowed to permanently station military personnel or equipment on Spitsbergen. The United States, the British Empire, Denmark, France, Japan, Norway, the Netherlands, and Sweden were the "high contracting parties," with rights to access and commercial activity. Russians and Russian enterprises were allowed. This a finesse of the fact that the Bolshevik regime in Moscow had yet to be recognized as the legitimate government.

76   Amundsen had been the first to reach the South Pole in 1911.

77   https://svalbardmuseum.no/en/

78   www.irex.org/

79   www.rferl.org/a/photographing-the-night-lithuania-declared-independence-from-the-soviet-union/30481214.html

www.rferl.org/a/lithuania-soviet-crackdown-1991-kremlin-rewriting-history/31043914.html

80   Source for section: *The Sami: an Indigenous People of the Arctic*, Odd Mathis Haetta, Published by D. Girji o.s., 1996

81   The King's speech to the Sami Parliament is reproduced in Norwegian at www.kongehuset.no/tale.html?tid=171065&sek=26947&scope=0

82   The American Field Service started in WWI as the American Ambulance Field Service, volunteers who helped France before America entered the war by ferrying the wounded from the battlefield to hospitals behind the lines. Between the wars the former volunteers organized a friendship program with France. The ambulance service was reprised in France prior to America entering WWII. After the war the friendship program became organized and grew into a very large and vibrant conduit of understanding by sponsoring students to come to American high schools for one year and live with a host family. The program sponsoring American students to go to high schools in foreign countries was added a short time later. There was an AFS student from Norway in my sister Wendy's class at Sun Prairie High School in 1969. The family of the local dentist was the host.

83   https://afs.org/archives/timeline/#afs-nav-2011

https://afs.org/2011/07/01/president-john-f-kennedys-speech-to-afs-students-1963/

84   https://english.mgimo.ru/structure/schools/school-of-international-relations

85   *Aftenposten*, March 18, 1995, translation by Embassy Oslo

86   *The Last Full Measure: The Life and Death of the First Minnesota Volunteers*, Richard Moe, Henry Holt & Co., 1993

87   *The Man From Clear Lake*, Bill Christofferson, University of Wisconsin Press, 2004

88   https://armscontrolcenter.org/fact-sheet-the-nunn-lugar-cooperative-threat-reduction-program-2/

89   After the July 4th celebration, Al Nadolski and I left for the military side of Fornebu airport to meet Sen. Sam Nunn of Georgia, the chairman of the Armed Services Committee. He is our houseguest at the Residence. I had met Sen. Nunn a few times during presidential campaigns, including in Atlanta in 1988 at the Democratic Convention where he was an official host. At breakfast with Foreign Minister Godal, the Nunn-Lugar program was the topic of discussion. Very important to Norway as the program was at work then in the Murmansk area. Nunn was passionate about securing nuclear weapons and reducing both American and Russian stockpiles. His focus was removing the threat of nuclear war. He managed to mention to the Foreign Minister, "Oh, by the way the artillery unit of the Georgia National Guard is dedicated to the defense of Norway and they have been here many times for the winter maneuvers." "Thank you very much," said Minister Godal and a glass of orange juice was raised for a Skål. Nunn when learning of my planned trip to Murmansk to move things along on the nuclear waste projects promised help should it be needed. "Just call me," he said.

90   My wonderful cousins include Helgatoni and Oddvar Fosmark, Ranveig and Egil Åsabø, and Vigdes and Ole Ravneberg. I had known Helgatoni as a playmate when growing up. Her father and mother, Karsten and Liv Bendickson, had lived and worked in Madison in the 1950s but returned to Norway. Karsten worked at the Gisholt factory

and Liv worked at Woldenbergs, a stylish woman's clothing store. Ranveig's mother was Sara and and Vigdes' mother was Asta, nieces of my grandmother.

91   *Svalbard*, Roger Norum & James Proctor, The Globe Pequot Press, Inc., 1991. Bradtguides.com

92   In 1971 a crew member had been attacked by a polar bear fifty yards from the building.

93   Published by Ad Notam forlag AS, Oslo, Norway 1991

94   *The United States and the Cold War in the High North*, Rolf Tamnes, Ad Notam, Oslo, Norway, 1991, p. 181

95   Tamnes, p. 181

96   Silins graduated from Princeton and entered the Foreign Service in 1970. He worked at the State Department Office of Soviet Affairs. President George H.W. Bush nominated him for ambassador to Latvia in 1992.

97   https://history.state.gov/departmenthistory/people/silins-ints-m

98   Translated by LuAnn Sorenson, who taught Norwegian in the UW Scandinavian Studies Department from 1998-2000.

99   Ann-Marit Sæbønes, the first female mayor of Oslo, was a Norwegian politician for the Labour Party. She was born in Porsgrunn. She worked as a physiotherapist in Norway and Kenya from 1969 to 1979 and studied sociology at the University of Oslo in 1979. She served as a deputy representative to the Norwegian Parliament from Oslo between 1985 and 1989.

100   The city of Oslo ended the Sister City relationship with Madison in 2004 by a letter Oslo Mayor Per Ditlev-Simonsen sent to Madison Mayor Dave Cieslewicz. Ditlev-Simonsen wrote that Oslo had been reviewing its "more formalized international contacts with a view to reduce the number, and to focus on relationships of maximum significance...While we highly treasure the history of our relationship with Madison, we have concluded that it will not be realistic to maintain this relationship on the basis of regular visits by official delegations." Paul Soglin's reaction was, "They divorced us." William T. Evjue, son of Norwegian Immigrants and founder of the Madison

newspaper *The Capital Times*, in whose pages Norwegians could do no wrong, rolled over in his grave.

www.channel3000.com/madison-magazine/columns/madison-looks-to-rekindle-relationship-with-oslo/article_17465cc2-4095-55b1-874e-777053195d74.html

101   The 17th of May is the date in 1814 when delegates meeting in the city of Eidsvoll adopted a constitution for a "free and independent Norway." The constitution was based on the U.S. and French constitutions in that there was a separation of powers: king, Parliament and judiciary. There would only be a king and he could not create any new titles of nobility. Male heirs would ascend to the throne. Male landowners and certain other males could vote, but not women. About 15 percent of the population had the right to vote for the Parliament. "The Constitution was not totally enlightened as it excluded all Jews, Jesuits and monastic orders from the Kingdom." The prohibition on Jews was removed in 1851, but the provision on Jesuits was in place until the 1950s. Women and all men got the vote in 1913. King Carl Johan of Sweden, also king of Norway, was none too pleased, especially since the Eidsvoll group planned on the crown prince of Denmark to be the new king of independent Norway. Carl Johan sent troops to the border. There was minor fighting but it all sorted out when the crown prince of Denmark bowed out and in 1815 an agreement was reached for a "dual monarchy, two countries with a common king, united in war, but otherwise independent." The union with Sweden ended amicably in 1905. Then Norway voted to have a constitutional monarchy with its own king.

History of Norway, John A. Yilek, Wasteland Press, 2018

102   www.artnouveau-net.eu/city/alesund/

103   I had visited a facility near Flekkefjord where Coach purses were handmade and the no-barbed-wire element was mentioned again as one of the reasons Coach was in Norway.

104   WHO was organized after WWII to address the public health crisis in a devastated Europe. It became part of the United Nations but nations must join it separately from their UN membership. These 190 member countries choose the director general. It has its own budget from dues assessed on each member country by GDP

rank. It is headquartered in Geneva with regional centers in Europe, the Americas, Asia, and Africa. Norway is a major donor for special programs, which make up more than half of WHO's activity. Norway is also an essential provider of specialized medical and policy staff at WHO.

105   It was not until 2003 that the book *Charlie's Wilson's War* was published and 2007 the movie of the same title opened with Tom Hanks playing Charlie Wilson. The book tells the story of Charlie using his seat on the House Defense Appropriations Subcommittee to help the Afghans drive out the Soviet occupiers. I knew none of this about Charlie at the time of our lunch. In fact, had never heard of him. Charlie served in the House from 1973 until October 8, 1996. On his Norway visit, the only schedule besides lunch was the two of us meeting with the chairman of the Parliament's Defense Committee, Hans Johan Røsjorde.

106   https://nsarchive2.gwu.edu/carterbrezhnev/docs_intervention_ in_afghanistan_and_the_fall_of_detente/fall_of_detente_transcript.pdf

107   *In Confidence: Moscow's Ambassador to Six Cold War Presidents*, Anatoly Dobrynin, Crown Publishing Group, New York, September 1995

108   https://www.congress.gov/treaty-document/101st-congress/20

109   *The Art of Norway 1750-1914*, Elvehjem Museum of Art. University of Wisconsin Madison. Nov. 5, 1978-Jan. 7, 1979

110   The King and Queen took a West Coast swing on which I did not accompany them. I spent October 20-28 in Madison doing press interviews, addressed the Assembly and playing golf, returned to D.C. on the 29th and reunited with The King and Queen for the State Dinner.

111   Menu translated by LuAnn Sorenson, with help from Google Translate

112   Part of the Marine Corps birthday proclamation: "Marine: This high name of distinction and soldierly repute we who are Marines today have received from those who preceded us in the corps. With it we have also received from them the eternal spirit which has animated our corps from generation to generation and has been the distinguishing mark of the Marines in every age. So long as that spirit

continues to flourish Marines will be found equal to every emergency in the future as they have been in the past."

113   In March of 1995, the Turkish ambassador in Oslo called Norway an "unreliable weapons supplier" and claimed Turkey had decided not to buy Norwegian weapons in the future. (*Arbeiderbladet,* March 18, 1995.) This was Ignored. The Pentagon continued to lobby Norway to sell the Penguins to Turkey.

114   I told Jorma that in the 1880s and early part of the 20th century many Finnish immigrants settled in northern Wisconsin in the counties along the southern shore of Lake Superior. They were loggers and farmers and dedicated to the co-op movement. I knew about this fine group of people because I had recruited a candidate of Finnish descent to run in the Assembly district in this area in the 1980s. I was campaigning for him and kept running up against the Republican charge that he and other Finns were "Red Finns." They voted Communist in presidential elections. An effective smear campaign. Well, somebody did vote Communist because Gus Hall, the Communist Party candidate for president in 1972, '76, '80 and '84 averaged about 700 votes in this part of Wisconsin. We lost the Assembly race. The Red Finn tag came from the Finnish civil war in 1917. http://countrystudies.us/finland/15.htm;

www.wisconsinhistory.org/Records/Article/CS2186 https://wep.csumc.wisc.edu/finnish-in-wisconsin/

115   "Most Americans don't realize that Finland was one of two European countries (the other was the United Kingdom) that were attacked and yet maintained independence and freedom during World War II. In 1939, Nazi and Soviet foreign ministers signed the Ribbentrop-Molotov Pact, which allowed Germany free rein to attack Czechoslovakia and Poland while giving Russia carte blanche to attack Finland. But the Finns mobilized and stalled the Russian invasion during what was called the Winter War. They filled vodka bottles with gasoline, placed rags in them, lit them, and hurled them onto Soviet tanks, coining the term 'Molotov Cocktails.'" Ambassador Derek Shearer.

https://washingtonmonthly.com/2022/03/09/as-war-rages-in-ukraine-finland-offers-answers/

116   www.lifeinnorway.net/nidaros-cathedral/

117   *Travel Memories From Norway 1860*, Aasmund Olavsson Vinje, Timber Window Publishing

118   Vinje here refers to the fact Norway is free under the Constitution adopted at Eidsvoll in 1814. It was a grand document, influenced by the Bill of Rights, but this freedom means little to the impoverished. The deal brokered shortly after Eidsvoll was that Sweden's king would be the Norwegian monarch.

119   In September 1991, President George H.W. Bush announced a Presidential Nuclear Initiative "to cease deployment of tactical nuclear weapons on surface ships, attack submarines, and land-based naval aircraft during "normal circumstances." In response, in October 1991 Soviet President Mikhail Gorbachev announced the "removal all tactical nuclear weapons from surface ships and multipurpose submarines. In June 1992 President Yeltsin reaffirmed these commitments. These initiatives were part of a historic and wide-ranging series of steps to end the deployment of tactical nuclear weapons in Western Europe and the former Soviet Bloc countries and begin the destruction of stockpiles of other nuclear weapons before the Strategic Arms Reduction Treaty (START) between the United States and the Soviet Union was signed in December 1991. START, governing the deployment and numbers of nuclear weapons, took effect in 1994.

www.armscontrol.org/factsheets/pniglance; www.armscontrol.org/factsheets/start1

120   I knew some things about nuclear submarines. Perhaps all one needs to know. In the 1980s, I was among the group in the Wisconsin Legislature trying to stop Project ELF: Extra Low Frequency. This was a Navy plan to lace tens of thousands of acres of northern Wisconsin with a web of antennas strung on telephone poles. The antenna would work by bouncing the signal off the very hard underground rock formation which would then form a larger antenna. Thus, the location in Wisconsin and the Upper Peninsula of Michigan over the Laurentian Shield was chosen. The antenna would signal to submerged submarines that it was war and they should come up and launch, since a sub cannot be contacted at cruising depth by normal frequencies. ELF could only be used to give a one-way signal—likely, a first strike, or

a launch of retaliation. But it was certain that the project would make northern Wisconsin a first-strike target of the Soviets.

121 In 1974, the EPA awarded Dyer a medal for his work in the development of international controls over the disposal of radioactive materials in the marine environment. Under the Ocean Dumping Act of 1972, EPA was responsible for regulating ocean disposal including radioactive waste.

122 "The Russian Northern Fleet: Sources of Radioactive Contamination," Thomas Nilsen, Igor Kudrik, Alexandr Nikitin. Bellona Report, Volume 2: 1996

123 See June 1993, FAFO Institute for Labour and Social Research report on living conditions in the Kola Peninsula.

www.fafo.no/zoo-publikasjoner/fafo-rapporter/environment-and-living-conditions-on-the-kola-peninsula

124 For a catalog of all nuclear submarine incidents from every nuclear navy since the first submarine, see Outrider Foundation report "Silent Dangers" at 2019-Outrider_report_FINAL.pdf

125 For background what I previously knew about Russian history, see Appendix C.

126 Operation Barbarossa was the code name for Hitler's secret plan to invade the Soviet Union that was launched in June of 1941. The capture of Murmansk was part of the plan. "There has never been a war fought in the high north...The region is unsuited to military operations...there are no roads..." This quote from German General Eduard Dietl was part of his argument to Hitler that taking Murmansk was not worth it. "In winter it was an icy hell on earth. The short summers were no better." Hitler would have none of it. It was the Soviets' only ice-free port and along with the strategic Murmansk railway this was the gateway for the USA and Britain to supply the USSR with war materiel. At Hitler's briefing of his generals before the invasion he pointed to a map and called the short distance to Murmansk from Occupied Norway "laughable." Furthermore, the Finns would help and attack from the east. Dietl argued that just cutting the Murmansk rail line would accomplish the same goal. Murmansk would be useless as a port. The Germans didn't need the port as they had ports in the fjords in Norway. Hitler said no and ensured failure.

Dietl was right: There were no roads. When the offensive from Norway started, the Russian maps he was using that he believed showed roads actually showed telegraph lines. The German offensive stalled. For the next three-and-one-half years the front moved little. Frozen.

Hitler's Arctic War: The German campaigns in Norway, Finland and the USSR 1940-45, Chris Mann & Christer Jorgensen, Brown Bear Books Limited, 2016

127 https://bellona.org/news/nuclear-issues/radioactive-waste-and-spent-nuclear-fuel/2012-09-lepse-nuclear-waste-storage-ship-endangering-murmansk-for-decades-finally-headed-for-dismantlement

128 In 1983, I was on a trade mission to China with Wisconsin Governor Lee Dreyfus and in two weeks every meeting, tour, and toast with plum wine went through an interpreter. In 1985, I led a trip to Nicaragua with former Wisconsin Governor and Ambassador to Mexico Pat Lucey, again for two weeks all through an interpreter.

129 The *Arktika* is a class of icebreaker of which there were five. All are commonly called *Arktika.* The *Yamel* is the ship referred to here.

130 He came under immediate attack. There was a litany of complaints about his pro-Western views from the KGB, the entrenched Soviet-era bureaucracy and the anti-Yeltsin political parties—the Communists and the others pining if not plotting for the return of the Soviet Union. (Ambassador Fokine, in Oslo, certainly a Soviet-era diplomat, had come over to the Kozyrev reform faction at the beginning.) A usual brickbat was that Kozyrev was suspect because he was not born in the Soviet Union. Always mentioned by his critics was that he was born in the NATO headquarters city of Brussels. Kozyrev's father, an engineer and member of the Communist Party, had been posted at the Soviet trade mission in Belgium for the years 1949-1951. I first was aware of Kozyrev by noticing he was not noticed. The ceremony at the White House announcing the Oslo Accords on September 9, 1993, became known as the "handshake on the White House Lawn" and the explaining symbol of it all became the photo of President Clinton standing between PLO Chairman Yasser Arafat and Israeli Prime Minister Yitzhak Rabin coaxing the handshake between the two. Also, on the stage that day was Kozyrev. *The New York Times* story of the event did not even mention that Kozyrev was there to

represent Yeltsin's support of the accords. I certainly took note as in a matter of weeks I would be in Oslo as the new ambassador and the Oslo Accords were the top priority of both U.S. and Norwegian foreign policy. www.nytimes.com/search?query=Mideast+Peace+Accords+1993

131   START: Strategic Arms Reduction Limitation Treaty. START I was an agreement between Gorbachev and Reagan. START II was an agreement between George H.W. Bush and Yeltsin. The treaties reduced the number of Russia's ICBMs and cut U.S. sea-based missiles and strategic bombers. START II also banned placing multiple warheads, each with their own target, on a single ICBM.

132   *The Firebird, A Memoir: The Elusive Fate of Russian Democracy*, Andrei Kozyrev, University of Pittsburgh Press, 2019

133   www.imo.org/en/OurWork/Environment/Pages/London-Convention-Protocol.aspx

134   William Nitze, the assistant administrator for international activities at the Environmental Protection Agency, was the key person supporting the project in Washington.

135   www.visitnorway.com/listings/visit-the-russian-border-and-king-oscar-ii-chapel-varanger/229398/

136   "U.S.-Russian Joint Commission on Economic and Technological Cooperation (Gore-Chernomyrdin Commission)," Department of State of the United States of America.

137   www.wilsonquarterly.com/quarterly/into-the-arctic/changing-climates-for-arctic-security

138   For Perry, being the secretary of Defense at the end of the Cold War was destiny. Looking back on his life it seemed to all lead to this. In the fall, of 1962 at the very start of what would be the Cuban Missile Crisis Perry, then 35, received a call at his home in Palo Alto from the CIA that he was to be in Washington the next day. He was the director of Sylvania's Electronic Defense Laboratories, developing reconnaissance systems directed at Soviet nuclear weapons systems. He was immediately made part of a small team of four weapons analysts and six experts to interpret the photos from U2 flights over Cuba. Within days they reported to President Kennedy that the missiles in Cuba were nuclear-capable and in a few weeks could be

operational. Whether in private industry or government, Perry was the expert on Soviet nuclear capability. At the start of the Carter administration in 1976 he was appointed undersecretary of Defense for research. His job was to close the missile gap with the Soviets. For the rest of us the threat of nuclear Armageddon became abstract, but not for Perry. It started in 1946 at age 19 when he was sent to Japan to be in the Army of Occupation after the war. He said several times that seeing what just one atomic bomb could do changed him forever.

My Journey at the Nuclear Brink, William J. Perry, Stanford University Press, 2015

139   Briefing paper prepared by U.S. Embassy Oslo

140   https://fromnorway.com/seafood-from-norway/cod/

141   www.norske-torske-klubben.com/

142   https://fromnorway.com/seafood-from-norway/cod/

143   Statement to the Storting on Nuclear Safety Issues by FM Godal, Oct. 29, 1996

144   https://barents-council.org/barents-euro-arctic-council

145   Dayton Accords negotiated by Holbrooke ending the war in Bosnia, a part of the war in the Balkans, Nov. 24, 1995

146   www.royalcourt.no/artikkel.html?tid=28678&sek=28571

147   *The Art of Legislative Politics*, Tom Loftus, Congressional Quarterly Press, 1994

148   The State Department had eliminated six positions since my arrival.

149   U.S. Department of State Office of Inspector General: Report of Inspection, Embassy Oslo, Norway, September 1996

150   Bob Stuart's life was an important part of the American story. In 1940 at age 24, he, along with a group of fellow Yale Law School students, which included future President Gerald R. Ford, the first head of the Peace Corps, Sargent Shriver, and future Supreme Court Justice Potter Stewart, founded the America First Committee to oppose American entry into World War II. Aviation hero Charles Lindbergh became the spokesman and face of the movement. It was

vilified as being pro-German but became one of the largest anti-war mass movements in American history. Bob and many others of his generation believed it was the false claims and duplicity of Woodrow Wilson that led America to enter World War I, a charge that crept steadily into credibility in the interwar years. The broken-down veterans and the Depression were evidence enough to conclude that never again should America get involved in a European war. After Pearl Harbor the movement ended and Bob enlisted, served in Europe and left the Army a major.

151   She was a "courtier," meaning a member of a royal family appointed by the monarch to assist The Queen in carrying out official functions. This title was not new to the Løvenskiold family. It was held between 1816 and 1845 by her husband's great-great-great-grandmother, Countess Karen of Wedel-Jarlsberg, and later by her husband's great-grandmother, Elise Løvenskiold, from 1887 to 1905. The Løvenskiold family's noble status and ties to the royal family dated from 1739. However, it was the family's holdings of large estates, lumber yards, industrial enterprises, and forest land that the newspaper readers in Oslo were familiar with. If you go to the observation platform on top of the ski jump on Holmenkollen, the mountain above Oslo, you look down on the city, but turn around and you will see seemingly to the horizon the forests owned by the Løvenskiold family.

152   Excerpts of Mikhail Gorbachev's speech in Murmansk on Oct. 1, 1987, relating to Norway: "The Soviet Union duly appreciates the fact that Denmark and Norway, while being members of NATO, unilaterally refused to station foreign military bases and deploy nuclear weapons on their territory in peacetime. This stance, if consistently adhered to, is important for lessening tensions in Europe...The following thought suggests itself in connection with the idea of a nuclear-free zone. At present the Northern countries, that is Iceland, Denmark, Norway, Sweden, and Finland, have no nuclear weapons. We are aware of their concern over the fact that we have a testing range for nuclear explosions on Novaya Zemlya. We are thinking how to solve this problem...we applaud the activities of the authoritative World Commission on Environment and Development headed by Prime Minister Gro Harlem Brundtland of Norway."

https://www.barentsinfo.fi/docs/gorbachev_speech.pdf

153   www.manhattanprojectvoices.org/location/los-alamos-ranch-school/

154   www.nytimes.com/2014/05/20/business/robert-d-stuart-jr-98-quaker-oats-chief-and-opponent-of-us-entry-in-wwii-is-dead.html?smid=nytcore-ios-share

155   www.nationalguard.mil/News/Article-View/Article/576122/minnesota-national-guard-in-norway-for-exchange-program/

156   www.forsvaret.no/en/organisation/home-guard

157   www.globalsecurity.org/military/facility/nalmeb.htm

158   www.blackpast.org/special-features/african-american-u-s-ambassadors-1869/

159   *Empire of Rubber: Firestone's Scramble for Land and Power in Liberia,* Gregg Mitman, The New Press, New York, 2021

160   Court of St. James's is the official name for the British royal court (The King or Queen and their family, officials, etc.). Ambassadors (senior representatives of other countries) in Britain are officially called Ambassadors to the Court of St James's.

161   Bob Farmer was campaign treasurer for both the Dukakis and Clinton campaigns. He invented "soft money" and enabled the Democrats to match the Republicans' spending. I first met him in Boston on one of the trips former Wisconsin Gov. Pat Lucey and I took to visit Gov. Dukakis about the 1988 primary campaign. When Ted Kennedy's campaign for the nomination failed and President Carter was nominated again in 1980, Illinois Congressman John Anderson entered the race as an independent. He chose Pat Lucey as his vice presidential running mate. Lucey had supported Kennedy against Carter, resigning as ambassador to Mexico to join the Kennedy campaign. Pat had been appointed ambassador by Carter in 1978. Wisconsin was a state Anderson could possibly win because Wisconsin had a history of supporting third-party candidates: Progressives, Socialists, and George Wallace in 1968, among others. A very young Bob Farmer raised the money for Anderson and was thought a genius, as he got banks to lend the campaign money based on the bet Anderson/Lucey would get more than 5 percent of the vote. If that happened,

public funding for the campaign would be paid retroactively and the banks would get their money. Anderson/Lucey got 6.6 percent of the vote.

162   Norway's ban on American beef was based on the use of growth hormones and other unnatural enhancements.

163   Linn Ullmann's highly praised first novel, *Before You Sleep*, published in 1998, fulfilled her promise as a writer.

164   I had met Liv Ullmann several times. The first was when I introduced her at an event at the UW in the 1980s. Liv acted in many Bergman films, including *Persona* (1966), *Cries and Whispers* (1972), *Scenes From a Marriage* (1973), *The Passion of Anna* (1969), and *Autumn Sonata* (1978). https://en.m.wikipedia.org/wiki/Liv_Ullmann

165   The governor of Minnesota, my friend Arne Carlson, came as part of a trip that included talking to the agriculture secretary in Denmark about the unfairness of the tariffs on the delicious ham from the hogs from his state. At his dinner, Arne, of Swedish descent, waxed eloquent about the fine Norwegians in Minnesota and presented me with a framed certificate making me an honorary citizen of the Gopher State. In my acceptance I said I was humbled more than he could know that I could be a Minnesotan but not have to live there. And, after reading it carefully, I noted that there was no mention of or even a hint that I would cheer for the Vikings in any game against the Green Bay Packers. Wisconsin Gov. Tommy Thompson visited as well.

166   My assistant Sue Meyer had given up correcting the spelling of my name except for airplane tickets, where my reservations in the name Lofthus, a common occurrence, was corrected because it did not match the name on my diplomatic passport. In 2022 on the embassy website on the list of former ambassadors, I am listed as Thomas A. Lofthus.

167   www.hotelullensvang.no/en/about-ullensvang/

168   I had a photo taken at this station holding a piglet, noting I had been instrumental in securing funding for a new swine facility. Bringing home the pork to my district being the not-too-subtle message.

169   *Ole Bull: Norway's Romantic Musician and Cosmopolitan Patriot*, Einar Haugen and Camilla Cai, University of Wisconsin Press, 1993. This book was a gift from my staff, friends who always made me look like I was in charge: Bob Lang, Sue Meyer, Michael Youngman, Susan Goodwin, Nancy McAdams, Carla Hillmer, Stephanie Riley, and Jeff Remsik.

170   *Marriage* was a gift from the Carter-Menil Human Rights Foundation in spring 1994.

171   HM would have first sailed on the *Norge* when he was a boy. Not his first experience on a yacht, as President Roosevelt took him fishing on the Presidential Yacht *Sequoia* when he was 9 years old. It was D-Day.

https://www.royalcourt.no/seksjon.html?tid=28712&sek=27324

No Ordinary Time: Franklin and Eleanor Roosevelt: The Home Front in World War II, Doris Kearns Goodwin, Simon & Schuster, 1994

172   www.nytimes.com/2011/07/24/us/24Shalikashvili.html

173   President Clinton replaced John Deutch as CIA director on Dec. 15, 1996.

174   United States Department of State, Office of the Inspector General. Report of Inspection, Embassy Oslo, Norway ISP/I-96-36. September 1996

175   For a short history of the Norwegian Resistance, see Appendix D.

176   https://www.dnt.no/

177   www.hydro.com/

178   The Telemark Canal opened in 1861, connecting lakes and rivers with locks to form a waterway from Dalen to Skien, where ocean-going ships could take on cargo. This was how the Norsk Hydro fertilizer got to European markets. Interestingly, however, the plant not the reason for the canal. The economics behind constructing the canal were two very valuable commodities: lumber and whetstone. The wealthy sawmill owners in Skien could now efficiently float their logs to the mills to be cut into lumber to then go by ship to build the houses of Europe; and the whetstone mines could cheaply move by barge this dense rock which was shaped into wheels and grindstones and shipped throughout the world to be used to sharpen knives, scythes, axes, and industrial cutting machines. Soon there were steam passenger boats

and the people of Telemark left the farms and boarded the boats and were on the first leg of their trip to America. Hiking the canal route, or lazing on an excursion boat through the locks, makes the canal today one of the most popular tourist destinations in Norway.

179   Here you can read of the "secret of Gaustatoppen Mountain." https://gaustabanen.no/en/hemmeligheten-i-gaustatoppen.

180   The Erdut Agreement ended the internal fighting after independence by establishing the minority rights of Serbs in the eastern part of Croatia.

181   *Ambassador's Journal*, John Kenneth Galbraith, Houghton Mifflin Co., 1969. The last line, "I a little wish I were going also" was handwritten by JFK, p. 45.

182   *The Art of Legislative Politics*, Tom Loftus, Congressional Quarterly Press, 1994. It was published for the market CQ press had with professors of political science as a complement to the textbook in courses on state and local government. Very popular. It sold out and was used across the country including at Harvard and the UW.

183   "We have given parties for a remarkable variety of American visitors and Indian guests. We had been in Delhi six weeks when Vice President and Mrs. Johnson, Stephen and Jean Kennedy Smith dropped in for three days. The temperature was just under 120 degrees, but they bore up nobly. Since then we have had the Harvard Glee Club, the Davis Cup players, the Joe E. Adams troupe, the World Council of Churches, the World Medical Conference, the Bairds and their marionettes, Mark Robson and José Ferrer, who were here to make a film on the death of Gandhi, the American polo team, Henry Luce, Winthrop Aldrich, museum directors, zoo directors, Nobel Prize winners, several senators, the presidents of Harvard and Princeton, two young girl graduates hitchhiking their way around the world for two years on $500 each, the Peace Corps, the crews of our C130s, who came to fly Indian troops and supplies to Nefa and Ladakh, James Farley, Yehudi Menuhin, Louis Untermeyer, Angie Dickinson, Averell Harriman, Luther Hodges, Arthur Schlesinger, Jr., Orville Freeman, Lowell Thomas, Norman Rockwell, Barbara Ward, and, of course, Mrs. Kennedy." cdn.theatlantic.com/media/archives/1963/05/211-5/132644583.pdf

184   The visit of Jackie Kennedy: "The Air India jet came in on time and I went aboard to find J.B.K. (Jacqueline Bouvier Kennedy) full of life and looking a million dollars in a suit of radioactive pink...we went to lay roses for Gandhi and to the Chancery to greet the Indian and American staff...I found myself worrying about the press reaction to things...and her own state of contentment because had she become tired (it would show)...one can hope to conceal some errors but not when they have to do with the President's wife." The first lady's trip lasted eight days. NBC did a full hour color prime-time special on her tour. *Ambassador's Journal*, John Kenneth Galbraith, Houghton Mifflin Co., 1969.

185   Thank you note translated by LuAnn Sorenson, with help from Google Translate

186   Svalbard is the archipelago, Spitsbergen the largest island, Longyearbyen the main town.

187   www.funkenlodge.com/explore/history/

188   https://archive.nytimes.com/www.nytimes.com/library/financial/020694mobil-noto-profile.html

189   Marton and Holbrooke were married in 1995. Marton's 1995 book on Raoul Wallenberg educated me on the Nazis, the fate of Jews in Hungary during WWII and the heroism of one incredible Swedish diplomat. It bolstered my advocacy for Hungary to join NATO. Marton, Kati (1995), *Wallenberg: Missing Hero* (1st Arcade ed.), New York: Distributed by Little, Brown and Company.

190   Richard C. Holbrooke, "The Baltics and Balkans: Speech to the Norwegian Atlantic Committee," Sept. 5, 1996. Security Policy Library No. 11/1996

191   *Beyond the Cold War: New Dimensions in International Relations*, Edited by Geir Lundestad and Odd Arne Westad, Oslo, Oxford, 1993

192   Liv Arnesen was the first woman to ski alone across the Greenland Ice Cap, which she did in 1992, and the first woman to ski solo to the South Pole, in 1994. Barbara was a friend of Liv's and a weekend skiing partner. In 1990 Erling Kagge and Børge Ousland became the first ever to reach the North Pole unsupported. In 1992 Kagge was the first to reach the South Pole unsupported and in 1994 reached the summit of Mount Everest.

193   Carl I. Hagen was an effective conservative populist in the vein of Ronald Reagan. The Progress Party, which Hagen founded and directed to prominence, was an alternative to the ideology of the Labour Party and the ineffectiveness of the Conservative Party. He questioned the status quo of high taxes, questioned liberal immigration policies and was an articulate, forceful speaker the media loved to cover. Unlike most of the other politicians he earned a business degree from a college in the UK. My lunches with him were great fun.

194   Derek Shearer, Finland; Chargé Jimmy Kolker, Denmark; Day Olin Mount, Iceland; James Swihart, Lithuania; Larry Napper, Latvia; Lawrence Taylor, Estonia. (Tom Siebert, Sweden, could not arrange his schedule to attend.)

195   From my notes: Is it now containment with a human face? Do we look at the Baltics from the West's point of view or the Russian? Swedish leadership is not a substitute for America leading. Ability to influence EU is substantial. Soviet constraints are gone. Should we do a little dance to exercise freedom or is that provocative? The promise of NATO membership and EU membership has an immense impact on the psyche of politics and society and influences thousands of daily decisions. The economy—financial regulations, establishing a stock market, banks connecting to the West's systems—all have to be done at once. The interest of the U.S. is to have the EU get new members in the fast lane now. Do Sweden, Finland, and Denmark act as agents for the Baltics in the EU? Assume Russia evolves into some sort of democracy? What promotes this. What hinders. Wish Tom Pickering (U.S. ambassador to Russia) were here.

196   www.newscancook.com/seafood/bergen-fish-soup

197   https://www.baroniet.no/en/

198   www.fvap.gov/citizen-voter

199   Niels Vik, the secretary of the Oslo Golf Club, was a UW alumnus. Told me he was "an old Badger fan."

200   Dear reader: In addition to Arnie's lessons my other guide can be found in the golf exploits of Bertie Wooster in the stories of P.G. Wodehouse. May I suggest *The Clicking of Cuthbert.*

201   www.oslogk.no/

202 www.foreignaffairs.com/articles/europe/1996-11-01/nato-and-have-nots-reassurance-after-enlargement

203 In 1997, His Majesty King Harald presented Tetley with the Knight of Royal Norwegian Order of Merit for his twenty years of work with the Norwegian National Ballet.

204 Speeches of note by the prime minister are circulated to embassies.

205 Rostropovich was laid to rest April 29, 2007, next to Yeltsin. Putin brought roses. www.nytimes.com/2007/04/29/world/europe/29iht-russia.4.5494244.html?searchResultPosition=7

206 He regained citizenship in 1990 under Gorbachev.

207 I suggest a memoir of this time: *The Gift Horse: Report on a Life*, by the German actress Hildegard Knef.

208 Bundestag is Germany's federal Parliament. The Reichstag was the Parliament of previous regimes before the war.

209 Petra Kelly was murdered in 1992 at age 44 by her partner and fellow Green Party politician.

210 The United States had diplomatic relations with East Germany from 1974 to 1990.

211 For more detail on Norway and NATO, see Appendix E.

212 United States Department of State, Office of the Inspector General, Report of Inspection, Embassy Oslo, Norway ISP/I-96-36. September 1996

213 *The Russia Hand: A Memoir of Presidential Diplomacy*, Strobe Talbott, Random House, 2002

214 Strobe Talbott on Russia, Baltics and NATO expansion

215 Bill Clinton's *Atlantic* article on Russia and NATO: www.theatlantic.com/ideas/archive/2022/04/bill-clinton-nato-expansion-ukraine/629499/

216 *Chances of a Lifetime: A Memoir*, Warren Christopher, Scribner, 2001, p. 273

217   The Norway Air Landed Marine Expeditionary Brigade (NALMEB) is the U.S. Marine Corps' pre-positioned stock of war-fighting supplies for the rapid reinforcement of Norway to protect NATO's northern flank. The storage of the equipment is governed by an agreement between the United States and Norway. The equipment is in six climate-controlled tunnels dug into mountains in central Norway. The pre-positioned stocks can support up to 17,000 Marines with 7,000 tons of ground and aviation ammunition, 1,000 vehicles, 40,000 cases of rations, and a number of pieces of artillery. In accordance with the agreement with Norway there are no tanks. There are no U.S. fighter jets permanently stationed in Norway. The Marines are to protect the airfields that arriving U.S. air forces (F-16s) would use in case of an attack on Norway and to also support a naval campaign. The pre-positioned stocks allow for the rapid deployment of Marines to Norway. Once landed they would retrieve the equipment that they have already been trained to use during yearly NATO war game exercises. The equipment has to be regularly updated and maintained, with the cost shared between the U.S. and Norway. During my tenure, in 1994, because of the end of the Cold War, the nine airfields to be protected were reduced to five. In 1995, Norwegian Minister of Defense Jørgen Kosmo proposed that Norway take over all of the expenses of the U.S. for storing and maintaining the equipment. U.S. Secretary of Defense Perry agreed to this change. The U.S. commitment to keeping the equipment in Norway was not changed.

218   France, Italy, and Spain told Norway: "Start buying our wine or we will stop buying your fish." One of the factors contributing to the end of prohibition in 1927.

219   The Leangkollen Security Conference is the Norwegian Atlantic Committee's (DNAK) annual two-day conference held during the first half of February. Every year, DNAK invites distinguished international and Norwegian researchers and senior officials to give speeches on current defense, foreign, and security policy issues - and has done so since the conference's inception in 1965. www.atlanterhavskomiteen. no/en/leangkollen-security-conference

220   www.rand.org/

221   https://news.wisc.edu/century-of-political-science-marked-at-uw-madison/

More recent alumni include former U.S. Secretary of State Lawrence Eagleburger and Major League Baseball Commissioner Bud Selig.

222   The Baltics include Estonia, Latvia, and Lithuania.

223   When Lithuania declared independence, Gorbachev imposed an economic blockade, including oil. There was a push to punish the Soviets with U.S. sanctions, but not wanting to hurt Gorbachev, Bush refused. The new head of Lithuania called it "another Munich." This followed on the January 1991 action when Soviet troops killed 14 protestors in Vilnius who were advocating independence. There was also a fight inside the Cabinet when Secretary of State Jim Baker resisted recognizing Lithuania. From: *The Man Who Ran Washington: The Life and Times of James A. Baker III*, Peter Baker and Susan Glasser, Doubleday 2020

224   *The Russia Hand*, Strobe Talbott, Random House, 2002, p. 94

225   www.ipsnews.net/1996/07/baltics-military-exercises-a-success-but-nato-still-far-away/

226   Zhirinovsky refers to American troops in Russia after World War I had ended when they were sent by Woodrow Wilson to fight with British troops in Murmansk and Archangel against the Bolsheviks in the Civil War. *The Armies March*, Ambassador John C. Cudahy, 1941

https://archive.org/details/TheArmiesMarch

227   www.globalsecurity.org/military/ops/baltic-challenge.htm

228   https://coldwarsites.net/country/estonia/soviet-nuclear-submarine-training-center-paldiski/

229   www.abandonedspaces.com/uncategorized/submarine-base-2.html?chrome=1

230   Severomorsk is just east of Murmansk and is the headquarters base of the Northern Fleet.

231   Interview with Admiral Oleg Yerofeyev, commander of the Northern Fleet, by Vladimir Gundarov, *Country and Navy*, Fall 1996. Translation by the U.S. Foreign Broadcast Intelligence Service.

232   https://www.uwalumni.com/news/fudge-bottom-pie-2/

233   Civilian control of the military, border disputes settled, ethnic minority rights addressed, and a presumption of EU membership first.

234   www.atlanterhavskomiteen.no/en/leangkollen-security-conference

235   West Germany had been a member of NATO since 1955. East Germany was folded into this membership upon reunification in October 1990.

236   www.newtraditions.de/

237   NATO ambassadors learned later the Clinton, Perry, Gore meeting was a showdown on NATO enlargement, with Perry coming away feeling he lost and convinced the decision was wrong: "Holbrooke was irrepressible and his proposal (adding now Poland, Czech, Hungary, and the Baltics to NATO) moved forward...I asked for a full National Security Council meeting...neither Secretary of State Christopher nor NSC advisor Tony Lake spoke out...Gore made forceful arguments in favor...He believed we could manage the problems this would create with Russia. I disagreed...I put a very high priority on maintaining a positive relationship with Russia, especially as it pertained to any future reduction in the nuclear weapons threat...I considered resigning but feared that would be interpreted as opposition to NATO membership for Poland, Hungary, and the Czech Republic, that I greatly supported—but not right away..." *My Journey at the Nuclear Brink*, William J. Perry, Stanford University Press, 2015, pp. 128-129.

238   Poland, Hungary and Czech Republic were invited to join NATO at the NATO Madrid Summit July 8, 1997. President Clinton, Chancellor Kohl, and Norwegian PM Jagland were present. www.nato.int/docu/speech/1997/s970708h.htm

239   https://emke.uwm.edu/

240   NUPI is the official Norwegian government international relations research arm. www.nupi.no/

241   The Norwegian participants included Sten Helland, state secretary prime minister's office; Martin Kolberg, state secretary Ministry of Defense; Tonje Westby, international secretary Labour Party; Bjørner

Per Olsen, chair, Finance Committee of the Storting; as well as Sverre Lodgaard.

242   www.prio.org/

243   Nicholas A. Rey of New York was ambassador to Poland from 1993 through 1997. He was born in 1938 in Warsaw. His family fled to the U.S. to escape the Nazi invasion in 1939 and he was subsequently naturalized a U.S. citizen. Rey was a director and vice chairman of the Polish-American Enterprise Fund between 1990 and 1993. Previously, he spent 25 years as an investment banker with Merrill Lynch and Bear Stearns. He was a member of the Council on Foreign Relations and a director of the Polish American Freedom Foundation as well as the National Democratic Institute for International Affairs. He passed away on Jan. 13, 2009.

https://www.washingtonpost.com/wp-dyn/content/article/2009/01/19/AR2009011903103.html

244   Anthony J. Drexel Biddle, Jr., of Pennsylvania was ambassador to Poland from 1937-1943. He was born in 1897. As ambassador, Biddle left Warsaw on September 5, 1939, and followed the government of Poland first to France (September 1939 to June 1940) and later to England (where Biddle arrived Mar 14, 1941). He was also commissioned to Belgium, Czechoslovakia, Greece, Luxembourg, the Netherlands, Norway, and Yugoslavia, and was resident in London during his service as ambassador to those countries. He left London on December 1, 1943, and later served with the U.S. Army with the rank of major general until 1961. He was named ambassador to Spain in 1961 by President John F. Kennedy. Ambassador Biddle died in 1961. https://pl.usembassy.gov/

Poland and the Coming of the Second World War. The diplomatic papers of A. J. Drexel Biddle, Jr. United States Ambassador to Poland 1937-1939, The Ohio State University Press, 1976

245   https://en.pafw.pl/about-us/

246   https://pl.usembassy.gov/embassy-consulate/embassy/ambassadors-residence-in-warsaw/

247   https://nara.getarchive.net/media/us-marines-conduct-quick-reaction-force-techniques-baltic-challenge-97-is-a-0f83d4

248   https://esm.ee/exhibition/general-johan-laidoner

249 www.nato.int/docu/speech/1997/s970709l.htm

250 https://sealiftcommand.com/

251 He is in his mid-forties and wears a bow tie. His parents fled Estonia when the Soviets came in 1940. Ilves grew up in New Jersey and was the valedictorian of his high school class. His degrees, in psychology, are from Columbia and the University of Pennsylvania. Ilves was the head of the Estonian Service of Radio Free Europe for ten years (1984-93) based in Munich. A colleague of Ron Asmus. Their times at RFE overlapped. https://pressroom.rferl.org/history

252 In my October 1996 trip to Estonia, my meeting was with Ilve's predecessor Foreign Minister Siim Kallas. Larry T. was not in the country on that visit.

253 *Opening NATO's Door*, Ronald D. Asmus, A Council on Foreign Relations Book, Columbia University Press, 2002, pp. 233-238

254 *The End of the Beginning: The Emergence of a New Russia*, Deputy Secretary of State Strobe Talbott. Stanford University, Sept. 19, 1997

255 https://1997-2001.state.gov/about_state/biography/talbott.html

256 *Opening NATO's Door*, Ronald D. Asmus. A Council on Foreign Relations Book, Columbia University Press, New York 2002

257 "As a young student I traveled across a continent divided by barbed wire and guard dogs. My son would never think twice about visiting Berlin, Warsaw, or Budapest. He would never know the divided Europe I had grown up with and what it was like to cross a Cold War boundary where great armies stood in an ideological and military standoff for four decades. Thank God, I thought to myself." (p. xxxii) (Asmus was commissioned by the State Department to write a book recounting the story of NATO enlargement. Published in 2002, it covers the period from Clinton's election in 1992 to the joining of NATO by Poland, Hungary and the Czech Republic in 1999.) *Opening NATO's Door*, Ronald D. Asmus, A Council on Foreign Relations Book, Columbia University Press, New York, 2002

258 Under the 1997 Assessed Contribution (the dues) based on GDP of member countries, the United States' share was 25 percent of the WHO operating budget. This constituted 20 percent of the total budget. The rest was from voluntary contributions from countries and foundations

for specific programs—polio eradication, malaria control, HIV, Ebola etc. The U.S. was and is also a major contributor to this programmatic budget.

259   Sir George Alleyne, head of the Pan American Health Organization (WHO regional office of the Americas); Dr. Nafis Sadik, head of the UN Population Fund; Dr. Ebrahim Malick Samba, head of WHO Africa Region; and Dr. Uton Muchtar Rafei, head of WHO Southeast Asia Region.

260   Universal human right is used here to mean she wants this incorporated into the Universal Declaration of Human Rights, one of the founding documents of the UN in 1948.

www.un.org/en/about-us/universal-declaration-of-human-rights

261   Gro's acceptance speech as director-general of WHO: https://apps.who.int/iris/bitstream/handle/10665/79896/eadiv6.pdf

262   www.legacy.com/us/obituaries/nytimes/name/william-nitze-obituary?id=14187366

263   Bruce was Clinton's national campaign director in 1992, director of the Office of Presidential Personnel in 1993, assistant to the president and deputy White House counsel in the first term.

264   At this time, Richard Holbrooke did not hold an official position with the State Department. He had left the position of assistant secretary of state for European and Canadian Affairs in February 1996 and would be appointed ambassador to the United Nations in September of 1999. Which didn't matter, as his position was to be Richard Holbrooke.

265   Jo Benkow was also well known, perhaps best known for two books that were bestsellers in Norway: his autobiography *From the Synagogue to the Løvebakken* and his book of conversations with his friend King Olav V, *Olav - Man and Monarch*.

266   Dear reader: I have to stop here and say again that with our small staff all this went off like clockwork. The interns were getting experience by trial by fire and performing like veterans. The talented staff, Mike Butler, Rhonda Ferguson-Augustus, Russ Trowbridge, DCM Sharon Mercurio, Ginny Phillips, and Sue Meyer were making sure all

was in order as well as and doing their regular jobs. Press attaché Mike Scanlon prepared media handouts, copies of my talks, and scheduled the many interview requests for Holbrooke. My driver Edmund was moving me about in the black Chevy like it was the Batmobile.

267 *America, Scandinavia, and the Cold War 1945-1949*, Geir Lundestad, Columbia University Press, New York, 1980, pp. 133-166.

268 www.marshallfoundation.org/the-marshall-plan/speech/

269 To read more on the economics of Marshall Plan in Norway, see *The Marshall Plan and the Modernization of the Norwegian Economy*, Helge Ø. Pharo, Institut de la gestion publique et du développement économique, 1993, https://books.openedition.org/igpde/14902

270 A political appointee of President Truman, both of Ambassador Bay's parents had immigrated to America from Norway.

271 Geir makes extended references to the writings on the Marshall Plan and NATO of two historians identified with the Wisconsin School of Diplomatic History, William Appleman Williams and Walter LaFeber, who received their Ph.D.s in history from the UW. Both were influenced by history Professor Fred Harvey Harrington, who became the president of the UW, serving from 1962 until 1970. The Wisconsin School is usually explained as promoting the thesis that economic reasons have been the driver of much of American foreign policy. (Williams was still on the faculty when I was at the UW. I did not have him as a professor.) The bestselling author of historical biographies Stephen E. Ambrose, his Ph.D. from the UW History Department, is also noted and quoted by Geir. "Ambrose argues the objective of the United States by entering the NATO alliance was that, Europe would become, for the American businessman, soldier and foreign policy maker, another Latin America and subjected to the same American domination." *America, Scandinavia, and the Cold War 1945-1949*, Geir Lundestad, Columbia University Press, New York, 1980, p. 171. LaFeber's influence on history students who went on to shape American foreign policy was significant. *America, Russia and The Cold War, 1945-1966*, Walter LaFeber, John Wiley and Sons Publisher, 1968. ww.nytimes.com/2021/03/10/education/walter-lafeber-dead.htm; www. historians.org/research-and-publications/perspectives-on-history/september-2021/walter-f-lafeber

272   I gave a readout to Holbrooke before breakfast on the recent trip to D.C. where I accompanied Godal to a meeting with the secretary of state, April 3-5. In a side conversation, I had updated Madeleine Albright on Gro's progress on WHO votes.

273   The members of the committee at that time included: Francis Sejersted, the chairman, representing the Conservative Party. He had a long-time affiliation with the Conservative Party starting in 1962 as president of the Norwegian Students' Association representing the student wing of the Conservative Party. In 1997, he was a history professor. Hanna Kvanmo, the member from the Socialist Left party, was the vice chair of the committee. She was convicted of treason for serving in the Nazi Red Cross on the Eastern Front. She was the leader of the Socialist Left Party in Parliament from 1977-1989. She had been on the committee since 1991. Sissel Rønbeck was from the Labour Party and was a former member of Parliament. Elected from an Oslo district. She served in three Cabinet posts under Gro Harlem Brundtland. Gunnar Stålsett represented the Centre Party. He was a theologian with the Lutheran Church of Norway and once headed the Lutheran World Federation. He chaired the Centre Party government from 1977-1979 and served as deputy representative from Oslo to Parliament from 1977-1981. Gunnar Berge was also from Labour. A former member of Parliament, he held three ministerial posts in Brundtland governments, including minister of finance. At the time, he was head of the Norwegian Petroleum Directorate, an arm of government dealing with offshore oil allocations.

274   Norway awards the Peace Prize while the other Nobel Prizes are controlled by Sweden. This is because Alfred Nobel stated in his will this prize be awarded by the Norwegian Parliament. Why? He didn't say. Best explanation is provided by Geir Lundestad: "He might have in fact, considered Norway a more peace-oriented and more democratic country than Sweden." www.nobelpeaceprize.org/nobel-peace-prize/history/why-norway

275   My role was witnessing and reporting on the discussion between the leaders of the Portuguese-speaking countries, including the prime minister of Portugal, and José Ramos-Horta, the prize recipient. Ramos-Horta was the leader of the revolutionary government in exile of the independence movement for East Timor and was expected to

become a leader of a future independent country. East Timor had been a Portuguese colony until 1975. Timor was then occupied by the Indonesians. The prize would give him legitimacy. See list of laureates: www.nobelpeaceprize.org/laureates/?offset2438=1

276 The lobbying of the Nobel Committee and a backstage look at politicians on the committee acting like politicians is laid out in *The World's Most Prestigious Prize, the Inside Story of the Nobel Peace Prize*, Geir Lundestad (former director of the Norwegian Nobel Institute), Oxford University Press, 2019

277 Finland and Sweden equip their militaries for NATO interoperability, meaning they could easily meld into NATO forces for war games, and if the time ever came to join NATO they would be ready.

278 www.operadeparis.fr/en/visits/palais-garnier

279 Paul Fanlund was now the assistant managing editor of the *Wisconsin State Journal.*

280 www.nytimes.com/1997/02/06/world/pamela-harriman-is-dead-at-76-an-ardent-political-personality.html

281 For example, the F-16 sold to a foreign country's military will not have all the technology and capabilities of the U.S. version. www.bis. doc.gov/index.php/other-areas/strategic-industries-and-economic-security-sies/offsets-in-defense-trade/54-other-areas/strategic-industries-and-economic-security/181-offset-definitions

282 A museum since 1880, the Carnavalet, "one of the rare examples of Renaissance architecture in Paris," started its provenance in 1548 as the mansion of the president of the Paris Parliament. www.carnavalet.paris. fr/en/museum/history

283 *Aftenposten*, Aug. 22, 1997

284 Princess Diana died Aug. 31, 1997, in Paris from injuries suffered in a car crash.

285 www.royalcourt.no/artikkel.html?tid=28708

286 King Harald's parents

287 *Norway and the Second World War*, Johannes Andenaes, Olav Riste, Magne Skodvin, 1966, Fourth edition 1989, Aschehoug, p.122

288 www.pbs.org/wgbh/masterpiece/specialfeatures/atlantic-crossing-fact-or-fiction-inside-episode-8/#8

289 www.royalcourt.no/artikkel.html?tid=28708

290 Amendment VIII: Excessive bail shall not be required, nor excessive fines imposed, nor cruel and unusual punishments inflicted.

291 *Norway and the Second World War*, Johannes Andenaes, Olav Riste, Magne Skodvin, 1966. Fourth edition 1989. Aschehoug, pp. 122-163

292 Andeneas, et al., p. 128

293 Andeneas, et al., p. 139. www.nationalww2museum.org/war/topics/nuremberg-trials

294 Andaneas, et al., p. 148

295 Andaneas, et al., p. 154

296 https://home.army.mil/wiesbaden/index.php/about/history

297 Donald Blinken is the father of future Secretary of State Antony Blinken.

298 www.wiesbaden.de/microsite/kurhaus-en/

299 www.americanacademy.de/about/mission/

300 www.einsteinforum.de/about/

301 www.aspeninstitute.de/aspen-history/

302 www.parlament-berlin.de/english

303 www.thepencompany.com/en-us/product/pelikan-souveran-800-fountain-pen/

304 www.royalcourt.no/artikkel.html?tid=28752

305 www.thehistorymakers.org/biography/anne-brown-41

306 https://nbl.snl.no/Anne_Brown

307 www.nobelpeaceprize.org/laureates/1997

308   I met Jody Williams in 1984 in Nicaragua when Patrick Lucey, former Wisconsin governor and ambassador to Mexico, and I led a delegation on a two-week fact-finding mission. I was the Speaker of the Assembly. We met with officials of the Sandinista government and opposition leaders. Jody Williams was a guide and translator working for the NGO that organized the trip. Many Wisconsin NGOs and some elements of the Catholic Church became active in development programs in Nicaragua after Wisconsin was assigned Nicaragua as its partner in President Kennedy's Partners of the Americas initiative. https://wisnic.org/nationalorganization/ This relationship intensified after the 1974 earthquake that devastated Managua and then-Gov. Lucey organized relief supplies that were flown to Nicaragua by the Wisconsin National Guard, which later formed its own partnership program. https://ng.wi.gov/topics/state-partnership-program

309   https://disarmament.unoda.org/anti-personnel-landmines-convention/

310   Signing a treaty means it is sent for ratification, usually to a legislative body. The U.S. president can ratify a treaty if the Senate first approves it with a two-thirds vote.

311   www.nytimes.com/1997/10/11/world/peace-prize-goes-to-land-mine-opponents.html?searchResultPosition=30

312   www.nobelprize.org/prizes/peace/1997/ceremony-speech/

313   www.nobelprize.org/prizes/peace/1997/williams/lecture/

314   www.nobelpeaceprize.org/nobel-peace-prize/about-the-nobel-peace-prize/nobel-peace-prize-celebrations/banquet

315   The Royal Norwegian Order of Merit was founded by King Olav V in 1985. It is conferred on foreign and Norwegian nationals as a reward for their outstanding service in the interest of Norway. His Majesty The King is the Grand Master of the Order. The Order of Merit is divided into three classes and two sub-classes: The classes are Grand Cross, Grand Officer, and Officer. Under Grand Officer is the subclass of commander, and under Officer is the subclass of knight.

www.royalcourt.no/artikkel.html?tid=28663&sek=28560

316   https://schiller.edu/

317 https://travel.state.gov/content/travel/en/us-visas/immigrate/family-immigration/immigrant-visa-for-a-spouse-or-fiance-of-a-us-citizen.html

318 www.state.gov/about-us-u-s-advisory-commission-on-public-diplomacy/

319 The three other Oslo interns recently reflected on their time as U.S. Embassy interns during the late 1990s. They tell of their experiences in their own voices:

Joel Hinckley, University of Utah, arrived June 13, 1997

"I served at the U.S. Embassy as an intern in the summer of 1997. I worked in consular affairs and the Political Economic Section. I was a little unique as an intern in that I had served a mission in Norway for the Church of Jesus Christ of Latter-day Saints in Norway from 1993-1995 and was fluent in Norwegian prior to coming there as an intern. As a result I did a lot of translation work for the rest of the staff and conducted a lot of visa interviews in consular affairs....I stayed in the small apartment above the garage. ...I enjoyed my time very much and probably the personal highlight for me was meeting Gro Harlem Brundtland at the Fourth of July party at the Ambassador's Residence."

Karen Febey, St. Olaf College, May 23, 1997

"I was already in Norway for study at the University of Oslo. A retired embassy staffer suggested I look into an internship. Russ Trowbridge (political officer) was my mentor. I spoke Norwegian and helped a lot in the consular section for those Norwegians who had trouble with English. The political officers Russ, Rhonda Ferguson, and Mike Butler showed me the ropes. I stayed three months."

Kim McDonald, University of Minnesota, Summer 1996

"I was at the University of Minnesota Humphrey School master's program and applied when in grad school. I stayed in the garage apartment. I worked in consular and the political sections. Russ Trowbridge and Ginny Phillips (deputy chief of mission's secretary) were my mentors. I was at the embassy for ten weeks. The big event I helped with was the meeting of Nordic and Baltic ambassadors hosted by Embassy Oslo, with all of the meetings in the Residence. I spoke Swedish so could do anything."

320   https://studylib.net/doc/14205183/alumni-notes-putting-the-wisconsin-idea-to-work-la-follette

321   *Ole Goes to War: Men From Norway Who Fought in America's Civil War*, Jerry Rosholt, 2003. Vesterheim Norwegian American Museum, Decorah Iowa, www.vesterheim.org

322   *Colonel Hans Christian Heg*, Odd S. Lovoll, Minnesota Historical Society Press, 2023.

323   Florence Jaffray Harriman, born in 1870, daughter of a wealthy New York ship-owning family, married into another wealthy family at age 19. She started adult life as a socialite; then the women's suffrage movement became her passion and entry to Democratic politics. Her first memoir was titled *From Pinafores to Politics*. In 1912 she supported Woodrow Wilson for president and led the Women's National Wilson and Marshall Association. President Wilson appointed her to the first Commission on Industrial Relations, where she made her mark by teaming with University of Wisconsin labor economist John R. Commons to write a minority report supporting labor unions. Prior to Wilson's campaign for re-election in 1916, Harriman famously told the president that if he did not support the constitutional amendment extending the right to vote to women, she would organize against him. This and other demands from the now-politically powerful suffrage movement caused Wilson to see the wisdom of changing his position. Her husband, J. Borden Harriman, died in 1914. The mother of one child, Ethel, Harriman never remarried. She remained a force in Democratic Party politics. https:en.wikipedia.org/wiki/Florence_Jaffray_Harriman

324   *No Ordinary Time: Franklin and Eleanor Roosevelt: The Home Front in WWII*, Doris Kearns Goodwin, Simon & Schuster, 2008, p. 254

325   Kearns Goodwin, p. 273.

326   Kearns Goodwin, p. 305.

327   Kearns Goodwin

328   https://en.m.wikipedia.org/wiki/Kråkerøy_speech

329   www.norwegianamerican.com/a-brief-history-of-norwegian-whaling/

330   https://www.rogerebert.com/reviews/reds-1981

331   Peter adopted the title emperor, replacing the title of tsar in 1721.

332   He gained the lands and a seaport on the Baltic (St. Petersburg). Sweden still nominally controlled Finland but in the Napoleonic Wars in 1809 Russia took back Finland.

333   Sources: *Norway: The Resistance Movement, 1940-1945*, Olav Riste and Berit Nokleby, Tano Oslo 1986. p. 59; *Norway and the Second World War*, Johannes Andeneaes, Olav Riste, Magne Skodvin, 1989 fourth edition, Aschehoug publishing; *Skis Against the Atom*, Knut Haukelid, 1989, North American Heritage Press; *History of Norway*, John A. Yilek, cited earlier. *The Guardian*, Obituary of Claus Helberg, www.theguardian.com/news/2003/mar/19/guardianobituaries

334   *Norway's Foreign Relations—A History*, Olav Riste, Universitetsforlaget, Oslo 2001

335   *Great Power Politics and Norwegian Foreign Policy, A Study of Norway's Foreign Relations November 1940 - February 1948*, Nils Morten Udgaard, 1973

336   Riste, p. 185

337   Riste, p. 186

INDEX

426

prime minister, first meeting with, 43–45. *See also* Brundtland, Gro Harlem

primogeniture, 343

Professor Logachev (Russian ship), 230–231

property restitution, 322

PT 109 (film), 88

Q

Quisling, Rolf, 78–79

Quisling, Vidkun, 79, 123, 319, 356

R

Rabin, Yitzhak, 153

radioactive waste. *See* nuclear waste

Radium Hospital, 135

Ragnhild (Princess), 172, 325–326

Rand, Lois, 150

Rand, Sidney, 150

Red Cross United World College, 210

Reds (film), 355

Reed, John, 355

Regal, Mary, 300

Reggie, Victoria, 194–195

reindeer, 33, 103

Reiten, Tor, 61

religion. *See also* Catholic Church; Lutheranism

    Brundtland's critique of reproductive health position, 74, 85

    church-state relationship, 21, 345

    immigrants fleeing persecution for, 343

    Lutheran Church in U.S., 344, 345

    under Olav (saint), 157

Rendalen, Barbara, 110

reproductive health, 85, 289

Residence (U.S. ambassador), 16, 25–29, 33–37

Restauration (Norwegian sloop), 343

Reuther, Walter, 197

Revang, Leonhard, 107

Rey, Nicholas, 66, 276–277, 278

Reynolds, Henry, 61, 127

Richter, Barry, 59

Richter, Pat, 59

Rignes beer, 36

Riley, John, 340

Riley, Stephanie, 340

Rinnan gang, 320

Risan, Leidulv, 87

Robertson, Cliff, 86–88

rocket launch, 95–96

Rød-Larsen, Terje, 45, 182, 334

Romantic art, 64

Roosevelt, Franklin Delano, 152, 348, 350

Rosendal, 238–239

Rosenkrantz Tower, 237–238

Røsjø, Endre, 295–298, 340

Rostropovich, Mstislav, 249–250, 252

royal yacht, 216

Rühe, Volker, 272

Ruksha, Vyacheslav

    Asmus dinner with, 282

    at follow-up Murmansk conference, 178

    at NATO Arctic contamination conference, 170

    as official host of Murmansk trip, 163, 165, *203*

    at Oslo conference on Murmansk initiative, 168

Ruppe, Loret Miller, 70

Rushdie, Salman, 236

Rusk, Dean, 226

Made in the USA
Las Vegas, NV
12 September 2024

95178480R00267